The Community Mental Health System

The Community Mental Health System

A Navigational Guide for Providers

Elizabeth L. Teed
Marist College

John A. Scileppi
Marist College

With

Monika Boeckmann
Northeastern New York Alzheimer's Association

Esther L. Crispi
Marist College

James Regan
Marist College

David J. M. Whitehouse, M.D.
United Behavioral Health

Boston   New York   San Francisco
Mexico City   Montreal   Toronto   London   Madrid   Munich   Paris
Hong Kong   Singapore   Tokyo   Cape Town   Sydney

Senior Series Editor: *Patricia Quinlin*
Series Editorial Assistant: *Nakeesha Warner*
Marketing Manager: *Laura Lee Manley*
Senior Production Editor: *Liz Napolitano*
Editorial-Production Service: *Pine Tree Composition, Inc.*
Composition Buyer: *Linda Cox*
Manufacturing Buyer: *Joanne Sweeney*
Cover Director: *Linda Knowles*

For related titles and support materials, visit our online catalog at www.ablongman.com

Between the time website information is gathered and then published, it is not unusual for some sites to have closed. Also, the transcription of URLs can result in typographical errors. The publisher would appreciate notification where these errors occur so that they may be corrected in subsequent editions.

Library of Congress Cataloging-in-Publication Data

The community mental health system: a navigational guide for providers
／ Elizabeth L. Teed . . . [et al.].
    p.; cm.
Includes bibliographical references.
ISBN 0-205-48665-7
1.   Community mental health services.   I.   Teed, Elizabeth Lee.
[DNLM: 1.   Community Mental Health Services—United States.
2.   Community Psychiatry—methods—United States.   3.   Mental Disorders
—therapy—United States. WM 30 C733422 2007]
    RA790.55.C568 2007
    362.2'0425—dc22

                                                                    2006029933

Printed in the United States of America

10 9 8 7 6 5 4 3 2 1   RRD-VA 10 09 08 07 06

CONTENTS

3   The Ecological Model: Person-in-Context   54

5 Individual Focus: Crisis and Coping   122

PREFACE

Sam Speers, a college chaplain, related a story about a Stanford University student writing his reflections after volunteering for a semester in a shelter for homeless men as part of a service/learning activity. The student described how much he learned through this experience and how he believed that he helped some of the men in the shelter. The student concluded his essay by stating that when he has children and when they go to college, he hoped they could volunteer in the same shelter. Reverend Speers noted the student's good intention but thought that a major point of the learning experience had been lost on this particular student. A goal of placing Stanford students in the shelter was for them to generate creative ideas and solutions so that society eventually would have less, or even no, need of such places in the future. Instead of seeing homelessness as a timeless problem, the student should have reflected on how potential solutions could be developed through an appreciation of the contextual forces surrounding the concern. This book is dedicated to that ideal. The mission statement of the community mental health system is to improve the quality of life and emotional well-being in society. The tactics to reach this goal involve both individual and systems level interventions. Some tactics include treating those already experiencing difficulties in living, and other strategies focus on keeping healthy people healthy so that they will not need extensive mental health care in the future.

The person-environment fit perspective described in depth throughout this book is perhaps the best approach to adopt to prepare mental health professionals for the challenges that present themselves in this young century. This orientation to the field combines the best aspects of the interpersonal therapeutic relationship and the efficiency of systems-level preventive interventions. Through this approach, professionals help individuals in need, work to remedy community problems, and in the process, serve to keep future generations healthy.

The aim of the book is to provide mental health professionals, both those in the field and those in training, with a better understanding of the service delivery system and ideas for how to work effectively in it. The text begins with an overview of the field, including the impact of deinstitutionalization, and provides a description of the ecological model and the prevention paradigm, both conceptualizations needed to navigate through the system. These concepts are concretized through discussing specific tactics useful to bolster individual coping strategies and provide social support. Individual-oriented tools include stress management to prevent debilitating effects of crises and brief therapeutic techniques. Systems-oriented tactics such as consultation strategies, community research methods, and change techniques are described to arm the professional with effective tools to produce large-scale reform. The values that community mental health professionals must consider include cultural competence, empowerment, and the ethical concerns unique to helping agency-affiliated individuals in the community. These are also discussed. The book concludes by exploring a vision of the near future of the system: a description of the needs of the elderly, the fastest growing segment of our population. Also covered are programs designed to help this population and dramatic changes expected in the types of mental health interventions that corporate employers and their insurance companies will support.

Throughout the book, examples of programs are presented as drawn from the communities nestled in the Hudson River Valley of New York State. Many institutions to serve individuals with mental illness or developmental disabilities were built in this area, and when deinstitutionalization occurred, community-based programs and agencies were created to assist those moving out of the large facilities. Similarly, because of its proximity to New York City, the Hudson Valley houses many correctional facilities. During the first half of the twentieth century, many individuals who suffered from psychiatric conditions or mental retardation and those who were deemed to be a danger to society were "shipped up the river" to institutions in Dutchess County and the surrounding region. These institutions were sufficiently distant from New York City to prevent escapees from returning to the city, but close enough to enable relatives or friends from the city to visit the patients or inmates. The visitors could travel relatively easily to the facilities by train, car, or boat.

We are a community of professionals and scholars, assembled to provide diverse and practical viewpoints on navigating the community mental health system. The authors of the book include (in alphabetical order), Monika Boeckmann, M.A., M.S., M.P.A., currently the Executive director of a regional agency serving the victims of Alzheimer's Disease and their families and a former senior administrator of the Dutchess County United Way and a former Director of Staff Training for two Veteran's Administration Health Centers; Esther (Lori) Crispi, Ph.D., a gerontologist, grant project administrator, and faculty member; James Regan, Ph.D., former C.E.O. of Hudson River State (NY) Psychiatric Center and current Director of a graduate training program in a community mental health field; John Scileppi, Ph.D., a member of numerous boards of directors of agencies assisting individuals with developmental disabilities, an author, and a faculty member; Elizabeth Teed, Ph.D., former Director of the Office of Community Research at Marist College, therapist, member of the Dutchess County Mental Health Association Board, and faculty member; and David Whitehouse, M.D., Th.D., M.B.A., Chief Medical Officer for Strategy and Innovation with United Behavioral Health, and former head of the Charles River (MA) Psychiatric Center, a private institution participating in Massachusetts's privatization of services program. Whereas the professors are expert in theory, the practitioners and administrators have a wealth of practical experience from which to draw upon when describing the community mental health system. We all agree on basic philosophy and orientation; however, the reader may find occasional times when two of us may support opposing viewpoints. Let these instances themselves be good training for navigating the community mental health system. We assure you it will not be the last time you encounter contradictory recommendations given by various stakeholders in the system!

Although all the authors have read and commented upon the material in each chapter, individual authors had primary responsibility in writing various chapters. Monika Boeckmann, utilizing her experience administering United Way, a human services agency, and a large staff training program, prepared the chapters on consultation, cultural competence, and managing change. Lori Crispi researched the chapter on gerontology, utilizing her 20 years of experience working as a developmental psychologist and teaching in this field. Jim Regan wrote the chapter on deinstitutionalization based on nearly 30 years of working in large state psychiatric centers, including the last twelve years as Chief Executive Officer. Jim also collaborated with John Scileppi in developing the chapter on empowerment and ethical considerations. John Scileppi has taught in a community psychology graduate program for over 30 years, and he also directed that program for 12 years. He has also published in the areas of systems approaches to education and community psychology. John authored the chapters on the overview of community mental health, the ecological model, and prevention. Beth Teed served as the Director of the Office of Community Research at Marist College and in this position learned a great deal not only about research but also about the community mental health system. She has also presented workshops on stress management in corporate executives' training programs, and she is a therapist serving those with substance abuse concerns and their families. On basis of these experiences, Beth prepared the introduction, individual focus: crisis and coping and brief therapeutic interventions, systems focus: social support, and outcome measurement and program evaluation chapters. Finally, David Whitehouse served as the CEO of a large private psychiatric hospital and for the past 10 years has been the Chief Medical Officer of an international health insurance company in charge of behavioral care. In these two positions, David learned the intricacies of reimbursement for mental health services from opposing positions, and he is deeply aware of the coming breakthroughs in the manner in which treatment and prevention will be supported. David prepared the chapter on The Evolution/Revolution in Health Care Insurance and Managed Care. Readers wanting to contact any of these authors should do so through the senior author, Elizabeth Teed, School of Social and Behavioral Sciences, Marist College, Poughkeepsie, NY 12601.

This book evolved out of an earlier one (Scileppi, Teed & Torres, 2000. *Community psychology: A common sense approach to mental health*, Upper Saddle River, NJ: Prentice Hall), and it extends beyond the one discipline to encompass all the professions that serve those in the community mental health system. We believe both current practitioners and students in fields such as social work, counseling, psychology, and psychiatric nursing can benefit from the perspectives and strategies discussed in the pages that follow. Many graduate students at Marist College have helped in the preparation of this manuscript, and we wish to publicly thank Michelle Wojtaszek, David Mack, Stacey Trapani, and Fallon Cunningham for their diligent and scholarly work.

As we explain throughout this book, none of us exists in a vacuum; rather, we live in a dynamic life space—a human ecology of family, colleagues, friends, and acquaintances. We thank our spouses, our parents, and our children for their support and encouragement.

INTRODUCTION

Since the beginning of time, wise men and women have struggled to conceptualize the significance of human existence. What is the knowledge we have gained from our own experiences and from the experiences of those who came before us, and how can that knowledge be applied to living more purposefully? The goal of community mental health is to assist mankind in ensuring that our time on this earth is as meaningful as possible by offering strategies for improving quality of life and by providing methods for minimizing the effects of problems in living. Community mental health is based on the assumption that life is rarely an easy journey along a path lined with lush green meadows. More often, it is as poets and philosophers have described: a process much like the experience of traveling a long and winding road. In the words of the late, great Harry Chapin, "There's no straight lines make up my life and all my roads have bends, there's no clear cut beginnings and so far no dead ends."

Community mental health recognizes that the road of life is often difficult to travel; that bends, potholes, and curves are part and parcel of the trip. As Joe Cocker said, "The road is long, there are mountains in our way, but we climb a step every day." In keeping with this philosophy, community mental health includes reactive interventions, but more often focuses on proactive approaches to mental health. Problems in living are viewed more as inherent in the experience we call "life" and less as a result of psychological pathology. Crisis situations are to be expected and prepared for, and they can be opportunities for personal development. Not only do we grow from each problem we resolve, but we also grow as a result of the problem-solving process.

A wise man once told one of the authors (Elizabeth Teed) that as a child, he put together wooden models during road trips with his family. After returning home, he always kept the scrap pieces of wood "because they were part of the trip." The author wondered for some time about such a practice and came to the realization that although the extra pieces of wood were not used to create the model, they were still valuable since they could be used for future projects. Similarly, some of the knowledge gained from experiences with crisis situations may seem irrelevant in solving the particular problem at hand. However, if we are careful not to discard or leave behind anything that we have learned, anything that has been "part of the trip," we are likely to find it useful elsewhere along the road.

Principles of community mental health teach us that although life experience provides both knowledge and problem-solving skills, the scope of problems in living is wide, and many of us at some point will encounter difficulties that require professional intervention.

According to the National Institute of Mental Health (NIMH) (2001), 22.1% of Americans ages 18 and older will suffer from a DSM-IV diagnosable mental disorder in any given year. This translates to more than 1 in 5 adults, and does not account for children who are diagnosed with mental disorders. In addition, many individuals are diagnosed with more than 1 disorder at a time. Earlier studies, such as one done by the

President's Commission on Mental Health in 1978, report that at some point between the cradle and the grave, 1 in 10 Americans experience some form of mental illness.

Given that no projection can be "perfectly accurate," let us consider the far more conservative "1 in 10" figure cited by the President's Commission. You are probably studying community psychology in a class of approximately 20 students. Ignoring the obvious "sampling error," the statistics suggest that at least 2 people in your class had, have, or will personally experience a mental illness that is severe enough to warrant professional intervention.

Consider the fact that there are approximately 300 million people living in the United States and that the average household contains 2.59 members (U. S. Bureau of the Census, 2000). That means that 30,000,000 people are suffering or will suffer from a mental illness. As we consider the impact on the family system, we become aware that 77,700,000 people, or almost 26% of the total population of the United States, already have experienced or will experience the impact of a psychiatric illness—and we know that this is an inappropriately low estimate. Going back to our classroom example, chances are favorable that 5 people in your class will be impacted by the effects of historically recognized mental health issues. However, it is important to remember that mental health is about much more than learning to manage or being lucky enough to avoid diagnosable mental disorders.

Stressful events are all around us. Holmes and Rahe (1967) created the widely used Social Readjustment Ratings Scale (SRRS), which has made its way into popular culture as well as scientific literature related to the mind-body connection. The SRRS was developed by asking subjects to rank-order a series of life-changing events in terms of the time necessary to adjust to them. It is interesting that even positive events such as marriage or the birth of a child were observed to produce high levels of stress. The test is administered by giving subjects a check-list with more than 40 major life events. Each subject is asked to note which of these events has occurred within a specified period of time. The ratings for these events are totaled to form a Life Change Unit Score. High scores on the SRRS have been related to heart attacks and other severe illnesses (Rahe & Lind, 1971).

The most stressful event listed on the SRRS is the death of a spouse, whereas the death of another close family member ranks fifth. It is not at all unusual for an individual to seek psychological services or to join a support group to deal with grief and loss issues and the accompanying life adjustments. These difficulties tend to be exacerbated when deaths occur suddenly, events that happen more often than commonly thought.

Annual Deaths in the U.S.

Suicide	30,622
Tobacco	435,000
Automobile Accidents	43,000
Cancer	553,768
Heart Disease	700,142

CDC, National Center for Health Statistics (2002)

Overall, there were 2,416, 425 deaths in the United States in 2001 (CDC, National Center for Health Statistics, 2002). Using our family multiplier of 2.59, that finding means that there were 6,258,540 people who dealt with one of life's most difficult and stress-producing events in that time period. This figure represents another 2.15% of the population, or another member of our class.

According to the SRRS, the second most stressful life event is divorce; marriage ranks seventh. According to the CDC, National Center for Health Statistics (2004), there were 1,110,000 divorces and 2,187,000 marriages in the United States in 2003. In all, there were 3,297,000 major changes in marital status, affecting 8,539,230 people—another 2.94% of the population, or perhaps the person sitting to the left of you. These figures do not include legal separations or other marital difficulties.

After deaths and changes in marital status, the next category of stressful life events on the SRSS is involvement with the criminal justice system. In 2000, there were at least 26,060,080 people who directly bore the impact of criminal behavior. This number does not include victims who do not report the crimes committed against them or the untold number of perpetrators who are on parole or probation. Referring back to our family impact factor, we are now talking about 67,495,607 individuals who experience the crisis of criminal behavior in one way or another. Roughly speaking, that number equals 23% of the current population, or almost 5 people in your class.

Annual Cases of Crimes in the U.S. in 2004

Violent Crime 1,367,009	(murder and nonnegligent manslaughter forcible rape, robbery, and aggravated assault)
Property Crime 10,328,255	(burglary, larceny-theft, motor vehicle theft, and arson)
Hate Crime 9,035	(crime motivated by offender's bias against a race, religion, disability, sexual orientation, or ethnicity/ national origin)
Total Cases	11,704,299

Source: Federal Bureau of Investigation (2004) www.fbi.gov/ucr/cius_04

Health-related issues are of great concern to all of us. In 2000, not including the millions of families that are dealing with disabilities and chronic illnesses, there were 98,613,000 visits to national emergency rooms and 59,505,000 outpatient care incidents—a mere fraction of the total number of individuals who require ongoing medical care for serious physical illnesses. In aggregate, there were 158,118,000 events resulting in a visit to a medical institution. This number alone, without the family multiplier, represents more than 54% of the current population, or 11 members of your class.

The SRSS lists many other significant life events that are major sources of stress, that test individual coping skills, and that may require some form of psychological intervention to facilitate a positive adjustment. Issues such as moving and unemployment, as well as changes in health and heavy consumer debt, also require adaptation. It is interesting to note that having a child leave home or celebrating the holiday season are also significant sources of familial stress. We will not "beat a dead horse" by including all of the calculations here; it is also important to recognize that the numbers reported do not account for the fact that many people experience *multiple* sources of major stress. Suffice to say that if you have not recognized yourself or a member of your family in any of these illustrations, then you are in a class by yourself.

Handling significant problems in living is normative behavior. If everyone experiences difficulties along the developmental journey, are we all "crazy," or are there inadequacies in our systems and approaches? Perhaps the purpose of life is to work through unforeseen difficulties in a manner that helps us build competency. The diagnostic categories or labels that we apply to situations are merely communication tools. Psychological and societal labels help us to understand the broad scope of human behavior in the same manner that a word demonstrates a concept. Should we think of the mentally ill or the unemployed as "lesser than" because of their label, or do we see them as "equal to," because as the numbers indicate, we all carry a placard? It is for these reasons that community mental health is more interested in prevention than in tackling what seems like an overwhelming number of problems on a one-to-one basis. In other words, if groups of individuals can be provided with a preventive safe-driving course for traveling the road of life, fewer individual road maps for those who are "lost" will be necessary.

From a practical vantage point, let us look at the actual number of potential providers of mental health services who are available to offer professional assistance with our problems in living. According to the United States Department of Labor (2000), there are approximately 95 individuals coping with mental illness for every 1 licensed mental health care provider. If every provider is employed full-time and if each spends 5 hours during the workday dealing with an individual's problems, then each client is able to receive only 12.5 hours of one-to-one assistance per year. Given that psychopathology represents only a small percentage of the total problems in living, the need for community mental health approaches and prevention in particular is critical.

Paraprofessionals who provide mental health services are classified as counselors, although 7 out of 10 individuals with this title work in school systems, as human service workers, or as psychiatric aides, and psychiatric nurses or psychiatric technicians. Taken together, these 1,471,000 individuals provide mental health services in typical clinical settings (U. S. Department of Labor, 2003) to a total of 294,250,000 clients. Given this 1:200 ratio of provider to clients, it is no surprise that government leaders are examining health care delivery systems in our country.

Community mental health recognizes that problems in living are everyone's problems and that intelligent, preventive, group approaches keep the bends in the road of life from becoming dead ends. Each of us will have to test our coping skills at some point, and solving problems one-by-one using traditional approaches and singular thinking cannot work. By simply looking at the number of problems that we face each day and the limited resources available to address them, it is clear that traditional one-on-one approaches designed for the rarest of problems will not sufficiently improve our lives.

Acknowledging this limitation is not to say that traditional or individual approaches are obsolete. There are many situations involving pathology that indeed require such interventions, but attempts to resolve problems in living that are not pathological have led to the realization that a community approach is the best road to improving the quality of life for all of us. It is simply the next step in the development of mental health services.

The Community Mental Health System

1 An Overview of the Community Mental Health System

OBJECTIVES

This chapter is designed to enable the reader to:

- Describe the community mental health systems approach.
- Describe the components of the community mental health system.
- Understand the difference between the community mental health systems approach and more traditional behaviorist or psychoanalytical approaches.
- Distinguish between prevention and treatment.
- Understand the importance of community mental health research in restructuring the system to improve its effectiveness.
- Understand the importance and impact of cultural diversity on mental health programs.
- Discuss the historical roots of the community mental health system.
- Discuss how social, economic, and political factors affect both the stigma and the treatment of mental illness.
- Recognize and discuss the challenges facing the implementation of the ideal community mental health service.
- Describe the community psychological/social work contribution to community mental health, and the Dohrenwend model.
- Discuss employment options in the community mental health system.

"We must learn to reawaken and keep ourselves awake, not by mechanical aids, but by an infinite expectation of the dawn, which does not forsake us in our soundest sleep. I know of no more encouraging fact than the unquestionable ability of man to elevate his life by a conscious endeavor. It is something to be able to paint a particular picture, or to carve a statue, and so to make a few objects beautiful; but it is far more glorious to carve and paint the very atmosphere and medium through which we look, which morally we can do. To affect the quality of the day, that is the highest of arts."

Henry David Thoreau

The mental health professional of the twenty-first century requires a new set of paradigms, principles, and intervention strategies to be able to meaningfully address the problems presented in contemporary society. A systems approach to community mental health, developed by community psychologists and social workers in the last part of the twentieth century, is such a strategy. By focusing on both the needs expressed by individuals and the context in which they live and work, community mental health practitioners can effectively enhance the psychological well-being of people in the community. This is a new approach that transcends the traditional views of focusing solely on individuals or environments. As will be seen, the community mental health systems approach is a more accurate model of human behavior, since it is based both on common sense and on empirical research. The interventions generated are also more effective and more efficient than the traditional perspectives they replace.

Traditional psychotherapy that was provided in an institutional setting cannot adequately address the problems encountered by persons in need in today's society. The difficulties encountered in our cities, towns, villages, and rural areas are too great, and they overwhelm the resources of individual therapists. Albee (1998, 2000) observed that the acceptance of the medical-organic explanation of mental disorder and the reliance on individual psychotherapy has created a mental health service delivery system incapable of providing for all those who need assistance. Former United States Surgeon General David Satcher (2000) reviewed over 3,000 research studies and found that in any given year, although one in five Americans experience a serious diagnosable mental disorder, only half of this number receive treatment. Satcher further reported that mental illness is the second leading cause of disability and premature mortality in the nation. Only cardiovascular conditions produce greater loss of productivity and well-being.

This inability to meet mental health needs has affected the nation's quality of life. Miringoff (1995) investigated the changes in 17 indicators of psychological and social health. In 12 of these areas, conditions worsened over the course of the previous 25 years. The costs of providing such care using individual psychological counseling are prohibitive, and American society is unwilling to provide the necessary financial resources to do so. In 1996, the direct treatment of mental disorders and substance abuse cost the nation nearly $100 billion, and indirect costs exceeded $80 billion (Satcher, 2000). For most people, the fees and premiums required to pay for individual treatment are staggering, and traditional insurance, managed care, and health maintenance organizations recognize the need to cap the cost associated with providing these mental health services. When one considers the number of sessions individual therapists need to treat each instance of illness and the relatively high cost per session, it becomes clear that improved and more efficient methods of service delivery are greatly needed. Employers who are eager to preserve their investment in "human capital," one of their most valuable resources, also demand cost-effective programs designed to reduce staff down-time due to illness.

Not only is the traditional model of individual therapeutic service delivery inadequate to meet the needs of persons in difficulty, but also its effectiveness is limited (Lewis, Lewis, Daniels, & D'Andrea, 1998), particularly if the treatment method does not match the client's need. Many traditional therapists still adhere to a psychodynamic or insight-oriented model of care. Such an approach, which relies on uncovering the inner workings of the psyche, might help healthy individuals achieve new understanding of their lives and might release a greater proportion of their creative potential and energies, but this approach is not able to help those with severe disorders in living. Mental health providers who use a behavioral approach with individual clients find that they can rarely alter the macrolevel societal factors that prevent these clients from achieving significant changes in their behavior. That is, such therapists can develop token economies, but they cannot enhance a community's sense of empowerment using behavior modification. Although there will always be a need for individual-oriented therapists, it is not conceivable that society can depend on this model to meet the mental health needs of all of its population. Thus, a new approach is needed, and one that will effectively meet the great and expanding needs in this area.

Even if traditional forms of therapy were successful, they would still emphasize treatment rather than prevention (Albee, 1990). Once individuals have succumbed to mental illness, their lives are already disrupted. The victim's job or family stability may be harmed by the episode. In addition, for each person who becomes mentally ill, the 2.6 others who live with the ailing individual experience stress as a result and may also need services. If the disorder in living is prevented, none of the related problems occur, and all the individuals involved can continue to lead productive lives. This is not to suggest that all mental illness, especially disorders with a biological component, can be easily prevented, but rather that there are many problems in living that can be ameliorated or minimized through prevention.

For example, there is a growing body of evidence (Hankin, 2002; May & Gossage, 2001; Ornoy, 2002) to support the idea that fetal alcohol syndrome can cause mental retardation. If even a short segment of an alcohol awareness lesson conducted in high school were devoted to the discussion of potential harm to the fetus by a pregnant woman drinking even a small amount of alcohol, it is possible that fewer individuals might be born with a developmental disability. Consider not only the financial savings but also more significantly the personal, familial and societal benefits that would be achieved by such a preventive program. Obviously, a new approach supplementing individual treatment and including a preventive component is surely needed.

In this chapter, the community mental health system is discussed. The components of the system are presented first, and then the historical trends that led to the development of the system are described. The challenges that inhibited the system from meeting its expected outcomes are also discussed. Finally, a solution to these challenges is defined and discussed: the paradigm of community psychology. This is an important approach that can be utilized by professionals in diverse disciplines within the community mental health system.

Components of the Community Mental Health System

When one is viewing the mental health system in the community, there are two main ways of describing its component parts. The first describes the types of agencies that comprise the system, and the second discusses the nature of the services provided. Former

U.S. Surgeon General David Satcher (2000), in the first ever Surgeon General Report that focused exclusively on the mental health system, noted that the system is "multi-faceted and complex, comprising the public and private sectors, general health and specialty mental health providers, and social services, housing, criminal justice, and education agencies" (p. 11). Satcher expressed concern that the components do not always interact in a cooperative manner and that providing a better coordinated service delivery system is a serious challenge to the nation.

In addition to the types of agencies cited by the Surgeon General, a comprehensive system serving the mental health needs of those in the community should include local transportation, as well as recreational and community gathering services. Also to be considered are the groups that fund the various services, such as governmental agencies at the federal, state, and local level; companies offering managed care and health insurance; and charitable sources such as private foundations, civic and faith-based groups, and individuals.

The second way of analyzing the system into its parts is to describe the types of unique programs or services that are provided under the umbrella of community mental health. The services should, of course, include the treatment and maintenance in the community of those who have already experienced episodes of mental illness and other disorders in living. The available services should enable these individuals to live productive and satisfying lives in the least restrictive setting. As a result of deinstitutionalization, many individuals who were previously "warehoused" in large mental hospitals or psychiatric centers have been discharged into the community, and their psychological and other human needs must be addressed by the community mental health system. In addition, the system should also provide "inoculation programs" (Seidman & French, 1998) that build and strengthen the skills of groups of healthy individuals to protect them from and prepare them for future difficulties. Promoting well-being is a form of prevention that will ultimately reduce the incidence of mental disorders in the community and consequently decrease the need for treatment.

The Need for Research

The mental health system should base the type of services offered on research. Prevention and health promotion services should be developed on the basis of empirically demonstrated research dealing with risk and protective factors. Large-scale epidemiological studies have shown correlations linking the prevalence of mental illness and various predictor variables, which either increase the likelihood of mental illness (risk factors) or reduce it (protective factors). Mental health interventions can target some of these factors through education and community change. The determination of the volume of mental health services offered in a community should be based on epidemiological surveillance (Satcher, 2000). This involves monitoring various population characteristics and social indicators to calculate the number of individuals who might need mental health services. Such monitoring should also study the level of access to services for those in need. Finally, research is needed to evaluate the effectiveness of specific individual and group prevention and treatment strategies in promoting health and reducing illness. Providers are currently experiencing increased pressure from public and private funding sources to demonstrate that their strategies are effective, the basis on empirical evidence.

Restructuring the System

Seidman and French (1998) list a final activity the new community mental health paradigm can provide—that of restructuring the system. Restructuring involves altering the standing rules of a setting to devise new procedures for offering mental health services.

Such restructuring may involve providing cultural amplifiers. These amplifiers encourage individuals from diverse cultures in the community to utilize the available mental health activities. Cultural amplifiers could include incorporating the traditions, customs, language, and activities of the neighborhood in mental health programs. For example, the absence of a Spanish-speaking counselor in a particular agency may discourage members of the Hispanic community from utilizing the services of that agency. The need for such cultural amplifiers in the United States is increasing. Using the trends supplied by the U.S. Census Bureau, the nation is becoming more of a global society in which half of all Americans will be from four ethnic groups: Asian American, African American, Hispanic American, and Native American. Agencies that do not embrace a multicultural perspective will be able neither to relate to individuals from these groups nor to benefit the community.

Restructuring can also include the review of funding criteria to determine whether any requirements are counterproductive to enhancing mental health. In the past, Medicaid assisted only those clients who lived in institutions. An individual living at home could receive Medicaid-funded psychological assistance only by being placed in an institution. Instead of providing the counseling needed to enable the person to continue to live independently, this federally sponsored program encouraged a more expensive living arrangement that very likely reduced the quality of life. Similarly, as many community mental health centers and service-oriented agencies make treatment decisions based on reimbursement criteria rather than on client needs (Heller, Jenkins, Steffen, and Swindle, 2000), restructuring can include advocacy to ensure that the needs of clients are met.

Restructuring may also modify the way an individual accesses the various services. Often the process of receiving services can be time-consuming because of the number of bureaucratic forms to be completed, the time needed to wait to be helped by a provider, and the lack of coordination among components of the system. Developing more efficient procedures will enhance the effectiveness of the community mental health system.

As can be seen from the preceding discussion, the community mental health system is indeed multifaceted and complex. Understanding and navigating the system requires consideration of this complexity. Each of the aspects that comprise the system is discussed in greater depth later in this book.

Restructuring the community mental health system is one application of the cognitive reframing approach used in business organizations. Although there are many types of reframing, the model developed by Bolman and Deal (2003) is very popular. In their view, any organization can be viewed from four frames or lenses. Problems occur when managers or change agents focus on only one of the frames or even only one viewpoint within a frame. This practice leads to misinterpreting critical situations and failing to comprehend the total "picture." The four frames include viewing the organization from each of the following perspectives, or frames:

a. Structural frame, which involves studying the goals, policies, and organizational charts;
b. Human resource frame, which focuses on viewing the staff and clients as an extended family, with each individual having specific needs, skills, and prejudices;
c. Political frame, which emphasizes an awareness of the conflicts, the competition for power, and the scarce resources within the company; and
d. Symbolic frame, which delves into the effect of metaphor on inspiring the staff to believe in the mission of the organization and to develop corporate loyalty.

Perceiving community mental health from a systems approach enables the practitioner to see all the frames. Through this perspective, one can generate creative and effective solutions to the challenges encountered in delivering mental health services.

These restructuring activities, such as the use of cultural amplifiers, advocacy, and reframing organizations, are themes that are described frequently in succeeding chapters of this book.

Historical Trends Leading to Community Mental Health

Deinstitutionalization

The deinstitutionalization process was a major contributor to the development of the community mental health system. The need for a community-based mental health system, in fact, was largely initiated by the preparation of many thousands of patients for discharge into the community. A number of historical trends led to this significant social change, including socio-political-cultural events that occurred during the 1960s in the United States. Although the deinstitutionalization movement was hailed as a humane reform, some individuals were released from the hospitals without adequate preparation, and this treatment led to new challenges for the nascent community mental health system. The deinstitutionalization process is covered in depth in Chapter 2.

Equal Educational Opportunity and the Civil Rights Movement

Social scientists in the middle of the twentieth century held to the belief that reducing inequity and psychological disorder could be accomplished to a great extent by altering the social environment. The roots of this belief can be traced back to the founding of the nation. Riegal (1972) and Gergin (1973) observed that social scientific theories emerge from the cultural beliefs of a society, and that these beliefs can be found in the documents held in high esteem by the citizens of that nation. In the United States, the Declaration of Independence is a seminal, almost a sacred, political statement of how Americans view the world as well as themselves. In 1776, Thomas Jefferson began this radical declaration by stating, "We hold these truths to be self-evident: that all men are created equal . . ." (Peterson, 1984). This statement implies that if we note there are substantial differences among individuals in that some are successful, healthy, intelligent, and contributors to society, whereas others are not, we can assume these differences could not be due to innate factors but must result from environmental causes. The founding fathers believed that oppressive political policies prevented citizens from achieving their full economic and social potentials. Perhaps we can observe how this environmental thrust implied in the Declaration of Independence has permeated American psychology by reflecting on the following statement of the behaviorist John Watson:

> Give me a dozen healthy infants, well formed, and my own specified world to bring them up in and I'll guarantee to take any one at random and train him to become any type of specialist I might suggest—doctor, lawyer, artist, merchant—chief and, yes, beggar-man and thief, regardless of his talents, penchants, tendencies, abilities, vocations and race of his ancestors. (Watson, 1924, p. 82)

The educational system was targeted as critical to restoring equality among racial, ethnic, and social classes. Equal educational opportunity became a national goal, and the sociologist James Coleman and his colleagues were charged by Congress with the task of investigating whether the funds and human resources provided to schools were being fairly allocated. Congress also wanted Coleman to study whether reallocating these resources had an impact on raising the academic achievement of poor and minority children (Coleman et al., 1966). Many educators and social scientists concluded that students from disadvantaged and minority cultures did not have the same access to educational resources as those from more affluent mainstream backgrounds. On the basis of the cultural belief that successful performance depends on the opportunities present in the social setting, the lack of access to resources was viewed as a significant reason for racial and ethnic differences in achievement.

The civil rights movement also focused on providing a level playing field so that all people would have equal access to resources. Mental health and human service advocates conducted research that found those most in need of services—the poor, the young, the elderly, minorities, and those who experienced mental and physical disabilities—received the least resources (Seidman & French, 1998). This finding led to many state and federal laws that prevented various forms of job discrimination. Legislation was also passed to promote residential integration, and public funds were channeled into reversing the long history of inequality that plagued the nation since the time of slavery.

Again, the national goal of the 1960s was to intervene in the social and political environment, usually by pouring funds into impoverished areas. Although the intention was noble, many believe the results were ineffective, as the programs were not fully thought out and lacked meaningful outcome evaluation measures (Levine & Perkins, 1987). Few politicians at that time would publicly state that the reason for poverty or low achievement involved any internal or individual factor. It was far more acceptable (politically correct) to emphasize the sociological causes of inequity. Currently, proponents of both models continue to debate this issue, as can be witnessed in the controversy regarding the accuracy of *The Bell Curve*, by Herrnstein and Murray (1994). This book was a major yet possibly biased review of literature concerning the basis of racial differences in intelligence. Psychologists realize the importance of limited access to resources and lack of political power as factors affecting behavior.

Crisis Intervention

Also during the middle of the twentieth century, views of the nature of mental illness and its treatment began to take an environmental emphasis. During World War II, many soldiers experienced symptoms of mental illness following involvement in a battle. Initially these soldiers were diagnosed as mentally ill and were confined to long-term treatment facilities. Appel (1999), a psychiatrist in the military at the time, was assigned to study the extent of the problem and "to prevent the seven million men in the Army from having nervous breakdowns" (p. 26). Appel noted that the number of days a regiment experienced combat was directly related to the percentage of men unable to fight because of mental trauma and other causes. Regiments that had been in combat for 120 days lost half of their members; and after 200 days, 90% of the regiment was unfit for battle. Appel further noted that all citizens were screened for mental disorders upon entering military service and that 12% of the men were rejected as a result. Thus, those who succumbed to "battle fatigue" had been judged to be mentally healthy at induction.

Some psychologists and psychiatrists began to provide these individuals with short-term, crisis-oriented counseling, and found that the soldiers could return to battle after a relatively brief time in treatment. Also, when they were discharged from the Army, they led normal and productive lives in the community. The diagnosis began to change from a mental illness with implications of genetic predisposition or character flaw to normal distress due to an unusual situation (Appel, 1999; Levine & Perkins 1987). As the rationale for these behaviors shifted, prognosis and intervention strategy changed dramatically. The "shell shock" or "battle fatigue" was understood to be caused by an abnormally stressful situation (combat), and once the individual was placed in a more normalizing setting, he could live a productive life in the community. This more optimistic prognosis was predicated on the soldier's receiving short-term treatment as soon after the traumatic experience as possible. Similarly, Lindemann (1944) found that swift crisis intervention reduced the grief of relatives of disaster victims. This research is described more fully in Chapter 5. Both these studies led to the view that many dysfunctional behaviors are situationally caused and can be reduced through brief counseling.

Medication Breakthroughs

The effectiveness of crisis intervention and other short-term therapeutic approaches increased the hope that long-term hospitalization could be avoided. At the same time, the discovery of many psychoactive medications such as the phenothiazines, which tended to reduce the intensity of psychotic symptoms and the frequency of deviant behavior, raised the possibility that mental patients could be discharged and return to the community (Seidman & French, 1998). The impact of these new medications is discussed in more detail in Chapter 2.

The Politics of Mental Illness

Various researchers began to link mental illness and social class. In a landmark study, Hollingshead and Redlich (1958) found that the label of schizophrenia was more likely to be given to lower social class individuals, whereas middle-class clients received a less severe diagnosis. Since the study was correlational, it must be noted that there are many plausible interpretations for explaining this relationship. The study, however, did initiate an important line of research that investigated social determinants of mental illness. With this study, the belief that mental illness resulted solely from individual pathology was challenged.

Others, such as Thomas Szasz (1970), postulated that labeling behaviors as being indicative of mental illness was a political decision rather than a scientific determination, and that treating an individual through institutionalization and medication was a method of deviance control. In time periods when conformity was encouraged, minor deviations from the norm were punished through the application of labels such as "mental illness." During more liberal times, a greater range of behaviors was seen as normal and acceptable.

Currently, the power to declare a behavior indicative of mental illness is held by the members of the American Psychiatric Association, who vote on what syndromes are to be included in the Diagnostic and Statistical Manual (American Psychiatric Association, 2000). Psychiatrists in the 1970s voted, for example, to no longer consider homosexuality a psychological disorder (Rappaport, 1977). These decisions typically are based not on research but on the mental health professionals' perceptions of cultural norms and tolerance for behavioral diversity.

Such decisions, regarding what constitutes deviant behavior, are embedded in the societal context. In the former Soviet Union, dissidents who opposed the communist principle that individual liberty should be subservient to the will of the community were diagnosed as having undifferentiated schizophrenia and were institutionalized. Whereas the rest of the world viewed this process as oppressive incarceration of political opponents, the Soviets interpreted this process as a scientifically based psychiatric intervention (Reich, 1983). This situation is by no means limited to totalitarian states. Meyer (personal communication, 1980), a practicing psychologist who worked in a state psychiatric center, noted that in the 1950s, an age of conformity, individuals were given psychiatric labels and institutionalized merely because of idiosyncratic personal preferences. In one instance, Meyer reported that a man who had no presenting symptoms except that he appeared disheveled and grew his hair long at a time when most other males had short hair cuts was labeled mentally ill and continuously institutionalized for over 20 years. Ruggiero (personal communication, 1980), a psychologist at a state developmental center, recalled a story told about an elderly woman. Apparently this woman, as a youth, was living at home and leading a reasonably productive life. Because she dated a man who was not liked by her family, her parents, to prevent the daughter's marriage, managed to have her placed in a "state school" for the mentally retarded. She remained institutionalized for many years, until the movement to return such individuals to the community occurred in the 1970s.

Applying a diagnostic label to a client demonstrates advantages and disadvantages. By diagnosing a client and attaching a psychiatric label, a therapist is better able to choose an appropriate treatment plan and assess therapeutic progress. In addition, applying a label enables the client to be eligible for relevant services. For example, once a student is assessed and found to have special needs, the school will provide beneficial programming not available to students not labeled. However, the client's individuality is lost, and the therapist tends to understand the person's behavior as being symptomatic of the developmental disability or mental disorder. The client becomes a "schizophrenic," and not a person who suffers from this disorder. Rosenhan (1973) studied the effect that applying psychiatric labels has on patients. This researcher recruited volunteers to serve as "pseudopatients." The volunteers were told to present themselves to the admissions unit of various mental hospitals and to tell the staff that they "heard voices." Each volunteer was admitted to the psychiatric center, usually with the label "schizophrenic." Rosenhan instructed the volunteers not to exhibit any further symptoms or unusual behavior once admitted. The staff, being aware only of the psychiatric label, interpreted any behavior as due to the mental disorder. One volunteer, a psychology student, thought it would be useful to keep a diary of experiences while on the ward. A staff member observed this practice and wrote on the patient's chart "compulsive note taker." Regardless of the fact that none of the pseudopatients had any episodes of hearing voices or any other symptoms of mental illness after being admitted, the average length of stay in the facility for these volunteers was over 70 days. The fixation on the labels prevented the staff from realizing that these individuals were normal. Thus, attaching the label of mental illness to individuals can have aversive effects on their freedom and can provide a rationale for others to exert control over their lives.

Observe how easy it is for staff trained in dysfunctional behavior to fall into the same problem pattern described in the Rosenhan study. Dr. Mayer Shevin described this concern well in this figure.

Language of Us/Them

We like things.
> *They fixate on objects.*

We try to make friends.
> *They display attention-seeking behaviors.*

We take a break.
> *They display off-task behaviors.*

We stand up for ourselves.
> *They are non-compliant.*

We have hobbies.
> *They self-stimulate.*

We choose our friends wisely.
> *They display poor peer socialization.*

We persevere.
> *They perseverate.*

We love people.
> *They have dependencies on people.*

We go for walks.
> *They run away.*

We insist.
> *They tantrum.*

We change our minds.
> *They are disoriented and have short attention spans.*

We are talented.
> *They have splinter skills.*

We are human.
> *They are . . .?*

Mayer Shevin

(Shevin, 1987, *used with permission of the author*).

Legislative Initiatives and the Mass Media

Regardless of the impact of new treatments, the most significant reasons for the great increase in deinstitutionalization during the 1960s and 1970s were not scientific breakthroughs or miracle cures. Legislative action at the federal level, judicial decisions, typically at the state level, and investigative reporting in the mass media served as the impetus to discharge mental patients into the community and create the community mental health system. Two significant trends dramatically altered the manner in which persons with either mental illness or developmental disabilities were viewed and treated.

The first trend was inspired by the federal government. President John F. Kennedy supported deinstitutionalization, partially on the recommendation of the Joint Commission on Mental Illness and Health (1961), and partially because of his concern for the treatment provided to his institutionalized sister (Rappaport, 1977). The recommendations of this Commission, which was established by Congress during the final year of the Dwight D. Eisenhower administration, were as follows:

- Provide improved care in small psychiatric hospitals for the chronically mentally ill.
- Provide improved aftercare services through partial hospitalization and rehabilitation.
- Provide intensive care for patients experiencing acute psychotic episodes.
- Offer increased public education regarding psychological disorders to reduce the stigma of mental illness.

President Kennedy's endorsement of these recommendations led to the passing of the Community Mental Health Centers Act of 1963, which encouraged mental health professionals to reintegrate the mentally ill into the community. Kennedy's political support for deinstitutionalization and community-based treatment, although controversial at the time, began a process that continues to the present. This legislation is detailed in Chapter 2.

Perhaps equally significant was the role of the mass media in affecting judicial decisions regarding the treatment of the mentally ill. In 1970, the network television reporter Geraldo Rivera conducted an exposé on the manner in which developmentally disabled adult residents of the Willowbrook State School in New York City were abused. He dramatically aired the dismal conditions, neglect, and mistreatment that were occurring. The public realized that disabled individuals were wasting away in this facility. The administration and staff were so unconcerned about the abuse of the clients that they did not object to the media coverage of the poor custodial care provided under their supervision. A group of parents brought suit against the state of New York (*A. R. C.* v. *Rockefeller*), and the presiding judge ruled that forced institutionalization without treatment was a type of illegal incarceration. The facility was ordered to provide treatment so that the clients could be prepared to return to the community as soon as possible. In order to speed up the treatment process, the "Willowbrook Consent Decree" required this state school to be dissolved and the 5,000 residents to be returned to the community within 5 years (Willer & Intagliata, 1984). This mandate, in modified form, was soon extended to all state schools (renamed developmental centers) and state hospitals (renamed psychiatric centers). This process significantly altered the manner in which those suffering from mental illness or developmental disabilities were treated. Similar judicial actions were taking place throughout the United States. At the federal level, a judge ruled in a 1972 landmark case, *Wyatt* v. *Stickney*, that institutionalized persons had a constitutional right to receive appropriate habilitation services. Normalization became the rationale for deinstitutionalization. It was felt that individuals with developmental disabilities and psychiatric conditions had the right to live in community settings free from unnecessary restraints (Willer and Intagliata, 1984). Over the years, through both judicial decisions and state and federal legislation, the nation began to realize that these individuals had civil rights, and hence statutes changed. These persons, originally called patients or residents, are now considered clients, consumers, program participants, and citizens. This significant change in thinking was evidenced more recently by the Americans with Disabilities Act, passed in 1990, which prohibited many forms of discrimination in the workplace. Also, in many states, mental health lawyers now advocate for the rights of those with developmental and psychological disabilities.

How the Willowbrook Decree Came About

This is a summary of an interview with lawyer Mickey A. Steiman, J.D.

No history of the community mental health movement would be complete without noting the tremendous influence of legislative actions and judicial rulings affecting the treatment given to consumers in the care of institutions and agencies. Among these landmark rulings is the Willowbrook Decree. In 1970, the Willowbrook State School in Staten Island, New York, housed nearly 5,000 adults and children who were diagnosed as having a developmental disability. In nearly all the cases, the residents were involuntarily admitted to this and to similar institutions. When individuals' liberty is restricted by the state through this admissions process, the state is expected to provide meaningful treatment. Otherwise, the forced incarceration reflects "cruel and unreasonable punishment," a violation of the Fourth Amendment to the U.S. Constitution. Treatment was nearly nonexistent at Willowbrook, as the residents were warehoused in an inhumane manner. Conditions did not change at Willowbrook because mental health professionals devised new counseling techniques. Rather, the situation improved because parents of the residents joined together with lawyers to sue the state, forcing it to provide better treatment. The following interview summary conducted in June 2004 is the story of one of the lawyers involved in litigating the case *NYS ARC & Parisi v. Rockefeller et al.* It is presented here so that psychologists and social workers can become more aware of the importance of the political process and the need to become involved in advocacy activities to assist their clients. In the process of reforming state institutions for both the mentally ill and the developmentally disabled, the role that the mass media played also unfolds. Mental health professionals can significantly improve the quality of life of the consumers by collaborating with print and electronic media journalists. From a systems perspective, intervening at the higher level of

the mental health system—reforming the minimum allowable standards of treatment—affects the clients' lives more completely than do many hours of individual one-to-one counseling.

In 1972, Mickey A. Steiman, a young lawyer recently out of the Syracuse University School of Law, landed a job with the Department of Justice's Office of Special Litigation in Washington, D.C. The Office of Special Litigation, with a staff of seven attorneys, was to protect the interests of the federal government wherever its interests were threatened. His supervisor, Michael Laughlin, had been involved in civil rights activities and learned about the plight of residents at the Willowbrook State School. In 1966, Burton Blatt wrote a book, *Christmas in Purgatory*, in which the conditions at this institution were described. The book included many photographs documenting the neglect and abuse of the patients and the extremely unsanitary facilities in which they lived. Geraldo Rivera, the television journalist, read the book and took a film crew to Willowbrook. His exposé of this state school on a national network brought great attention to this inhumane situation.

At about the same time, the parents of one of the residents, aware of the poor treatment at Willowbrook, contacted the New York Chapter of the American Civil Liberties Union (ACLU) and began litigation against the New York State Office of Mental Health and Developmental Disabilities. The suit was moved to a federal court and revolved around the issue of whether one of the original civil rights statutes passed in the aftermath of the Civil War had been violated. This law stated that no one shall be deprived of any privilege guaranteed by the U.S. Constitution by order of a state law. In this case, the New York state agency, acting in accordance with New York state law, restricted individuals' freedoms through involuntary admission to Willowbrook without providing meaningful treatment. The ACLU lawyer Bruce Ennis argued that

(continued)

How the Willowbrook Decree Came About   (Continued)

this action violated the civil rights of the Willowbrook resident, a right guaranteed by the preceding federal statute. A parents' group, the Association for Retarded Children (ARC), had been recently formed, and this group joined the lawsuit with the Parisi family. The lawsuit became a class action suit, and all individuals admitted to Willowbrook between certain specified years, whether still residing at Willowbrook or elsewhere, were included in the class of plaintiffs. The federal judge assigned randomly to the case, Orren Judd, a civil rights advocate, concurred with this change. This modification was crucial in that any judgment resolving the suit would be applied to thousands of consumers rather than to just one individual. This created a systems level change.

As the suit dragged on, the plaintiffs, largely the parents of residents, were running low on funding. The lawyers for the New York state agency were willing to have the case drag on, as this outcome would eventually bankrupt the plaintiffs. Defense adopted this strategy, as the state realized that an unfavorable decision, such as being forced to provide meaningful and humane treatment, would be extremely costly. The defense discounted all the witnesses' stories of neglect and abuse as isolated incidents. At that point, Mr. Laughlin's Office of Special Litigation decided to become involved. The first obstacle to overcome was that to become involved, the Office needed to show the state violated a federal statute or a congressional mandate and that no law was directly relevant. Just prior to this lawsuit, however, the Office had become a party to another landmark case, *Wyatt v. Stickney* in Alabama that stopped the forced sterilization of mental patients. The Office argued that in an 1899 case, In *Re Debs*, the federal government was judged to have the right to halt a railroad strike led by Eugene V. Debs's labor union because the interest of the federal government was threatened by the loss of rail service even though no federal statute protecting rail service existed. (It is ironic that a ruling restricting the rights of union members would

be used seventy years later to uphold the rights of institutionalized citizens.) The Office of Special Litigation argued in the *ARC & Parisi v. Rockefeller et al.* that federal Medicare and Medicaid funds were used at Willowbrook and thus the federal government had a legitimate interest in the case. Justice Judd accepted the argument and made the Department of Justice a litigating amicus curiae, a "friend of the court." This ruling allowed the vast resources of the U.S. Department of Justice to be used to support the plaintiffs, and thus the case was revitalized.

In developing its legal strategy, the Office of Special Litigation reasoned that proving inadequate treatment was a subjective judgment that could be challenged, delaying any eventual settlement, but that describing nonfunctioning physical facilities was far more obvious and objective. Ten FBI agents were sent into Willowbrook to document that toilets and showers were not working for months at a time, and logs were kept. The agents photographed staff members wheeling groups of typically naked residents on a "cripple cart." Because the residents were unable to use the broken plumbing facilities, they were forced to urinate and defecate on the floor as they were wheeled around. Later in the day, the floor—and often the residents— were hosed down. The Office of Special Litigation hired experts who described how good institutions could be run, and how the conditions at Willowbrook were deplorable and unnecessarily inadequate. Parents documented substandard medical treatments. One resident broke his leg in a fall and died because of infection caused by woefully incompetent follow-up. Others documented that residents were used in Hepatitis B experiments and that some contracted the disease and died as a result.

Justice Judd, after hearing the testimony, strongly recommended that New York state settle the case. Over a weekend, after two years of litigation, the Willowbrook Decree was hammered out. The state was required to reduce the census of patients at Willowbrook to prevent

(continued)

How the Willowbrook Decree Came About   (Continued)

overcrowding and also to increase the number of staff treating the residents there. So as not to enable the state to farm out residents to other facilities, thereby creating the same overcrowded and inadequate conditions elsewhere, the decree required that certain minimum staff-to-patient ratios be maintained in any facility in which a Willowbrook class client resided. Ultimately, this decree meant that every facility in the state had to provide a minimum level of physical, occupational, and speech therapy, and psychological service. All residents were assessed regularly and treatment plans were developed and revised as clients' level of functioning improved. A Willowbrook Review Panel was established to oversee the state's compliance with the Decree, and this panel continued to operate until Willowbrook was finally closed. Mr. Steiman, after leaving his position with the Department of Justice, was hired as the counsel for the panel, and he reviewed the monthly reports prepared by the state. At one point, the state failed to meet its requirement to fund the mandated services, and the panel filed suit to hold the state in contempt—with the intended remedy being that the then Governor, Hugh Carey, would be forced to live at Willowbrook for a month. The state swiftly provided the funding, and the lawsuit was withdrawn. Finally, the parallel agencies of other states observed what happened in New York, and many decided to upgrade their services in anticipation of similar suits and decrees. The Willowbrook decision had far-reaching effects on the system, extending throughout the entire nation.

One may wonder what would have happened if the Office of Special Investigation had not become involved in the case. Perhaps the original plaintiffs would have limped on; but without adequate funding, their arguments, lacking expert witnesses and extensive objective documentation, would not have been as compelling. It is likely that the resulting decree would not have as significant an effect on the treatment of institutionalized residents.

One also might wonder how this Office of Special Investigations would have functioned had the Nixon Administration been more aware of its activities and the implications for enhanced services. During the time of this litigation, the administration was preoccupied with winning the 1972 presidential election, and then with managing the resulting Watergate scandal. Five successive attorneys general were in office throughout the case, since many of them were forced to resign in the aftermath of this scandal. Few in the Department of Justice cared what the nearly invisible office of seven lawyers were doing, yet they changed the community mental health system, perhaps forever.

Mental health professionals typically were reluctant participants in these dramatic "sea changes." Psychologists and psychiatrists had no training in deinstitutionalization, and they were content to provide custodial service in the large state facilities. Szasz (1970) and Breggin (1991) noted that psychiatric drug administration to patients seemed to be primarily directed toward helping the staff manage disruptive patients, rather than to enhance the clients' ability to lead a productive life. Many, such as Yoosuf Haveliwala, former director of the (now closed) Harlem Valley Psychiatric Center in Dutchess County, New York, realized that the professional staff themselves had become institutionalized and that they required additional training to learn how to facilitate the clients' movement into the community (Levine & Perkins, 1987).

Later Developments in Community Mental Health

Unfortunately, the hoped-for changes to the delivery of mental health services in the community have not been fully realized. During the more than four decades since the passage of the Community Mental Health Act of 1963, a series of factors occurred that prevented the aims of the system from being fulfilled completely. Heller et al. (2000) identified these difficulties as follows:

- Beginning in the 1980s, during the time when the public seemed to be intent on reducing the size of the national debt, federal funding for mental health and human services was reduced dramatically. The financially well-off clients were able to receive private psychotherapy, whereas the poor and chronically mentally ill had access only to barely adequate basic supportive care.
- Since most mental health professionals were trained only in clinical psychotherapy, they felt uncomfortable providing preventive interventions and performing consultative and public educational activities that lay outside their area of expertise. Funding for such retraining was meager at best, and few universities developed programs for the next generation of professionals to be prepared for these nonclinical activities.
- Ambiguity existed regarding who was responsible for providing community mental health services. Prior to 1960, the states assumed the major part of the burden of providing mental health services, and the state mental hospital was the main location in which these services were dispensed. As described in Chapter 2, the Community Mental Health Act of 1963 initiated a new service delivery system, and the federal government provided much of the funding for its implementation. When federal funding sources dried up during the Reagan era, the states were reluctant to increase their share of the financial burden. The states did not accept ownership of the community-based programs, since the system had originally resulted from federal legislation.
- Advocates of the community mental health system assumed that the local communities would mobilize to protect the programs and would fight to reinstate the higher funding levels. Instead, community residents were more concerned that group homes and other programs and facilities for individuals suffering from mental illness would be placed in their neighborhoods. These citizens were relieved to learn that lower funding levels might mean that fewer community-based facilities would be opened. This pattern of community residents' being concerned that their quality of life and property values might decline if community mental health programs were established in their neighborhoods has been called the NIMBY ("not in my back yard") syndrome.
- When the boundaries of the 1,500 catchment areas were drawn, natural communities were not considered. As a result, some communities were split between two service areas, and in other cases neighborhoods that differed ethnically and socioeconomically were combined into the same area. This result caused great diversity within a community mental health center's service area, and no one community group could speak for the needs of the 75,000 to 200,000 people in a

particular catchment area. This outcome reduced citizen involvement and lack of local ownership for the programs offered. Professional mental health center staff were left to decide what services were to be provided. The professionals had not been taught how to collaborate with community residents in problem-solving activities, nor how to incorporate a concern for community traditions and needs in the services provided, and many of these professionals felt relieved when community input was not expressed.

Not all the problems facing the community mental health system were due to technical and funding issues. Heller et al. (2000) noted that the system failed to meet its expectations because of unexamined societal assumptions regarding mental health services. In other words, the public and their elected representatives as well as many mental health professionals held to an ideology more consistent with the pre-1960 mental health system. Some of the problematic assumptions are as follows:

- All individuals should be evaluated according to one standard. That is, there exists one acceptable normal behavior pattern, and all others are indicative of mental disorders. This belief leads to great conformity, and individual differences in behavior and preferences for diverse lifestyles are viewed as symptoms of disorder. The public frowned on diversity. Meanwhile, clinicians, who were trained to detect illness, tended to over-diagnose psychopathology.
- Similarly, community residents overgeneralized from extreme examples. Of course, it is true that *some* former mental patients behave impulsively and even in a violent manner. The overgeneralization—that all discharged individuals could be dangerous—was frequently used as a reason not to allow group homes to be placed in the community. Given proper predischarge skill preparation and adequate supervision in the community facility, such behaviors are much less likely to occur. Professionals concerned about liability were also reluctant to discharge individuals into the community. Energy should have been directed toward dedicating greater resources to ensure drug compliance and toward providing activities for daily living (ADL) training for the former patients, and to offer public education for the community rather than to discourage or prevent deinstitutionalization.
- Although research has pointed to multiple causes of mental disorders, many professionals adhere to a favorite therapeutic approach that emphasizes only one particular cause of psychopathology. Although psychological paradigms can enable practitioners to understand a problem deeply from one perspective, these paradigms also act as a type of blinder and thus can cause individuals to be unable to see the same problem from other viewpoints. Accepting a multiple causation approach to disorders in living leads to the development of multiple prevention and treatment options. Such flexibility in intervention alternatives increases the likelihood that the unique needs of those requiring assistance in the community can be met.
- Similarly, federal legislation tends to mandate and fund uniform solutions to mental health problems. Local communities that want access to these federal

dollars find they are not allowed to modify the funded programs to account for cultural differences or even geographical differences. A program designed with an inner city urban population in mind might not be appropriate for use on a rural Native American reservation.

■ Frequently, funding priorities and the training most mental health professionals have received tend to produce a nearly exclusive focus on treatment and rehabilitation. Swift (1987) found that only 2.5% of all the hours worked by staff in community mental health centers are dedicated to prevention. Until more graduate programs offer instruction on developing, implementing, and evaluating preventive interventions, the near absence of prevention programs offered through community mental health centers is unlikely to change.

The Community Psychological Approach to Community Mental Health

The preceding assumptions had to be challenged. A new paradigm was needed to provide a better theoretical basis upon which to build innovative services for the community mental health system. Community psychology is an approach that provides this alternative strategy. All professionals working in the community mental health system—whether they be social workers, psychologists, mental health or school counselors—can utilize components of this paradigm.

Community psychology views mental health problems or disorders in living as being caused by a poor person-environment fit (Levine and Perkins, 1987). This model considers that focusing only on persons psychodynamically or only on settings behavioristically leads to ineffective treatment and solutions that can cause worse problems later on. The community psychological approach instead looks at the relationship between persons and their social settings. It accepts that there are individual differences among people and that each setting has its own strengths and weaknesses. No one setting is conducive to the happiness and productivity of every person, and no one person can exist or develop well in every setting.

Using an example from education, a highly conforming child would do well in a structured school but would do poorly in an educational setting that called for a great deal of individual initiative and creativity. Similarly, a curious, active child interested in exploring his/her own world would be frustrated and nonproductive in the traditional school but would be a leader in the more freestyle program. It is possible to label either child, who simply attended the wrong type of school, as a poor learner or an underachiever, or even in the case of the active child, a behavior problem. Such labels are stigmatizing and self-fulfilling. By focusing on the child's inappropriate behavior alone, a proponent of the traditional paradigm would create a worse problem. Individual counseling for the child could imply that the child is at fault and has an intrinsic character flaw or psychological disorder. The same is true if we label either of the preceding schools as being bad. If all schools were judged according to how well they met the traditional standard of structure, they would become uniformly structured and unable to meet the needs of active, nonconforming children.

Continuing with the preceding example, a mental health professional utilizing the community psychology model would attempt to investigate the fit between the needs of the child and the resources and opportunities presented by the available schools. If no reasonably good fit were available, the provider would have many strategies for developing a better fit. One might use social or coping-skill training to increase the range of settings in which the child can function, or one might alter the school by providing diverse kinds of learning activities to increase the range of children with which the school system can help. In this way, the social worker, counselor, or community psychologist need not label either the child or the school as being problematic, but rather could place emphasis on forging a comfortable match between the two. In this example, an ecological approach is utilized, in which both the needs of the individual and the resources available to the person are considered together. The focus is on this person-setting unit, and not on just the person or just the environment. More specific examples of this ecological perspective are presented in Chapter 3.

Community Psychology's Central Thesis: The Dohrenwend Model

Perhaps the most significant statement of the orientation of community psychology was presented by Barbara Dohrenwend (1978). This internationally recognized scholar and then president of the American Psychological Association's Division for Community Psychology provided a blueprint for understanding problems in living and for developing intervention strategies to promote mental health. In doing so, she opposed the medical model. Dohrenwend noted that traditional medical models of mental illness view psychopathology as inherent within some individuals and as being due to early childhood experiences. This view is far too limiting in developing the types of treatment that can be utilized to reduce illness. The medical model sees symptoms as the effects of illness, and it stipulates that the root causes must be identified and treated in order for the individual to be healed. This view forces the helper to utilize only psychodynamic therapy or medication as treatment methods. The Dohrenwend model differentiates psychosocial stress from psychopathology. Psychosocial stress is the normal emotional reaction to a traumatic life event and does not imply that an individual is mentally ill. Rather than viewing the stress as a symptom of illness, it can be viewed as a self-contained process. Dohrenwend noted that if the stress is treated as soon as possible, the emotional reaction does not typically degenerate into psychopathology (Dohrenwend, 1978).

When an individual experiences psychosocial stress in response to a crisis, three outcomes are possible. First, the person might grow as a result of having mastered the crisis. In this case, the "survivor" learns that the coping skills utilized were successful and thus can feel a greater self-confidence when encountering similar stressful situations in the future. Second, other individuals could return to their precrisis state and consider the crisis as passed, and could feel that they can resume their normal routine. The third possible outcome is that the person could succumb to the stress and develop psychopathology. This outcome usually occurs because the individual's coping strategies, social supports, and other resources are either insufficient or nonexistent, and the stress reaction changes from acute to chronic as a result. This third outcome is similar to Selye's (1956) more biologically based general adaptation syndrome. Stress-inducing agents cause an alarm reaction in the victim, and physiological changes occur in the body to mobilize its resources to deal with the stressor. After a relatively brief time, the body enters a resistance stage. During this stage, an attempt is made to return to a normal precrisis physiological state. If the stressor has not been eliminated or successfully confronted, a state of exhaustion results, and an abnormal pathological physiological state can occur. At this point, removing the stressor does not reverse the process, but rather, the abnormal psychological state or mental illness itself needs to be addressed.

In the Dohrenwend model, the timing of the intervention is critical if the third outcome, psychopathology, is to be avoided. Generally, the more swiftly the intervention is applied following the onset of the crisis, the more likely it will be successful in providing effective help. Psychopathology will be avoided, and the individual can lead a normal, productive life.

According to this model, there is no need to wait for a crisis to occur before intervening. Many developmental or life stage crises can be anticipated, and a community mental health practitioner can plan the type of resources and programs in a community to meet the likely needs of persons about to enter these developmental crises. The entire system of the delivery of mental health services can be analyzed to determine whether gaps exist in meeting these likely needs. For example, Scileppi (1976) used Erikson's (1950) stage theory of development to anticipate psychological crises and to ensure that agency services were available to meet the needs of individuals before and during these life-cycle milestones. This particular position paper focused on the Native American Reservation in Pine Ridge, South Dakota, and involved programs designed to meet developmental needs of individuals who were going through transitions, as well as the needs of their families. The services were designed to prevent healthy individuals from succumbing to stress as well as to treat those who had already been adversely affected by the crisis.

Additionally, by using the Dohrenwend model, the likely cyclical crises individuals encounter in institutions like schools, colleges, and hospitals can be considered. Gibbs, Lachenmeyer, and Sigal (1992) discussed how programs could be established in residential colleges to deal with expected needs of students at different times during the academic year. During the first weeks of school, students, particularly those in their first year at college, need to make friends and to experience a sense of belonging. Programs designed to teach social and interpersonal skills and various group activities can be provided. Enhancing listening and self-expressive techniques may reduce the fear of initiating a friendship and may increase the likelihood that such a relationship might develop. Later on, students might feel imposed upon by peers, and possibly exploited or abused, and the staff might provide assertiveness training workshops or date rape awareness programs. Stress management and time management workshops can help students during examination periods, and programs designed to prevent loneliness and separation fears are particularly useful for graduating students at the conclusion of the academic year.

The Dohrenwend model encourages the providing of services in the community that are proactive rather than reactive. Proactive services are available prior to the onset of the crisis, with individuals having access to these programs as soon as (or even before) stress is encountered. Examples of such proactive programs and their outcomes are presented in Chapter 4 on prevention. Preparing patients for surgical procedures, primary school students for middle school, employees for retirement, and couples for marriage are a few proactive-type programs. Such prevention-oriented programs require that the individual has at least a minimum level of motivation to participate, or else the effectiveness of the service will be limited.

Similarly, the model favors a seeking rather than waiting mode of service delivery (Rappaport, 1977). The traditional clinician sits in an office "waiting" for clients who have already succumbed to stress and are experiencing chronic disorders in living to present themselves. This method of service delivery is less effective, as typically the clients' symptoms are in an advanced stage, and these symptoms have already disrupted the social and occupational aspects of their lives. The range of services provided in this waiting mode is also frequently restricted to individual psychotherapy and medication. Instead, community mental health providers utilize a seeking mode. Service providers anticipate crises and subsequently develop targeted programs in the community. They conduct needs assessments and analyze the programs offered in the community to determine what unmet needs or gaps in services exist. The community mental health professional then consults with agencies, schools, businesses, and neighborhood groups to provide enhanced services and to ensure that the persons needing these services have access to them. The mental health professional travels to the school, workplace, group home, and neighborhood organization. In a sense, the community practitioner's office *is* the community.

In the seeking mode, some interventions might be focused on individuals. Conducting psychotherapy and developing individual behavior plans to enable an emotionally disturbed child to interact appropriately in school would be examples of person-oriented treatment, particularly if these services were provided in the child's school setting. Other interventions could be offered to groups, such as to employees in their work setting. Scileppi and Montalto (1986) discussed the value of offering workshops on topics such as interpersonal communication and problem solving to workers in large corporations. The trainees learn skills that can be useful in their lives, both at work and at home. As will be seen later on in Chapter 6, having good interpersonal skills improves one's social support network, and a worker who later experiences a crisis is more likely to have friends to assist in managing the crisis. Companies generally support such workshops, since they enhance the productivity of their employees.

Interventions could also be geared to changing social systems. Allen, Chinsky, Larcen, Lockman, and Selinger (1976) described a program in which community psychologists consulted to school administrators and collaboratively developed a multilevel intervention to promote students' social problem solving, enhance their social skills, and reduce behavioral problems. Others have sought out persons occupying key roles in the community and have designed training programs that enable these citizens to become nonprofessional mental health providers. When encountering a crisis, it is highly likely that individuals will (either voluntarily or not) discuss their situation with a police officer, a clergy member, a teacher, or others. The result of this interaction could be pivotal in determining whether individuals will grow from or succumb to the crisis. Offering training in crisis intervention, stress management and similar skills to these key community leaders could help the individuals in need to resolve the crisis in a positive manner. In addition, it could enhance the productivity of the helper. Police officers may have fewer repeat calls, and clergy members may become better pastors as a result of this training.

Such social system level intervention that utilizes the seeking mode is very cost-effective. A two-day interpersonal communication workshop training 20 clergy whose congregations each average 100 families will provide service for about 5,000 individuals, at a minute fraction of what individual psychotherapy would cost. Of course, as with any other workshop, the trainers must be sensitive to the cultural background and individual preferences of the trainees, and must encourage the trainees to do likewise with those they serve.

In studying the implications of the Dohrenwend model, the need for social workers, counselors, and psychologists to become involved in politics or the mass media becomes evident. The mental health professional must ensure that services are available in the community and that those persons in need have access to them. Communities, states, and nations must be made aware of the needs and the benefits of providing services to prevent mental illness and enhance the quality of life in society. Either through public funds, private foundations, insurance companies, or some combination thereof, financial resources must be provided. During a time when politicians get votes by striving to reduce expenditures, mental health professionals need to advocate the provision of more services that are cost-effective. This effort requires influencing voters by using the mass media and consulting with legislators regarding the sponsorship and passage of strong laws enhancing mental health services. There are many hidden (and overt) costs associated with not preventing substance abuse, domestic violence, school dropouts, and related social concerns, and the benefits of prevention programs must become more visible to attract funds and public support (Perla, 1997). Psychologists, counselors, and social workers need to make citizens more aware that cutting back services has detrimental long-term financial and social effects.

Finally, the Dohrenwend model does not lose sight of the individual in this person-environment fit paradigm. Each of the interventions mentioned earlier should be tailor-made to fit the needs of individuals. In many cases, the personality style of potential clients may clash with programs. Introverts, for example, may not seek out social skills training workshops. Some groups of suicide-prone individuals might not be inclined to call a telephone "hotline" service. Bereaved senior citizens who encounter the loss of their peers and the resulting shrinking social support network might not believe that joining a new social group is appropriate for them. Practitioners must develop creative programs for each of these groups. Some successful programs might involve multifaceted interventions. Encouraging older Americans to join volunteer groups, for example, might provide new opportunities for socializing that could be appealing to those who would not think of joining a group just to relieve their own loneliness. Research is needed to study utilization patterns of existing programs and to ensure that barriers to participation are removed for those in need of the service.

Frequently the barriers to participating in programs result from cultural differences. Programs established for rural teens may not be appropriate for inner-city youth. The values of Hispanic families differ from those of African American families. Social networks of blue-collar workers are structured very differently from those of more affluent individuals. The community provider cannot generalize from the success of a program involving one population to a different group without modifying the program to make it amenable to the norms, values, perceptions, and traditions of the newly targeted culture. Rather than imposing one culture onto another, one needs to be sensitive to these differences and adopt the value of cultural relativity. To enhance this aspect of person-environment fit, it is useful to collaborate with leaders in the targeted community when planning interventions.

When utilizing the Dohrenwend model, ethical questions need to be raised. The seeking mode of service delivery should be balanced by a respect for the freedom of individuals to choose not to participate in a program. Although it is certainly appropriate to provide access to a program and to develop strategies to ensure that all those in need are aware of the program and its benefits, it is usually not appropriate to force individuals living in the community to participate. In addition, it is necessary to inform program participants of possible aversive effects. Providing assertiveness training for women is usually beneficial. However, a compliant woman who learns how to be assertive may find that a relationship with an exploiting boyfriend or husband may suffer (Foa & Emmelkamp, 1983). Another ethical question concerns whether the goal of an intervention is a desirable one. Beliefs regarding the proper styles of parenting vary from culture to culture and from time to time. What was once thought of as discipline is now considered child abuse. As previously suggested, community mental health experts should consult with local community leaders to ensure the intervention is not an imposition on the culture.

Social Work, Community Psychology, and Mental Health Counseling

Social work and community psychology share a common ecological framework, and practitioners in the field, regardless of title, are truly "kindred spirits" (personal communication, Murray Levine, 1990), who are united in attempting to enhance the quality of mental health in the community. Mental health counselors—whether they are school, community, or pastoral—draw freely from both social work and psychology.

Perhaps the major difference between social work and community psychology is that the latter is an approach within psychology. It is affiliated with psychology, as it supports this field's emphasis on enhancing the mental health of individuals. Social work emphasizes a sociological approach, noting how structural role characteristics of organizations, systems, and communities affect the mental health of groups. Although community psychology focuses more on individuals, it draws on other disciplines such as sociology, anthropology, and political science. Both disciplines acknowledge that behavior occurs only in a context. All behaviors, both healthy and symptomatic of disorder, are influenced by the quality of the match between a person's needs and abilities *and* the setting's resources and opportunities. Both social workers and community psychologists view the person-environment fit as the appropriate unit of study, and each discipline contributes its distinctive orientation to this understanding.

In either discipline, behavior is seen from a system's perspective that allows for interventions to be generated at many levels: individual, family, groups, institution, and community. This approach enables practitioners to predict likely problematic transitional periods, allowing them to plan programs that not only treat but also prevent difficulties in living.

Both social work and community psychology focus on the community. Interventionists are sensitive to the local cultural norms and traditions, and they develop programs in cooperation with community residents and organizations.

Finally, proponents of this joint perspective note that many difficulties in living are intensified by lack of access to resources and political inequity. Programs that empower communities to remedy these problems are encouraged. As can be seen, many of the defining qualities of community psychology and social work have the Dohrenwend model as their basis.

Work Settings in the Community Mental Health System

The Dohrenwend model provides the blueprint for developing many useful interventions to promote mental health in the community. A question might be raised regarding where community practitioners are employed to implement these ideas. Although this question is discussed in many of the succeeding chapters, it is beneficial to introduce the issue briefly here.

Professionals can be employed in community mental health centers. Ruth Schelkun (2000) recently described activities such as consultation, education, and prevention that she performed while being employed in a community mental health center in Ann Arbor, Michigan. For example, she collaborated with a local neighborhood group to design enhanced community resources to meet the needs created by a sudden influx of people when a 2,000-unit, low-income project was opened. In another activity, Dr. Schelkun designed a program to teach school staff and administrators how to collaborate with members of students' families to create school-level change. In addition, she also worked with the staff of agencies that served homeless populations, and she developed video and live in-service programs to teach such community competency skills as how to manage difficult situations. Finally, Dr. Schelkun offered programs to train the staff of volunteer organizations and social service agencies in organizational development skills. In these activities, she worked with teachers, school administrators, outreach workers, agency staff, and local residents to promote the well-being of those who live in the community. Although Dr. Schelkun was a psychologist, knowing the professional's title or discipline does not always identify the type of work activities performed. In different centers, the same activities described before—and many more—could have been done by social workers or counselors as well as psychologists.

Social workers, counselors, and psychologists can be employed in a variety of other settings; some are university- and school-based, others are agency, government, or corporation affiliated, and the remainder are self-employed as private consultants and practitioners. In these settings, most are employed primarily in other roles such as educator, administrator, program evaluator, researcher, or therapist. In each role, practitioners who are knowledgeable about the community psychological perspective and strategies creatively search for opportunities to utilize this approach.

Teachers at any level, for example, could incorporate topics related to mental health enhancement in the educational curriculum. Teaching interpersonal communication and problem-solving strategies not only helps students to become better learners but also enables them to deal more effectively with the common stressors in life. Administrators and program evaluators, in pursuing their usual duties, might develop new programs that provide easier access to needed resources in the community. These new programs might be designed either to keep healthy citizens well or to enable those already affected by mental illness to lead more productive lives. Staff at various levels of government might facilitate the enacting of legislation, the setting of public policy, and the funding of proposals to implement productive community psychological principles more fully. Finally, private consultants and practitioners might work with grassroots groups, support groups, and any of the preceding staff to offer workshops and to design and implement programs to enhance the quality of mental health. For example, a consultant might offer stress management programs to managers and employees of corporations. Therapists could consult to area clergy to develop empathy skills for use with members of their congregation. Still others might use mass media to disseminate practical mental-health-enhancing techniques to area residents. The list of employment opportunities is dependent largely on the level of creativity of the community provider. As more mental health professionals learn about this approach, it is expected that the list of possible applications will grow larger.

The Organization of This Book

The remainder of this book elaborates on many of the issues discussed earlier. Since deinstitutionalization is so central to the community mental health system, the following chapter is focused on this process. After the deinstitutionalization chapter, the book is divided into sections that deal with theoretical perspectives, the values of practitioners in the field, methods and techniques used in community mental health, and projections regarding the future of this service delivery system.

The major theoretical perspective in community mental health is the ecological approach. Recognizing that the quality of the person–environment fit is the appropriate unit of study, preventive interventions can be devised to enhance this fit. Each aspect of the fit can be studied. The process describing how individuals encounter crises and the types of coping skills they can be taught emphasize the person component. Community mental health counselors also conduct forms of brief psychotherapy to assist those in crisis. The role that the social support network plays in making the setting more conducive to mental health targets the environment side of the fit. The therapeutic and social system interventions are aimed at enhancing an individual's ability to remain in the community. Thus, the chapters on ecology, prevention, crisis and coping, and social support and systems level interventions form a unified approach to the field.

Community mental health practitioners are not value-neutral. Interventions that increase sensitivity to diversity, empowerment, and ready access to needed resources are viewed as desirable, and their opposites are discouraged. The ethical principles involved in creating and implementing interventions at all levels are discussed, along with the ethical implications of nonintervention.

The methods and techniques utilized by practitioners to concretize the theory base follow. Community mental health professionals consult with staff of other agencies, organizations, and institutions in the community, and this consultation allows for both individual- and systems-oriented interventions. Following the chapter on consultation, the next technique discussed is research. This is consistent with U.S. Surgeon General Satcher's encouragement that all interventions in the mental health system be based on empirical studies. Thus, program evaluation and outcomes assessment techniques are described. The final method concerns how to reform the system and to develop new programs. Frequently, service components need restructuring, and community mental health practitioners need to be aware of the many strategies to create change. The ability to secure funding through grant-writing is also covered.

The final section projects into the future. The elderly population is the fastest-growing segment in the United States and elsewhere. The needs of this group and the types of new services to meet their emerging needs are explored in a chapter on gerontology. The costs of behavioral care are rising swiftly, and it is likely that managed care and health insurance companies policies will dramatically change during the next ten years to find and fund cost-effective methods of enhancing the quality of mental health in the community. The strategies likely to be adopted are discussed, and the implications for how this outcome will affect the delivery of mental health services are considered. In its entirety, this text is intended to provide a more complete awareness of the community mental health system and will enable practitioners to navigate the system more effectively.

DISCUSSION QUESTIONS

1. What is the community mental health approach? Is it likely that this approach will be effective in producing positive change in the mental health field? If not, what are the impediments? Why did the traditional model of psychotherapy need to be replaced?

2. How would a community mental health interventionist use the Dohrenwend model to design and implement a needed program? How might the cultural diversity in the locality affect the way the program is designed and put into practice?

3. What benefits can community mental health impart to the mentally ill? What are some benefits and detriments of applying labels? Are they necessary? Are they helpful?

4. What is the purpose of epidemiological surveillance? Why is it important to monitor population characteristics?

5. How did the deinstitutionalization process spur the movement toward reforming the mental health industry? What events contributed to the shift? How did the state of behavioral health care in the past differ from the methods that are commonly used today? How might these methods change if the community psychological approach becomes implemented more fully in the future?

2 Deinstitutionalization

O B J E C T I V E S

This chapter is designed to enable the reader to:

- Gain an overview of the history of institutionalization.
- Identify factors that contributed to the initiation of the institutionalization movement.
- Identify the role of government in the institutionalization and deinstitutionalization movements.
- Describe the "moral approach" and its roots.
- Identify events that contributed to the "psychiatric revolution" in the 1950s.
- Describe the ways in which a preventative viewpoint contributed to the deinstitutionalization process.
- Identify three perspectives from which to view the impact of reduced hospitalization.
- Document the roots of somatic treatments, psychosurgery, and other methods used in the past to treat the mentally ill.
- Understand the importance of the Community Mental Health Act of 1963.
- Identify different types of antipsychotic drugs and their importance to deinstitutionalization, along with their benefits and side effects.
- Understand the bio-psycho-social model of schizophrenia.
- Define evidenced-based practices.
- Outline the ideas behind the mental hygiene movement.
- Understand the impact of World War II on the mental health industry.
- Gain a general understanding of relevant mental health legislation, on both the state and the federal levels.

"Those who cannot learn from history are doomed to repeat it."
George Santayana

The topic of deinstitutionalization can serve as a lens to review the past treatment of the severely mentally ill. Starting with the history of institutionalization and tracking its progress can provide a focal point as to why the deinstitutionalization process became necessary. It also discloses both positive and questionable outcomes for persons with mental illness. Understanding what produced these negative events provides an important lesson in future program considerations. Current practices that utilize "evidenced-based" psychosocial interventions for the severely mentally ill offer renewed hope that those with mental illness can achieve not only symptom reduction but also a significant improvement in their quality of life.

The Beginning of Institutionalization

Any discussion of deinstitutionalization must begin with an understanding of how the institutional process itself began. The story of the treatment of the mentally ill in America is a troubled one. The care of the mentally ill has indeed had a difficult past, ranging the spectrum from no treatment at all to brain sectioning, or lobotomy. In the broader picture, it is possible to understand that most attempts to treat the mentally ill were well-intentioned but in many ways doomed. The core problem is that even today there does not exist a thorough understanding of what causes severe mental illness. Schizophrenia affects 1% of the worldwide population, but the precise etiology and course remain elusive. Scientists can describe the disorder and its symptoms and can indicate what neurotransmitters are askew, but they are yet unable to indicate a cause. Treating a disease symptomatically can be dangerous or ineffective. Severe colds are a good example. Symptoms include aches, runny nose, and maybe fever. We can treat the symptoms in many ways: rest, antibiotics, fluids, cold remedies, and so on. On the other hand, good medicine looks to the etiology and treats accordingly. Antibiotics treat bacterial infections but have no effect on viruses, and thus are ineffective if prescribed for a viral ailment that is misdiagnosed as bacterial. Psychiatry, similarly, continues to look for a root cause of severe mental illness in an effort to develop an effective treatment.

People with severe mental illness have difficulty functioning in the world. They often have difficulty thinking, and they may show inappropriate emotions or may not socialize. In colonial days, without treatment or institutions, the mentally ill could be found in various locations. The obvious place was home. Families were called upon to take responsibility for their loved ones. In many cases, the home setting proved somewhat effective. Rothman (1971) described the home environment for the mentally ill as a loving setting where people were looked after and taken care of. Deutsch (1949), on the other hand, found life for the mentally ill much more difficult. Individuals would wander freely and wind up in jails, or be dropped off in different towns like unwanted cats. Unfortunately, in today's world, there still exist mentally ill individuals who are homeless or in jail. The progress made in over 300 years is questionable. Deutsch (1949) discussed other colonial day practices such as building small residential units (in one case, 5 by 7 feet) where the mentally ill would live. Auctions were held to sell off "lunatics" to the highest bidder. Beatings and floggings were commonly documented. In spite of this practice, there were people who wanted to help. Almshouses or poor houses were designed to help the mentally ill by providing room and board, and in some cases by creating employment opportunities. Work in colonial times was viewed as essential and seen as a way to contribute to the developing society. In writings of the day, the mentally ill were referred to as "distracted," a reference most likely indicating that they were distracted from work. Colonial Americans implemented the English poor laws of 1597 and 1601, which gave community officers the responsibility to force families to take care of their sick or assign them to workhouses. Although these workhouses were ostensibly for the poor, they were really inhabited by the social deviants of the day, including the developmentally disabled, physically handicapped, homeless, and mentally ill. Since work was stressed and seen as part of a normal life, people who could not work were stigmatized as being poor and needing help.

Over time, those with an illness were separated from the other poor. In 1752, the first hospital to provide a separate unit for the mentally ill was opened in the Pennsylvania Hospital, in Philadelphia. It wasn't until 1773 that a separate facility for the mentally ill was opened in Williamsburg, Virginia. Interestingly, this public hospital was modeled after the Bedlam Hospital in England, which was originally called "Bethlehem Hospital." It only later became known as "Bedlam," a word now used in common parlance to describe out of control activities, such as those that occurred in the hospital at that time.

As the 18th century was coming to a close, an international movement for the treatment of the mentally ill was beginning. Benjamin Rush, the American Father of Psychiatry, was convinced that mental illness was caused by clogged cerebral blood vessels, and he prescribed bloodletting (a process that drained blood from the individual in the hope that new, "good blood," would form, and consequently the "bad blood" would be eliminated). Meanwhile, a much broader and more enlightened view of the mentally ill was taking place in Europe. In France, Philippe Pinel was not impressed with either the incarceration or the treatment approaches of his time. He saw such practices as bloodletting and chaining patients as not only ineffective but also inhumane. Instead, he sought to work with the patient and to instill hope and confidence. His work became known as "moral treatment," words that reflect a weak French translation but had profound effects on the treatment and care of the mentally ill for hundreds of years. This approach, perhaps better called "psychological treatment," treated the mentally ill with respect. Pinel was known for removing the chains from the incarcerated mentally ill. His "moral treatment" began to spread to other European countries (Grob, 1994). In Italy and England, respectively, Vincenzio Chiargui and William Tuke took up the new approach. Most notable was Tuke, who founded the York Retreat in 1792. His methods relied on assisting patients in gaining self-control and self-restraint. Tuke was a Quaker, and his religious background allowed him to expand upon the concepts of moral treatment. He often described the treatment of the mentally ill as akin to the treatment of children. Although the cause of mental illness was not known, Tuke and others saw that their treatment made people well enough to return home. In effect, they had a workable treatment approach that utilized a hospital or an asylum, as they were known at the time (Grob, 1994). Soon, others in the

United States saw the potential of this approach, and the humane hospital treatment and a number of hospitals throughout the United States were initiated. Among the first were Bloomingdale Hospital in New York City, the Public Asylum in Williamsburg, Virginia, and McLean Hospital near Boston, Massachusetts. The excitement and optimism generated at this time were further enhanced by claims of cure rates that ranged from 40% to 100% (Quen, 1975). These claims were publicly pronounced and created quite a positive stir. It would appear, however, such claims were exaggerated and over time may have led to disillusionment with this new, more humane approach. Quen (1975) noted that Woodard, in 1834, reported an 82% cure rate and that Galt and Awl in 1842–1843 reported an astonishing 100% recovery rate, but Quen indicated these claims were impossible and exaggerated. Nonetheless, momentum was building for the treatment of the mentally ill in settings other than homes and almshouses. Asylums were developing and in some cases, thriving. States that heretofore had avoided the use of tax funds were now beginning to invest in publicly funded state mental asylums. The initial asylums were mostly privately financed, but both Massachusetts and New York were working toward developing institutions in the 1820s and 1830s. There was a growing feeling that government now could and should take care of the less fortunate. The reasons for this shift in thinking were multiple, one being the desire for government to improve an expanding and emerging society. It was important for established economic progress to be maintained. It would appear, however, that the motivation of government was not as pure and singular as that of Tuke and Pinel. Early state-funded asylums for the mentally ill were, unfortunately, less interested in the moral treatment approach and instead focused on custodial care. The stated goal was to remove the mentally ill from society. The unspoken comment was that society could get on with its economic production and not be plagued by "distracters." New state asylums in Virginia and Kentucky were underfunded from their inception, and as a result the concept of "moral treatment" was never implemented. Some of the rationale for this shortcoming was stated as being due to a lack of funds, a seemingly endless cry of public facilities. Not all was lost, however, as Massachusetts was about to develop its first hospital in Worcester (1833). Under the esteemed leadership of Samuel Woodward, this asylum flourished and drew a national reputation for its care and success in treating the mentally ill. Claiming an 82% cure rate (Quen, 1975), this hospital provided a pilot study for other states to use as justification to begin developing their own asylums.

Serendipitously, at about the same time, one of the most influential of all mental health advocates was about to change the national landscape. Dorothea Dix made the care and treatment of the mentally ill a national issue. In the 1840s, she exposed the poor quality of care that the mentally ill received in almshouse and jails. She argued local governments could not afford the proper treatment, and so she called upon the states to fund the needed care. Her advocacy was impressive. By 1860, 28 of the 33 states had at least one public mental hospital (Rothman, 1971). This surge was based on a confluence of factors. The Pinel-Tuke moral approach, coupled with the Massachusetts cure rates and Dix's charm, changed the scope and focus of treatment for hundreds of years. This was the true beginning of institutionalization. In an amazing show of confidence, optimism, and perhaps naïveté, the New York State Senate reported that "Science, aided by humanity, has dispelled ignorance, overcome prejudice, conquered superstition, and investigated the causes, character and curability of mental disease, and had gloriously demonstrated that insanity can be made to yield to the power of medicine and medical treatment, and to moral discipline. The mystery which once enveloped it has vanished." (New York State Senate, 1856).

Such optimism seemed to be doomed. Or was it? Certainly the intent of government was to help treat the mentally ill in a therapeutic environment, a noble mission that should not be forgotten. However, a major variable was overlooked. The United States was undergoing rapid population growth with a significant immigration influx. Many of these individuals had difficulty dealing with the stress of a new culture as well as a new life. Political groups were concerned and somewhat fearful that some of these new residents who were struggling, and perhaps genuinely mentally ill in some cases, would be dangerous and perhaps more significantly, would be seen as not contributing to the then booming economy. The appeal to remove those individuals to a place that would provide "moral treatment" was great—so great, in fact that the institutionalized population swelled. This burgeoning group of hospitalized individuals created space issues from the inception. If the Massachusetts cure rate data were even half-correct, what made the model effective were the smaller, more intimate, respectful institutions that could attend to individuals in a beautiful, heartwarming environment.

How big is big? Let's jump ahead quickly to the mid-1950s, the peak of institutionalization, when there were 558,000 people hospitalized (Meyer, 1976). Pilgrim State Hospital on Long Island in New York had a population of over 16,000. Imagine the magnitude of implementing the respectful moral treatment approach to 16,000 people. Clearly, the model can be easily lost in a sea of people, staff, and the mundane aspects of daily life. It appears in hindsight that the concept of moral treatment may have had value but the enormity of individuals in need overwhelmed the approach.

It is interesting to note that as new asylums were being built and expanded upon, there was a consistent architectural character to the buildings. These developments, however, should be kept in perspective. In less than 50 years, the mentally ill were unchained, moved out of jails and almshouses, and placed in fine new institutional settings. In New York State, the legislature wanted to insure the finest architecture and paid for world-class architects. The Buffalo Insane Asylum was designed by H. H. Richardson, known for many magnificent buildings (including the New York State Capital) worldwide. The Hudson River Insane Asylum in Poughkeepsie contracted with Vaux and Whiters (who designed the Natural History Museum in New York City) for the buildings, and with Frederick Law Olmstead (Central and Prospect Park, New York City) for the landscape. At some level, it was clear the political winds were supporting the moral treatment concept.

One of the early asylum superintendents (today known as the Director, or as in some cases, the new business appellation of Chief Executive Officer) became influential in helping existing institutions expand. Dr. Thomas Kirkbride was so influential, in fact, that almost all public hospitals conformed to his conceptual approaches and architectural standards. Simply put, Kirkbride envisioned a central area for staff and "spokes" of long corridors, emanating from the center. The spokes were long, rectangular buildings with a hallway that led to a large open area at the end (later known as wards or dayrooms). Any trip to a state hospital in the United States built before 1900 (and many after) will reflect the Kirkbride influence. His architectural influence became particularly significant as space became a premium, due to the increasing numbers of people being institutionalized. Although the Kirkbride layout did not provide an easy solution to the increasing numbers, it was an accepted approach and thus utilized in many expansion plans. No model would, in reality, be able to handle a tenfold increase in need. This trend of insufficient space was a theme of state hospitals throughout the twentieth century. The most problematic time for state mental health professionals was the early 1950s. Not only had the number of people increased dramatically (to almost 600,000 nationwide), but the care at overcrowded facilities had become scandalous. As an example, at many state hospitals a single paraprofessional (therapy aide) had responsibility for over 100 patients on a daily basis. This included daily showers, eating, and programming. These daily tasks were often not completed, as it was overwhelming for the staff. The patient, at this time, was far removed from the individual, humane, and respectful treatment provided in the 19th century.

The Psychiatric Revolution and the Beginning of Deinstitutionalization

It was time for a change, and a number of significant events began to unfold in the 1950s, causing what some have called a "psychiatric revolution." These events were to usher in a significant period in the history of psychiatry, namely, the deinstitutionalization process. Others have more succinctly used reinstitutionalization (U.S. General Accounting Office, 1977), dehospitalization (Geller, 2000), or transinstitutionalization (Talbott, 1975) to describe the process.

The process of deinstitutionalization/dehospitalization occurred as these five major forces came together:

- The extraordinary development of psychotropic medications, most notably chlorpromazine. This new medication was marketed as Thorazine and was able to modify symptoms, most notably the positive symptoms of schizophrenia (so-called because they can be seen or witnessed, for example, hallucinations and delusions), while at the same time not entirely tranquilizing an individual. This new drug therapy was so effective that for the first time in years, professionals considered discharging people from the hospital. In addition, this breakthrough coincided with a developing national policy of prevention and preventive medicine.
- During the 1950s, there was discussion at the federal level of developing programs, policies, and medicines that would prevent illnesses from developing. Children throughout the United States were being inoculated against various medical illnesses such as polio, smallpox, and even measles. These services gave policy makers a newfound appreciation for funding preventive programs and interventions. The new drug Thorazine was not only effective as a treatment to help hospitalized individuals, but could also prevent hospitalization if prescribed early in the course of illness.

- There was, at this time, a growing movement to support individual rights. Initially, patients did not have the power to refuse hospitalization. The news that state hospitals had lost their humane touch and tipped the scales toward inhumane experiences became more public, and in response, advocates supported the rights of individuals to not be exposed to such abuse. As discussed by Brooks (1977), over time the legal action filtered these thoughts into a policy of "least restrictive environment." This meant that an individual had a right to be in the least restrictive (involuntary hospitalization being the most restrictive) environment his or her medical condition allowed. It became illegal to continue to hospitalize someone against his or her will if the person could manage outside a hospital setting. Also around this time, the criteria for being hospitalized underwent significant change. Because of the aforementioned restrictedness criteria, only those people who were a danger to self or others as a result of a mental illness would continue to be admitted.

- These changes also dovetailed with a major change in the insurance world. A major policy shift occurred, whereby Blue Cross/Blue Shield began to cover inpatient hospital costs for psychiatry in a general hospital. Insurance companies were swept up in the idea of prevention and early intervention. It was reasoned that a hospitalization at a general hospital would be short (although expensive) and perhaps would ward off longer-term stays in the future. State government was supportive for the first time and found some nontax support for the treatment of the mentally ill. It is not coincidental that as general hospitals developed new "psychiatric wings" in their medical-surgical complexes, the number of patients admitted to state facilities began to drop.

- "It's always about the money" is a common sentiment. Well, when a cost rises beyond what legislatures can support (and what will allow them to get reelected), something usually transpires. It should not be overlooked that the amount of money a society wants to spend on a need is relative. As recently as 1995, the United States spent 14% of its Gross National Product (GNP)—the total dollar value of all final goods and services produced for consumption in society during a particular time period—on health care (Lewit, 1996). This cost would be equal to 14% of all the income generated in an economy. It would be possible for the government to spend, for example, as much as 20% of the GNP on health care, but this would mean 6% less spent on other areas like defense, housing, or food. Is that what the population would desire? The answer lies in how far elected officials want to push their agenda and still retain their chances of reelection. In the case of the mentally ill and state hospitals, cost had moved beyond the point of support.

Budgets had skyrocketed as the price of care and housing moved upward. A growing concern was the condition of the then almost 100-year-old campus structures and infrastructure. How expensive was the care? In New York State in 2004, the actual cost for all state care expenses for adults, including administration for the mentally ill locally and statewide, was approximately $650 a day. For children and adolescents, the cost was $951 per diem (Rifton, personal communication, 2004). This amount equals $237,250, or $347,115 per person and per year, respectively. Something had to give.

For reasons that now seem logical, the movement of people out of institutions for therapeutic, legal, and political reasons began in the late 1950s and early 1960s. The impact of this movement has been felt by individual patients, the local community, and decision-makers at the federal level. The discussion of the positive and the negative aspects of this decision needs to be balanced. Deinstitutionalization could be considered a positive experience by the severely mentally ill. The ability to live in the community with state of the art bio-psycho-social supports drastically improved the quality of life for many people. Unfortunately, it is common for those who have not fared well in the process (the homeless and jailed mentally ill) to be seen as the rule rather than the exception. Geller (2000) says it best: "We remain entrenched in our concerns about the locus of care, confusing it with the humanness, effectiveness and quality of care."

Implications for Today

What remains today is the need to focus on implementing interventions that improve a person's quality of life. The need for such improvement implies that the entire system of care needs attention, not just the locus of care. The significant policy decision of a reduction in hospitalization impacts all aspects of the system.

We will review the impact of this decision from three perspectives:

- The individual
- The community/organization
- Political and social policy

The Individual Perspective

The United States has a record of treating the mentally ill that spans over 200 years. Unlike the situation with other major diseases such as polio, tuberculosis, and smallpox, medical research has yet to identify a specific etiology for mental illness. Even when effective treatments are discovered, moving those treatments to both the public and the private patient has been slow. As stated earlier, the United States Surgeon General reported that only half of the severely mentally ill in the United States receive treatment. Treatments that have shown evidence of efficacy are not being implemented. Why not? As previously discussed, the treatment of the severely mentally ill over the past two hundred years has undergone enormous change. The initial response to this patient group was to provide moral therapy in a safe place (asylum), but even as new asylums were built, the need continued to grow. The rate of constructing additional buildings could not keep up with the burgeoning need. Another new stream of persons requiring hospital treatment exacerbated the problem: that of the elderly. The institutionalization of elderly patients was to become a major unresolved problem for years. "Senility" was frequently seen as an admitting diagnosis at the turn of the 19th century. Elderly people who could not be cared for by families were sent to almshouses, but without sufficient funds, these homes were poorly kept. Since elder individuals were unable to work, they became a burden. According to Grob (1994), in 1920, 18% of all first admissions to public hospitals were diagnosed as psychotic because of senility. This number rose to over 30% by 1940.

It should also be noted that another major diagnostic category of the time was paresis, the third and terminal phase of syphilis. Paresis eventually led to death, and the behavioral symptoms were significant and dramatic, since the infection destroyed areas in the central nervous system. The characteristics and symptoms of this disease presented enormous issues for staff, as the behaviors were unremitting. According to Grob (1994), in 1920, about 20% of all first admission to New York State mental hospitals had a diagnosis of paresis. Grob (1994) also reports that between 1913 and 1922, 88% of all first admission patients died during confinement. The focus of treatment needed to be moved from the milieu to the individual.

The admittance of individuals suffering from dementia and paresis sidetracked the movement to develop asylums into treatment facilities. It wasn't until the 1890s that insane asylums began to provide real "treatment," and as a result, the asylums changed their names to state hospitals to better reflect this medical treatment orientation. The chronic populations of people with senility and syphilis impacted the general public in a negative way. The concept of the state hospital as a moral treatment center with positive results had shifted to that of a place where people who were "out of their mind" lived, and where many went to die. The advent of antibiotic medication (after World War II) eliminated the syphilis population, yet the elderly remained. It wasn't until the 1990s that more appropriate treatment and institutional settings like nursing homes began to accept what heretofore had been a state hospital population. This change came about with the understanding that senility is, in fact, a dementia. Dementia is a generic term for a medical condition that is not reversible, such as Alzheimer's. The state hospital began to shift to an "active treatment" facility; maintenance, respite, and housing were no longer part of the state hospital mission.

Dr. Adolf Meyer returned to the movement from asylum to hospital, and he was instrumental in implementing a new conceptualization of mental illness. Nineteenth-century physicians saw mental illness as an either/or condition; a person was either sick (mentally) or healthy. Meyer, in the early twentieth century, supported the notion that mental illnesses lie on a continuum from so-called normal behavior to abnormal behavior. Meyer also stressed that people become "more" mentally ill as a result of maladaption to the environment. It was reasoned that in some cases, early intervention could lessen further exacerbation. Meyer returned the focus to the individual by gathering the facts of a person's life, including behaviors that existed before the person became ill. He helped reinforce the role of the physician in the personal treatment of the individual (Johnson, 1990).

As hospitals became crowded with more difficult-to-treat patients, hospital officials came under pressure to treat more effectively. The growing population of dementia and paresis patients added to the pressure. Physicians looked to Europe for new and innovative approaches. Dr. Wagner-Jouregg from the University of Vienna made an observation that has impacted treatment of the mentally ill to this day, by starting a series of interventions that were troubling yet seemed to be effective in some cases. He came to call his protocol "malaria therapy." Malaria therapy was based on the observation that people with mental symptoms who became ill with typhoid fever would sometimes shed some of their psychotic symptoms. Wagner-Jouregg reasoned that the effects of fever had a palliative effect on mental symptoms (Grob, 1994). American physicians were quick to apply the new fever therapy to paresis patients. Over time, subsequent research and outcomes indicated that the procedure was not effective. During the same period, another somatic observation was linked to mental symptoms. Manfred Sakel, a Viennese physician of the 1920s, observed that administering insulin to a point where a seizure or "shock" occurred reduced the symptoms of mental illness. This new "shock therapy" was another attempt to deal with difficult symptoms. Sakel did not provide a rationale as to why the treatment worked, and his interventions were seen as dangerous and risky. Some patients did, in fact, show improvement, but the mortality rate was as high as 5% (Grob, 1994). Despite this outcome, there was a brief use of metrozol to induce seizure, which was soon replaced with electroshock. Fever, coma, and seizure all seemed to effect a change in the brain that was sometimes beneficial. Indeed, the rationale for the use of these extreme measures was that some patients were improved. However, there were many who expressed concern, since there was little or no understanding of why these intrusive methodologies worked. Of all of the methods, only electroconvulsive therapy (ECT) is still in use today. It is given in cases of severe depression, but with many fewer sessions than were initially used. A "course" of ECT today could be as low as 8 to 10 "shocks" or treatments, whereas 60 years ago, individuals may have received up to 100 treatments. Recent literature suggests that the seizure produced by ECT may give the patient a burst of serotonin, the neurotransmitter often linked with depression (Sasa, 1999).

Somatic treatments reached their peak with the use of psychosurgery. Both prefrontal and orbital lobotomies were performed, with mixed results. Although this surgery was touted as a lifesaver, many patients were left in an emotionless state. It is also worth noting that the statistical evaluation of treatment outcomes at this time was premature, at best. Many claims of the success of seizures as effective treatment were merely anecdotal. Patients who were simply emotionally dulled by the scalpel were in some cases referred to as "improved." Other hands-on treatments were tried, but often yielded poor results. Hot baths, cold baths, hydrotherapy, sleep, and so on were all attempts to find, at the very least, symptom reduction; yet it is safe to say individual treatment before the 1950s provided only minimal improvement for a small number of patients. State hospitals were overcrowded and understaffed, and abuses were common. Treatment efforts were minimally effective, and the general public viewed the use of extreme measures (shock, psychosurgery) as proof that people with mental illness were of a different type.

Revolutions in Treatment: Psychotropic Drugs

Revolutions, even psychiatric revolutions, occur only when the timing is right. It was an opportune time for the introduction of a pill that would help control behaviors and permit previously hospitalized individuals return to the community. Although there were many factors that synergized to make deinstitutionalization occur, there were none more critical than this new treatment approach: the use of phenothiazines, especially chlorpromazine. In 1952, two French psychiatrists, Jean Delay and Pierre Deniker, noted that chlorpromazine dramatically tranquilized people with schizophrenia. They used the term "neuroleptic" to describe the effects, because it caused a reduction in nervous activity rather than a paralysis (drugs before this, such as barbiturates, were but pure sedatives) (Swazey, 1974). Drug companies were quick to respond and began to market these neuroleptics as "antipsychotics." Chlorpromazine was given the trade name Thorazine. Soon, Thorazine was seen as a miracle drug. The main contribution of this pharmaceutical was its effectiveness in relieving the positive symptoms of schizophrenia without totally sedating a person. Shedding thought disturbances allowed patients to function more effectively.

Not only had physicians focused on effective treatment, but government officials also became hopeful that there was a means to decrease costs associated with hospitalization. As mentioned previously, the new antipsychotic is often given major credit for the deinstitutionalization movement. However, there were complications; from the patient's perspective, the new medication was generally well received but not without problems. It became evident over time that long-term use of Thorazine-like medications (phenothiazines) had lasting, irreversible side effects. These drugs have a common neurotransmitter effect: they all reduce the amount of dopamine, a major neurotransmitter that has pathways through the brain's frontal lobes and two major motor sites. Reducing the amount of dopamine below sufficient levels impairs the motor areas in the substantia nigra, and as a result, certain motor movements become impaired. Side effects developed that were similar to Parkinson's disease, which results from damage to the same motor brain site areas and is precipitated by low dopamine levels. Motor palsy and "shuffling feet" were becoming common side effects of persons on phenothiazines for long periods of time. These movement disorders were called dyskinesias, and because they occurred after long-term use of medications, they were termed "tardive" dyskinesias.

Without question, however, the new medications reinforced the prevailing concept that people could be released/discharged into the community. In addition, those not yet hospitalized could be treated in their natural setting and never need a hospital stay. It should be clearly understood that patients were not "cured," but rather they had a lessening of the symptoms to the degree that a hospital stay was not necessary. There arose no new knowledge of the cause or etiology of schizophrenia, just an awareness that symptoms in some individuals could be reduced, thus allowing people to be moved to less restrictive settings.

Bio-Psycho-Social Considerations

Researchers have come to understand that schizophrenia, one of the major mental illnesses, is a bio-psycho-social disorder. All three areas are disrupted to some extent and need attention or repair. Medication management handled some of the biological repair needed, but individuals with schizophrenia had additional personal and inter-personal issues that needed to be addressed. Merely reducing symptoms and expecting the "psychosocial" skills of people to return was and is naïve. In the early 1960s, there was little thought given to this aspect, and patients were discharged with the hopes that these skills would return. In some cases, initial placements were made to support-ive living arrangements such as family homes; but to this day, there are not enough smaller, supportive housing arrangements for all those discharged. Despite this, life was better from most patients' perspectives. Medication controlled troubling symp-toms, housing was less crowded and more comfortable, and many people believed the quality of their life had returned. Individuals who returned to the community could continue treatment at outpatient clinics, where they received medication and some-times individual or group therapy. These psychotherapies were found to be helpful in addressing the psychosocial aspects of the disorder. It wasn't until the 1980s, however, that specific research on social skill acquisition became available (Liberman, DeRisi & Mueser, 1989).

The PORT Study

From the latter part of the 1960s on, the programs offered were a result of the Com-munity Mental Health Act of 1963. There were now a number of community pro-grams that would treat individuals both before and after hospitalization. Community mental health centers held out the promise that mental illness could be treated in the community, and only exceptional cases would need long-term hospitalization. Still, without a full understanding of the disease process, programs and treatments were designed primarily to treat symptoms. It wasn't until 1992 that both the Agency for Health Care Policy and Research and the National Institute of Mental Health funded the Schizophrenia Patient Outcomes Research Teams (PORT). The purpose was to gather all available scientific evidence related to the treatment of schizophrenia. The PORT study, which was compiled and published in 1998, paved the way for later "evidence-based" practice literature (Lehman & Steinwachs, 1998). It made 30 recom-mendations, covering all aspects of a bio-psycho-social approach.

Eighteen of the 30 recommendations related to medication usage. These recom-mendations capitalized on advancements in developing medications that had produced a new series of antipsychotic medications, termed "atypicals." These new antipsy-chotics provided both positive symptom abatement and, in some cases, a therapeutic effect on negative symptoms, all without producing dyskinesias. These drugs avoided the motor pathways when reducing dopamine, thus lessening or negating any motor involvement. The most prominent of the new atypicals was Clozapine. Clozapine became an important treatment alternative, especially for treatment refractory patients (those not responding to previous medication trials) as well as patients who displayed violent behavior. It was also a boon to patients who developed motor side effects from the more typical antipsychotics.

Recommendations 19–21 of the PORT study related to the use of electroconvul-sive therapy (ECT). The study reported there was sufficient evidence to show ECT reduced acute symptoms of schizophrenia, yet it was also noted the positive effects were short-lived. The number of treatments was ideally listed as 12, as studies had shown no significant change with more treatments. Recommendations 22 and 23 reported individual and group therapy were supportive and had shown some benefit, but that psychodynamic therapies should not be used in the treatment of persons with schizophrenia. Recommendations 24–26 suggested patients who had ongoing contact with families should be offered an intervention that was education and skill-learning-based, and these interventions could be given to families that had high "expressed emotion" (EE). There were, in the literature, reports that families with high expressed emotion (family members who were hyperactive, loud, etc.) were not suitable for people recovering from schizophrenia (Butzlaff & Hooley, 1998). As the "high EE" concept was discarded (Cheng, 2001), so was the notion of the anxious family.

Recommendations 27–28 gave public credibility to the positive impact of vocational rehabilitation. Vocational rehabilitation was recommended for people who had an interest in working, a history of work, and the potential for good work skills. Provided opportunities would include prevocational, transitional supported employment, and vocational counseling. The last two recommendations made two service system recommendations—assertive case management and assertive community treatment. Both service components had evidenced positive outcomes by molding program offerings to the patient and not making the patient fit a program mold or be turned away.

Evidence-Based Practices

These 30 recommendations were well received by the mental health community, and public programs began, albeit slowly, to modify treatment and program offerings.

Although there was heavy reliance in the PORT study on the biology of schizophrenia, all the components of a bio-psycho-social model were addressed, giving credence to the concept that schizophrenia involves all aspects of the bio-psycho-social continuum. It follows that current day treatment approaches address all aspects of the bio-psycho-social continuum. This position was supported by a meta-analysis of effective community-based treatments for schizophrenia (Mueser, Bond, & Drake, 2001), a study indicating psychosocial interventions and psychosocial treatments have positive treatment outcomes. These interventions provide to the clinician a number of varying treatment practices research has found to be effective. These practices, as mentioned earlier, are generally referred to as "evidence-based practices."

A number of observations are worth noting:

- Currently accepted practices for the treatment of the severely mentally ill produce positive outcomes. These results and subsequent reconfirmations give new hope to individuals and families who have dealt with mental disease for generations.
- Effective treatments support a bio-psycho-social model. Neither medication nor skills-building alone will return a person to a better quality of life.
- Clinicians are now more research- and evidence-based. Previous practices (lobotomies, insulin, shock, etc.) that were drastic attempts at symptom reduction have been replaced with workable, effective interventions that deal with all aspects of functioning and greatly improve quality of life.

Currently, there are six areas of practice where research evidence has indicated positive treatment outcomes with the severely mentally ill (Mueser, Bond, & Drake, 2001).

- *Medication:* It is understood individuals with severe mental illness have a chemical neurotransmitter imbalance. Whether it is too much dopamine or glutamate or too little serotonin remains to be determined. However, there is sufficient evidence to indicate that following medication guidelines leads to an increased chance of positive change (often symptom reduction) over a short period of time.
- *Illness self-management training:* Perhaps better labeled "wellness self-management," it involves several sub areas. Psychoeducation, another term needing some redesign, is at the cornerstone of self-management. Nothing is more empowering than understanding the impact that actions have on future behavior, and stressing an individual's ability to exercise personal control in order to avoid negative consequences. The literature is now consistent in reporting that conveying basic information about psychiatric disorders, including their history, course, symptoms, methods of relapse, and prevention, as well as knowledge of medication effects and side effects, has reduced relapse and has improved the quality of life for many (Mueser, Bond, & Drake 2001). Social skills training has been a staple of treatment for some time, with patients being taught social skills that either were forgotten or never learned. Social interaction while hallucinating is difficult at best, and short circuits valuable life experiences. Skill development can be achieved through role-playing, modeling, social learning principles, and other methods (Lieberman, DeRisi & Mueser 1989). Cognitive remediation is an additional sub area and a relatively recent development. Beck (1979) successfully demonstrated the use of cognitive therapy for the amelioration of depression, and this therapy is now also being applied to the treatment of psychotic disorders. Working with individuals to change their thinking about both themselves and their options in life can have a positive effect (Chadwick, Birchwood, & Trower, 1996).
- *Case management and assertive community treatment (ACT):* ACT is a modification of typical case management highlighted by the offering of services in natural settings, around the clock/seven days a week availability, direct service provision (as opposed to the prescription of services), team rather than individual caseloads, and low caseloads (as low as 10 in some programs). Additionally, some ACT teams are incorporating concepts of empowerment and individual responsibility as philosophical substrates in what is termed "the road to recovery." ACT teams and services have been extensively researched since the initial programs were developed in the 1980s (Stein & Test, 1980). Research has continually found ACT teams reduce hospitalization (Mueser, Bond, & Drake, 1998).
- *Family psychoeducation:* As fewer individuals are hospitalized and therefore spend more time in the community, it is more common for families to be involved with the severely mentally ill. Talbott (1984) reported that between 30 to 60% of the severely mentally ill at this time lived with their families. A number of interventions have proven effective, especially at preventing relapse and maintaining

community living. McFarlane, Lukens & Link (1995) reported lowered relapse rates with multiple family groups. These are group sessions in which a number of families constitute the meeting, and family members eventually learn to provide support to each other as they deal with the illness.

■ *Supported employment:* The current approach to employment is a radical change from previous years. It was originally thought that prevocational experiences and training were necessary before a person entered an employment position. Current thinking moves individuals into competitive employment directly and provides supports at the work site. Bond, Drake & Mueser (1997) found supported employment programs show superior levels of competitive employment, 58% versus 21% seen with more traditional approaches.

■ *Integrated substance abuse treatment:* Individuals with severe mental illness have been frequently known to develop substance use disorders and thus be dually diagnosed. Common treatment approaches in the 1980s would treat each disorder separately and sequentially. A review of the literature by Drake, Mercer-McFadder & Mueser (1998) indicates integrated treatment, in which both disorders are simultaneously treated, has positive clinical outcomes. According to Drake, these programs "lead to amelioration of both mental illness and substance use disorder, and reduce the risks of negative outcomes that have been associated with dual disorders."

The Community/Organization Perspective

As was discussed, the first asylums, such as McLean, the Hartford Retreat, and Bloomingdale Hospital, were all initiated through the use of private and/or corporate funds. It wasn't until after the 1820s that individual states began to consider themselves responsible for the care and treatment of the mentally ill. Policy makers, again, were not responding solely to humanistic concerns; from their view, the mentally ill were a problem in that they were not able to work or participate in the expanding economy. In order to fully understand the import of community organization, it is necessary to review the influence of governments in the establishment of programs for the mentally ill.

Individual states such as New York and Massachusetts led the way in establishing publicly funded mental hospitals. Dorothea Dix, in the 1840s, advocated for all states to have publicly funded state asylums. Her arguments, as touched on previously, were predicated on the deteriorating condition in the poor or almshouses that provided residence for many mentally ill individuals. As early as 1806, the New York State Legislature appropriated money to erect an asylum for "lunatics." These dollars went unspent, but the concept was revisited in 1830 when Governor Throop called attention to the legislature that there were "345 lunatics in the various counties unaccounted for. . ." (New York State Senate, 1856). The background was set for Dix's concerns, most notably the idea that counties could not afford to care for the increasing number of mentally ill in almshouses. Hence began a complex dance of accountability and responsibility for the mentally ill. County, state, and eventually federal involvement all had a role in leadership or lack thereof. Dix specifically requested that five million acres of federal land be given to the states for the purpose of building asylums. Although Congress passed a bill in 1854 allocating ten million acres, then President Pierce set a precedent for years to come when he vetoed the bill (Grob, 1994). This veto kept the federal government out of financing for the mentally ill for almost a full century. Some states forged ahead despite this setback. In 1873, New York created the State Commission of Lunacy. The goal of this group was to send all of the current mentally ill persons in almshouses to a centralized state asylum. Interestingly, the state required the counties to contribute to the cost. This process became formalized when in 1890, the New York State Care Act was passed, requiring the mentally ill to be sent to the state asylums. An immediate result of this action was a large increase in the population of existing asylums but without sufficient funds for expansion. This began an unfortunate trend that followed the history of public mental institutions, perhaps even to this day.

As was mentioned, Adolph Meyer was an influential psychiatrist at the turn of the 19th century who developed a number of interesting inpatient treatment approaches. He stressed the professionalization and medicalization of psychiatric care. In addition to his more personalized approach to the individual, he was also responsible for developing a new approach to community treatment, the aftercare clinic. Meyer envisioned that some state hospital patients could in fact be discharged and yet still get care at a community clinic. This idea was not well received, since other hospital superintendents saw this as a threat to their jobs. Hence, the aftercare clinic concept was never fully implemented, since the larger state hospitals held considerable political influence. The clinic concept did continue despite this outcome, through a number of privately funded, mostly child guidance clinics. Unfortunately, a number of practices were allowed to flourish that eventually became problematic. To begin with, hospitals used the term "parole status" for those who could leave the hospital and attend aftercare clinics. This term formed a link between the mentally ill and the criminal justice system that persists until this day.

In another questionable practice, it was not uncommon for patients to be "put in charge" of other patients, to augment increasingly lower levels of staffing. Superintendents were reluctant to release patients to aftercare status because they could utilize the help that the patients provided.

The Mental Hygiene Movement

It would not be until the 1960s that aftercare clinics would return in full form as an adjunct to state hospital care. Meyer's ideas, which included treating an individual in the community before the person became severely ill, became known as the mental hygiene movement. This word "hygiene" became associated with prevention and eventually moved psychiatrists from working in solely inpatient settings to community settings. It was this community prevention focus that also ushered in the beginning of what we now call advocacy. Through the efforts of Clifford Beers, a former hospital patient, a more critical view of the provision of care was begun. Beers chronicled his mental illness (he experienced grandiose delusions and had symptoms that would most likely be associated with bipolar disorder) for others to read. He was Yale educated and was able at times to speak eloquently about his treatment and mistreatment. He eventually wrote a book, *A Mind That Found Itself* (Beers, 1908), that started a call for reform. Beers wanted to start a national organization that would promote his ideas and calls for reform. He spoke with Meyer, who also wanted such an organization, but under the sponsorship of "professionals." Meyer convinced Beers that to focus on mental hygiene would be the best option for people with mental illness. In 1908, the Connecticut Society for Mental Hygiene was formed. Beers and Meyer did promote mental hygiene, but soon would break apart, and in 1909 the National Committee for Mental Hygiene was founded. Its purpose was to "protect the public's mental health and promote research into the etiology of mental illness" (Johnson, 1990), goals that the group held for many years, although the research outcomes were slim.

The psychiatry specialty's organization, which before 1921 was known as the American Medico-Psychological Association, became the American Psychiatric Association in that year. The American Psychiatric Association was to some extent a struggling entity, as its place within the American Medical Association (AMA) was often in question. In 1931, the AMA decided to formalize the approach to institutionalization, and through the efforts of John Grimes, a nonpsychiatrist physician, formed a committee to review the conditions at state hospitals. Grimes and three colleagues visited 600 of the 631 state mental hospitals (Johnson, 1990) and also supplemented the visits with a written evaluation by the hospital superintendents. Grimes found that as he was preparing his report, word had leaked out that his findings would expose terrible and embarrassing conditions, and members of the American Psychiatric Association lobbied to have him revise it. His reluctance led to his termination. Determined, Grimes prepared his report despite this, and he provided new information on the worsening conditions. He wrote that hospitals were overcrowded, that patients basically worked for hospital staff, and that others were locked up for staff convenience. Of most importance, Grimes was offended that these so-called "hospitals" were not providing treatment but rather mere residence. His recommendation was prophetic. As Johnson (1990) states, "he proposed what he called 'deinstitutionalization' to include immediate parole of all suitable patients to aftercare clinics where they would be seen by social workers under medical supervision." His other recommendations were equally prophetic: conversion of state hospitals to acute care facilities, teaching of skills of daily living, and development of mutual arrangements with community agencies. His concepts were to be realized, but not for over 30 years.

Needless to say, his recommendations were not heeded, and hence overcrowding, physical plant deterioration, and somewhat drastic attempts at new treatment "cures" (shock therapy, psychosurgery) prevailed. This was, however, the beginning of a movement to shift care to the community. Karl Menninger, a well-respected and popular physician of the time, was supportive of community care, and his voice, in 1945, prompted others to listen. Things took a different turn, however, as psychiatrists were about to be sidetracked by their involvement in World War II.

The Impact of World War II

The economic depression of the 1930s and the impending World War proved to be a devastating time for the state hospital system. Deprived of capital dollars to either fix or expand buildings, the wards continued to fill. Overcrowding was exacerbated by a shortage of doctors, about 1 doctor to 500 patients, and an even greater shortage of nurses, about 1 nurse to 1,320 patients (Group for the Advancement of Psychiatry, 1946). Unfortunately, this was a trend that would not easily abate. Increased pressure was developing to allay symptoms and to create improvement sufficient enough to warrant discharge. Despite the now worsening conditions and drastic treatment measures, the policy of institutionalization continued to be supported. In 1945, the Mental Hospital Survey Committee (jointly created by the American Psychiatric Association and the U.S. Public Health Service in 1936) began to identify concerns with state hospitals and overcrowding, but the committee reported optimistically on the impact of the new somatic treatments within institutional settings (Grob, 1994). Hence, the impact of World War II and its effect on the treatment of the mentally ill was significant and yet often unrecognized.

As mentioned in Chapter 1, psychiatrists were involved in the screening and assessment of recruits to help determine whether individuals were suited for active duty. As war unfolded, the effects of stress were witnessed and studied. The relationship between stress and mental deterioration was seen as a significant variable in the treatment of the mentally ill. Environmental factors, if controlled, were recognized as something that could potentially limit the severity of illness. A new theoretical model of community treatment was developing. The concept was simple: prevent circumstantial stress from occurring in the community and individuals would not deteriorate to such a degree that hospitalization was necessary. Government response was not far behind. After World War II, the U.S. health care system reemphasized research. Robert Felix, who was trained in the public health approach to mental illness, initiated an effort to rekindle federal involvement in the mental health field. Although psychiatry was not a major influence at this time, research in the medical arena pointed to success with controlling such diseases as smallpox. As such, a wave of sentiment for prevention programs was pervasive. On the basis of the new medical findings, President Truman passed the National Mental Health Act of 1946, which provided funds for research, training, and grants to states instituting pilot projects dealing with prevention and treatment of mental disorders. The National Institute of Mental Health (NIMH) was established to carry out the mandate. Felix had orchestrated the support of the federal government on the conceptualization that mental disorders were a public health issue. The immediate outcomes of the new funding policies were such that by the 1950s, many states had initiated community-oriented prevention programs. NIMH conducted a survey in the mid-1950s and found that nearly 1,300 outpatient clinics were in operation (Bahn & Norman, 1957). The popular therapeutic approach centered on early detection, but little data or supportive evaluation revealed program effectiveness. A community approach was becoming particularly common as well. Then Senator John F. Kennedy cosponsored a bill, the Mental Health Study Act of 1955, to study the treatment of the mentally ill. The bill established the Joint Commission on Mental Illness and Health (note the tag word "Health"), which completed a major study in 1961. This report concluded that "the nation could more than double the number of chronically ill mental patients returned to the community" (Johnson, 1990). Sentiment and action were now moving toward changing the state hospital system. Mary Jane Ward's *The Snake Pit* (1947) and Albert Deutsch's *The Shame of the States* (1948) were popular exposés that compelled the public and politicians to take action.

Also as mentioned in Chapter 1, Kennedy, who was by then the President, read the Joint Commission report and developed a task force to draw up recommendations to implement the suggested recommendations. The task force had wide representation from individuals both within the field and outside, including representatives from the Defense Department and American Legion. An ideological split developed within the task force, thereby leading, perhaps more than any other aspect, to the negative outcomes of deinstitutionalization. The issue at stake was the role of the state hospitals. It was a crucial time that necessitated a clear direction, either advocating a continued role for state hospitals or calling for their abolishment. Unfortunately, there was no consensus, and thus an opportune time to develop a progressive policy for the severely mentally ill was lost. A large contingent of the committee felt that the concept of prevention was so strong that the need for long-term care would not be necessary. In hindsight, the committee failed to either understand or appreciate the needs of the severely mentally ill. They failed to consider these conditions affect an individual in many different spheres and that patients require support and treatment throughout much of their life. Again, in retrospect, it is clear a comprehensive community program for long-term patients was needed but not considered. What did develop from the committee was a program based on prevention and on the acute treatment of mental illness. The role of the state hospital was simply to "get smaller." The community mental health program that developed was designed for the more acute cases, and the long-term patients were returned to a system that was not designed to meet their needs. Over 50 years later, there is still discussion of the severely mentally ill and their needs; an opportunity was lost, and attempts are still being made to rectify a flawed policy. Without a clear policy direction, state hospitals survived but were to be of diminishing use. Some state hospital closures were rapid. In 2003, The Olympian, a popular Washington State newspaper, reported that over forty state hospitals were closed between 1990 and 1997 alone. Closures were precipitated not only by fuzzy philosophy but also by federal reimbursement policy, the "institution for the treatment of mental disease," or IMDs, which would exclude federal reimbursement to state hospitals.

Community Mental Health Act of 1963

The Community Mental Health Act of 1963, the direct result of the commission's report, was developed essentially around a strong public health orientation. It was predicated on local development of services provided to a geographic section of 75,000 to 200,000 people. The Community Mental Health Act of 1963 mandated the provision of five essential services: inpatient acute care, outpatient care, partial hospitalization, emergency care, and consultation and education.

- *Inpatient acute care:* "Acute" was initially understood to be several weeks to months, although recent managed care mandates have reduced this number to "days." Linkages needed to be developed with long-term hospitals for those requiring further care and treatment. These linkages were generally with state hospitals. This system exists today, yet the access to the long-term facilities is seen as limited.
- *Outpatient care:* This was the core treatment approach. It was envisioned that a number of clinics, geographically accessible by transportation, would be part of the Community Mental Health Center (CMHC). Such programs did develop, but they were not prepared for the long-term patient.
- *Partial hospitalization:* This was a new program designed to prevent a hospitalization by providing intensive services throughout the day. Either someone at risk or someone reentering the community from a hospital stay would be a candidate for a partial hospitalization program. Typically, the program ran five days a week, eight hours a day. An individual would essentially spend an entire day at the partial site. Variations of this program included some weekend stays and evening hours to help accommodate those with different schedules.
- *Emergency care:* Emergency mental health services were to be available every day, 24 hours a day. This was a logical extension of the public health approach. Reaching out at all hours to individuals in acute stress was seen as central to the new community approach. Although these services continue to exist, they are often restricted to an area in a general hospital's emergency room.
- *Consultation and education:* Again, this is the public health approach. An informed populace would, in effect, be preventative. Mental health staff were, as part of the legislation, to consult with schools, hospitals, and the general public on mental illness and its treatment.

It is interesting to note the Act of 1963 also included five secondary services: diagnosis, precare and aftercare, rehabilitation, training, and research and evaluation. These secondary services were not required but were encouraged. It is noteworthy that another opportunity for the long-term client was missed. The "rehabilitation" service was designed to prepare those who needed skills in community living and in vocational services. Rehabilitation was recognized as a need but not seen as a mandate. Both social and vocational types have proven to be an essential component in current treatment approaches to the severely mentally ill.

Deinstitutionalization, unfortunately, was neither legislated nor planned. Without this sense of direction, it would produce significant problems. Action at this time, at the federal level, would begin a momentum that could not be stopped.

It would be 10 years before the community mental health act was revised. In 1975, expanded funding and new essential services for CMHC were enacted by Congress. The new essential services included the following:

- *Mental health services for children and the aged:* The childrens' services were an outgrowth of the prevention model.

- *Follow-up services for discharged patients:* There was recognition that services were needed for this population. In addition, there had been concerns that the new CMHCs were not treating the "sickest" of the mentally ill. Some people claimed that the new federal money was being spent on the "worried well." In 1974, Ralph Nader wrote a report titled the "Madness Establishment" (Chu & Trotter, 1974) and in which he stated, "the community mental health centers have been neither accountable backward to NIMH nor forward to the consumers and citizens in the community they allegedly service." This report was prescient not only in 1974, but currently as well. What was lost was a focus on providing the best possible treatment (evidence-based) to individuals in need. It is not the "where" of treatment, but instead the "what" of treatment that is essential. This new service, to follow individuals after hospital discharge, was an important step to refocus the mental health system on those most in need.
- *To provide treatment for substance abuse and mental illness in designated geographical areas:* In some ways this was a reaction not only to the "worried well" criticism but also to the disappointment that CMHCs were not more numerous and more specifically, that many were not developed in high-need areas.

These additional dollars and new service elements were an attempt to bolster a system that was not meeting the needs of the severely mentally ill. With the Carter administration, a renewed interest in the severely mentally ill came to pass, through advocacy from Rosalyn Carter as she helped push the "mentally ill agenda." The National Institute of Mental Health awarded contracts to sixteen states for a project called "Community Support Program" (CSP). These programs were designed as pilot projects to help assimilate long-term hospitalized individuals into the community. They included various skill level training and prevocational experiences. Also, they offered a focus on the person with severe mental illness and used what were, at the time, therapeutically effective practices. Psychosocial skill development was particularly emphasized. CSP programs were, to a large extent, on target with a need, but the funding was too little and 15 years too late.

Hopes were raised again in 1977 when President Carter commissioned a group to review mental health policies, particularly in light of the now numerous underserved deinstitutionalized individuals. Chaired by Rosalyn Carter, the group developed a framework for the Mental Health Systems Act of 1980. This Act, which had significant promise for the severely mentally ill, was repealed by the Reagan administration. The repeal returned the responsibility for mental health leadership to the states, something that had not been the case since President Pierce. In essence, the leadership the federal government had provided since the 1950s was now in other hands. After a gap of almost 20 years, the federal government has recently shown some leadership on issues of priorities for the mentally ill in areas of health coverage, and more generally on a patient Bill of Rights.

Programmatic modification, from the 1980s to current practice, was vested with the states. As such, there developed great variability in implementing any change in program design. Quite frankly, without any clear direction, the states generally muddled along. Some states, such as New York, have still, for various reasons, not set a direction for the state hospital system. As recently as 2004, the New York State Public Professional Union sponsored a full-page newspaper ad opposing closure of a state hospital. The stated concern was to not inconvenience families to have to travel an additional 50 miles to the next state hospital. State hospital policy aside, current public hospitals have begun to incorporate, on a national level, evidence-based practices.

Political and Social Policy Perspective

As mentioned earlier in the chapter, the role of the federal government has changed over the years. President Pierce was the most outspoken opponent of federal intervention or direction, as he believed mental health policy was a state issue. He vetoed legislation that Dorthea Dix had advocated, and he stated, ". . . I cannot find any authority in the Constitution that makes the federal government the great almoner of public charity throughout the United States" (Foley & Sharfstein 1983, p. 647). The federal movement toward prevention and public health in the early 1950s helped rekindle the political role of federal government. In 1954, President Eisenhower passed Title II of the Social Security Act: the Disability Income Program. This title would be the groundwork for further titles: XVIII, Medicare; XIX, Medicaid; and XVI, Supplemental Security Income Program. These would ensure federal financial involvement for programs for the mentally ill for future years. Eisenhower spoke at his State of the Union Address in 1955, ". . . I shall propose rigorous steps to combat the misery and national loss involved in mental illness" (Sharfstein, 2000). Up to this time, few states had authorized funds for community service. The first attempt to fund community care by the states came in 1954 when New York State passed the Community Mental Health Service Act, which proposed state fiscal support for local communities to develop community programs. Governor Thomas Dewey's state budget message alluded to reducing the state fiscal commitment to inpatient care (Johnson, 1990).

The cost to the states for institutionalized care has become enormous. The median annual cost per patient in a mental hospital in the nation was $246 in 1939 and $636 in 1949 (Johnson, 1990). As discussed, in 2004 the estimated cost per adult person per year was $237,615 (Rifton, personal communication, 2004). This enormous fiscal burden forced government officials to look for cost-cutting measures, as New York State did in the 1950s.

The fiscal policy issues that states face today relative to funding mental health programs were determined over 40 years ago. The first significant legislation that began to impact the mentally ill was in 1960, when the federal government agreed to subsidize general and chronic hospital care through medical assistance to the aged, which today is called Medicare. This regulation was incorporated under Title 1 of the Social Security Law and exempted from state-run institutions reimbursement (the IMD exclusion). The exclusion of state-run institutions would be a significant oversight for the future of many individuals with severe mental illness. The exclusion concept was carried forward to 1965 under Title XIX and Title XX of the Social Security Law, which provided for Medicare and Medicaid, a new reimbursement mechanism for the poor. Medicaid is now the nation's largest public insurance program (Rosenbaum & Teitelbaum, 2002). The enactment of Medicaid included an exclusion known as "Medicaid IMD exclusion." The exclusion bars federal contributions to the cost of medically necessary inpatient care incurred in treating Medicaid beneficiaries from ages 21 to 64 who receive care in certain institutions that fall within the definition of an "institution for mental disease" (Rosenbaum & Teitelbaum, 2002). An "institution for mental disease" is defined as "a hospital nursing facility or other institution of more than 16 beds that is primarily engaged in providing diagnosis, treatment or care of persons with mental disease, including medical attention, nursing care and related services." It should be noted that in subsequent legislation, Medicare provided funding for the under 21 and over 65 population, but the IMD exclusion remained.

This fiscal incentive to release long-term state hospital patients into the community was significant. States moved quickly (although in hindsight, not quickly enough) to develop community housing and programs. Generally speaking, the federal government paid between 50% and 78% of the costs on Medicaid eligible individuals. Given such fiscal incentives, states looked to shift the financial burden to the federal government by moving long-term patients from state hospitals with no federal reimbursement, to other institutions (often nursing homes) that were Medicaid eligible. The *Chicago Tribune* reported that the State of Illinois "dumped thousands of mentally ill patients into nursing homes in order to collect Medicaid, which paid half the cost" (Berens, 1998). The article goes on to say that state workers "quietly reclassified" many patients to disguise the portion who were mentally ill. This transinstitutionalization resulted in the state's receiving an additional $50 million from Medicaid. This was based on the early promise that the adult ages 21 to 64 population should be excluded from reimbursement for public institutions. It was hoped that all individuals in this group would move to community settings.

To compound matters, Medicaid was originally a medically based service. In other words, all reimbursable services were to be prescribed by a physician, and non-physician-based services were not reimbursed. As previously illustrated, services such as rehabilitation, self-help, case management, and so on are essential elements in the treatment regime for the severely mentally ill. These services are often provided by professionals, but not necessarily by physicians. Program priority was directed toward reimbursable services, and thus some of the evidence-based services (assertive case management, etc.) were slighted. More recently, states have reversed this trend by incorporating some of these services under the reimbursable rehabilitation designation.

As has been repeatedly shown, the lack of vision for a coordinated treatment approach to the mentally ill created a void filled by other opportunistic fiscal and political agendas. In 1972, another federal amendment aided this trend. The Social Security Amendment of 1972 was a new entitlement to provide a certain level of guaranteed income called SSI. SSI eligibility was generously applied to people with a "disability" that prevented them from entering the workforce. Unlike Medicaid, which was only half-supported by the federal government, SSI was 100% federal funds, although states were allowed to supplement the amount if they felt it was necessary. States saw this entitlement as yet another vehicle to help institutionalized persons return to the community. Armed with sufficient funds and with new reimbursable programs available in the community, a "push" was evident. In 1974, the first year SSI was available, states saw the largest decrease in state hospital population (13.3%) of any single year (Johnson, 1990). SSI has been a mixed blessing. In a similar fashion as fee-for-service, reimbursement methodologies in which repeated visits are rewarded financially, SSI created an uncomfortable dependency. There was no incentive to recover or to return to the workforce. Also, the money savings of the Social Security programs of 1965 and 1974 gave no attention to the treatment needs of the severely mentally ill. The hope was that if the locus of care shifted to the community and people had enough money to live, they would be "better off." As has been indicated, it is not the locus of care but the attention to the disorder and application of evidence-based treatments that are necessary (Geller, 2000).

Another significant yet unfortunate outcome of the new federal policy was a lack of accountability for treatment implementation. As patients left the institutions, there was no consistent management of the ongoing treatment, something that is essential to recovery, and no assurance of the critical interface between hospital, community treatment, and individual needs.

This unfolding myopic approach to the severely mentally ill did not go unnoticed. David Mechanic spoke frequently about the "need to overcome the debilitating efforts of decentralization of an uncoordinated system of treatment, care and financing" (Grob, 1994, p. 305).

The National Institute of Mental Health was also aware of the existing fears, and given its mandate to promote research, launched a community support program in 1977. In some ways it was an add-on to the original 1965 legislation, as it added components for housing, income, psychiatric and medical treatment, and support services, including vocational rehabilitation. The CSP, as previously mentioned, was to be a partnership with the states, and was designed to fill in gaps, where needed, for those who were no longer in state institutions.

In many ways, CSP was successful. It provided a renewed focus on the individual and his or her needs. For states that took advantage, such as Wisconsin, it provided the necessary impetus for better, more coordinated treatment.

The Wisconsin model, through the foresighted efforts of researchers such as Leonard Stein and Mary Test, suggested it was possible for highly impaired persons to be able to not only survive in the community but also to be satisfied with services involving less hospitalizations (Stein & Test, 1980). A number of replications of this model were attempted throughout the United States, and the most consistent outcome was that the "assertive community care" did reduce hospitalization. As illustrated, Assertive Community Treatment (ACT) teams have been demonstrated to be an evidence-based practice for the treatment of the severely mentally ill.

To some degree, it is unfortunate the motivation to implement such programs was left to the states. President Reagan's repeal of the Mental Health Systems Act of 1980 contributed to this outcome. Yet another attempt to force states to at least plan for the SMI was enacted in 1986, as the Comprehensive Mental Health Service Act (CMHS). This Act required states to plan and implement a comprehensive, community-based program of care for the severely mentally ill. Failure to do so jeopardized other funding, and as a result, states included annual plans to the federal government to ensure funding (Geller, 2000).

From a financial perspective, there has been little change in the role of the federal government. There is still no clear accountability for patient care. There are, however, a vast number of uncoordinated fiscal incentives that may or may not facilitate evidence-based practices.

Justice

There have been significant changes in the mental health commitment laws in recent years. One of the first laws to address involuntary commitment was in California, the Lauterman-Petris Short Act of 1968. This legislation dealt with the civil rights of psychiatric patients being hospitalized against their will, and made hospitalization more difficult. In addition, it challenged the renewed commitment once someone had been admitted. This Act was a follow-up to the 1966 judicial decision, *Lake* v. *Cameron*, in which an appellate court ruled that a person could be admitted to an institution only if a less restrictive facility could not be found. These two rulings drastically changed the admission policies of all state hospitals and, of course, could be used not only to protect civil rights but also to foster cost-savings measures that some states craved.

Along with these new admittance protocols, the thrust of civil rights protections for the mentally ill continued. In 1970, the *Wyatt* vs. *Stickney* (ruled by state of Alabama) ruling mandated adequate and effective treatment in public psychiatric hospitals. In addition, it insisted on a humane psychological and physical environment and enough staff to administer adequate treatment, including individualized treatment plans. This statute was significant for many states. Those individuals who remained in hospitals now had a civil right to effective and humane treatment with adequate staffing. It is interesting, that this continued the process of discharging more and more patients to the community, as the cost to provide care for those remaining became a fiscal burden. Still, further protection continued to be granted. In 1972, in *Lessard* vs. *Schmidt*, the court ruled persons facing involuntary commitment were guaranteed legal procedure safeguards similar to those for someone who was charged with a crime. In effect, each involuntary committed person had a right to legal aide. In New York State, attorneys were assigned to state hospitals to implement such a mandate and to meet with each admitted individual. Another suit had a quiet but significant impact on state hospitals and discharges. In 1973, in *Sauder* vs. *Brennan*, the court ruled patient-workers are covered by the Federal Fair Labor Standards Act, entitling them to the minimum wage and overtime compensation. Patient workers were, for many hospitals, a euphemism for "free help." Many long-stay patients who were relatively stable had become part of the working fabric of the hospital, so much so that some patients were often confused with staff. These workers "earned their keep," socialized with staff, and worked long and hard. Generally, patients in these positions did not want to leave the hospital, as this had become their "real" home where they felt protected and productive. The Sauder Act changed that, and vocational rehabilitation became a more treatment-oriented element in hospital practice.

In *Donaldson* vs. *O'Connor* (1974), and later confirmed by the Supreme Court (1975), it was ruled that a state cannot confine a nondangerous individual who is capable of living by him or herself or with a family member. This significant act again made involuntary hospitalization more stringent. It added to *Wyatt* vs. *Stickney* and made the admitting criteria to hospitals what they are today: evidence of a mental condition that cannot be treated in a less restrictive environment and/or evidence the person is a danger to self or to others as a result of such mental condition.

Although not impacting hospitals directly, in 1976, *Tarasoff* vs. *Regents of the University of California* ruled, "if a patient presents a serious danger of violence to another, the therapist incurs an obligation to protect the intended victim against the danger" (Geller, 2000). Although at the time it was thought that this ruling would greatly impede the therapeutic alliance, generally speaking, this has not been the case.

In 1990, more important legislation that helped protect those with mental illness was passed. The American with Disabilities Act (ADA) pushed to eliminate discrimination against disabled persons. For the mentally ill, this legislation was an important boost for those entering the competitive job market.

In 1996, advocacy groups that argued on behalf of psychiatric coverage as part of health insurance were rewarded with the Domenici Wellstone Mental Illness Parity Amendment. This amendment forced employers of more than 50 workers to provide coverage for mental illness.

Lastly, in 1999, 30 years after *Lake* vs. *Cameron*, the Supreme Court ruled in *Olmstead* vs. *LC and E.W.* that the ADA would mandate states to provide community placement for persons with mental disabilities. This was a somewhat belated recognition that without supported community placement, successful community placement was compromised.

Conclusion

The history of treatment interventions for the mentally ill has shown movement from a focus on institutionalization to community-oriented, evidence-based practices. The deinstitutionalization movement helped foster a more community-oriented approach, although not without some negative consequences. Current evidence-based practices and the psychosocial interventions they provide offer new hope for an emerging recovery-oriented field.

DISCUSSION QUESTIONS

1. What was the state of mental health inpatient care in the 1950s? How did this differ from the standard of care commonly given in the 19th century? What contextual factors contributed to a shift in mental health care administration?

2. How has the treatment of the mentally ill changed since the 1950s? What prompted these changes? How has the role of the state hospital changed during this time period? What sociopolitical events in modern times might be contributing to the state of the current mental health system?

3. Why have mental health programs traditionally been designed to treat only the symptoms of the disorder? Has this protocol changed? If not, what would have to happen to cause it to change?

4. Outline some of the contributions that Adolph Meyer made to the treatment of the mentally ill and the way in which these contributions manifest in modern treatment protocols. How did his ideas contribute to the design of community mental health approaches?

5. How have admittance procedures changed over the years? What were some social issues that contributed to this shift? What were some important pieces of legislation that affected this change? To whom were these changes beneficial, and why?

3

The Ecological Model: Person-in-Context

OBJECTIVES

This chapter is designed to enable to reader to:

■ Describe the ecological perspective as it applies to the community mental health system, child development, education deinstitutionalization, and other important areas.

■ Describe some of the more significant ecological models.

■ Identify the research tools needed to evaluate an adequate person-environment fit.

■ Understand the need for synergy.

■ Explain the importance of Lewin's Field Theory.

■ Define driving forces and restraining forces.

■ Understand the influence of environment on behavior.

■ Identify ways in which the recycling of resources can be beneficial.

■ Explain why stigmatizing labels tend to be setting specific.

■ Explain how the expansion of niche breadth is beneficial to both mental health clients and society.

■ Distinguish achieved roles from ascribed roles.

■ Explain how Kelly's ecological perspective can be applied to organizational structure, and why this application is relevant to the community mental health system.

■ Understand the levels of Bronfenbrenner's model of child development in a context, and the components of his revised lifespan system.

> "Whenever you start measuring somebody, measure him right, child, measure him right. Make sure you done taken into account what hills and valleys he came through before he got to where he is."
>
> Mama, in the play A Raisin in the Sun, by Lorraine Hansberry

Community mental health professionals should view human behavior from an ecological perspective. This perspective acknowledges that all behavior occurs in settings and that it is necessary to investigate both the person and his/her environment to understand why a particular behavior occurs. The word "ecology" is derived from a Greek word meaning "house." Ecologists realize that the study of an organism's behavior can be understood only by considering the habitat in which the organism functions. Viewing the "person-in-context" allows us to approach behavior more holistically. It enables us to understand normal activity and to explain abnormal or pathological behavior by focusing on the setting. It therefore reduces the need to apply stigmatizing, deviant labels to people. Furthermore, the ecological perspective enables us to generate many more interventions to reduce problems in living and to create a better person-environment fit.

In this chapter, some of the more significant ecological models are presented, along with an explanation of the research tools needed to evaluate good fit. Interspersed throughout are various community mental health applications showing how this model can improve the effectiveness of offered services.

Lewin's Field Theory

In psychology, Kurt Lewin (1951) popularized the ecological approach with his famous equation $B = f(P, E)$, which states that behavior is a function of both the person and the environment. Lewin elaborated, stating that there are many additional forces operating on behavior. Some of these factors (or vectors) originate within the person, such as the individual's abilities, needs, hopes, goals, memories, perceptions, personality, and beliefs. Some variables are applied on the individual from the outside, and they include social setting characteristics such as family, peer group, culture, norms, and laws, and also physical influences such as temperature, lighting, pollution, available nutrients, and potential toxins. Lewin borrowed the analogy from field theory in physics, which states that the behavior of a particle traveling through space is influenced by the interaction of many vectors. Any attempt to describe this behavior accurately without knowing the dynamics of all vectors is doomed to failure. Similarly, humans travel through a life space or a subjective world of experience, and they are influenced by many vectors, as is the particle passing through space. The difference, however, is that people are affected not only by external stimuli but also by conscious experiences and perceptions. The vectors in the life space interact, as do the vectors influencing the particle, but a person interprets stimuli before responding to them. In the life space of a human being, some environmental forces are emphasized, some distorted, and others ignored. In a sense, the person responds to the setting as he/she sees it, not as it really is.

Applying Lewin's Model to Deinstitutionalization

Following Lewin's formula, $B = f(P, E)$, community mental health professionals realize that to change behavior, it is necessary to alter both the perception and the abilities of individuals, as well as the characteristics of the environment. For example, if the desire is to reintegrate institutionalized psychiatric patients into the community, three types of concerns must be addressed. First, it is necessary to teach the client more effective coping skills. Some of these skills might be aimed at reducing psychotic episodes, or at least providing information and support to deal with these episodes. Other targeted skills might involve working on routine behaviors needed to live in the community such as cleaning, cooking, practicing personal hygiene, and using public transportation. Second, it is necessary to help change the patient's perceptions, enabling the person to believe he or she can survive happily and successfully in the community. Issues such as personal empowerment, self-esteem, and the belief that the community will accept the person needs to be addressed. Third, community mental health professionals need to ensure that environmental factors such as adequate housing, jobs, and services are available in the community, and that deinstitutionalized persons have access to them. One of the environmental factors affecting formerly hospitalized individuals involves the willingness of the community to accept them into the neighborhood. Community educational programs need to be devised to encourage this acceptance.

An effective policy of deinstitutionalization can be introduced by focusing on all three concerns. If any are omitted, the program is likely to fail, resulting in patients never being discharged or swiftly returning to the institution in a "revolving door" fashion. Perhaps it was a lack of consideration of all factors that led Rosenfield (1991), in a review of research literature, to find that half of all discharged hospital patients reenter the facility within one year. Rosenfield also noted the type of housing in which a discharged person was placed affected the rate of reinstitutionalization. Individuals who were discharged into stable housing were significantly less likely to be rehospitalized than were the homeless mentally ill. In fact, Rosenfield found the ability to meet housing needs had a greater impact than the provision of enhanced psychiatric services when attempting to prevent relapse.

The Need for Synergy

Rosenfield's research points to another principle derived from the ecological perspective. If all the forces (both personal and environmental) are directed toward maintaining a former patient living in the community, then deinstitutionalization can work. When all factors in a system are lined up with each other, "synergy" is said to result (Murrell, 1973; Scileppi, 1988). When a synergistic situation is created, the effect of all the factors working together is greater than the sum of each force working separately. Following from Lewin's life space approach, to ensure all vectors are moving toward the same goal creates synergy, and hence the desired goals are more likely to be realized.

Release Driving Forces by Weakening Restraining Forces

When a mental health professional is considering strategies to reintegrate individuals into the community, another aspect of Lewin's field theory can be utilized. As mentioned earlier, Lewin conceptualized that a person moving through the life space encounters many vectors. Some of these vectors propel the individual toward a desired goal. These vectors are called "driving forces." Other vectors, called "restraining forces," hold the person back from achieving the goal. Lewin (1951) found that efforts to weaken restraining forces created more movement toward the goal than energies directed at bolstering the driving forces. Thus, it would be useful for an advocate to ask former patients what they view as obstacles preventing good community habilitation, and then to address these issues. For example, if clients fear failure, concerns can be addressed by reminding them of former successes or by having them work on a task at which they can succeed. If clients believe they lack needed social skills, these skills can be taught.

In the face of a lack of community acceptance, it is consistent with the preceding preference toward the weakening of restraining forces, as well as generally beneficial, to determine why community residents may be concerned. Gray (2001) provides an interesting insight into this process. This researcher studied the attitudes of members of a conservative Christian church congregation in the United Kingdom. The group was expected to have less favorable attitudes, since mental illness might be associated with sin or demonic possession. Gray found this church group actually had more favorable attitudes and were less judgmental toward the mentally ill than the general population. It was also found, however, that many in the church sample were concerned about dangerousness and unpredictability. Gray suggested public education directed at these concerns is likely to enhance community acceptance. Regarding faith-based organizations and community acceptance, Koenig (2000) noted that 40% of Americans (over 100 million individuals) attend religious services, on a weekly basis or more. Such groups could be key resources for mental health professionals to utilize when attempting to meet the needs of clients in the community. Koenig cautioned, however, that religious beliefs may not always be supportive of mental health efforts.

Even though Lewin's research was conducted in the 1940s, the approach is still used today. For example, Agazarian and Gantt (2003) use Lewin's field theory as a way of understanding behavior in any human social system. They note that weakening restraining forces to release driving forces helps to move an organization toward its next level of development, and can help social support and therapeutically oriented groups to advance toward their goals. Others have noted the impact of Lewin's field theory approach in providing a significant framework for understanding both individual and group behavior. Recently, Ellen Berscheid (2003) presented an in-depth review of Lewin's contribution to the fields of social psychology, industrial-organizational psychology, and child development.

Applying Lewin's Model in the Schools

In understanding the community mental health and education systems, Lewin's B = f (P, E) has evolved into the person-environment fit model described in Chapter 1. Laursen and Williams (2002), using Lewin's model, noted ethnic identity and group membership affect person-oriented factors or vectors that influence behavior. Thus, when devising synergistic interventions in the schools and the community mental health system, the ethnic values and traditions of the targeted individuals must be incorporated into a program if it is to be successful.

Other researchers have applied Lewin's person-environment fit concept to shed light on student progress at each level of school. Eccles et al. (1993) studied the negative effects caused by the typical move from elementary to middle school on students' academic motivation. These authors noted a lack of good fit between young adolescents' need for autonomy and the teachers' emphasis on control and discipline. Compared with elementary school, classes in middle school are larger and more formal. The large class size reduces the likelihood that teachers will get to know students personally. Without this rapport, the authors reasoned, teachers do not develop trust in the students, and this lack in turn inhibits teachers from granting sufficient autonomy to the students. The poor match that results can cause a deterioration in academic motivation and performance.

Another study, involving the academic motivation of sixth graders, was conducted by Turner, Midgley, Meyer, Gheen, Anderman, Kang, & Patrick (2000). These researchers studied how an environmental factor, such as the teacher's perceived emphasis on mastery goals, affected student goals. Specifically, the focus was on the interest in using avoidance of learning strategies in mathematics. A teacher's emphasis on mastery goals includes a tendency to encourage students to try hard, to explore new ideas without worrying excessively about making mistakes, and to enjoy mathematics. This teaching style was differentiated from that of performance-focused teachers. The latter type of teacher places emphasis on comparing student test scores, pointing out which learners did well and who performed poorly. Student avoidance of learning strategies includes self-handicapping (for example, putting off the studying of mathematics and not trying hard) and not seeking help. Turner et al. found teachers who emphasized mastery goals rather than performance resulted in students who were less inclined to use avoidance of learning strategies. Thus, if teachers are perceived as supporting the learners' efforts, students are less likely to adopt defensive measures and will likely do better in mathematics. To apply this study, mental health professionals might enhance client motivation to succeed in the community by adopting a supportive style, parallel to the mastery-goal-oriented teachers.

Orstroff (1993) studied the relationship between person-environment congruence and organizational effectiveness in 29 high schools. Using an innovative method, Orstroff operationalized personal orientation as a set of preferences, values, and beliefs held by students, teachers, and parents in the school. Organizational climate was defined as the summary perception of these individuals' responses to the same questionnaire for each school. In some schools, the degree of shared preference was greater than in other schools. The higher the proportion of values that were shared in the school, the better the person-environment fit was considered to be. Organizational effectiveness was measured by a variety of outcomes, such as the percentage of high-achieving students; the frequency of behavior problems; and student, parent, and teacher satisfaction rates. Orstroff found the greater the degree of person-climate congruence, the higher the academic achievement and rate of satisfaction in high school.

Joniak, Puccio, and Talbot (1993) investigated the relationship between person-environment fit and stress in college students. The personal characteristics studied involved whether students prefer to work within existing paradigms (adaptive style) or to challenge existing paradigms (innovative style). The environmental factor concerned the perceived style (adaptive or innovative) required in specific courses. Students reported high satisfaction and low levels of stress in courses in which their preferred style was encouraged. When the student-course style was incongruent, students reported a high need to conform and high stress levels.

Chartrand (1990) focused on the unique problems of nontraditional college students. Older individuals often have multiple roles including parent, employee, or spouse that may conflict with their student role. For example, an adult female student may be torn between caring for a young child at home and attending classes. Chartrand found that high role-conflict was correlated with lower academic performance and higher personal distress. The academic adjustment of nontraditional students could be influenced greatly by this aspect of person-environment fit. Lewin's formula has far-reaching implications in many aspects of life, as can be seen in the preceding studies.

Lewin's B = f (P, E) model has stimulated the development of interactionist approaches in many other disciplines, including managerial and organizational development. One such model is Fiedler's (1964; 1996; 2002) contingency model of leadership effectiveness. Although the usual applications of Lewin in community mental health involve enhancing the behavior of clients and students, it is important to recognize the agencies that comprise the mental health system have organizational structure. Mental health professionals are frequently called upon to participate in the selection process of supervisors in agencies, programs, projects, and task forces. Choosing well can make an important difference in the degree to which the agency runs smoothly and accomplishes its mission to serve clients. Therefore, discussing the qualities that result in leadership effectiveness is relevant to community mental health.

Over the past 50 years, Fred Fiedler has studied leadership effectiveness in thousands of group settings including military units, corporate offices, nonprofit agencies, and informal social groups. He found that leadership is not an inherited trait or ability, but is the result of a complex interaction between the leader and the organizational environment, parallel to Lewin's person-environment fit model. Leadership effectiveness, or the ability to marshal the energies of a group to accomplish its objectives, depends on the match between the personal qualities of the leader such as personality, ability, and managerial style, and the environmental factors such as task structure, goal objectivity, and leader-member and member-member relationships. Fiedler differentiated the degree to which the group situation is favorable to the leader. Groups with structured tasks and objectively assessible goals in which the workers are friendly to each other and with the leader are considered to be favorable to the supervisor. Fiedler has found that a more employee-centered leadership style, characterized by a considerate and socioemotionally oriented approach, results in greater productivity when the group situation is moderately favorable. The more task-oriented or job-centered leader is more effective when the group situation is either very favorable or very unfavorable to the leader. When choosing a supervisor, organizational consultants can diagnose the prospective leader's preferred style and intellectual abilities, as well as the group situation. In addition, the chosen leader can then regularly assess the match between style and setting and can either change the group situation or adjust leadership style to maintain the best fit as conditions evolve.

Barker's Behavior Settings

Up to the time Lewin presented his famous equation, most psychological research had focused on the individual, and little attention had been given to developing models of the environment. Barker (1964) was one of the first to fill in the gap. Barker assumed that some behavior patterns remain constant in a setting even as the people in the setting change, and the setting itself generates these "standing rules of behavior." Barker and Gump (1964), for example, found the size of a school affects the degree of student participation. Students are more likely to join activities in a small school than in a large one. It was noted that in large schools, even though there are more athletic teams, musical bands, and social clubs, only the best students in these areas are encouraged to join such groups. Tryouts for sports teams can be humiliating, and those not confident in their ability rarely even come to a team screening. On the other hand, in small schools the teams need members to fill their rosters, and all students, regardless of ability, are encouraged to participate. In large schools, teachers often complain about student apathy, yet this lack of involvement is usually due to school size factors and not to individual student characteristics.

It is interesting to consider the significance of Barker's standing rules of behavior concept when reflecting on how an individual's behavior changes over the course of a day. For example, a college student might be silent in class but animated at a sport stadium during a game. A young child might be respectful at home but misbehave in school, or vice versa. The varying behavior of the college student or the young child is not due to some personal variable, but to the demands or standing rules of the setting.

Barker's Four Circuits

Barker observed that it is useful to study homeostatic processes that keep behavior patterns constant. He found there are four processes, or "circuits," in social settings that tend to maintain behaviors even when the persons in the setting change. Barker borrowed the "circuit" metaphor from electronic equipment. Each electronic circuit is designed to perform a specific function, and all the circuits together keep the appliance running smoothly under a variety of circumstances. In applying this analogy to a social setting, Barker identified four circuits: program, goal, deviation-countering, and veto.

The program circuit consists of the meeting agenda that connects people to a required behavior. The ritualized activities that occur each day in a school or during every Alcoholic Anonymous (A. A.) meeting are examples of the program circuit. All clients in a human service agency follow these routine behaviors, as do all members of a church congregation during a religious service. Tension or embarrassment may occur when a newcomer is unaware of the group's program, and most are motivated to learn the appropriate cues and to perform the required behaviors.

Gibson and Werner (1994) investigated factors that encourage compliance with a program, by studying the effect of visual cues in communicating the "no-smoking" regulation in airport waiting rooms. They found the presence of no-smoking signs and the absence of ash trays significantly increased compliance. Interestingly, the clarity and legibility of the cues also encouraged other occupants of the same setting to voluntarily enforce the program regulations by asking smokers assertively to refrain from smoking in these areas. In this way, the bystanders became maintenance mechanisms (Barker, 1968), acting to restore the setting's program. Gibson and Werner found that in the absence of cues, the bystanders merely withdrew to other waiting rooms rather than confront the smoker's inappropriate behavior. Thus, clear and unambiguous visual cues can enhance compliance with the rules of the setting, a finding of value when designing the physical layout of a mental health program. It should be noted also that from a person-oriented perspective, an individual smoking in a nonsmoking area is viewed as being seriously addicted to tobacco, whereas from an environmental approach, the interpretation is focused instead on the clarity of the signs in the room.

The program circuit should help to facilitate the goal circuit. The goal circuit represents the purpose for which the social setting was formed. For instance, the goal of A. A. is to have its members refrain from drinking alcohol. Schools are established with the goal of helping students learn and become socialized into a culture. If an agency does not seem to be meeting its goals, the problem may be that the program circuit is not encouraging behavior consistent with these goals. Serving alcohol at an A. A. meeting would be an obvious example of a program circuit being out of harmony with a goal circuit. Occasionally, complications might arise if staff and clients disagree regarding the purpose of an agency, and this lack of consensus will typically reduce the ability to meet objectives.

The deviation-countering circuit involves any strategies used to reduce or eliminate nonprogram behavior. Ushers in a movie theater, for example, use certain strategies to quiet noisy movie-goers, and teachers apply certain classroom management techniques to deal with students who act out and do not attend to academic lessons. At times, the deviation-countering circuit may not be effective, and thus the frowned-upon behavior will continue. Additional problems may arise if the strategy conflicts with the goal circuit. For example, a minister who scolds the parent of a crying child while preaching love and tolerance is violating the basic tenet of this specific goal circuit.

When a deviation-countering circuit fails, the veto circuit comes into play. The veto circuit consists of rules governing the ejection of a deviant person from a particular setting. A habitually misbehaving student, for example, might be suspended or expelled from school, a member of a religious congregation may be excommunicated, or a child might be dropped from an agency's roster. Frequently, the expelled member is considered to be the source of the problem, and may earn labels such as "disruptive" or even "incorrigible."

Using Barker's Model to Assess Mental Health Settings

Barker's model can encourage mental health professionals to explore alternatives when considering why a program is or is not effective. If a particular setting necessitates the ejection of many members, it is useful to investigate which circuits may be at fault.

Environmental psychologists, for example, study social settings and programs to determine whether (a) all program circuits are consistent with goal circuits, (b) the goal circuits are understood and accepted by all setting occupants, and (c) the deviation-countering and veto circuits are effective and in agreement with the goal circuit. Altering any of these factors will affect the standing rules of behavior.

Many research studies have been conducted using Barker's framework, the most significant having explored the functioning of wards in psychiatric centers. A common goal of most wards is to enhance the social interaction of the patients, yet many day rooms have been designed in a manner that reduces socializing. Chairs were often positioned in a straight line along the wall of the day room. Although such an arrangement may facilitate house cleaning, it makes it difficult for patients to carry on a group discussion. Environmental psychologists Sommer and Ross (1958) observed that this type of arrangement was sociofugal (reducing interactions), and they suggested the chairs instead be arranged in small circles so as to allow patients to look at each other while conversing. Such a sociopetal (increasing interaction) arrangement was designed to encourage social contacts, and patients in wards utilizing this arrangement were in fact observed to interact more frequently. Once these adjustments to the setting were made, the program circuit became more consistent with the goal circuit, and consequently, the patients' behavior improved. Some individual therapists might overlook such an effective strategy and instead label patients as withdrawn instead of recognizing the profound effect of the setting on their social behavior.

Health psychology research also supports Barker's main contention that environments influence behavior. Investigators have found living near toxic waste sites or in violence-prone communities can affect the psychological health of youths. O'Leary and Covell (2002) studied adolescents who lived near the Sydney Tar Ponds of Nova Scotia, Canada. These 12- to 14-year-olds reported higher environmental and health worries, predictive of clinical depression, than a comparison sample of adolescents living elsewhere. Similarly, Stiffman and Hadley-Ives (1999) found heightened depression and anxiety among children living in dangerous and highly violent neighborhoods. Thus, it can be inferred that the standing rules present in these types of communities generate anxieties that can adversely affect the mental health of those who reside there.

Moos's Perceived Social Climate Scales

Whereas Barker demonstrated how social settings influence behavior, Moos (1994) was interested in developing an instrument to measure the differences among settings of the same type. One of his goals, for example, was to measure how various psychiatric wards compare with each other. In a similar line of thought, Murray (1938), the developer of the Thematic Apperception Test (TAT), believed that the "presses" or demands of the environment, as well as individual differences in personality, affected behavior. Murray speculated that although presses could be due to objective aspects of a setting, they could also refer to the subjective perception that each person has of the environment. Murray developed the TAT to measure individual personality differences, and hoped that others would devise a similar method to study differences between settings.

The Moos's Social Climate Scales

Moos developed a series of scales to fill the need specified by Murray, as he considered settings to have "personalities" that differentiated similar environments. Moos devised numerous scales, including the Ward Atmosphere Scale (WAS) to assess a psychiatric ward's social environment, the Community-Oriented Programs Environment Scale (COPES) to measure the psychosocial environment of transitional community-oriented psychiatric treatment programs, and the Family Environment Scale (FES) to measure perceived family qualities. In all, there are nine social climate scales, described in detail in *The Social Climate Scales: A User's Guide* (Moos, 1994). Each of these scales consists of approximately 100 statements to be rated, such as "members' activities are carefully planned" or "members here are very strongly encouraged to be independent," and each scale takes about 30 minutes to complete. These particular items appear in the COPES (Moos, 1972, p. 10), and they are administered to both members (clients) and staff. All the questionnaires measure the perceived "presses" of a particular setting. A pattern or profile of the ward, community program, or family environment emerges from the sum of the responses to these questionnaires. In this way, wards can be compared with other wards. To illustrate the utility of such a comparison, consider the example of a consultant finding that the program circuit of a particular ward does not align with the goal circuit of the psychiatric center. Another possible application of data obtained through these measures might be the placement of patients into specific wards, on the basis of both their individual needs and their abilities, as well as the WAS profiles of the setting.

Each of the social climate scales measures slightly different attributes. The COPES instrument, for example, has 10 subscales that assess three types of dimensions. The dimensions are relationship, personal growth, and system maintenance and change (Moos, 1972, 2002). The relationship dimension assesses the extent to which the members are involved with and support others in the program, and the degree to which they are encouraged to be spontaneous and open in their emotional expressiveness. Some programs encourage such interactions, whereas others treat clients more individually. The personal growth dimension focuses on types of programs that vary from agency to agency, and is concerned with the ways in which members of a program are encouraged to be autonomous, to deal with practical concerns, or to work on personal problems. For example, some programs tend to emphasize socioemotional activities, whereas others emphasize specific task-oriented behavioral objectives for each client. The system maintenance and change dimension considers the degree to which a program's clarity of goals, staff control, and order and organization are emphasized. Some programs are highly structured, whereas others allow for greater member input in establishing and modifying the daily routine. This dimension also assesses a program's responsiveness to change. Moos (2002) believed these three dimensions comprise the social climate of any setting.

Research on Mental Health Settings

The Moos Social Climate Scales have been used by many researchers and consultants. They offer a practical and reliable method for studying Barker's social settings, as well as for operationalizing both Lewin's and Murray's concerns that behavior results from the goodness of the person-environment fit. Holahan (2002) reported the social climate scales have been applied worldwide "in hospital- and community-based treatment programs, in educational settings such as classrooms and student living units, in community settings such as families, the workplace and small groups, and in institutions such as correctional facilities and [the] military. . ." (p. 65).

Cruser (1995), for example, used a then-recent version of the WAS to capture the distinct features of two types of hospital programs, the admissions unit and the resocializing ward. He also utilized these scales to measure the degree of consistency between patients' and staff's perception of each type of unit. The first type of ward generally attempts to stabilize a patient after an acute psychiatric episode, whereas the second attempts to reintegrate the patient into the community. Patients and staff of resocialization units tended to perceive their programs as being more orderly and as having fewer aggressive incidents than their counterparts on the admissions unit. Staff in both programs, however, reported lower levels of support than those perceived by patients. Through this study, Cruser (1995) confirmed the potential of the WAS as a useful instrument in developing profiles for specific psychiatric programs.

In another study utilizing Moos's scales, Roberts and Smith (1994) attempted to enhance the therapeutic environment for a group of inpatients, with the hopes of facilitating societal reintegration. These change agents redesigned the ward to stimulate enhancement of interpersonal skills, daily functioning, expressiveness, and community orientation. According to WAS testing that was done both before and after the intervention, the social environment of the ward did change significantly. Of the 22 chronically ill patients admitted to the unit, all were able to be discharged, and only one was readmitted. This study employed a Moos's social climate scale to pinpoint environmental characteristics needing modification, and then to evaluate whether the changes made actually altered the perceived condition on the therapeutic unit.

Anderson (1981) used a Moos-type scale to examine the placement of developmentally disabled adults into various types of group homes. The Resident-Environment Analysis by Level (R.E.A.L) scale, which was developed by Heiny, Stachowiak, and Shriner (1975), is generally used to study the effect that Lewin's goodness of fit has on client improvement. Anderson noted both the level of functioning of the client (person variable) as well as the degree of client autonomy that a particular community residence allowed. Some clients were relatively low-functioning and required a great deal of supervision, whereas other clients could function at a higher level and were able to perform such activities as using public transportation, preparing meals, and using money. Some group homes were operated in an institutional manner, in which meal preparation and cleaning tasks were performed entirely by staff. In contrast, other homes were run to a great extent by the members, who took turns shopping, cooking, and cleaning.

Anderson compared the level of client functioning before and after community placement, using Nihira, Foster, Shellhaas, and Leland's (1974) Adaptive Behavior Scale. The rate of improvement for high-functioning clients was significantly greater when they were placed in homes that allowed for more (rather than less) client autonomy, whereas low-functioning clients improved more in homes that were staff (rather than client) controlled. As predicted by the ecological model, an increase in the goodness of fit was correlated with a more rapid progression in the clients' ability to learn adaptive behaviors needed to live in the community.

Anderson also found that poor fit produced emotional and behavioral problems. He noted that high-functioning clients placed in staff-controlled residences tended to become hostile in such a restrictive setting, and frequently they attempted to "test the limits" of what they could do. Staff labeled these ensuing reactions as "behavior problems" and recommended that the individuals exhibiting these behaviors be returned to the institution, because of their "acting out." On the other hand, low-functioning clients placed in highly autonomous settings were overwhelmed and incapacitated. Although an ecologist would easily recognize these problems as being caused by poor fit, most of the staff interpreted them in a more individual or person-oriented manner. The blame for the "bad" behavior was transferred to the client, and commonly recommended intervention strategies included traditional approaches such as medication and reinstitutionalization. These individual-level interventions were observed to be both ineffective and counterproductive. Anderson's study found the ecological strategy, which concentrates on finding the best client placement, to be substantially more effective. As a general rule, understanding and treating problems at the correct level of analysis results in client progress and growth. Focusing on the wrong level is ineffective and often produces a "game without end" (Watzlawick, Weakland, & Fisch, 1974).

The Fundamental Attribution Error

Not only is it counterproductive for staff to hold clients responsible for problem behaviors caused by a poor person/environment fit, but it is also likely to be inaccurate. Ross (1977) found that observers often overestimate the degree to which dispositional factors affect behavior, a bias he called the "fundamental attribution error." In this type of error, behavior is attributed to personal characteristics rather than setting variables. In other words, abnormal behavior is not seen as being triggered by a dysfunctional setting or a poor person-environment fit, but simply as the action of a mentally ill person.

This error is very pervasive. Gifford and Hine (1997) found that research participants tended to perceive workers as more responsible for their productivity than they actually were. This bias could result from the observer's focusing on the actor's behavior and allowing the setting to blur in the background (Baron & Byrne, 1987). This type of inaccuracy can also be self-serving. Examples are the tendency of teachers to blame students for not learning instead of taking some measure of responsibility, or the tendency of residence managers to blame clients for acting-out behaviors rather than reflecting on needed changes in the environment.

The Current Behavior Inventory

Whereas Anderson measured both the individual's level of functioning and the presses of the setting for already discharged clients, Margolies (1997) performed the same assessment for clients preparing to reenter the community. A new, multifaceted instrument was developed for this purpose: the Current Behavior Inventory (CBI) (Margolies, Glickman, & Devine, 1993). The CBI, based on the goodness of fit psychiatric rehabilitation model of William Anthony and his colleagues (Anthony, Cohen, & Farkas, 1990; Anthony, Cohen, Farkas, & Gagne, 2002), consists of two 75-item forms. The first form, completed by clinical team members, assesses the individual's skills and abilities relevant to four areas of functioning: independent community living, interpersonal behavior, work or training, and symptom management. The second form, filled in by gatekeepers of various types of community residences, identifies the entry skills required for an individual to succeed in a specific residence, on the basis of the same four areas. Examples of items include "crosses streets safely as a pedestrian," "respects the living spaces of others," "dresses appropriately for work setting," and "complies with medical treatment recommendations" (Margolies 1999, 2000).

The results of both the clinician and the provider response forms are combined, and then they are used to establish skill-training goals for each participant. This process can aid discharge planners in selecting a good fit. It is expected that individuals prepared for discharge using the CBI will be more likely to make successful adjustments to the community than those placed without use of the instrument.

To date, a number of CBI studies have been completed. Two such studies (Margolies, 1999; Margolies & Columbia, 1997) found that staff of various community residences identified different entry-skill needs for clients, even within the same type of setting. This finding resulted from the fact that each residence had unique characteristics. The study reported that between 23 community residences, the number of skills required for entry varied from 5 to 51, out of the 75 assessed. This information implies that discharge planners and clinicians need to target the specific residence when preparing a patient for reentry into the community. It should be noted, however, Margolies (2000) found 17 particular skills listed by 75% of the gatekeepers. It was thus inferred these 17 skills could become the core of any training program designed to prepare patients for discharge.

Traditionally, the CBI has been used to improve client competencies and to create a good placement fit, and in theory this instrument could also be used to adjust setting presses as well. In other words, the characteristics of group homes could be modified to more closely mirror the level of skills possessed by the clients about to enter these residences. Indeed, the use of the CBI encourages this modification to take place. Margolies (2000) reported the average number of skills needed for entry at four state-controlled community residences dropped from 28 in 1997 to 21 in 2000. The reduction in the number of required skills resulted from the provision of more support in these settings, which in turn increased the likelihood of successful client discharge into the community. An added advantage of using the CBI is that patients, after visiting a prospective community residence and reviewing promising CBI data for that home, tend to be highly motivated to participate in pre-discharge skills training programs (Margolies, 1999). The ecological model has provided practitioners with many new and effective tools for forging a good person-environment fit, and the process of deinstitutionalization has improved greatly through the use of this approach. Fewer patients are simply "dumped" into any available slot outside the facility, and more are prepared to be discharged into appropriate settings where they can function effectively in the community.

As mentioned previously, the CBI is based on Anthony's (Anthony, Cohen, & Farkas, 1990; Anthony, Cohen, Farkas, & Gagne, 2002) psychiatric rehabilitation model, an ecological approach that has helped individuals with psychiatric disabilities transition back to the community. Practitioners using this model are trained to assist clients "in choosing, getting and keeping their desired living environments and preferred social activities" (Kramer, Anthony, Rogers, & Kennard, 2003, p. 414). The CBI can help them assess both individual readiness and skills needed for competence in the desired setting.

Kramer et al. (2003) blended Anthony's training model and the assertive Community Treatment (ACT) program. The ACT program, developed by Stein, Test, and Marx (1975), utilizes multidisciplinary treatment teams available on a 24-hour basis, assertive outreach, and in vivo rehabilitation in the community. These researchers investigated the treatment benefits of the combined intervention on individuals hospitalized with a severe and persistent mental illness. Over a four-year period, the average number of days the clients were hospitalized decreased by over 90%, from 365 to 17 days, and over half of the clients were able to eventually live independently in the community. Thus, by incorporating an ecological approach and being careful to assess the fit between the person and the setting, a good P-E fit can occur, and deinstitutionalization can be accomplished successfully.

Kelly's Principles of Ecology

Like Lewin, Kelly (1966) provided a framework for utilizing the ecological perspective to understand the principles and forces affecting an individual's functioning in the community. More recently, Kelly and his colleagues (Kelly, Ryan, Altman, & Stelzner, 2000) described how this ecological model can be used to understand and change any social system, including the community mental health system. The original model is presented first, and then the updated application. In the 1966 formulation, Kelly outlined four processes that describe how a social system operates and how an awareness of these processes can assist a community psychologist in developing effective strategies for helping individuals who have difficulties in living. The four processes are interdependence, cycling of resources, adaptation, and succession.

Interdependence

Since all components of a social system work together, changes in one sector affect all aspects in some fashion. This process indicates that, as mentioned earlier, many parts of the social setting need to be considered before discharging a psychiatric patient.

Cummings' Closed Ranks

Since medication and psychotherapy are aimed at reducing symptoms and gaining insight, respectively, they are not sufficient to address the problems of reentry into the community or even rejoining the family. Cumming and Cumming (1957) observed a common phenomenon occurring during community reentry, which they termed "closed ranks." They used a military analogy to describe it. As an army unit loses members in battle, other soldiers step in to take the place of their fallen comrades. Similarly, when a family member becomes hospitalized, other individuals fill the gap created. If the individual in question had been performing a needed chore or providing some unique social or emotional support, someone else would take over that particular duty. The "closed ranks" phenomenon may occur in employment settings as well. A supervisor may promise to hold a job open for a hospitalized individual but needs to hire a replacement as work piles up. When the individual's mental illness is under control and the person is discharged, the family and the work unit may no longer be receptive. The former patient has lost his/her place due to a "closing of the ranks." Thus, a community psychologist needs to work with a patient's family to ensure that a role can be found and the returning member will be accepted. The psychologist also needs to determine how the client might earn a living and whether training for a new job is needed. Merely treating the intrapsychic mental illness is not enough; the client's interdependence with family, work-place, and community must be reestablished.

To expand on the concept of interdependence, it is necessary to note that any intervention affects all sectors of the social system. Releasing former patients into the community will affect nearly all aspects of life in a neighborhood. If these individuals move into group homes, local laws regulating zoning need to be reviewed. Strategies to promote community acceptance and to reduce any fear on the part of potential neighbors need to be devised. Transportation requirements for the newcomers need to be worked out. Fire and police department personnel need to be consulted. Shopkeepers, political leaders, medical doctors, restaurant managers, clergy, beauticians, recreation facility operators, and many others in the community will be affected, since all participants of the neighborhood are interlocking. Changes in one sector, such as increasing the number of discharged individuals, will inevitably impact all other sectors.

General Systems Theory

The principle of interdependence is not unique to Kelly's theory of ecology. It is also an essential construct in General Systems Theory (GST), a multidisciplinary approach originated by Ludwig Bertalanffy (1968). GST studies how a system achieves goals in its environment. A system acts as a whole organism that exchanges resources, energies, and outputs as it adapts to its setting. Systematic interventions are more likely to be successful than changes that focus only on an isolated element. Hearn (1969) viewed the community as a social system. A system is made up of a set of elements and includes the relationships among the elements. If one element is altered, the relationships between it and the other factors are also likely affected, and such a modification places stress on the entire system. If all interrelated components can be made consistent with the reformed element, the change is accepted, and the system will stabilize with resulting synergy. If, however, the interaction is inconsistent with the other components of the system, the change will be rejected as the system strives to reestablish the status quo following disruption. This feature of social systems is often called "equifinality" (Hearn, 1969). This refers to a tendency within the social system to produce identical results even when some of the components within the system have been altered. To relate back to a previous example, if a group planning to reintegrate clients into the community considers and accounts for all the dynamic effects such an action might have on the entire social system, the change will likely be accepted, and the individuals will be apt to lead productive lives. If the planners fail to obtain a zoning variance, do not attempt to gain community acceptance, or neglect to provide transportation or access to a job or day program, the process of deinstitutionalization will fail. The system, in such a case, will "buffer" itself to resist the change.

The purpose of systems thinking lies not only in understanding how systems change but also in intervening to improve them. Checkland (1997) noted that when systems theory is applied to social organizations concerned with mental health, education, or business, it should be remembered that each stakeholder in the system may have a unique perspective on what purposes the system should serve. To use the reintegration example, perhaps not everyone in the community wants a particular client to succeed. Interdependence implies that all stakeholders are "lined up" and agree to support the planned change, yet this is not always the case. As a result, political and persuasive skills are essential when attempting to initiate a change in a system (Melan, 2004).

Interdependence in the Criminal Justice System

Systems theory and the principle of interdependence have been applied to many fields in the social sciences; among them is criminal justice. Roesch (1995) advocated for multilevel interventions in the community to reduce crime. In his presidential address to the American Psychology and Law Society, Roesch noted the drawbacks of a person-centered approach that views delinquent behavior as a result of only individual factors. Such an approach fails to consider the exposure to critical social conditions on the part of the individual. Problems are multifaceted, and effective solutions must be as well. Roesch stated the best interventions, from an ecological perspective, should include both individual and systems-level components.

In an example of a systems-oriented intervention, Henggeler, Melton, and Smith (1992) described the multisystemic therapy (MST) program, designed as an alternative to incarcerating serious juvenile offenders. This program targets both the individual and the family, and it is directed toward problem solving at the peer, family, school, and neighborhood levels. Ongoing care is provided in the home and in the community settings and is individualized to meet the characteristics of the juvenile, family, and community. Borduin et al. (1995) performed a four-year follow-up on the effectiveness of the MST. Participants included 176 juvenile offenders who were at high risk of committing additional violent crimes. Compared with matched controls who received individual therapy, the MST juveniles were better adjusted and significantly less likely to be rearrested. Tate, Reppucci, and Mulvey (1995), in reviewing the effectiveness of interventions with violent juvenile offenders, found multicomponent, systems-oriented interventions such as the MST were relatively promising in terms of reducing crime and recidivism.

Cycling of Resources

Kelly's second ecological principle concerns how resources are utilized. Within any social system it is useful to consider how resources and energy are transferred through the system. Wastes from one sector may become the raw materials for another sector. As an example, recently retired workers who may suddenly find themselves with too much free time on their hands could be very useful to agencies that need volunteers. Additionally, parents of adult children who experience depression due to the "empty-nest syndrome" may find great satisfaction in becoming actively involved as grandparents. Psychology graduate students who need inexpensive off-campus housing may be useful as roommates and companion role models to recently deinstitutionalized adults with developmental disabilities who are living alone in the community. Parents of school-aged children may have free time during lunch hours when they can help supervise students during recess. In all these cases, opportunities exist to utilize otherwise wasted human resources, and to do so in a manner that permits agencies and institutions to benefit from such cycling of resources. This process, although often operating on a volunteer basis, is sometimes initiated out of necessity. One of the authors (JS) learned about a useful example that occurred during World War II. During this time, many young adults were serving in the military, and many citizens were involved in the war effort as well. Because of this state of affairs, individuals available to work in old-age homes and orphanages were few and far between. As a result of this worker shortage, a plan was devised to have elderly citizens spend some time each day with the abandoned children. This arrangement was warmly received by both groups. The elderly experienced less loneliness and greater satisfaction with their lives, and the youth had access to the adult interaction and guidance they needed. It was apparent the plan worked, and even though it was formally dismantled after the war emergency had passed, many elementary schools and adult homes have continued such voluntary intergenerational programs.

In another interesting application of cycling resources, Broadhead, Heckathorn, Grund, Stern, & Anthony (1995) used former drug addicts as street-based outreach workers in an AIDS prevention program. These former IV drug users became cost-effective peer community health educators in an Eastern Connecticut program. Through this intervention, former clients became nonprofessional service providers, creating a new and an available human resource in the fight against AIDS.

The cycling of resources is not limited to human resources. Facilities, equipment, and food supplies can also frequently be transferred throughout a system for the mutual benefit of all involved. For example, church halls and school buildings can be used during off-hours as meeting places for many types of community groups. This use provides an obvious benefit for the neighborhood groups, but it also provides an additional opportunity for a church to implement its social mission or for a school to reduce the "town-gown" barrier that restricts the community's participation in education. As another example; technologically oriented businesses need state-of-the art computers. Every three years or so, the level of sophistication of newer machines increases so greatly that the older models become obsolete and must be replaced. These three-year-old computers are no longer useful to the company, but they would be greatly beneficial as learning aids in local classrooms. Again, rather than discarding resources, they can be put to use in another section of the social system.

A final example concerns food. Farmers' surpluses can be used to feed the hungry, in both inner cities and developing nations. Moreover, restaurants and culinary schools often prepare food in greater quantity than can be realistically consumed, and these "leftovers" can be donated to local agencies to feed the poor. Many other opportunities exist to exploit unused and discarded resources for the betterment of the community. Although in nature this process occurs automatically in the food chain, society needs clever interventionists to conceive of such arrangements and to plan strategies that can overcome barriers to implementing such programs.

Levine and Perkins (1987) noted the cycling of resources is frequently needed because of sociopolitical change in the community. When a psychiatric center closes, employment patterns in a community are disrupted. Out-of-work staff represent wasted resources, and the system should retain these individuals or relocate them in expanding agencies or businesses that meet the needs of those being discharged. Frequently this sort of redistribution of resources requires "seed money," but the intervention pays for itself by providing many dividends to the community in a relatively short period of time. Kelly's interdependence principle interacts with the cycling of resources in this type of situation, since the entire system is affected by the decision to close a hospital, or downsize a corporation.

Adaptation

Kelly's third principle of ecology is adaptation. Adaptation refers to an individual's ability to live and grow in a specific habitat or environment. Adaptation can be improved either by enhancing the competency of individuals, enabling them to thrive in a wider range of habitats, or by making the environment more "friendly." Adaptation clearly represents the community mental health professional's central theme of creating a better person-environment fit. The adaptation principle allows for both person-oriented and setting-oriented interventions to be conceived in a manner that will enhance the goodness of fit.

Psychiatric and Other Stigmatizing Labels as Setting Specific

Adaptation uses a higher unit of analysis than traditional psychotherapy. Rather than focusing only on the person, ecological psychologists view the "person in a setting" as the unit of study. By doing so, they reduce the need for stigmatizing person-oriented labels. For example, traditional psychology might label an individual as mildly mentally retarded as a result of poor academic performance in a school. That same individual, however, might perform well in a simple 1950s style farm setting where only repetitive routine tasks (picking fruit, collecting eggs, feeding animals, etc.) are required. Such a person who always lived on a farm might not have been labeled retarded, because his/her adaptation to the setting was adequate.

Few psychiatric labels can be applied independent of a setting. An accountant concerned about detail at work would not be called obsessive, whereas a similar behavior performed by a child at play might be considered so. A football player who is aggressive during a game is not typically labeled antisocial or violence-prone. A mystic might have a vision during a religious service, but few would apply a psychotic label to an individual in this situation. A behavior that in one setting is seen as desirable may be inappropriate in another setting, and so the activity itself cannot be accurately evaluated outside the context in which it occurs.

Research supports the concept the person-environment fit influences the degree to which individuals with mental disorders can be successful in daily life. Van Ornum (1997) investigated the perceptions of individuals who suffer from obsessive-compulsive disorder and scrupulosity (OCD/Scrup). Such persons can be successful in life as long as they have formed a good fit with their environment. Van Ornum found, according to responses from a national survey of over 1,000 members of Scrupulous Anonymous, that a large number of participants noted favorable aspects of their disorder, particularly those who chose professions in the areas of health and public safety. A compulsive surgeon, for instance, checks twice to be certain no sponges are left inside the patient, and an obsessive detective conducts a very thorough and meticulous criminal investigation. Among the survey findings, 56% of the total respondents described themselves as hardworking, and 50% stated they were college graduates or professionals. Specifically, 18% indicated OCD/Scrup made them more moral, 11% more caring, and 7% more honest. Presumably, these individuals had found an acceptable niche that allowed them to lead productive lives in the community.

Increasing Niche Breadth

As mentioned previously, adaptation allows for both individual- and setting-oriented interventions. Person-oriented programs attempt to widen the range of settings or "niches" in which an individual can function. Ecologists use the term "niche" to refer to settings in which a person can live and grow. As the range of niches increases, so does the chance of survival, particularly when niches change quickly. When long-term institutionalized patients are encouraged to leave a facility (sometimes because of political public budget cutting), staff must teach these patients activities for daily living (ADL) skills. These include areas such as cooking, practicing personal hygiene, and using money. By learning these skills, former patients are better able to live independently in the community. Of course, such person-oriented programs are not limited to the deinstitutionalized. All individuals can adapt more comfortably to a niche by learning abilities such as better problem solving, time management, and interpersonal skills, among others. Colleges, for example, attempt to increase the niche breadth of new first-year students by offering a series of relationship-building workshops and seminars.

Adaptation also involves making a setting more "habitable." A common example is the ability for physically challenged individuals to enter buildings if they are wheelchair accessible. The Americans with Disabilities Act of 1991 requires businesses to make reasonable adjustments in the workplace to accommodate the needs of disabled employees. Desks can be raised to enable their use by workers in wheelchairs. Employers can provide specially adapted computer hardware and software to users with various disabling conditions. Without these adjustments, the workplace would not be available as a niche for these individuals.

Frequently, niches are constricted or expanded as a result of political and economic forces. In the past, for example, if a developmentally disabled adult was living at home and family members were able to care for this individual, little or no federal funds were available to help maintain the person. If the individual was a wheelchair user and the family home was not wheelchair accessible, he or she would be required to enter an intermediate care facility or a nursing home in order for the federal Medicaid program to provide assistance. Usually this move was very costly, and the care received was institutionalized and impersonal; it was certainly better to add an entrance ramp or make a door frame wider. Recently, state developmental centers were authorized to request waivers allowing the utilization of Medicaid funds to make reasonable changes in the homes of persons with developmental disabilities. This was done in order to maintain more normalized living arrangements. Under this program, the case manager and the client were to cooperate and create a unique program to meet the client's needs (McGarrity, 1993). Medicaid waivers allow for greater independence and choice at a reduced cost to the system. The original regulations reduced the person's niche breadth, but the revised waiver of regulations expanded it and thus opened up far more housing opportunities than previously available. Note also that financial resources in the system were cycled or transferred so that the disabled adults and their families could receive funds that were previously available only to nursing homes and institutions.

Another setting factor that affects adaptation is the degree of social support available to the individual. Although this topic is discussed extensively in a later chapter, it is worthwhile to present a brief example of a study that demonstrated the benefits of social support on an individual's ability to adapt to a health crisis. Christensen, Raichle, Ehlers, and Bertolatus (2002) investigated the mental health and social functioning of patients who received kidney transplants. Patients who reported having a supportive family exhibited fewer symptoms of depression and greater mobility and social functioning than similar patients who had less supportive families.

Frequently, new programs enhance adaptation by targeting both the setting and the person, and they result in a significantly greater niche breadth. When the deinstitutionalization process was under way in the early 1970s, adults with developmental disabilities were not prepared to enter the workforce and become economically productive citizens. Work training centers and sheltered workshops were developed to teach these adults needed work skills and attitudes. Laws were modified to allow such individuals to work for pay below the minimum wage, and usually based salary on the rate of productivity. In other words, if a "regular" worker could produce 10 units of a product per hour and a disabled person could make 5, then the latter individual would be paid half the salary of the regular worker. Additional legislation encouraged companies to accept bids for "piecework" contracts from sheltered workshops. Adults with disabilities were empowered in the process. Such interventions required staff to train clients with a person-oriented strategy, agency administrators to establish sheltered workshop programs with a setting-oriented strategy, and state and federal legislation to ensure that the programs were accepted by the social system. This would be considered a higher-order system-level strategy.

Niche Building in Work Settings for Individuals with Developmental Disabilities

Although these types of interventions gradually increased the range of niches available, many adult clients believed working in sheltered programs was somewhat demeaning. Polls were conducted among workers in these programs, and the majority indicated they would rather work in regular businesses. A 1991 poll of adult employees with developmental disabilities at Rehabilitation Programs, Inc. (Rehab) in Dutchess County, New York, found that 60% would opt for community work situations if they were available (Carroll, 1993). As a result, both at Rehab and many other agencies throughout the country, new programs have been established to enable clients (now called consumers or participants) to work with their "able-bodied" neighbors. In these programs, staff members called "job coaches" contact managers of businesses whose workers typically perform routine and repetitive tasks. Fast food establishments, hotel and company cleaning services, factories with assembly line functions, and mail rooms of corporations tend to respond favorably and accept individuals with developmental disabilities on a trial basis. The job coaches learn the tasks required for a particular job, usually by performing them in the workplace for a short time, and then teaching these skills to an interested program participant. The participant then practices the skills in the workplace, under the supervision of the job coach. After a brief time, a regular worker (called a "job buddy") is invited to volunteer to provide minor assistance and guidance to the trainee, and the job coach leaves. The developmentally disabled adult "graduates" through the process, from being a Rehab client to a "McDonald's employee," for example, and works side-by-side with other employees. Through these programs an individual, formerly limited to participating only in sheltered workshops, can work in a variety of settings, having gained the ability to adapt to a wider range of niches. In a sense, the only limitation is the ability of the system to create new niches, and not that of the individual. Perhaps agencies that place unnecessary restrictive limitations should be named "disabled," rather than the individuals traditionally identified with such a stigmatizing label. However, although the intervention described above is available for individuals with mild or even moderate disabilities, it cannot be readily applied to those with severe or profound disabilities. As community mental health professionals become more creative, perhaps niches can be found for more severely disabled program participants as well.

Sarbin's Achieved versus Ascribed Role Status

Adults with developmental disabilities who graduate from agency clients to business employees gain an achieved role status that has many psychosocial benefits. Sarbin (1970) discussed the differences between ascribed and achieved role status. Ascribed roles are passively acquired. Being a male or a female, young or old, or a member of a particular ethnic group are examples of ascribed roles, as are psychiatric labels. Achieved roles, on the other hand, are those that persons strive to attain. College student, medical doctor, worker, public official, athlete, and volunteer are examples of achieved roles. Individuals can become personally involved in achieved roles, and the value associated with the status of the role can range from neutral, at worst, to positive. Athletes, therapists, and home gardeners, for example, can devote their time and energy to participating in activities related to these roles. They can take pride in their work, because the public respects a soccer player, even a player who loses a game, in recognition of the effort involved in becoming an athlete.

Individuals cannot become involved in ascribed roles, and the public views the status of ascribed roles as neutral at best, to "very unfavorably." It is very difficult to take pride in "being" schizophrenic or mentally retarded, and to add to the stigma, family members or neighbors are often relieved if an individual with a disorder in living has merely avoided a relapse or the display of inappropriate behavior in the recent past.

By calling individuals "agency clients," service providers are inadvertently making the ascribed role more salient, which not only stigmatizes but also reduces the likelihood of psychological improvement. Client apathy and stagnation are often partially due to acceptance of the ascribed role, and this trend runs counter to intended treatment goals for the person. Because of this tendency, the move from Rehab client to McDonald's employee, for example, becomes far more significant, since it involves a change from ascribed to achieved role. Arns and Linney (1993) found that for individuals with mental disorders, a change in vocational status affected self-efficacy, self-esteem, and life satisfaction. Hence, the enhancement of individual adaptation through the teaching of meaningful vocational skills can provide new achieved role status and improved mental health.

Succession

Kelly's fourth and final ecological principle is succession. As environments change, a more adaptable population will tend to replace a less adaptable one. In the animal world, for example, as rain forests in South America are reduced in size, some species become extinct while others thrive. Sometimes the environmental changes are the result of purely natural processes, whereas in other cases, they are the result of human intervention, intentional or not.

Settings are not "behavior neutral" (Levine & Perkins, 1987). Environments tend to favor some populations and constrain others. Using the preceding work example, it can be understood why programs that provide new employment niches for various client populations work in times of low unemployment but fail when unemployment increases. This is a natural result when the economy slows, since fewer jobs are available and many out-of-work adults compete for scarce positions. Public sentiment for the developmentally disabled becomes relatively less favorable during these times, and government directives encouraging businesses to hire these clients are suspended.

Transinstitutionalization as a Form of Succession

Another example of succession is as follows: as the deinstitutionalization process becomes more universal, individuals must be more severely disabled before they can be admitted. This requirement strains the resources of service systems within the community, since these agencies must accept those with more serious problems and yet frequently cannot provide sufficient services. Clients "fall through the cracks" and may become homeless and jobless. These individuals often engage in criminal behaviors such as loitering, shoplifting, or prostitution, either because they have to meet survival needs or because they are not trained in understanding social norms or performing ADL skills. As a result, mentally ill and developmentally disabled persons are arrested and incarcerated. In this case, the population of individuals with disabling conditions is moved from the psychiatric and developmental centers to the inner cities, and then to jails and prisons. This succession, sometimes called "transinstitutionalization" (Talbott, 1975), occurs largely due to public policy changes that affect the community.

Prior to the 1960s, rich and poor alike lived in relatively close urban proximity across the nation. As the automobile became accessible to the middle class, wealthier individuals began to move out of the cities. Shopping malls were developed in the suburbs to accommodate the needs of affluent consumers. Urban businesses declined, and as a result, fewer jobs were available in the cities. This outcome strained the urban tax base, causing city transportation and other services to deteriorate and the housing market to evaporate. Many central cities were left with a high concentration of powerless, unemployed, and poor people who lived in run-down buildings with inadequate public services. As the wealthy moved out, the poor began to occupy their neighborhoods. In the previous example of succession, only some inner cities deteriorated greatly. As a result of better urban planning and the use of public funds and private foundation support, some urban areas continued to attract middle-class populations by encouraging new businesses through tax-reduced economic development zones and small business incubators. In these areas, services were maintained, and community gathering opportunities were provided.

The principle of succession, along with Kelly's three other principles, enables ecological psychologists to view the entire community as a social system and to perceive the macro-level trends that exist in the system. As a result, effective interventions in both natural settings and through political policy can be made to ensure that populations in need have access to resources and services.

Kelly's Ecological Approach to Systems Change

Whereas Kelly's original 1966 model focused on how individuals interact with settings, the more recent approach is concerned with how systems and agencies change. Kelly, Ryan, Altman, and Stelzner (2000) offer an ecological perspective for facilitating large-scale development and change. This approach is ecological in that it is based on the premise that individuals and systems affect each other. In community mental health, a system could refer to a program or programs within an agency, to an agency or to a group of agencies, or to the entire system of service delivery in a geographical area.

Kelly and his colleagues encouraged change agents to investigate eight concepts, consisting of four structural and four process attributes. The structural components refer to frameworks, policies, and procedures within the system, whereas the process factors consist of the series of social activities performed as a result of the structure. To simplify, the structure reflects the "what," and the process the "how" of the agency.

The four structural concepts include the following:

- Personal resource potentials, or the abilities, expertise, and skills of the members of the agency;
- Social system resources, or the services, procedures, and groupings designed to help members achieve the system's goals;
- Social settings, or the actual places in which the agency functions; and
- System boundaries, which define the nature of the relationship between agency participants and individuals not in the agency.

Kelly et al. urge prospective interventionists to investigate whether all members are encouraged to contribute their personal resource potentials in a free exchange, whether the social system resources are known to and accessible by all participants, whether the standing rules of the setting (Barker, 1968) are appropriate given the values of the agency, and whether participants can easily establish relationships with those outside the agency to achieve group objectives.

The four process concepts include the following:

- Reciprocity, or the amount of mutual exchange among members;
- Networking, or the actions taken to establish communication among members of the agency;
- Boundary spanning, or the establishing of relationships with those outside the agency to identify and share resources; and
- Adaptation, or the processes used to respond to new demands within the agencies or to requirements of the outside environment.

Change agents could study the quality of reciprocity by assessing whether a hierarchical organization might restrict openness and thus limit the sharing of knowledge or skills. Similarly, networking can provide members with an appreciation of other members' functioning at the boundaries of the system, which will raise awareness of how a new program might affect others' ability to provide services. Organizational consultants might investigate whether there are sufficient exchanges across system boundaries, while ensuring that the integrity of the agency is not compromised. Finally, the change agent might explore the degree to which the agency monitors changes in the environment. In light of these examples, it is easy to see how restricting networking may create ineffective interventions.

In addition to the eight concepts, Kelly et al. encouraged those seeking to improve the functioning of an agency to investigate values, norms, and roles. Values refer to the ideological beliefs that justify behavior. For instance, does the agency have a clearly described mission statement that is understood and accepted by agency participants? Norms are the general expectations of the system participants. An important question is whether the norms are consistent with agency values: are they discussed frequently, and are there appropriate methods for enforcing member adherence to them? Finally, roles are the specific behaviors associated with each position in the agency. It is important to assess whether new members are aware of and trained to perform their roles: are members given feedback on the quality of role performance, and are the roles consistent with norms and values and with the roles of other members who occupy complementary positions in the agency? Finally, when members perform multiple roles, are the requirements of each role consistent with the others?

These are only a sample of the questions that Kelly, Ryan, Altman, and Stelzner (2000) suggest to help assess an agency's structure and functioning. As can be inferred from these macrolevel concepts, Kelly's ecological perspective can assist in creating more effective interventions in the community mental health system.

Bronfenbrenner's Ecological Theory of Child Development

Bronfenbrenner (1979) noted that most theories of child development treat the child as an individual entity without sufficient concern for the context in which the child develops. The principles derived from individual psychology cannot be easily modified to account for setting level variables, but the models of Lewin and Kelly can be readily applied.

Bronfenbrenner viewed the social context as being composed of four systems, varying from the relatively small micro-level to the more global macro-level. These systems are of a nested nature, analogous to a series of concentric circles of varying size.

Microsystems

The smallest unit of analysis is called the microsystem level. This unit includes the people with whom the child interacts on a regular and frequent basis, including family members, classmates, and friends. A child's behavior and development are greatly influenced by the structure and dynamics of his or her family, classroom, and close social network. The microsystem level of analysis also allows for the investigation of second-order effects, such as the effect of the birth of a new sibling on the mother-child dyad, paternal influence, or the role of birth order.

Many researchers have investigated the effects of each of the three microsystems across the life span. For example, Repetti, Taylor, and Seaman (2002) reviewed the literature on the effect of "risky families" on children's psychosocial functioning, social competence, and incidence of later substance abuse. Risky families are defined as those "characterized by conflict and aggression and by relationships that are cold, unsupportive and neglectful" (p. 330). On the basis of a review of over 75 studies, it was found that children raised in risky families had a greater incidence of mental and physical illness than those who grew up in more functional families, an effect that was observed to last far beyond childhood.

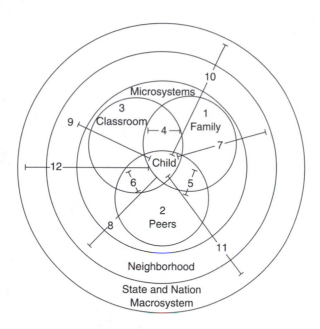

EXAMPLES OF FACTORS IN A NESTED SYSTEM

A. Microlevel
   1. family, nuclear and extended
   2. peers and neighbors
   3. classroom and school

B. Mesolevel
   4. parent-teacher conference
   5. child's sibling and next door friend
   6. friend who dropped out of school

C. Exolevel
   7. parent's work supervisor
   8. local curfew ordinance
   9. school board

D. Macrolevel
   10. economic recession
   11. discrimination, cultural norms
   12. mandatory education law

Bronfenbrenner's ecological model of human development.

FIGURE 3.1

Regarding peer groups, other researchers examined the effect of neighborhood on prevalence of mental illness in adult residents. Silver, Mulvey, and Swanson (2002) found, on the basis of socioeconomic and other demographic data, disadvantaged neighborhoods were associated with higher rates of depression and substance abuse. They also found resident mobility in a neighborhood resulted in higher rates of schizophrenia, depression, and substance abuse.

The classroom microsystem can also affect behavior. Scileppi (1988), in a review of the literature, found classroom social atmosphere, or "value climate," has a strong effect on a child's academic behavior and interpersonal development. Bronfenbrenner's model provides the rationale for focusing on this pattern. The way in which a child views his or her family, peer group, and school affects development and thus is an important issue to explore therapeutically at the microsystem level.

Mesosystems

Bronfenbrenner's next level is called the mesosystem. The mesosystem consists of the links between two or more microsystems. Murrell (1973) studied the effect of the degree of synergy among home, peers, and school on children. If the members of all three microsystems agree on values and goals, the child is more likely to accept these priorities and exhibit more focused and effective behavior in meeting these objectives. On the other hand, if the microsystems are in conflict, the child will be less certain about career choices and his or her direction in life. In middle-class neighborhoods, the three systems are usually synergistic, but in lower-class or minority culture this is often not the case. A lack of synergy can create tension and ambivalence in children, affecting development.

De La Sierra (2001) studied the relationship between family and school microsystems on the academic performance of primary-grade students in a predominantly Hispanic public school in South Florida. This researcher found students who perceived a positive (i.e., consistent) school/family mesosystem had better scores in mathematics, conduct, and effort than those who noted conflicts between the mesosystem components. To reduce inconsistencies in such cases, school psychologists and other school change agents can encourage teachers and administrators to interact and cooperate with community leaders and parents, working to include "cultural amplifiers" (Rappaport, 1977) in the curriculum. Cultural classroom amplifiers can include discussing processes, events, and things common to the ethnic background of the students, or the development of after-school peer group activities that validate the productive aspects of subcultural values. In this way, teachers, parents, and peers can each be affected by cooperative programs. Studies demonstrating the positive effects of parental involvement in education on learning (Herman & Yeh, 1980; Ordovensky, 1986) could be due to the enhancement of synergy among the three microsystem structures. The celebration of cultural differences (as opposed to the practice of "culturocide," which attempts to eliminate or derogate locally held values and beliefs) is an intervention not likely to be derived from individual psychology.

Other researchers have studied the mesosystems of adults. Grzywacz and Marks (2000) investigated the work/family interface of employed adults. These researchers studied whether stress and conflict in one microsystem can affect an individual's perception of the other microsystem, and whether success or personal enhancement in one area can "spill over" to the other area. They found both stress and success in either microsystem do, in fact, affect the other. In a practical application, this finding suggests prevention programs to train individuals in skills such as stress management, conflict resolution, and interpersonal communication can have beneficial results for both work and family microsystems of the participants.

Exosystems

Bronfenbrenner's third level of analysis considers the exosystem. The exosystem focuses on the interconnection between an individual and the settings that are rarely experienced directly by the individual. Exosystems such as the school board, parent's place of employment, or local legislative bodies have significant effects on the child's life, yet usually leave the child feeling powerless. For example, the child is indirectly but profoundly affected if a desirable school program is cut from the district budget, or if a parent's boss reduces some work benefit.

Anderson and Mohr (2003) studied the effect of the system of care for children with emotional disturbances (ED) on the well-being of the youth involved. This type of program is an example of an exosystem, since the children rarely meet the decision-makers in the service delivery system yet the policies developed can affect the lives of these youth. These authors expressed the concern that the "fragmented nature of the U.S. mental health system with its historic focus on tertiary care [results in] a large percentage of children with mental health needs receiving little if any intervention in schools or communities" (p. 53). Children with ED have the poorest long-term outcomes in terms of educational performance, social and economic behavior, and overall functioning out of any disability group. Anderson and Mohr note that adopting a developmental ecological perspective based on Bronfenbrenner's model could remedy this situation.

Exosystems, as mentioned in a previous example, also include the parent's work-place. In towns where one employer dominates the workforce, if that company down-sizes the number of local employees, the youth experience tension as the result of these massive layoffs. This tension results in lower academic performance, more frequent physical and mental illness, and increased vandalism and student aggression. Such a pattern emerged in Dutchess County, New York, when the IBM Corporation reduced its local workforce by several thousand employees in 1993. It would have been beneficial for community mental health practitioners to collaborate with community and school leaders and to establish support groups for both children and their recently unemployed parents, advocate for resources to fund job-retraining programs, and develop programs to attract new businesses to enter the community.

Macrosystems

The fourth and most global level of analysis in Bronfenbrenner's nested systems ecological model of child development is the macrosystem. The macrosystem includes large-scale societal factors such as ideology, culture, and economic and political conditions. Changes in these processes (particularly rapid ones) affect the lives of every person in the society. Some examples of significant macrosystem events include the worldwide depression of the 1930s, religious and ethnic genocide, the rapid fall of Communism in vast areas of Eastern Europe and Asia in the early 1990s, the breakdown of the family structure, and the increased fear of terrorism that has occurred in the United States during the past fifty years. These events affected the psychological well-being of all the people in the cultures involved. On a smaller scale, public policy changes such as school desegregation or changes in public assistance to poor children can affect cognitive development; and on an even more localized level, rapid economic growth or decline can affect children as well (Luria, 1976).

Lerner's (1995, 1998, 2002; Lerner, Castellino, Terry, Villarruel, & McKinney, 1995) developmental contextualism model complements Bronfenbrenner's concepts.

Lerner noted the temporal dimension of the political/economic/historical context is the broadest setting in which an individual matures, and that understanding the linkage among all the levels of a system over the lifespan is essential both to an understanding of human development and to the planning of desirable interventions. Lerner viewed these linkages as multilevel, dynamic, and reciprocal. For example, not only is a child affected directly by public assistance programs, but so are parent-child interaction and the family structure. The effects of the historical context are not limited to children. Individual workers, for example, are impacted by equal rights legislation, but so are employer/employee and employee/employee interactions. Finally, the relationship is reciprocal or bidirectional in that the individual contributes to either maintaining or changing the political context. According to Lerner (Whitbourne, 2005), the real challenge in fully understanding development is in bringing together experts from all disciplines involved in this systems model, to investigate all significant interactions in longitudinal research. Developmentalists should be able to adopt an optimistic stance, since systemic change is possible, and that mental health professionals can develop programs that will enhance positive development across the life span.

Federal legislation is an important macrolevel factor that affects behavioral incentives, funding priorities, and methods of service delivery. Laws affect nearly every aspect of contemporary life, and to illustrate typical ways that public policy can affect behavior, two issues are presented next. The first issue focuses on legislation affecting parental involvement in determining early childhood intervention services, and the second demonstrates how laws affect teen pregnancy.

As mentioned, it is inevitable that public laws will affect the manner in which services are to be provided. Public Law 99-457 requires that children with disabilities receive assistance and that parents be essential members of the treatment team process (Nash, Roynds, & Bowen 1992). This macrolevel factor supports a family-centered approach to early intervention. Such an approach is consistent with the community psychological perspective of empowering parents while treating children in their social context. Able-Boone, Goodwin, Sandall, Gordon, and Martin (1992) conducted a survey to determine whether the services provided because of P.L. 99-457 were favorably perceived. These researchers found both parents and professionals who were involved in home-based early intervention programs reported higher satisfaction than those who participated in center-based programs. Bradley et al. (1994) and Blair, Ramey, and Hardin (1995) also evaluated the effectiveness of home- and parent-centered early interventions on the development of premature and low-birth-weight infants. In both studies, the intellectual and social competence of infants in programs was significantly higher than that for infants who did not receive an intervention.

Plotnick (1993) reviewed the effect of legislation and social policy on teenage pregnancy and childbearing outcomes.

The rate of babies being born to teenage mothers is influenced by laws that

- limit adolescent access to contraceptive devices;
- regulate the types of allowable abortions; and
- restrict the public funding of abortions.

These laws, along with social customs and religious beliefs, affect the availability of family planning services, sex education in the schools, and the types of information available through the mass media and on the Internet. As the political climate swings, public policy changes, and the consequences of behavior are affected. Conservatives tend to support "abstinence only" programs for unmarried teens, whereas liberals advocate for sex education programs that discuss contraceptive methods and abortion options. In order to provide objective data on the values of the differing approaches, the Teenage Pregnancy Reduction Act of 1996 (Lowey, 1996) was proposed. Congresswoman Nita Lowey described this bill as providing funds to evaluate the effectiveness of teen pregnancy prevention programs and to disseminate, through the National Clearinghouse on Teenage Pregnancy Prevention Programs, those interventions found to be successful.

Legislation, of course, is not the only factor that affects the teen pregnancy rate. Corcoran, Franklin, and Bennett (2000) used Bronfenbrenner's model to discover a combination of factors that predicted adolescent pregnancy. This study investigated the role played by individual-level factors such as self-esteem, stress, depression, and substance abuse; microsystem variables such as family functioning, problems with peers, and in school; mesosytem level interactions among these microsystems; and macrolevel issues such as socioeconomic status, culture, and race. Using an advanced goodness of fit statistic, Hosmer and Lemeshow (1989) found that the model predicted the pregnancy status of 86 of the 105 research participants; in other words, 82% of the adolescent women were correctly classified. The best predictors of teen pregnancy were household income and race, the quality of communication in the family, individual stress level, alcohol abuse, and relationship with the school.

In both Bronfenbrenner's and Lerner's models, there is interaction between levels of systems. For example, Szcipocznik, and Krutines (1993) described their work with troubled Hispanic youth and their families. A major area of difficulty concerned how these parents attempted to manage their children by using traditional practices and values. The children often sought autonomy and no longer accepted traditional values, and therefore they became embedded in the context of two systems: the microsystem culture of the particular Hispanic family and the mainstream pluralistic macrosystem. The youths' problems originated, in part, from the nonsynergistic interaction between these two systems.

Regarding system-level interactions, researchers have used Bronfenbrenner's nested systems approach to gain an holistic understanding of large-scale problems and design-effective interventions to address these problems. Eamon (2001), for example, investigated the effects of poverty on the socioemotional development of children. This study addressed a major concern, since 20% of all children in the United States are living in poverty. As a group, these children have higher levels of depression, have lower levels of sociability and initiative, and exhibit more problematic peer relationships and disruptive classroom behavior. Eamon used Bronfenbrenner's nested system model to organize the available research literature and understand the processes that mediate the effects of poverty on children at each level.

Research at the microsystem level has primarily but not exclusively focused on the family. Family-level stressors can be classified as either discrete life events, such as a temporary loss of income, or more chronic strains, such as persistent poverty that prevents a family from meeting its financial or other role obligations. Chronic strains require continuous readjustment. Economic deprivation can reduce the types of coping skills available to children, thus overtaxing their ability to cope and leading to a sense of powerlessness.

Regarding peer group variables, research found that compared with other youth, poor children are more likely to be rejected by their peers and stigmatized because of their poverty. Poor children are likely to exhibit fewer resources in the classroom microsystem as well, a finding that is empirically associated with a higher rate of adolescent behavioral problems and distress. Eamon (2001) also noted that children living in poverty are more likely to have biological concerns such as chronic health problems, undernutrition, and higher levels of lead in the body—additional factors that can negatively impact socioemotional development.

Factors at higher system levels also affect child development. Although studies of mesosystems interactions are rare, Eamon (2001) found low maternal/school involvement was higher for poor children, a factor associated with an increase in school adjustment problems. Critical exosystem variables may include parental workplace stressors that threaten the financial well-being of the family, or inadequacies in parental social support networks. Low-income adults, despite their greater need, tend to have fewer social contacts and therefore receive lower levels of social and material support than adults of higher income levels. These factors, along with other conditions such as neighborhood violence, a relative lack of social and economic opportunities, inappropriate role models, and sporadic adult supervision affect a child's socioemotional development. At the macrosystem level, economic resources and access to employment vary according to race and ethnicity, and have at least an indirect influence on child development. Macro social policies impact children's socioemotional development by affecting equal employment opportunity and universal access to health care, as well as other essential resources. Eamon's intent was to arm mental health professionals with the ability to identify factors hindering the development of children living in poverty. It was hoped that a mental health professional could assess these conditions and then intervene to correct the most problematic factors.

Trickett and Mitchell (1992) integrated Kelly's four ecological principles with Bronfenbrenner's child development-in-a-context model, postulating that in order to understand a child's behavior, it is useful to study the interdependence of factors within the youth's microsystem. The demands of the social setting affect behavior, and as the child grows, both the number and the nature of microsystems change. Family dynamics, peer groups, norms, and classroom activities all interact to affect child development.

The relationship between child development and the cycling of community resources is commonly bidirectional. As children grow older, their resource needs change, while at the same time their behavior is affected by how well relevant resources are cycled within a community. Macrolevel factors such as economic conditions, racism, and discrimination all affect child development through their impact on access to quality schools, adequate nutrition, and recreational activities. On the other hand, a child's own strengths and abilities increase during maturation, and this change enables the child to contribute resources to the community.

Many types of volunteer programs can be beneficial to both providers and the community that receives the service. Youth clubs benefit children by providing opportunities to develop interpersonal skills, leadership, and responsibility, as well as a sense of belongingness and community awareness. Through this process, the activities performed by the club become resources available to the community. The relationship is dynamic; if children did not have access to the youth groups, this cycling of resources would not have occurred. In another illustration of dynamics, it can be expected that as the children mature, their incentive and ability to join such groups change. In addition, youth need to possess some initial level of social skills in order to form volunteer groups, and so these groups will tend to flourish in areas where the community provides access to learning such skills. The relationship between child development and the cycling of resources is indeed a complex and an interactive process, and community psychological interventions targeting either component can enhance both.

The principle of adaptation is a useful tool to understand how children find suitable niches. A child needs to exhibit certain attitudes, behaviors, and knowledge in order to successfully exist in each microsystem encountered. Assessing a child in only one setting (the school, for example) is not an accurate indication of how the child behaves in the home or at the playground. Interventions designed to teach needed skills or to change setting dynamics may help a child to form niches in the three major microsystems.

Succession operates as the setting changes, or as a child moves from one setting to another. The family structure, for example, can change with the birth of a sibling or a parental divorce. Neighborhoods can change as a result of macrolevel factors, causing peers to move out of the area for a variety of reasons. In a common example, a child graduates to new levels of school and learning. As these transitions occur, some children will be helped and others hurt by the change. Skills that were useful in one setting might not generalize to a new one; obedient behavior might be more rewarded in an elementary school than in a high school. Community psychologists can investigate the type of problem-solving skills needed in the new setting and then teach these skills to the youth before the transition has occurred. For example, Elias, Gara, Schuyler, Branden-Muller, and Sayette (1986) planned an intervention to reduce stress in children going from elementary school to middle school. As was mentioned previously (Eccles et al., 1993), this sort of transition is a time of great stress for many children, because of the larger size of the middle school, the increased academic and peer pressure, and the less personal relationship with the teachers. In this study, training in social problem-solving skills was provided to two groups of students during the year prior to the transition to middle school. One group received extensive instruction in problem solving, coupled with the opportunity for the children to discuss typical problems and the way that they could use the techniques learned to solve them. The second group received only the instructions. Both treatment groups were compared with students who made the transition during the previous year and without any special training. As expected, the children in both treatments reported significantly less stress than the previous year controls, and the instructions plus application/discussion treatment group experienced lower stress than the instruction-only treatment group. It can thus be inferred that by planning programs that provide needed skills and resources to individuals in transition from one setting to another, the potential problems related to succession can be reduced or eliminated.

Succession can be helpful to a child's development. The stigma of a pejorative label might not carry over to a new habitat. A family, for example, might consider moving to a new community in order to help a child escape a past inappropriate action and the unfavorable label accompanying it. Changing schools, making new friends, and exploring new volunteer and vocational opportunities are all potentially effective interventions derived from the succession principle. Trickett and Mitchell (1992) demonstrated that linking Kelly's ecological model with Bronfenbrenner's focus on child development in a context can assist psychologists in both understanding human development and in planning effective interventions to enhance a child 's growth and well-being.

Bronfenbrenner's Current PPCT Bioecological Model

Bronfenbrenner more recently expanded his approach into a more comprehensive bioecological model (Bronfenbrenner & Ceci, 1994; Bronfenbrenner & Evans, 2000; Ceci, 2000). In this model, the emphasis is on how biologically oriented heredity and setting-oriented environment interact to produce development and behavior. Bronfenbrenner and Ceci (1994) noted that genetic material does not produce behavior by itself but must interact with the setting. The model was designed to help in understanding the mechanisms or processes through which genetic potentials are actualized. These authors, along with Williams and Ceci (1997), argued our ability to interpret and explain behavior can be enhanced by adding two concepts, context and time, to psychology's two biological foci of person and process. This treatment creates a Process/Person/Context/Time (PPCT) ecological model. "Person variables" refer to biologically rooted dispositions, states, and innate abilities. "Process factors" refer to the stream of activities and interactions performed by the person to either maintain or change a state. "Context" refers to the physical and social setting in which the behavior occurs. Finally, "time" refers to at least three dimensions:

- Developmental time in which behavior and abilities change as the person grows;
- Historical effects due to events that shape the nation, such as the end of the cold war or the outbreak of the HIV/AIDS epidemic; and
- Cohort effects, or shared experiences of those growing up in the same subculture.

Williams and Ceci (1997) stated that empirical studies considering all four factors will produce more valid explanations of behavior. For example, although an individual's IQ is influenced by heredity, it may be lowered during periods of economic scarcity. It may be increased if an individual's family values education highly and encourages the frequent practice of challenging mental tasks. The relative influence of each factor on IQ depends on the qualities of the other variables. Heredity has less of an effect, for example, in extremely stimulating or severely deprived settings.

Tudge, Odero, Hogan, and Etz (2003) utilized the PPCT approach to understand the transition to school more fully. They studied school-relevant activities (processes) of children (person) drawn from two social classes (context) prior to and after entering preschool (time) over an entire waking day. The students were then followed over a two-year period to observe the quality of their transition into elementary school. Trickett and Buchanan (2001) also studied transition from an ecological perspective. They observed a variety of transitions: middle school to high school, high school to college, adolescent motherhood, and migration to a new country. These researchers noted transitions tended to strain relationships and that these stresses were affected by personal, process, and contextual factors.

Bronfenbrenner and Evans (2000) identified three propositions framing the expanded model. These propositions are useful not only for understanding children but also for understanding development across the life span.

> *Proposition I.* Human development takes place through a process of reciprocal interactions between an active and evolving biopsychological human organism and the persons, objects, and symbols in his or her environment. This interaction occurs on a regular basis and over time. Two outcomes are possible: competence, the acquisition or further development of a skill; or dysfunction, experiencing difficulties in maintaining control and integration of behavior.
>
> *Proposition II.* The developmental outcome is a function of the form, quality, and directionality of the proximal processes, the characteristics of the person, the immediate and remote context in which the behavior takes place, and the social continuities and changes occurring over time.
>
> *Proposition III.* In order to develop competence, an individual requires active participation in progressively complex reciprocal interactions with persons to whom he or she develops a strong, mutual, irrational attachment. Over time, these individuals become committed to each other's well-being and development (adapted, p. 122).

Conclusion

The ecological perspective provides the rationale for a more holistic understanding of human behavior, and it is the basis for diverse and effective strategies that enhance the quality of mental health in the community. This paradigm can be applied on a larger scale as well, to many aspects of society. To frame problems in an ecological perspective is beneficial to such areas as academic achievement, crime reduction, work productivity, neighborhood involvement, service delivery, system effectiveness, and overall smooth community functioning. The ecological perspective is a major theoretical advance and provides the foundation for prevention, as discussed in the next chapter.

DISCUSSION QUESTIONS

1. What is an ecological perspective? How can it improve the efficacy of mental health services?

2. How is Lewin's Model applied to deinstitutionalization? What are some concerns that must be addressed to reintegrate institutionalized psychiatric patients into the community, according to this model? What are the different personal and societal factors that need to be addressed?

3. What is synergy? What are driving forces and restraining forces? Why are they important?

4. What are Barker's four circuits? How is this model useful in the assessment of mental health environments? List and explain some examples of each type of circuit.

5. How might Moos' social climate scales be used to a) help high school students and their families choose the right college *or* b) help recently retired couples select a meaningful residential community *or* c) help families decide on an appropriate assisted living community for an elderly relative?

6. What are "closed ranks"? In what social situations might this phenomenon occur? What are some possible alternatives? How might a client's interdependent status be reestablished in the community after a hospitalization?

7. Identify ways to increase the niche breadth for youthful offenders.

8. Show how an understanding of Bronfenbrenner's nested system model might help in planning a preventive program of your choosing.

4 Prevention

OBJECTIVES

This chapter is designed to enable the reader to:

- Explain the importance of prevention and the way that it fits with the ecological model used in community mental health.
- Describe the origin of prevention and its relation to the public health system's study of epidemiology.
- Identify the three levels of prevention of mental illness.
- Define and explain epidemiology, incidence, and prevalence, and the way that they relate when applied to the study of mental health.
- Define and identify risk factors and protective factors that could contribute to or decrease the incidence of mental illness.
- Compare and contrast different models used to categorize prevention programs.
- Understand the influence of early intervention programs on children and other age groups.
- Identify specific examples of early intervention-prevention programs in the community.
- Explain how technological advances can affect the delivery of programs in the future.
- Understand the importance of considering multiple causes for difficulties in living to ensure prevention programs designed address those causes and are comprehensive.
- Understand why it is important to consider multiple causes for difficulties in living when designing and implementing prevention programs, and how a comprehensive program, multiple component design is useful in this regard.
- Identify prevention opportunities in health care settings.
- Understand how socioeconomic context affects federal policies regarding the structure of prevention programs and their funding.

> *"An ounce of prevention is worth a pound of cure."*
>
> *"Take charge of your life! . . . To act intelligently and effectively, we still must have a plan. To the proverb which says, 'a journey of a thousand miles begins with a single step,' I would add the words 'and a road map.'"*
>
> Cecile M. Springer

The prevention of mental illness and the promotion of mental health are central themes in community mental health, and they are probably the most efficient ways of helping millions of citizens remain healthy and happy. Emory Cowen (1996), a leader in the field of prevention over the past 40 years, observed that this method was far more effective than the traditional clinical techniques in which he had originally been trained. Early on in his career, Cowen noted that if a disorder had crystallized in an individual, efforts to treat the person were often very costly and ineffective, and their implementation tended to be time-consuming as well. On the other hand, the prevention of a disorder would allow the individual to continue to live productively in the community without disruption, misery, or stigma. In addition, scarce human resources would be conserved.

Prevention is not only very efficient but also consistent with the ecological orientation and essential to community mental health. If difficulties in living are the result of a poor fit between a person's needs and his or her environmental resources, it is possible to prevent these disorders by either bolstering the individual's competence or enriching the services available in the community. The first strategy focuses on enhancing the person's skills. Providing training in problem solving, social skills, anger and depression management, and stress reduction are examples of this approach. The second strategy targets the social milieu. Intervening to enhance school or human service agency programs, to develop better social networks and support systems, and to provide better access to resources typify this approach. With these two strategies, community mental health professionals have more techniques on hand to promote mental health than do traditional clinicians.

Berman and Jobes (1995) also identified a third intervention approach, called "sensitizing proximal agents." Proximal agents are people in the community who have close and regular contact with members of populations likely to face specific challenges in life. Ways to implement this approach include consulting with significant individuals (proximal agents), alerting them to signs of potential problems, and teaching them how to prevent problems from occurring.

Parents, teachers, coaches, and pediatricians are examples of proximal agents for children. Clergy can also be proximal agents for members of their faith-based communities experiencing emotional problems. These individuals might first turn to a member of the clergy for assistance, rather than to a mental health professional. Benes, Walsh, McMinn, Dominguez, & Aikins (2000) describe two models in which mental health professionals and a member of the clergy can collaborate. In the first model, the direct service approach, the clergy member counsels the distraught individual and decides whether to refer the person to a professional. In the second model, the indirect service delivery approach, the mental health professional consults a member of the clergy with the purpose of strengthening the resources available to the congregation. This type of consultation may involve training clergy and lay ministers in listening skills, forming support groups, or offering workshops on mental health issues relevant to the congregation.

It can be seen through the preceding examples that community mental health professionals have many strategies available to enhance the person-environment fit and thus to prevent mental illness. All three strategies can be combined to prevent problems in living. An example of a social problem that can be successfully addressed through prevention efforts is domestic violence. Local resources can be utilized; religious organizations can use their moral suasion to encourage respect, concern, and toleration for family members; and mediation centers can be established or enlarged to resolve domestic disputes. Proximal agents such as police officers, members of the clergy, and even work supervisors can be sensitized to warning signs of abuse and educated about appropriate actions to take when these signs are observed. Individuals and groups in general can be taught assertiveness, conflict resolution, and impulse control skills to bolster their competencies with regards to the issue. Since community mental health practitioners have many alternative interventions available, the likelihood is increased that problems will be averted before significant damage is done.

It can be readily concluded that prevention has many benefits, yet only small portions of mental health service budgets are allocated for prevention programs. This is due to several factors. First of all, most clinicians are not adequately trained in designing and implementing preventive interventions. As a result, many practitioners are more comfortable with a one-on-one therapeutic approach and choose individual treatment strategies over interventions that utilize group prevention. Second, from a political perspective, it is difficult to divert relatively scarce resources away from treating those who are obviously suffering from various mental disorders, and instead to dedicate these funds to help keep healthy people productive. Individuals typically do not fund prevention programs; usually, elected officials propose legislation to do so (Albee, 1996). Encountering an ill person needing immediate assistance tends to have a dramatic impact on voters and politicians alike. An intellectual reflection might reveal that a higher proportion of healthy individuals will probably become ill if a preventive program is not implemented. However, an abstract concept is not as profoundly motivating as a tangible example.

A third factor concerns social scientific models that view mental disorders as having multiple causes. The ecological paradigm, as discussed previously, views difficulties in living as resulting from a poor person-environment fit and involving multiple factors. Therefore, a prevention program that targets only one factor may not produce the expected benefit. Few prevention programs were evaluated prior to 1975 (Cowen, 1977), perhaps because existing programs tended to be single-dimensional and interventionists were unable to demonstrate the success of their programs. A major review of prevention research was performed more recently by the Institute of Medicine (IOM), at the request of the U.S. Congress (Mrazek & Haggerty, 1994; Munoz, Mrazek, & Haggerty, 1996). With these findings, it became apparent that programs targeting multiple rather than single risk factors were far more effective. Since the earlier single-factor programs failed to yield strong results demonstrating effectiveness, governmental agencies and private foundations were reluctant to fund later prevention programs.

As a final complication, it is challenging to perform definitive research demonstrating the benefits of interventions, even on programs that do target multiple factors. Cuipers (2003) noted that since the percentage of the general population who suffer from each specific form of mental illness is relatively low, research seeking to show that programs aimed at preventing typical currently healthy individuals from becoming mentally ill must have sample sizes in the tens of thousands in order to find statistically significant differences. However, if the program targets either those at risk or those who already have some symptoms of the disorder, the numbers needed for significance are much lower. It should be pointed out that large-scale programs targeting entire populations can result in statistically significant reductions in mental illness. As an example, McGrath (2000) noted that obstetric complications, prenatal exposure to viruses, and inadequate prenatal nutrition have been linked to an increased incidence of schizophrenia. In light of these findings, it is plausible that widespread vaccination, health education, and enhanced antenatal care programs could reduce the probability of schizophrenia in a targeted area. Another research problem to be addressed when assessing the outcomes of prevention programs, whether related to mental illness or other concerns, is that expensive, long-term follow-up is needed. Evaluation of a pre-school program to prevent juvenile delinquency, for instance, requires at least 15 years of research. Over such a long time period, some participants will drop out of the study, or the funding for the intervention along with the research assessing its effect may be terminated. For these reasons, most prevention researchers have opted to monitor short-term proximal outcome indicators (such as improved social and problem-solving skills) that reduce risk factors, rather than the more distal ultimate outcome objectives (Heller, 1996). Such proximal and proxy measures, however, seem to be less convincing evidence to use when attempting to gain support for prevention programs.

These empirical concerns are being currently addressed. Preventive programs today are more likely to be multidimensional rather than targeting a single component or cause, and research designs are utilizing instruments to monitor intermediate criteria of success rather than relying on only ultimate outcomes (Cowen, 1996). In addition, some preventive programs have been in operation for a sufficiently long time as to allow for adequate follow-up studies (Schweinhart, Barnes, & Weikart, 1993). Community mental health professionals are beginning to gather data where previously they had only promises and beliefs built on logically constructed models. As outlined later in this chapter, certain prevention programs have been able to demonstrate their cost-effectiveness.

The Origin of Prevention

Just as ecological psychology borrowed its model from biology, prevention in mental health has its roots in the public health field. The idea of prevention as applied to mental health originated in the public health system's study of epidemiology, and it adapted the strategies commonly employed to stop the spread of physical disease. Public health system experts realized early on that the best way to control the spread of disease was to prevent healthy people from coming in contact with the causes of the illness. At that time, medical treatment was largely ineffective, and becoming infected with a serious disease usually led either to an early death or a long period of disability and misery. Prevention is still a preferred strategy with regard to physical disease. One reason for this preference is that certain medical treatments, such as those for viral infections, are still less than ideal. The best methods available simply attempt to bolster the victim's immune system and reduce symptoms and secondary infections.

The average human life expectancy increased from 47 years in 1900 to 77 years in 2000, primarily due to innovative preventive interventions rather than advances in medical treatment (Johnson & Millstein, 2003). Measures such as immunization for childhood infectious diseases, providing clean drinking water, and early detection of cancer (nearly unheard of in 1900) effectively and dramatically lengthened the human life span.

To prevent illness, public health officials seek to eliminate the causes of illness. For example, a famous prevention program reduced the spread of malaria by draining swamps (Ross, 1910). Mosquitoes that carry a certain germ spread malaria, and they reproduce by laying eggs in stagnant water. If a source of stagnant water is eliminated, mosquitoes cannot multiply as quickly. Similar environmental strategies include the provision of adequate sewer systems and safe drinking water. Through these efforts, malaria became a much less common disease (Albee, 1996).

In addition to prevention programs that target the environment, some forms of medical prevention focus on the individual. Vaccines have been developed to build up the body's ability to resist diseases such as polio, measles, and influenza, and must be given prior to exposure to the disease. Some diseases are associated with high-risk behaviors. For example, HIV/AIDS is spread in part by unprotected sex with infected partners. As the number of partners and the frequency of encounters increase, the probability of being infected increases. Public health officials have used the mass media to educate the community about avoiding such risky behaviors. Note that in each of these cases, effective prevention is far more beneficial than treatment after the fact, which has minimal effectiveness and is disruptive, costly, and time-consuming.

Epidemiology, Incidence, and Prevalence

Public health specialists need to be able to monitor how disease or epidemics are spreading through a population. The study of the rate at which disorders increase or decrease is called epidemiology. Epidemiologists describe disease rates by using concepts such as incidence and prevalence. Incidence refers to the number of new cases of a disease that occur in a population during a particular time period, and prevalence refers to the total number of people afflicted with the disorder at any specific time.

Incidence is a more sensitive measure of an intervention's preventive effects. If the incidence is increasing, the epidemic is becoming more widespread. If the incidence is decreasing, the epidemic is beginning to recede, thus indicating that the targeted interventions have been successful to some degree. The relationship between incidence and prevalence is affected by many factors, one being the length of time that it takes for an ill person to get better. Disorders such as mental retardation are lifelong, whereas others, such as the common cold, take only days or weeks to run their course. In a typical community, the prevalence of mental retardation is always far greater than its incidence. The monthly incidence of new cases of colds, however, can be very close in number to the prevalence rate that month, particularly at the onset of the cold season.

Epidemiologists and public health officials have broadened the concept of a "disorder" beyond only biologically based or infectious diseases. For example, the National Center for Disease Control now regularly monitors the incidence and prevalence of various types of violent crimes and accidents. These scientists study population characteristics to investigate which groups of people are more likely to develop a disorder. Teenagers, for example, tend to commit more crimes than other age groups (Zigler, Taussig, & Black, 1992). From an epidemiological standpoint, it can thus be logically assumed that the frequency of crime will increase if the percentage of teens in a population increases, all other things being equal. Many politicians have taken credit for lower crime rates during times when the relative number of adolescents in a population has decreased, yet the major reason for the decline in criminal activity may be the demographic change itself.

Epidemiologists also study behaviors that are at high risk for spreading a particular problem. Intravenous drug users who exchange used needles are likely to spread HIV. Therefore, the incidence of HIV/AIDS can be lowered through programs that educate these individuals about the dangers of sharing dirty needles (Guydish, Bucardo, Clark, & Bernheim, 1998). If teens are more likely to cause accidents because they drink alcohol and then drive, the frequency of accidents can be reduced by raising the drinking age or by limiting teen access to alcohol. In many situations it is not necessary to target specific populations when attempting to reduce high-risk (or to increase safe) behaviors. Society at large can benefit from preventive interventions focusing on risky behaviors. For example, the campaign to increase the use of automobile seat belts has reduced the rate of serious injuries for all segments of the population (Robertson, 1996).

Finally, epidemiologists investigate which environments are associated with the spread of disorders. Public health officials have observed a relationship between various pollutants and illness. Substances present in air, water, and soil; contaminants in paint and other building materials; high-intensity noise; and other environmental factors are correlated with a higher rate of many diseases in affected geographical areas. Efforts by the Environmental Protection Agency and other federal and state "environmental clean up" groups have reduced these pollutants, and through such programs there has been a decrease in the incidence of certain types of cancer and even some forms of developmental disabilities.

Risk and Protective Factors

Although it is beyond the scope of this book to discuss specific prevention programs in public health, it is important to note that community mental health professionals have adopted the personal, behavioral, and environmental prevention strategies of public health and have applied these to mental health concerns. The association between community public health principles and the prevention of mental disorders is a continuing trend. To illustrate this, it should be noted that an IOM report (Mrazek & Haggerty, 1994) included guidelines that applied public health concepts to the practical prevention of mental illness.

An important component in the reduction of the incidence of illness is to identify factors that influence the likelihood of individuals' becoming ill. Characteristics associated with an increased spread of disease are called risk factors. In the mental health field, risk factors can be personal (such as a family history of alcoholism), behavioral (such as teenage use of street drugs), or environmental (such as an abusive home with intense social stressors). U.S. Surgeon General David Satcher (2000) identified risk factors for developing childhood mental disorders. These included biological factors such as genetic predispositions, infections, poor nutrition, exposure to toxins (including environmental pollutants such as lead), maternal substance abuse during pregnancy and breast feeding, and low birth weight. Psychosocial factors included severe parental marital discord, parental psychopathology or criminality, overcrowding, economic hardship, exposure to violence and stressful life events, and poor caregiving practices. Programs that are designed to reduce the level or frequency of these risk factors can also in turn reduce the incidence of mental disorders.

Other qualities, called protective factors, tend to reduce the likelihood of mental disorders. Again, these can be personal (such as a strong commitment to a value system) (Kobassa, 1979), behavioral (such as the use of good coping skills), or environmental (such as a nurturing family or access to effective problem-solving training programs). Catalano, Berglund, Ryan, Loczak, & Hawkins (2002) developed a list of criteria for positive youth development and described programs that bolstered these protective factors, all of which yielded empirically demonstrated mental health benefits. Among the protective factors identified by Catalano et al. were promoting bonding, fostering resilience, promoting social, emotional, cognitive, behavioral, and moral competence, fostering self-determination and self-efficacy, fostering clear and positive identity, providing opportunities for pro-social involvement, and fostering pro-social norms (p. 15).

In a theoretical example, if community mental health professionals knew all the risk and protective factors that influenced depression, and if effective programs could be developed to reduce every risk factor and bolster every protective factor, the incidence of depression would drop to zero. Note, however, that targeting only one risk factor will not eliminate the disorder (Horwath, Johnson, Klerman, & Weissman, 1992).

A number of researchers have considered spirituality and active participation in faith-based communities to be protective factors. Catalano et al. (2002) included the fostering of spirituality and the promoting of belief in the future as criteria for positive youth development. Merrill and Salazar (2002), using a random telephone survey design, administered the Utah Health Status Survey to 6,188 adult residents of that state. They found that Mormons who attended church services weekly reported fewer mental health problems than those who were less active in this church. The authors considered that some of this effect may be due to health and lifestyle choices (such as abstinence from alcohol) associated with Mormon practice. Swisher (2001) found that Methodists who attended a series of sermons and positive coaching seminars expressed higher levels of personal well-being. Although more research is needed, preliminary data indicate that spirituality and religious faith may contribute to mental health cognitively, behaviorally, and affectively.

Attributable Risk

It is possible to measure the relative importance of each risk factor for an illness. The term "attributable risk" describes the "maximum proportion of cases that would be prevented if an intervention were 100% effective in eliminating that risk factor" (Munoz et al., 1996, p. 1119). For example, Horwath (et al., 1992, 1994) studied the impact of depressive symptoms on the risk for first-onset major depression. Depressive symptoms include insomnia, weight or appetite change, fatigue, inappropriate guilt, diminished concentration, and other behaviors. Although these symptoms themselves do not meet the criteria for a diagnosis of major depression, they contribute to the diagnosis. The researchers found that in a sample of 9,900 adults, those with depressive symptoms were 4.4 times more likely than average to develop a first-onset major depression within one year. From these data, Horwath et al. (1994) calculated that the attributable risk of depressive symptoms is over 50%. Therefore, a program that effectively eliminated these symptoms would be expected to reduce the incidence of depression by 50%. Munoz et al. (1996) noted that such research is in its infancy and that further investigation will enhance understanding of this concept. For example, recent attributable risk studies do not consider the interactive effects of two or more risk factors that contribute to the same disorder, but despite such issues, this particular line of research offers the potential for more convincing evaluations of preventive research.

Cost-Effectiveness of Prevention and Funding

The Institute of Medicine (IOM) recommended that funding for mental illness prevention programs should increase to 50 to 60 million dollars per year (Mrazek & Haggerty, 1994). This recommendation was not based so much on demonstrated cost-effectiveness as it was on the conclusion that prevention reduces emotional pain, personal disruption, and aversive social impact associated with mental disorders. Mechanic (1995, 1996; Mechanic, Schlesinger, & McAlpine, 1995) of the Institute for Health, Health Care Policy and Aging Research echoes this view by noting the benefits of prevention to the human and social capital of the nation. These benefits, in terms of direct outcomes as well as wider effects that ripple through the community, are huge and extremely challenging to calculate. After reviewing the IOM report and listening to the testimony given by researchers and interventionists, Congresswoman Nancy Pelosi (1996), member of the House Appropriations Committee on Human Services and Education, concluded that prevention "is not only humane, it is cost-effective" (p. 1128).

A number of researchers have demonstrated a reduction in future medical costs that result from various psychological interventions, including preventive programs. The expenses connected with the reduction in expected medical costs, due to lower medical utilization following successful psychological intervention, are known as "medical offset costs." In 1998, the Congressional Prevention Coalition and the Institute of Science, Technology and Public Policy held a conference on stress prevention and its impact on health and medical savings (Institute of Science, Technology and

Public Policy, 2004). Presenters at this conference cited studies that found that 90% of all disease is caused or complicated by stress. Heart disease is the single most frequent cause of death in the United States, and the primary risk factor for this disease is hypertension. Together, high blood pressure and advanced heart disease cost Medicare over $100 billion per year, and yet hypertension can be prevented and even reversed through psychological stress reduction techniques. At the same conference, a study by Orme-Johnson (1987) was cited. In this study, Blue Cross/Blue Shield statistics were reviewed to compare the medical utilization rates of participants who practiced Transcendental Meditation (TM) against a group of matched controls. The TM participants averaged 50% less medical utilization across each of 16 disease categories including mental disorders and nervous system, heart, and respiratory illnesses. The Canadian Psychological Association commissioned a report on the medical offset costs due to psychological interventions in that country (Hunsley, 2002). Health care costs for depression and psychological distress in Canada exceed 14 billion Canadian dollars annually and are greater than the costs associated with heart disease, diabetes, or chronic back pain. Hunsley's review of the literature found that psychological interventions such as cognitive behavioral therapy were 10% to 50% less costly than pharmacological treatment and were just as effective. The psychological interventions also resulted in lower overall health care costs in the future. Although the Canadian study included only patients with symptoms of mental illness, the reduction in later medical utilization implied that the psychological interventions prevented further illness and promoted health. Hunsley (2002) reported on a stress management program designed to treat hypertension. Symptoms in over 50% of the patients were well controlled without drug treatment, resulting in a savings of $1,300 total medical costs per person over a five-year period. To reinforce the potential cost savings of preventative programs, Hunsley cited another study in which five dollars were saved for each dollar spent on stress management.

These interventions can utilize a seeking mode of service delivery. Groth-Marnat and Schumaker (1995) reviewed the literature and found that psychological interventions for disease prevention and health promotion in the workplace can be very cost-effective. They noted that stress management and smoking cessation programs using techniques like relaxation training, time management, biofeedback, and cognitive behavioral therapy were most cost-effective. Studies demonstrating cost-effectiveness are not limited to mental-illness prevention. Catalano et al. (2002) discussed the results of the Quantum Opportunities Program (QOP), a high school–based program that attempted to address 13 of the Positive Youth Development categories described earlier. The QOP included peer tutoring, computer assisted instruction, community service projects, college and job planning, adult mentoring, and life and family skills training. Participants consisted of 25 ninth-grade students selected each year. These youths attended high schools in which the typical student came from a single-parent ethnic minority family on welfare. Results indicated higher rates of high school graduation and college attendance, among other benefits. According to a cost-benefit analysis, $3.68 was gained for every dollar spent.

It is useful to calculate the cost-effectiveness of specific prevention programs through a formal cost/benefit analysis when attempting to increase federal funding levels. Demonstrating cost-effectiveness may also motivate behavioral managed care and health insurance companies to support prevention efforts. These organizations may find it less expensive, for example, to fund employee stress management workshops than to pay for later psychotherapy. Furthermore, corporations may discover added benefits such as lower staff turnover, less sick day utilization, and increased productivity that can result from such workshops. These benefits, as well as the changing policies of health insurance companies, are discussed more fully in Chapter 13.

One approach to cost-effectiveness is to use attributable risk. To link changes in intermediate success criteria and projected decreases in the incidence of mental disorders will allow for the calculation of the expected dollar savings of the prevention program. Later in this chapter, examples of successful prevention programs are described, and available cost-effectiveness results are provided as well.

Levels of Prevention: The Caplan Model

In 1964, Gerald Caplan presented a three-level model of psychiatric prevention, which served as the primary research basis in the field for 30 years. This model was eventually replaced with a newer categorization system that encompasses both prevention and treatment methods. However, the Caplan model was highly influential to the field and warrants discussion.

Caplan identified the three levels of psychiatric prevention as primary, secondary, and tertiary. Primary prevention is aimed at helping healthy people maintain their health. Interventions at this level target individuals who have no symptoms of emotional or mental disorder. Primary prevention programs generally supply additional environmental resources or bolster personal competencies in order to decrease the likelihood that the target individuals will succumb to difficulties in living.

Secondary prevention programs attempt to help individuals at high risk of developing psychological disorders. The targeted individuals typically show some initial symptoms of distress. These programs attempt to "nip the problem in the bud," and as a result they reduce the severity and duration of the illness. Whereas primary prevention reduces incidence, secondary prevention attempts to reduce prevalence through early intervention.

Tertiary prevention aims at alleviating the harmful consequences of long-term illness. Individuals already suffering from chronic disorders are targeted in these programs. Although similar to clinical treatment, the objective of tertiary programs is to help individuals return to as normal a lifestyle as is possible. The goal of clinical treatment is often to reduce illness, whereas tertiary prevention programs rarely attempt to do so. Psychiatric diagnoses are not usually changed. Instead, the goals of tertiary programs include placing institutionalized patients into the community as swiftly as possible and preparing them to live in suitable neighborhood housing and to work in local business settings. These programs strive to avoid the "closed ranks" (Cumming & Cumming, 1957) process. Community psychologists and social workers realize that the longer an individual is away from home, school, and work, the more challenging it is for that person to return to a normalized lifestyle. Tertiary programs focus on teaching individuals to live with their illness and to improve the quality of life in spite of the disorder.

Although Caplan's three-level model had been used in the research since 1964, many psychologists found it challenging and often arbitrary to categorize specific programs as primary, secondary, or tertiary. In practice, most interventions cross over these boundaries. The Caplan model is still useful, however, since it enables interventionists to conceive of and develop many program alternatives to prevent mental disorder.

The Institute of Medicine Model

Since precise definitions and boundaries are ideals that social scientists strive to realize, a new system for categorizing types of prevention was developed (Mrazek & Haggerty, 1994; Munoz et al., 1996). The new system was presented in a major report from the federal government's Institute of Medicine, and it "established rigorous standards for prevention research, highlighted the scientific credibility the field has achieved, and prompted constructive debate regarding priorities for future research, practice and training" (Weissberg, Kumpfer, & Seligman, 2003, pp. 425–426). In the new category system, the spectrum of mental health interventions included prevention, treatment, and maintenance. Prevention programs were further divided into universal, selective, and indicated interventions, focusing on the population to be targeted. These categories and subcategories are described next.

A New System for Categorizing Prevention Programs

Preventive programs aim to reduce the incidence of mental disorder and are presented to individuals or groups prior to the onset of the disorder. Treatment programs, on the other hand, are applied to those already displaying the criteria and symptoms of a diagnosable mental illness. Finally, maintenance programs are implemented after the acute episode of the disorder has subsided. Maintenance programs aim to reduce relapses and reoccurrences and to provide rehabilitative services.

Universal Prevention

Prevention is divided into three subcategories. Universal preventive interventions target general populations who have not been identified as being at increased risk. Generally, a good universal preventive program should have little risk of negative side effects, be acceptable to the public, and have a low cost per individual targeted. Examples of universal prevention programs are stress management workshops or problem-solving-skills training programs administered to all employees in an office or all students in a class or school. Universal prevention is similar to Caplan's primary prevention concept.

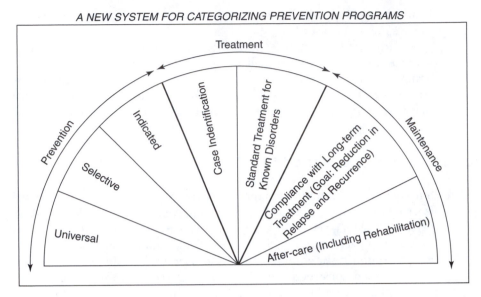

FIGURE 4.1   A New System for Categorizing Prevention Programs The mental health intervention spectrum.

Note: From Reducing Risks for Mental Disorders: Frontiers for Preventive Intervention Research (p. 23) by Patricia J. Mrazek and Robert J. Haggerty (Editors), (1994), Washington, D.C.: National Academy Press. Reprinted by permission.

Two Forms of Primary Prevention

Cowen (1996) differentiated between two forms of primary prevention. The first type attempts to reduce the likelihood that healthy individuals will experience psychological dysfunctions. Risk factors are targeted, and the aim is to reduce the incidence of mental illness. Cowen, however, favored the second form, which seeks to promote psychological health and wellness. Programs that target protective factors benefit everyone and enhance positive mental health in the community. Although this distinction is one of degree, promoting health has the added value of aiming for a higher objective. Successful programs designed to enhance health will also achieve the slightly lesser goal of preventing illness. By analogy, many of those who participate in various aerobic exercise programs in health clubs are hoping to gain fitness and to look and feel better. Others who work out to reduce the likelihood of cardiovascular disease have different motivations and perceptions of these activities. Similarly, students who enroll in college or graduate programs are not trying to reduce their ignorance, but rather are attempting to improve themselves and to obtain more meaningful employment. It is likely that more individuals will want to become involved in programs described as "wellness enhancing" than in those presented as "illness preventing," since there is no stigma involved in the former distinction.

The Prevention Task Panel recommended both forms of primary prevention in 1978, in its report to the President's Commission on Mental Health. This report noted the dual objectives of lowering the incidence of mental disorders while promoting conditions that reinforce positive mental health. Unfortunately, more recent government-sponsored commissions have deemphasized the wellness enhancement approach. Albee (1996) noted that reports published by the National Institute of Mental Health (1994) and the IOM concluded that since mental health promotion does not target specific disorders listed in the DSM-IV, it is not as important as risk reduction. Although the two reports did not call for a halt to such research, their conclusions reduced the likelihood that interventions based on wellness enhancement would receive increased funding by governmental agencies. Also, wellness promotion activities are excluded from the category of universal prevention.

Criteria for Good Universal or Primary Prevention Programs

Cowen (1980) noted that many activities have been called "primary prevention" even though they were not true examples of this approach, and that the concept was too vaguely interpreted to generate meaningful programs. He established the following criteria for considering a program to fall at the first level of prevention.

Cowen stated that primary (or universal) prevention programs must be

- offered to groups and not individuals;
- applied before any symptoms of maladjustment appear in the targeted population; and
- intended to strengthen psychological adjustment; and
- empirically demonstrated to be effective.

Initially, few programs met these criteria, and by 1988, the American Psychological Association found only 14 programs that could be considered as model (Price, Cowen, Lorion, & Ramos-McKay, 1988). Since that time, many programs meeting these criteria have been implemented, examples of which are presented later in this chapter.

Weissberg, Kumpfer, and Seligman (2003) identified six characteristics for effective and well-coordinated prevention programs. The six are as follows:

- *Uses an empirically derived risk and protective factor basis that targets multiple outcomes and allows for participation by many in the community.* Diverse outcomes enable the program to address interdependent issues to increase the beneficial outcome.
- *Is long-term and both culturally and age appropriate.* Programs for children should continue across the youth's development, and activities should relate to the child's interest, experiences, and cultural tradition.
- *Fosters development through encouraging participants to apply socioemotional skills and ethical values.* Programs should enhance the ability of individuals to manage their emotions, establish goals, and communicate well, and also to perform other skills needed to interact successfully in the community.

- *Aims to establish policies that enhance environmental supports to nurture optimal development.* Interventions will be more effective and will be long-lasting if they target community structures such as families, schools, and neighborhoods, and also encourage processes consistent with healthy development.
- *Selects, trains, and supports staff who have good interpersonal skills and the appropriate expertise.* Choosing the correct individuals to implement the program is essential if the program is to achieve its intended effects. The ability of program personnel to interact effectively and smoothly with the participants is also very important.
- *Uses evidence-based programs adapted to local needs, and incorporates an ongoing evaluation strategy for continuous program improvement.* Interventions should be based on well-researched ideas and should be consistent with the ecological perspective. Ideas need to be adjusted to the cultural traditions of the targeted group.

Nation, Crusto, Wandersman, Kumpfer, Seybolt, Morrissey-Kane, & Davino (2003) identified nine characteristics that have been consistently associated with effective prevention interventions. These components included programs that "were comprehensive, included varied teaching methods, provided sufficient dosage, were theory driven, provided opportunities for positive relationships, were appropriately timed, were socioculturally relevant, included outcome evaluation, and involved well-trained staff" (p. 449). As can be seen, the lists of Cowen, Weissberg et al., and Nation et al. overlap. When one is planning a prevention program, these criteria provide a good checklist of attributes to include.

A Checklist of Characteristics Useful to Include When Creating Successful Universal Prevention Interventions

- Program should be offered to groups, not individuals.
- Program should be designed for healthy individuals.
- Program should be theory-driven.
- Intervention should be based on empirically derived risk and protective factors.
- Intervention should strengthen psychological adjustment.
- Program should enhance socioemotional skills.
- Program should bolster environmental supports.
- Program policies should apply ethical values.
- Activities should be culturally and age-appropriate.
- Intervention should utilize varied teaching methods.
- Intervention should be comprehensive, including multiple outcome goals.
- Intervention should be empirically demonstrated to be effective.
- Program should be long-term.
- Targeted groups should receive sufficient dosage of the activities.
- Program should utilize staff proficient in interpersonal skills.

Selective Prevention

Selective preventive interventions target those whose risk of disorder is greater than average due to some biological, psychological, or social risk factor. The individuals chosen to participate in these programs have not yet displayed any symptoms of the disorder. For example, a school psychologist might develop a selective prevention "banana split" group designed for students whose parents are in the process of divorce or separation. The students are not displaying any symptoms, but it is likely that without adequate peer social support, they might later exhibit maladaptive behavior. Selective prevention is similar to Caplan's secondary prevention concept, in that the participants are symptom-free but are high-risk candidates.

An Example of Selective Prevention: The Primary Mental Health Project

Perhaps the most famous and selective prevention program, and the one that has been in operation for the longest time, is the Primary Mental Health Project (PMHP). This program, started by Emory Cowen in 1957 in the Rochester, New York, School District, has grown to include 2,000 schools in over 700 school districts throughout the country (Cowen, 1996). The PMHP was aimed at the early detection and prevention of school adjustment problems. Cowen initiated the program in reaction to his discovery that many individuals currently presenting themselves for treatment had histories of psychological maladjustment dating back to their early years in school. Cowen reasoned that by assessing children psychologically in the primary grades, mental health professionals might identify at-risk children. Together with teachers and parents, professionals could then design programs to help these students. Also, paraprofessional volunteers such as college students could be recruited and trained to provide inexpensive direct care to children in the program.

Satcher (2000) noted that the PMHP produced significant improvement in participating students' grades, achievement test scores, and behavioral ratings. The program was relatively expensive though, since the screening instruments were unable to differentiate which students were truly at risk. Levine and Perkins (1987) listed problems common to both the PMHP and most other selective or secondary prevention programs that tend to limit effectiveness. The early detection of problems led to many false positives; many children were identified as being at high risk when in reality, they were not. Consider that children's behavior in the first grade is affected by many transient factors. A teacher, parent, or even a psychologist observing a student on a "bad day" might interpret a temporary behavior as an early warning sign of illness. In the original version of the PMHP, fully one-third of all first graders were classified as needing services offered in the program, yet by another estimate (Levine & Perkins, 1987) over 80% of the identified children did not really need treatment, and if they were left alone, would develop into healthy adults.

Treating many false positives is very costly, since as a result, only a small percentage of the consumed resources are helping those who truly need the service. A more significant concern arising from the identification of false positives involves labeling.

As was discussed in Chapter 1, labeling affects how a child is viewed. Parents might lower their expectations concerning the child's future upon learning that the child is at risk for developing a psychiatric condition. Teachers and classmates might isolate the child, and even the identified child might begin to act in a way consistent with the label—a type of self-fulfilling prophecy. This cycle leads to a great deal of emotional turmoil, and the faulty diagnosis itself may cause the problem that the program was designed to prevent.

Unfortunately, the percentage of false positives increases the earlier that the diagnoses are made. If problems are allowed to continue for a longer period of time prior to the diagnosis, the observed behavior becomes more apparent and consistent, and confidence in the accuracy of the assessment increases. However, with a prolonged period of time prior to the diagnosis, the behavior becomes more resistant to change. Although some selective prevention programs are effective, universal preventive strategies applied to groups of individuals who have not yet displayed any symptoms are the methods of choice. Universal prevention does not require labeling, and the services offered are not stigmatizing.

Indicated Prevention Programs

The indicated preventive interventions target high-risk individuals who have minimal and detectable symptoms, but not all the diagnostic criteria of a mental disorder. Schoolchildren who already display some conduct disorder behaviors might be singled out for a conflict-resolution training program. These programs are worthwhile even if they only delay rather than prevent the onset of the disorder. Generally, the public accepts these programs even if the cost per targeted individual is high or if there are some risks associated with the intervention. This type of strategy is not a separate category in the Caplan Model, and most of the programs at this level would have been "forced to fit" into the secondary prevention concept. Caplan's tertiary prevention is more similar to the IOM treatment and maintenance strategies.

The IOM model has provided a framework for reviewing the full range of programs present in the mental health system. It has also encouraged rigorous empirical evaluations of preventive and treatment-oriented programs. However, no model is perfect. It is likely that specific programs will still straddle two or more categories. A participant may be chosen for a selective preventive program and then display initial symptoms of the disorder. At that point, the intervention will include both selective and indicated individuals. It is unlikely that the indicated students will be required to leave the program to maintain the research boundaries. The real value of the system is not to differentiate types of prevention. Instead, the major benefit is to encourage creative thinking on the part of intervention planners to devise alternative programs that can meet the needs of all segments of the population.

Examples of Prevention Programs

The programs presented are typical examples of what has been done with various populations to reduce the incidence of specific disorders or problem behaviors. Hopefully, they will serve to arouse the reader's imagination regarding potential interventions to implement. In addition, some researchers have conducted meta-analyses of many similar studies. These researchers sought to find factors that consistently resulted in significant beneficial effects, and these meta-analyses are presented as well. The program that has generated the greatest interest and controversy over the past 40 years is the Head Start Program.

The Head Start Program

Perhaps the most significant large-scale example of universal prevention, Head Start was initiated in 1965 as a preschool program designed to overcome the effects of "cultural deprivation." The program had a number of lofty goals: to improve the physical health and social and emotional development of young children, to improve the level of their mental processes, to raise their expectations for success, to instill responsible attitudes toward family and society, and to increase dignity and self-worth (Zigler & Valentine, 1979). Over one-half million children participated in 3,000 local projects in the first Head Start summer program, and Head Start swiftly expanded to a 12-month program affecting millions of preschool students.

Both the development of the program and its near early demise were affected greatly by politics at the national level. The Head Start concept originated as part of President Kennedy's "New Frontier," and it was implemented through the Johnson Administration's "War on Poverty" and the Office of Economic Opportunity, during a period when liberal politics dominated. Medicare, Medicaid, community mental health, and civil rights legislation were either initiated or strongly supported at this time (Moynihan, 1969). By 1969, a more conservative administration had been elected, and support for these initiatives waned. Early evaluations of Head Start yielded disappointing results. This outcome, coupled with the publication of Arthur Jensen's (1969) *Harvard Educational Review* article defending the position that innate racial differences in IQ cannot be changed, supported President Nixon's attempt to dismantle Head Start. As was mentioned in Chapter 1, political and economic ideologies affect social scientific theory and research, and as the nation's mood changes, so does the nature of conducted and published studies (Rappaport, 1977; Riegal, 1972).

In its early days, Head Start, like other federally funded programs, was mandated to include some degree of parental involvement to enhance the community's sense of empowerment and ownership of the program. Parental involvement, however, had an unintended consequence that affected evaluation. Local control converted Head Start into a large number of separate projects, each with its own unique curriculum and other characteristics. There was not just one national and uniform program, and evaluation studies ended up either summing the results of many diverse projects or focusing on only one small-scale local intervention. The former alternative increased error variance, which made it harder to detect real effects of the program, while the latter choice reduced the ability to generalize the findings. Early research utilized the first approach, and the results were disappointing. In a controversial evaluation called the Westinghouse Study, Cicirelli (1969) found no lasting IQ effect due to participation in Head Start. When measured just after completing the program, the IQ scores of the Head Start children were significantly higher than that of the controls, but after three

In the IOM system, programs implementing Caplan's tertiary prevention concept are now seen as examples of maintenance. Since this chapter concerns prevention, such programs no longer fit into the new framework. However, maintenance programs do prevent mental disorders from becoming more disabling. Also, maintenance is valuable not only to the patient but to society as well. The ability to provide care in the community is far less costly than institutionalized care, and the economy benefits when the disabled return to productive employment. Of course, mental health strategies that include prevention are preferable, but failure to include maintenance programs creates a large and an unacceptable gap in the service delivery system. Thus, a description of both residential and employment maintenance programs helps to round out an understanding of the range of possible services.

Perhaps the most significant early example of maintenance was a program started in the 1960s by George Fairweather, called the "Fairweather Lodge Society" (Fairweather, 1980). This program attempted to return long-term institutionalized mental patients to the community. The lodges provided both supportive living arrangements and productive employment opportunities. To encourage empowerment, the residents had control over their daily routine. Each resident took responsibility on a rotating basis for providing basic services such as cooking, shopping, and cleaning. A janitorial and gardening business was established, which provided employment to the participants. The business required varying levels of social responsibility, and patients were assigned duties according to their functioning level. Staff provided consultation and supervision for the residents.

Fairweather, Sanders, Maynard, & Cressler (1969) performed a 40-month evaluation of the program, comparing recidivism rates of the recently deinstitutionalized lodge residents against a matched control group who were still living in the psychiatric hospital at the beginning of the study. The groups were matched by demographics, length of hospitalization, and diagnosis, among other variables. After 40 months, 80% of the lodge participants continued to live in the community, compared with only 20% of the control group. Over 40% of the lodge residents were employed as compared with 2% of the control group. At the beginning of the study, the lodge cost per participant was only one-third of the hospital expenses, and at the end of the 40 months, the lodge was self-sufficient. In addition, the lodge residents had become tax-paying citizens. Although the diagnoses had not changed, the lodge residents successfully moved into the community and were living productive, purposeful lives. As an example of Caplan's tertiary prevention and the IOM maintenance, the Fairweather Lodge Society continues to be an effective model program.

In addition to the many Fairweather Lodges throughout the nation, other local maintenance programs have been established independently by county, state, and private agencies. These programs typically target either the residential or employment needs of patients moving into the community. In both areas, programs differ by the level of structure and the intensity or extent of the services offered. In theory at least, the wide range of programs available can create good matches between the varying needs of ex-patients, if the placement is sensitive to the individual's level of functioning and the services provided.

Residential Services

Residential programs include intermediate care facilities (ICF), group homes, supervised apartments, supportive apartments, and "uncertified" private homes. An ICF is a self-contained "mini-institution" and provides total care for relatively low-functioning and sometimes violence-prone clients. Since it is much smaller than a traditional institution, the care provided can be more personalized. Group homes encourage greater client input in performing chores and deciding on group activities. These group homes are not self-contained service units, and typically, residents leave during the day to go to work or to attend other day programming activities. Supervised apartments allow greater client freedom and responsibility. In this type of program, an agency leases an entire apartment complex. One apartment unit is reserved for staff members to occupy on a 24-hour basis. The agency pairs two clients to live as roommates in each of the remaining apartments. Roommates are screened to ensure compatibility. The participants take care of managing their own apartments, and the staff is available to deal with any emergency that may arise. In addition, the staff might train the participant roommates in practical skills such as budgeting, using the local transportation system, and cooperating with each other. Supportive apartments are similar, but these apartments are located throughout the neighborhood, and the clients and staff communicate by phone on a regular basis, and in person only if needed.

Uncertified homes are the most normalizing of options. In this program, high-functioning clients find their own housing. The residence is uncertified, meaning that it need not meet the regulatory standards of any human service agency. Of course, all local fire, building, and occupancy codes must be followed as is the case with any other apartment or home offered for rent or sale in the community. Participants live on their own, and contact staff only when needed or for nonresidential services.

In good maintenance-type residential programs, client functioning is reassessed on a regular basis, and habitation plans are prepared for each participant. As clients increase their ability to function freely in the community, they move to the next level of independent living. The process is impaired whenever a compatible housing option is not available. In such situations, staff members have two options. They can keep a participant in an overly structured setting that often leads to client rebelliousness, or in the second option, staff might place a client in a housing situation that requires too much personal responsibility. Much of the local community's unfavorable attitude toward deinstitutionalization is due to this dumping of unprepared clients into the community. Frequently, clients fail, and so need to be reinstitutionalized, and they are understandably reluctant to seek a new community-based housing option in the future.

Employment Programs

As with residential services, employment programs also vary with differing levels of client ability. Lower-functioning clients might begin at a day training program, and as they improve their vocational skills and attitudes, move to sheltered workshops, enclave work units, or community-based competitive employment situations. Day training programs offer intensive preoccupational therapy. Clients are taught ADL and social skills and attitudes that relate to the workplace. The values of acceptable grooming and the need to report to work on time are examples of types of attitudes learned at this level. In some cases, the day training program is located in a neighborhood where clients are encouraged to volunteer for short periods of time to perform real tasks like returning shopping carts or assembling pizza boxes. All activities are conducted under appropriate supervision and are aimed at teaching skills rather than performing productive work.

Sheltered employment offers the first true opportunity to work productively, although teaching skills is still a priority. In these settings, agencies operate workshops and bid for work contracts from manufacturing companies. Clients are taught how to perform repetitive tasks and are paid to assemble a product or insert an item in its packaging. Clients work at their own pace, and staff closely supervise to ensure that safety standards are met and that the quality of work is acceptable. Staff members also regularly assess the appropriateness of the work duties in terms of the client's functioning level. Sheltered workshops are segregated from the rest of the community, and coworkers are often clients rather than business employees. Some workshop clients are permitted to travel to business establishments in the community. They are organized as a work unit or an enclave to perform a specific task under supervision. Such a work enclave might be assigned the job of cleaning an office building after hours or maintaining the grounds of a local business facility. Although the employment is more community-based, the clients are not truly integrated into the neighborhood, and most contact is with other clients only.

(continued)

As clients improve their work abilities, they move into integrative competitive jobs in the community. The agency hires staff to serve as job coaches who first learn the duties required in a specific position and then teach these tasks to a client. When the client performs the task duties at an acceptable level, the staff leaves, and the participant becomes a regular employee at the business. Sometimes a fellow worker is asked to be a "job-buddy," assigned to help the employee perfect the skills needed on the job. The participant is no longer viewed as a client and is interacting regularly on an equal basis with other employees.

These residential and employment programs are examples of maintenance-type interventions, since they are aimed at returning the patient to the community as a fully functioning person as soon as possible. It is not likely that the diagnostic label will change, but the disabling consequences of the disorder have been alleviated, and the individual is able to live a normalized lifestyle.

Before concluding this section, it is worthwhile to consider how clients are placed in both residential and employment settings. In the current mental health system, an Assertive Case Treatment (ACT) team assists clients in locating housing appropriate to the client's functioning level. The ACT approach has been described in both the ecology and deinstitutionalization chapters. This model does not include a vocational specialist, and the placement of clients into specific employment settings is not as precise a process. Furlong, McCoy, Dincin, Clay, McClory, & Pavick (2002) sought to determine the value of adding a vocational specialist to the ACT Team. These researchers and providers conducted a 21-month study of clients with the most severe psychiatric disorders. The clients were members of Thresholds, a psychosocial rehabilitation program in Chicago. In this maintenance type program, the vocational specialist assisted members in getting jobs. Possible placements ranged from agency-controlled sheltered employment to community-based group and individual competitive jobs. Choice of placement was guided by the member's preference. If the client chose to accept the agency placement, upgrades to competitive positions were always possible and encouraged, if consistent with the member's employment goals. On-the-job support in the community was provided. Compared with a control group of similar Thresholds members, at the end of the 21-month period, those in the intervention group were three times as likely to be employed, and they earned nearly three times the salary. They were twice as likely to hold competitive jobs in the community. Consistent with the findings of other research, although the psychiatric diagnoses did not change and there was no difference in rates of hospital utilization between the two groups, adding a vocational specialist to the ACT team had a positive benefit on enhancing the quality of life and employment status of individuals with the most severe psychotic disorders.

years of attending public school, the initial IQ gains disappeared. Some social scientists have criticized this study. Given the multifaceted goals of Head Start, perhaps IQ was not the correct outcome to measure. Even if an educator believed that improving mental processes was the most significant objective, intelligence is too stable a measure to be affected by a short-term program such as Head Start. It is normal for any temporary IQ changes to disappear over time. Haggard (1954), for example, found that "prepping" a naïve child on how to take an intelligence test can result in a temporary gain, but that this gain disappears as the control group children gradually gain more experience in test taking. Achievement test scores and even school grades are better measures of intervention-sensitive mental processes than are IQ scores.

Other critics of the Westinghouse study believed that its findings demonstrated the faults of the public school system and not those of Head Start (Zigler & Valentine, 1979). The participating children gained from the program, but their initial enthusiasm for learning was dulled by the public school experience. Consider that Head Start is highly responsive to the needs of the targeted minority children, whereas public schools follow a state-mandated curriculum. Parental involvement and local control guaranteed that Head Start met local needs of participating families. Although public schools have school boards, the members of the board might be more concerned about school taxes and administrative issues than about the quality of education. Also, boards rarely represent minority cultures, and typically there are fewer cultural amplifiers in public schools than in Head Start programs.

Stanley Murrell (1973) viewed the problems that minority children encounter when they enter public school, as caused by the lack of social system synergy. As mentioned in the ecology chapter, a child belongs to three systems: the family, peer group, and school. When members of all three systems are encouraging the same goals and values, synergy exists and a child is likely to behave in a manner consistent with these forces. When the systems conflict, the child is less certain about goals and so feels confused. Behavior appears more erratic and less focused. In Head Start, the three systems are more synergistic, but in public school, the minority child confronts an alien culture, and the school system is no longer in step with peers and family.

Perry Preschool Project

Other researchers have found permanent gains from Head Start when they focused on evaluating individual well-run programs, rather than summing over the outcomes of many different projects. The Head Start program that has been researched most extensively using the best experimental design is the Perry Preschool Project in Ypsilanti, Michigan. This program targeted African American children from low socioeconomic backgrounds whose initial IQs ranged from 60 to 90. The program consisted of a child development curriculum geared toward intellectual, physical, and social development, along with weekly home visits. Children attended half-day classes during a 30-week period (Schweinhart & Weikart, 1989). The research participants were assigned randomly either to the program or to a no-preschool control (Levine & Perkins, 1987). Various researchers followed these children over a 23-year period and observed them to age 27 years. On the basis of empirical evidence from a variety of studies, the Perry Preschool Project has been a huge success. Darlington, Royce, Snipper, Murray, & Lazar (1980) found that children who participated in the preschool program were far less likely to be labeled as mentally retarded (35% of the controls versus 15% of the preschool children) and less likely to need special education classes. Berreuta-Clement, Schweinhart, Barnett, Epstein, and Weikart (1984) and Schweinhart et al. (1993) listed the statistically significant benefits of participation in the Perry Preschool Project as including fewer teenage pregnancies, lower arrest rates, higher school grades, higher rates of graduation from high school, and overall level of educational attainment, as well as higher income, lower welfare, lower unemployment, and greater social responsibility. The researchers estimate that seven dollars were saved for each dollar spent in this one-year preschool program. While the empirical data is striking and the economic cost/benefit analysis impressive, the total gains in promoting wellness and preventing pain and misery are incalculable.

Statistical significance in research is often not sufficient to sway policy makers and the general public. For example, the U.S. General Accounting Office (1997) reviewed 22 Head Start evaluation studies and concluded that there was insufficient evidence of long-term effects. The GAO noted that large-scale studies demonstrating significant benefits had not been performed. As a result, a consortium of researchers began to conduct a national study to evaluate Head Start (Ripple & Zigler, 2003). A parallel program called Early Head Start was designed to assist preschoolers and their parents, and it has been evaluated on a large scale. Love, Kisker, Ross, Schochet, Brooks-Gunn, Paulsell, et al. (2002) performed a national random assignment study of 3,001 families who participated in 17 Head Start programs. They found the toddlers in the program developed more swiftly in cognitive, socioemotional, and language areas, and that the families' home environment, parenting, and economic condition improved. Although the empirical debate continues, political interests are more likely to sway policy. President George W. Bush expressed the position that Head Start should focus more exclusively on literacy learning and it should be transferred from the Department of Health and Human Services to the Department of Education. This change would transform Head Start from a national- to a state-directed program, and the comprehensive scope and national orientation of the program might be lost (Ripple & Zigler, 2003).

Even though the Head Start Program is the most significant program studied, there are many other examples of successful primary prevention programs. These programs are presented next and are arranged according to the life span developmental stage of the targeted population.

Prevention Programs for Infants and Young Children

From a therapeutic perspective, the earlier the intervention, the more likely it will succeed (Cowen, 1996). The following programs focused on infancy and early childhood, and the first study started even before the children were born.

The Elmira (NY) Prenatal/Early Infancy Project

This project began in the early 1980s and demonstrates Cowen's perspective well. In the Elmira Prenatal Early Infancy Project (Olds, Eckenrode, Henderson, Kitzman, Powers, Cole, et al., 1997), young women pregnant for the first time were given developmental screenings, transportation to health care, and nurse home visits every 2 weeks during pregnancy and then on a diminishing schedule for 2 years after the child was born. Issues such as parenting style, the mothers' support systems, and the utilization of community services were explored. The program is of the selective preventive type, since the women were at high risk due to their young age, single-parent status, and/or low socioeconomic level. From those meeting the criteria, the assignment of the women participants to the intensive treatment group was random, which allowed for appropriate program evaluation. Early results showed that families in this treatment group had fewer instances of child abuse and neglect; the mothers punished their children less frequently and provided more appropriate play materials. A cost-benefit analysis conducted two years after the program ended (i.e., when the children were 4 years old) showed that the direct cost per family for the nurse visits, transportation, and services was $1,582, but the benefit in reduced Medicaid, Aid to Families with Dependent Children, food stamps, and child protective services was $1,762, a dividend of $180. The families were followed until the children reached 15 years of age. The women in the intensive treatment group had fewer subsequent pregnancies, used welfare less frequently, were less likely to be abusive or neglectful of their children, used less alcohol, and had fewer arrests. Their children also had fewer arrests, convictions, and probation violations; had lower alcohol and cigarette use; and exhibited fewer behavioral problems. Even though the program ended when the children were 2 years old, the benefits of the program continued through adolescence.

Focusing on a slightly older group of children, a second early intervention program involved the parents and teachers of 4-year-old children enrolled in Head Start in Seattle, Washington. In this program, 272 parents and 61 Head Start teachers participated in 12 weekly workshop sessions in which various parenting and classroom management skills were discussed. Results both immediately after the program ended and one year later indicated that compared with Head Start controls, the mothers utilized a more positive parenting style, and their children displayed fewer conduct problems both at home and in school. The teachers in the program displayed better classroom management skills and had greater parent-teacher bonding than those in the control group (Webster-Stratton, Reid, & Hammond, 2001).

There are many successful prevention programs that help young children. Durlak and Wells (1997) performed a meta-analysis of 177 primary prevention programs for youth. Of these, 168 were deemed effective in preventing behavioral and social problems in children and adolescents. These researchers found that preventive interventions for youth produced better outcomes than other treatment and prevention programs in medicine and the social sciences. For example, they reported that many programs to prevent delinquency, smoking, and alcohol use among school children produced higher magnitudes of effect than did medical interventions to encourage aspirin use to prevent heart attacks. In Durlak and Wells's (1997) meta-analysis, "the average participant in a youth oriented primary prevention program surpasses the performance of between 59% and 82% of those in a control group" (p. 115). Particularly effective were programs that provided affective education to young children and promoted their emotional and social development, as well as programs helping first-time parents during difficult transition periods.

Elementary-School-Based Primary Prevention Programs

There are many benefits to be gained by locating prevention programs in schools. Elementary school "is the first point in the lifespan when the majority of children enter a service system that includes a broad cross section of the population" (Eddy, Reid,

& Fetrow, 2000, p. 167). Cowen, Hightower, Pedro-Carroll, & Work (1989) noted the audience is captive and available and that these programs can reach populations that may not actively seek out therapeutic help in the community. Also, school-based programs allow the interventionists some options regarding how to deliver the program. They can choose either to train regular teachers to present the program or to present the program to the children themselves. In the latter case, the program developer can be more confident that the intervention is being properly implemented. There are also great benefits to training teachers. Typically, students know and like their teachers, and therefore rapport building is an easier process. Also, if the teachers believe the program is effective, they are inclined to offer it repeatedly in future years, and the preventive program becomes more accepted by and integrated into the school. Finally, a secondary effect of many prevention programs is to enhance the students' ability and motivation to learn, a benefit consistent with the goals of the school. Educators are eager to embrace programs after viewing data demonstrating that the programs improve academic achievement and reduce classroom management problems. Prevention need not take time away from traditional learning; psychologists, working with teachers, can integrate a program's objectives into regular academic lessons. For example, a problem-solving curriculum can be built into the typical selection of short stories read during literature class. Having the students brainstorm alternatives available to the hero at a critical moment in the story adds to the students' motivation to read, as well as to their understanding of how to solve social problems and cope with crises. Examples of specific preventive programs in the school are described next, arranged by the type of behavior targeted by the intervention. The first two programs addressed some of the antecedents of delinquent behavior.

The Seattle Social Development Project

The Seattle Social Development Project is an elementary-school-based program designed to promote academic achievement and pro-social bonding, and to prevent crime, teen pregnancy, drug abuse, and school dropout (Hawkins, Catalano, Kosterman, Abbott, & Hill, 1999). The program is both selective and universal, since it is targeted to all students in Grades 1 through 6 in schools located in high-crime, high-poverty neighborhoods. The program consists of teacher training in classroom management, parent training, and social competence workshops for the youth. The behavior of students was assessed at age 18, 6 years after they completed the program. The treatment group differed significantly from the controls; they had stronger attachments to the school, less involvement in school misbehavior, and higher scholastic achievement. In addition, the treatment group committed fewer violent acts, drank alcohol less heavily, engaged in sexual intercourse less frequently, and had multiple sex partners less frequently.

Linking the Interests of Families and Teachers (LIFT)

Another elementary-school-based program that targeted antecedents of delinquency and violence is the LIFT Program. LIFT, designed and evaluated by Eddy, Reid, and Fetrow (2000), targeted child oppositional, defiant, and socially inept behavior, as well

as parental styles of disciplining and monitoring their children. The program participants were chosen from the general population of students in elementary schools in
the Eugene-Springfield, (Oregon), metropolitan area. The three-month-long program consisted of three components: (a) classroom-based training sessions in social
and problem solving skills for the children, (b) playground-based behavior modification, and (c) group-delivered parent training sessions. The classroom modules for
both the children and the parents utilized lecture, discussion, role play, and practice
methods. The playground component consisted of teachers and other adults rewarding students for using pro-social and positive relationship behavior while playing a
game. In a three-year follow-up evaluation, it was observed that compared with controls, program participants delayed the time they first became involved with antisocial
peers, their first alcohol and marijuana use, and their first police arrest. Also, behaviors
such as inattentiveness, impulsivity, and hyperactivity, which are empirically predictive
of later delinquent and conduct-problem behavior, were decreased in severity at the
three-year assessment compared with the behavior of the controls.

Curwin and Mendler (2002) add a system-level factor to enhance the effectiveness
of programs aimed at preventing violence. These authors argued that schools should
include, as core to their mission statement, the values of finding nonviolent expressions
of resolving conflict and of challenging hostile and disrespectful acts directed at others
throughout the school community. Curwin and Mendler believed that programs would
be more effective if they were embedded in a value-based school system.

In reviewing the results of 84 studies that teach children social skills to prevent
antisocial behavior, Losel and Beelmann (2003) found that while many treatment
modalities were effective, cognitive behavioral programs had the strongest impact on
students' behavior. Consistent with other researchers, these authors found that tar-
getting at risk groups had a greater likelihood of achieving significant differences
than programs that included all students. This finding is probably due to an artifact in
the assessment process, since there is a much lower frequency of serious antisocial
behavior in the general as opposed to the high-risk populations. They concluded that
more research using well-controlled studies, larger samples, and long follow-up periods was needed.

In addition to elementary school programs that teach students to behave more
socially, other programs are designed to prevent children from becoming victims of
sexual abuse. Davis and Gidycz (2000) reviewed 27 programs focusing on this issue
and found most programs to be effective. "The average effect size for all programs was
1.07 indicating that the children who participated in prevention programs perform
1.07 SD [standard deviations] higher than control group children on the outcome
measures used in the studies" (p. 257). For example, on a measure in which 50% of the
control group members scored favorably, 69% of the treated children would have met
this criterion. These researchers also found that the best programs had children participate actively and attend at least four sessions. In other studies, it was found that students attending abuse-prevention sessions become more knowledgeable about abuse
but that they did not always learn how to respond appropriately in potential abuse situations. Ko and Cosden (2001) surveyed high school students about an abuse program
they attended in elementary school. Those who participated in the earlier program

were more knowledgeable about abuse and reported fewer incidents than controls, but their responses to abuse were not significantly better.

Among elementary-school-based prevention programs, those dealing with assisting children with emotional disturbance (ED) are particularly important for community mental health professionals, since success with these children early on may reduce the later incidence of adults with a parallel diagnosis. A number of prevention programs have focused on this population. Kamps, Kravitz, Rauch, Kamps, and Chung (2000) reported on a program for students at risk or with ED that was conducted in the Kansas City, Kansas, Public Schools. The intervention spanned one-and-a-half school years and included weekly social-skills training, peer tutoring, and classroom behavioral management using token economies and student contracts. The students in the program ranged from 5 to 10 years old when the intervention started and were assessed over a 4-year period. Compared with a delayed control group, participants showed a decrease in inappropriate behavior such as aggression, out-of-seat and negative verbal acts (like teasing or threatening peers), and increased appropriate behaviors, such as academic engagement and behavioral compliance. The effect improved over time, and the greatest effectiveness occurred in classrooms with high structure and with those students who attended more sessions.

Similar findings were reported by McConaughy, Kay, and Fitzgerald (2000). These researchers evaluated a prevention program for first and second graders at risk for ED. The program utilized collaborative teams of parents, the teacher, and a mental health professional for each child, as well as classroom-wide social skills training. These teams met monthly, on average, and assessed each child's strengths and problems, set goals, and designed and monitored the intervention. Children were assessed at the end of the first and second year of the program. Compared to matched controls who received only the social skill training, the participants' problem behaviors decreased somewhat after the first year with more pronounced benefits after the second year. Consistent with other researchers, McConaughy et al. found that the longer the program was maintained, the greater the effect tended to be.

Prior to concluding the discussion of prevention programs for children at risk for ED, one final program will be touched upon. McArdle, Moseley, Quibell, Johnson, Allen, Hammal, and leCouteur (2002) reported on a program that used an innovative treatment method, drama-group therapy. Their research compared the drama group, consisting of 12 one-hour sessions, against a curriculum studies approach and a waiting list control group. At-risk students were randomly assigned to the various groups. The behavior of the drama group therapy treatment participants improved significantly compared with that of either of the other two groups, and this effect carried over a one-year follow-up assessment.

School- and Community-Based Prevention for High School and College Students

As students get older, many behavior patterns, both good and bad, have been established and are more resistant to change. Although it becomes more challenging, it is still possible to design effective prevention programs to meet the needs of high school and college-aged students. If one considers the effect of a program on the future generation, it is easily seen that these programs have multiple benefits. For example, effective programs targeting drug abuse among adolescents can reduce, in a relatively few years, the likelihood of fetal alcohol syndrome or the birth of cocaine addicted babies. Similarly, programs addressing impulsive or violent behaviors of teenagers about to become parents can reduce the likelihood of later child abuse. From this perspective, such programs are preventive in nature and very useful to society. Following are some examples of prevention programs that focus on high school and college students. Issues such as antisocial and violent behavior, adolescent suicide, and drug abuse behavior are discussed.

Consistent with other areas of prevention, effective interventions in programs for adolescents should be multifaceted and multilevel. For example, Speaker and Peterson (2000) recommended that programs to prevent juvenile violence and suicide should include family participation and involve school staff as well as the adolescents themselves. The school staff should be trained in values education, and the youth should be encouraged to develop success-oriented self-identity and utilize nonviolent conflict resolution skills. Finally, programs should advocate for the use of media in both the schools and the community that stress appropriate, respectful social interaction. Huey and Henggeler (2001) have echoed a similar theme of targeting multiple components of the youths' life space to prevent antisocial behavior and juvenile delinquency. These authors cited a number of programs that were found to be cost-effective on a long-term basis. Among the most beneficial was multisystemic therapy (MST). As previously described in the ecology chapter, MST is an alternative to incarcerating youthful offenders and involves problem-solving activities at the peer, family, school, and neighborhood levels. In terms of the IOM categories, this intervention can be viewed as both indicated prevention and maintenance, in that it reduces the risk that juvenile delinquents will become career criminals and enables the youth to remain in the community without committing additional offenses. The MST program involves individualized ongoing care and supervision both in the home and in community settings.

Substance abuse prevention programs may be the most common school-based interventions. Nancy Tobler and Susan Ennett and their colleagues have performed a series of meta-analyses over the past 15 years (Ennett, Ringwalt, Thorne, Rohrbach, Vincus, Simons-Rudolph, & Jones, 2003; Ennett, Tobler, Ringwalt, & Flewelling, 1994; Tobler, 2000; Tobler, Lessard, Marshall, Ochshorn, & Roona, 1999; Tobler, Roona, Ochshorn, Marshall, Streke, & Stackpole, 2000; and Tobler & Stratton, 1997). Summing up their empirical findings are the following points about the effectiveness of universal substance abuse (tobacco, alcohol, marijuana, other street drugs) prevention programs.

- DARE (Drug Abuse Resistance Education) is almost completely ineffective.
- Regarding the content of prevention programs, teaching interpersonal social skills such as assertiveness is far more effective than teaching knowledge about drugs in reducing drug abuse.

- Interactive programs are more effective than lecture-oriented sessions. Tobler (2000) cited a 21% reduction in the prevalence of drug abuse among adolescents in schools where an interactive approach was presented.
- Small-scale programs are more effective than large-scale interventions, perhaps because the program protocol is more closely followed in smaller programs.
- Unfortunately, teachers in the substance-abuse programs have not been utilizing the research findings. In a study of 1,800 teachers of middle-school prevention programs, Ennett et al. (2003) found that although the majority of teachers used effective content, few (17%) used an effective delivery system, and even fewer (14%) utilized both effective content and delivery. This last finding is particularly important, since mental health providers in both the school and the community are urged to utilize evidence-based treatment methods as part of best practice guidelines.

Other researchers generally agreed with Ennett's and Tobler's findings. In a separate meta-analysis, Wilson, Gottfredson, and Najaka (2001) found that self-control and social-competency instruction utilizing cognitive behavioral and behavioral training methods were more effective than interventions based on other therapeutic techniques. Also, Cuipers (2002) found that among interactive programs, peer-led interventions were somewhat more effective than adult-led sessions. Peer-led programs are probably more interactive than adult-led classes and thus may be better received by the adolescents.

Prevention programs can also target college students and adults at risk for mental illness. Kenardy, McCafferty, and Rosa (2003) evaluated an innovative, Internet-delivered program for anxiety disorder. In this indicated type intervention, university students with elevated anxiety sensitivity, a risk factor for anxiety disorder and other pathologies, were randomly assigned to either a six-week Internet-based program or a wait-list control. The Internet program utilized a cognitive-behavioral and behavioral approach. At the end of the six weeks, those in the Internet program experienced fewer anxiety-related cognitions and symptoms of depression. Internet therapeutic delivery is still in its early development, and both practical and potentially ethical concerns need to be resolved before widespread use of on-line therapy is possible, but programs such as this demonstrate the promise of this approach.

Programs for Adults and the Elderly

Adults continue to face new challenges and developmental crises throughout life, and existing coping mechanisms may need to be enhanced to deal with new stressors. In this section, programs dealing with marital discord, stresses associated with receiving public assistance, and challenges facing older adults are discussed.

Markman, Renick, Floyd, Stanley, and Clements (1993) examined a program designed to prevent marital distress by training couples in communication and conflict resolution skills. The intervention, called the Prevention and Relationship Enhancement Program (PREP), consisted of five 3-hour sessions that focused on active listening, expressive speaking, and distinguishing between problem discussion and problem solving. Couples practiced these skills and reviewed feedback from the consultants. The researchers assessed the effects of the program after 5 years. Intervention couples had higher levels of positive communication skills and lower levels of violence compared with no-treatment controls. Program participants also had higher levels of marital satisfaction and lower levels of relationship instability. These results demonstrate that marital discord is partly due to a lack of training, which can be remedied through interpersonal communication and conflict-management skill-building.

Low-income adults on welfare are at high risk for a variety of psychological disorders. Albee and Ryan-Finn (1993) described a program designed to prevent stress, depression, and anxiety among women receiving public assistance. The program, conducted over a 2-year period, provided training in problem solving and stress management. Consultants also helped the women become more aware of their existing attitudes and capabilities. Results indicated that program participants were more self-confident, were less anxious or depressed, and had higher ego strength and increased social contact than did the no-treatment controls. Such a preventive program is an effective way to help needy adults change the direction of their lives.

As adults grow older, they encounter new obstacles in life that if not mastered, can lead to both psychological and physical problems. Lopez and Silber (1991) evaluated the effectiveness of a stress management program for 39 older adults living independently in the community. Participants were randomly divided into 3 groups: a stress inoculation training condition, an information/attention control condition, and a no-treatment control. The two treatment conditions received 12 hours of training conducted by psychology graduate students over a 6-week period. Results showed that the stress inoculation group reported less anxiety and stress than either of the other two groups. Stress inoculation training demonstrated to be an effective tool in teaching coping skills to the elderly. Prevention programs can also address the serious risk of accidental falls that affect many elderly. A fall can incapacitate an older adult, forcing the individual to live in a nursing home; therefore, preventing falls is of great psychological and economic benefit. Hornbrook, Stevens, Wingfield, Hollis, Greenlick, and Ory (1994) evaluated a program designed to reduce the risk of falling. Called the Study of Accidental Falls in the Elderly (SAFE), the program sought to reduce accidental falls by addressing cognitive and behavioral domains. Study participants, 3,182 people over 65 years old, were visited in their homes, and fall hazards were assessed and recorded. All subjects were informed of existing trouble spots and given a safety booklet. The intervention group received further treatment. They were advised to make specific repairs and informed on how to apply for technical and financial assistance to do so. Also, these individuals were invited to attend 4 weekly group accident-prevention classes conducted by a health behaviorist and a physical therapist. Self-reported falls were recorded for two years. Compared to the minimum treatment control group, the intervention group reduced the risk of their falling by 85%. Most of the benefit, however, was confined to the prevention of noninjury falls, as opposed to those that required medical treatment. Apparently, other methods were needed to reduce the risk of these more serious falls. This evidence highlights the concern that difficulties in living often have multiple causes. Many serious falls may be due to acute medical emergencies such as strokes, and these are less likely to be prevented by environmental changes.

The studies presented here are representative of the hundreds of researched and effective prevention programs. It is beyond the scope of this book to provide an exhaustive review of interventions in each area of interest. Additional resources for those wanting in-depth descriptions of a greater range of case studies in prevention include Price, Cowen, Lorion, and Ramos-McKay (1988), a 2-volume review of programs for children by Weissberg, Gullotta, Adams, Hampton, and Ryan (1997a and b), and a more recent overview of prevention across the life span by Gullotta and Bloom (2003).

The Future of Prevention

Throughout the twentieth century, prevention in the areas of physical and mental health have demonstrated effectiveness in reducing both the incidence and the prevalence of illness and in promoting health. It is expected that preventive interventions will continue to flourish in the current century. Topics to be discussed in this section include opportunities to offer preventive interventions in health care settings, the value of increasing community-based prevention, and the federal government's role in funding prevention.

Prevention Opportunities in Health Care Settings

Providers in health care settings are becoming increasingly aware of the value of offering behaviorally based preventive interventions for improving health. Johnson and Millstein (2003) noted that interventions can be conducted in hospitals and outpatient and school-based clinics, and even through outreach programs into the patients' homes. Interventions can target health care professionals as well as patients and their families.

Most health care providers are aware of the role that preventable risky behaviors play in the illnesses of their patients. For example, the leading cause of death among children and adolescents is injury resulting from accidents or violence. Substance abuse and reckless driving are preventable behaviors that contribute greatly to these injuries. Among adults, half of the deaths due to chronic illnesses such as cardiovascular disease, respiratory and liver disorders, cancer, HIV, and diabetes are related to high-risk behaviors. Behavioral interventions that target smoking, diet, exercise, substance abuse, and sexual practices can prevent or delay the onset of chronic illnesses (Johnson & Millstein, 2003). Health professionals aware of these statistics are more likely to discuss behavioral issues with their patients.

Mental health professionals can consider pediatricians and other primary care health professionals as proximal agents in the lives of their patients. The vast majority of children and adolescents visit a health care provider at least yearly. These visits typically occur in the doctor's office but can also take place in emergency rooms, agency, school or special service clinics, community health centers, and dental offices. Workshops that educate health care professionals about screening for risky behaviors and methods of behavioral change and persuasion can help prevent these behaviors and promote healthy ones in their place. Public health nurses who perform outreach to the community, visiting the homes and apartments of individuals, can also be offered behaviorally oriented prevention workshops.

Programs can focus on the patients themselves and their families in each of the settings previously mentioned. Effective preventive interventions have targeted reducing pre- and post-surgical stress, and some of these programs have taught parents to be "coping coaches" for children preparing for a hospital stay, immunizations, or even dental work. Other mental health professionals have taught visiting nurses to help improve health-related behaviors that are important during pregnancy and in parenting. Genetic testing for a variety of physical illnesses is increasing, and as a result, interventions that prepare tested individuals for psychological trauma that is likely to occur with positive test results are in greater demand.

Although Johnson and Millstein (2003) stated that more cost-effectiveness studies are needed, it is likely that even modestly successful programs will be cost-effective. It was noted that a smoking cessation program for pregnant women, which increased the cessation rate by a modest 14%, had a benefit-to-cost ratio of from 18:1 to 46:1, depending on which benefits were included in the calculation. It is clear that the cost of health care can be dramatically reduced if more behaviorally oriented preventive interventions are utilized.

Conducting More Community-Based Prevention Programs

Many of the prevention programs mentioned earlier in this chapter were school-based. Although schools offer the benefit of easy access to large populations of students, there are many concerns that cannot be addressed solely in the schools. The problems of high-risk pregnancies, substance abuse, violence, and crime are too large, and they often deal with individuals not connected with the schools. The best interventions are those that target multiple domains (antisocial behaviors, violence, substance abuse, etc.), are applied across multiple settings, and use multiple strategies and components. This method creates a system of programs that is more likely to generate synergistic effects.

Wandersman and Florin (2003) cited several community-based prevention programs that were empirically demonstrated to be effective. For example, a successful substance abuse program included public service announcements and interviews in the mass media, social skills training for youth, parent communication skills training, municipal laws affecting access to and use of tobacco and alcohol and penalties for alcohol-related accidents, and a community task force to mobilize all segments of the community. An effective adolescent pregnancy and parenting program included hospitals; public libraries; public schools; the United Way; neighborhood organizations; and local, state, and federal funding. An immunization program included most of these components and added strategies aimed at business organizations.

Even though there are many benefits to community-wide prevention programs, there are barriers to increasing the use of these programs. Wandersman and Florin (2003) noted that evaluation research methods need some improvement. In addition to the problems of measuring universal and selected-type programs, as mentioned earlier in this chapter, community-wide programs have unique challenges. It is difficult to measure outcomes in an entire community, because comparable control groups are problematic. In addition, not all community residents will receive the needed "dose" of media announcements, and without this exposure, the program may not be sufficiently effective. Finally, although there are many benefits to community building, developing the needed collaborative relationship with all the opinion leaders in the neighborhood can be time-consuming and difficult.

The Federal Government's Role in Funding Prevention and Setting National Policy

The federal government is a great resource in funding prevention programs, but ambivalence and politics tend to dilute the effect. For example, the federal government spent over $55 billion on Head Start since 1965, but only half the eligible children are enrolled (Ripple & Zigler, 2003). Even beyond the funding, the policies set by the government establish the national agenda, but as presidential administrations change, so do the national thrusts. Ripple and Zigler identified the following three aspects of the current sociopolitical context that affect federal policies regarding prevention:

■ Partly because of a desire to support states' rights and partly because of the government's ambivalence about its role in affecting family life and parenting style, pressure is being exerted to move prevention programs from federal to state control. The benefit of this process is that the programs can be "tailor fit" to the needs of each state. The drawbacks to this devolution process are that the program can lose its national integrity, the funding for many programs is bundled together into block grants, and funds can end up being used for other purposes.
■ Politically, it is easier to fund programs that target a severe problem, resulting in a tendency for programs to target high-risk groups. Although this policy seems to be a commonsense approach, it results in marginalization and stigmatization of the targeted group. After a short time, the targeted "have-nots" are separated from the policymaker "haves." When the initial period of funding expires, the policy makers are able to politically sidetrack the program, and funding either stops or is sharply decreased.
■ Similarly, it is easier to gain federal funding support for specific problems, such as lead poisoning. Yet high-risk factors tend to cluster, and targeting one concern without addressing related concerns results in nonsynergistic, piecemeal programs with limited effect.

Ripple and Zigler (2003) recommended directions for the federal government to take to remedy some of these concerns. First, adopt a universal prevention approach; all children can gain from Head Start. This step reduces the likelihood that low-income or ethnic minority children will be marginalized. Also, the energies and expenses consumed by checking eligibility requirements can be spent more productively. In addition, voters everywhere can experience the benefits of the program, and hence the program is easier to defend politically. Second, rather than targeting individual problems or specific groups of persons, target communities or neighborhoods and then develop multiple component programs to deal with the cluster of problems present in that community. Poverty is associated with poor nutrition, substandard education, inadequate housing (where there is a higher likelihood of peeling lead paint causing poisoning), high unemployment, and the like. Joining the programs to address all the needs in the community allows for the possibility of spillover effects, in that the solution for one concern could also remedy a related one. In conclusion, Ripple and Zigler recommend that the government sponsor comprehensive programs with universal access.

Conclusion

Prevention is a highly effective strategy for enhancing the quality of mental health in the community, and all mental health professionals should attempt to design and implement prevention programs in their work. Prevention is a hallmark of the community mental health movement, and it is useful to apply this principle whenever possible.

DISCUSSION QUESTIONS

1. What is a proximal agent? What are some examples of proximal agents, and how might they help an individual at risk? Give examples.

2. Why is it difficult, in some cases, to secure funding for the implementation of community prevention programs? What are some possible solutions to this problem?

3. How has the community mental heath field borrowed from the public health model of disease transmission and prevention? What are the benefits of prevention as opposed to treatment after the fact?

4. What are the benefits of universal prevention? What are some different types of primary prevention? What are the criteria for a good universal prevention program? What are some difficulties or possible detrimental effects stemming from the administration of a universal prevention program?

5. Explain why it is of concern that difficulties in living are often the result of multiple causes. How can these influences be examined and addressed, in order to design effective prevention programs? Give some examples of targeted difficulties in living that may be due to more than a single cause, and of some possible program components that might help to reduce these variables.

6. Why is it advisable for health care providers to be aware of the importance of prevention? What role can educators and school officials play in encouraging prevention? What type of behaviors can be targeted through these interventions? Do you feel that these programs are effective? If not, how could they be made more effective?

5 Individual Focus: Crisis and Coping

OBJECTIVES

This chapter is designed to enable the reader to:

- Understand the community mental health approach to crisis theory.
- Identify six considerations that contribute to succesfully coping with a life crisis.
- Describe the stages of the General Adaptation Syndrome.
- Understand the concept of resilience and identify character traits that might contribute to resilience.
- Identify different stages of stress and the way they progress toward illness.
- Explain why a community approach can be effective for stress management.
- Explain how the expansion of niche breadth is beneficial to both mental health clients and society.
- Define what constitutes a crisis.
- Explain how family members can take an important part in mitigating a crisis on the part of an individual.
- Identify different types of personal resources and the way they relate to the ability to cope with stress.
- Understand how the subjective perception of an event determines the emotional response.
- Identify practical steps that can help an individual coping with stress.
- Identify distortions in thinking and ways in which they can contribute to stress and maladaptive coping, as well as the importance of positive thinking.
- Understand how the maintenance of physical health is important to coping with stress.
- Describe different types of brief therapy interventions.

"When written in Chinese the word crisis is composed of two characters. One represents danger and the other represents opportunity."

John F. Kennedy

"You gain strength, courage and confidence by every experience in which you really stop to look fear in the face. You are able to say to yourself, 'I lived through this horror; I can take the next thing that comes along.' You must do the thing you think you cannot do."

Eleanor Roosevelt

From the descriptive nature of ancient Chinese etymology to the various situations each of us have faced in our own lives, the intricate yin and yang dance that a crisis situation poses is both a challenge and an opportunity for growth. Most of us can recall a time when a difficult circumstance or a series of unfortunate experiences that occurred within a short period of time made us feel out of place or confused in our surroundings. The death of a friend or relative, a violent crime occurring in our neighborhood, or a change in the status of an important relationship are but a few brief illustrations of unplanned events that can tax our inner resources and detract from our usual abilities to navigate curves on the road of life. Usually, this sense of being off-kilter, the overwhelming feeling that we "just can't handle any more," is short-lived. The good news, according to Chung, Labouvie, Langenbucher, Moos, and Pandina (2001), is that managing crises successfully can actually improve the quality of one's life.

Most of us can remember adversities that generated a great deal of personal stress and required major adjustments in our thinking, but we can often point to these critical moments in our lives as times when we maximized our mayhem and resolved a situation in a growth-producing manner. For example, starting college can be viewed as a crisis situation. Transitioning into an academic institution frequently requires difficult tasks, such as moving to a new area and adjusting to one or more roommates, experiencing a dip in role status in the move from "accomplished high school student" to "novice freshman," and adjusting to increased academic demands. Most college students seriously consider withdrawing from school at some point during their first six weeks (Jewler & Gardner, 1987). Although the environmental shift may be difficult, most students manage to adapt to their new surroundings, and ultimately they resolve their crisis by experiencing tremendous intellectual and personal growth.

Looking at the challenges in living we all face, including positive and negative situations like starting school or recovering from a serious accident, it is abundantly clear that crises are natural and expected parts of the life cycle. Indeed, prominent personality theorists, such as Erikson and Freud, characterized human development in terms of crisis or stage resolution. One choice (opportunity) will likely lead to developmental growth, and the other (danger) will likely lead to fixation and psychopathology. Turner and Avison (1992) described how the central propositions in crisis theory can be traced back to Erikson's work, with the mastery of certain predictable and pivotal events building competence toward the mastery of the next difficult stage. These turning points in our lives, the resolution of the dance suggested by the ideographic symbols of the ancient Chinese, form the foundation of crisis theory. The basic tenets of this body of literature help to mold the theoretical underpinnings of community psychology, which is one of the disciplines guiding the activities of community mental health professionals. Rather than focusing on treating those already affected by crisis, professionals can instead work to prepare individuals for upcoming crises and to bolster resiliency and coping ability. It should not be forgotten that community psychology itself was borne as a direct result of what clinical psychologists perceived as a crisis in results-oriented human service delivery within their own profession.

This chapter focuses on the historical context and theoretical basis for crisis intervention, and the ways one can help himself/herself to cope with stress and crisis.

Several professional brief treatment approaches are presented, and current research on the efficacy of such treatments and interventions are also described.

Historical Developments in Crisis Intervention

The introductory chapters of this book have detailed the historical contexts from which community mental health emerged. Prior to World War II, problems in living were conceptualized through the looking glass of diagnosable mental illness. Individuals were viewed as having neurotic, unresolved (and often unconscious) issues that could be managed only through either custodial care in a mental institution or, for those with the means and necessary supports, lengthy psychoanalysis. As mentioned earlier, military psychology clearly demonstrated the traumatic reactions of ordinary people experiencing extraordinary circumstances and the way that brief, well-timed interventions could return individuals back to their prior level of functioning. This groundbreaking model of "situation blaming" versus "person blaming" meant individuals were beginning to be viewed within a context and that interventions were starting to develop on the basis of "here and now." This change helped lay the critical foundation for scientific research on crisis theory.

Erich Lindemann is in many ways considered the father of this area of community mental health, mainly for his landmark study of natural reactions to unnatural disasters (Hoff, 1984; Levine & Perkins, 1987). Lindemann (1944) published an article on the grief reactions of 101 subjects who experienced the unexpected death of a close relative. Among the persons in his study were bereaved disaster victims from the Coconut Grove Melody Lounge fire (a nightclub in Boston, Massachusetts, where 492 people were killed), members of their immediate families, and the relatives of soldiers who died during military service in World War II.

Lindemann found the outcome of such a serious and an unexpected life occurrence, whether or not the persons involved were in "danger" of succumbing to psychopathology or had the "opportunity" to move on as stronger individuals, depended upon the success with which the person completed what he called "grief work." This concept of grief work is characterized as a series of important stages of activity the bereaved individual must pass through, including letting go of the lost relationship; managing the accompanying feelings of guilt, anger, and sadness; and paving the way for the formation of new attachments (Golan, 1978).

Stages of Crisis and Crisis Resolution

Moos and Schaefer (Balk, 1996) proposed that the resolution of coping with any life crisis involves six considerations.

These considerations are as follows:

1. Background and personal factors
   - gender, race, religious beliefs, age, and intelligence;
   - temperament, personal development, self concept, and previous experience with this type of crisis.

2. Event-related factors
   ■ anticipation of and preparation for the crisis
   ■ personal responsibility for the crisis
3. Physical and Social environmental factors
   ■ supportive family and social networks, availability of mental health care services, and sympathetic work and/or school environment
4. Cognitive appraisal
   ■ how one perceives or interprets the crisis
5. Coping skills
   ■ The strategies one employs in dealing with crisis
6. Adaptive tasks
   ■ The challenges associated with adjusting to crisis.

In order to successfully emerge from crisis, Moos and Schaefer found that individuals must complete the following five adaptive tasks (Balk, 1996, p. 373):

1. Establish the meaning of the event and comprehend its personal significance;
2. Confront reality and respond to the situational requirements of the event;
3. Sustain interpersonal relationships;
4. Maintain emotional balance; and
5. Preserve a satisfactory self-image and maintain a sense of self-efficacy.

Similar to the predictable stages referenced by Golan (1978), Balk identifies coping skills as the means by which an individual carries out adaptive tasks. In turn, the completion of adaptive tasks further develops one's ability to cope and to build resilience (Bonanno et al., 2002).

The ability to manage crisis is particularly important for children and adolescents today, since increasing numbers of young people have to face one of the most traumatic facts of life: the death of a loved one. United States census data indicate death rates rise rapidly from early through middle and into late adolescence (Balk, 1996). In 2000, more than 40,000 adolescents died in the United States, and the majority of deaths were a result of accidents, homicides, and suicides (U.S. Bureau of the Census, 2000). Given the number of adolescents struggling through the bereavement process, it is likely that many are forced to cope without the support of psychological services.

Children are not the only population experiencing limited psychological services. The availability of services is one part of the problem. However, knowledge is another. The impact of stress, crisis, and other threats on the individual has been an area of study for only the past 25 years or so. Although war veterans as far back as the sixth century B.C. demonstrated what was once called shell shock or battle fatigue and now called post traumatic stress disorder (PTSD), the Vietnam War in particular produced large numbers of veterans returning home with symptoms that required psychological treatment (Dohrenwend, Neria, Turner, Turse Marshall, Lewis-Fernandez, and Koenen, 2004). In addition, rape trauma, child abuse, and battered wife syndrome

http://www.september11news.com/AttackImages.htm

have generated more inquiry about the effects of trauma. More recently, the terrorist attack of September 11, 2001, illustrated the traumatization of a whole nation.

Lindemann recognized that given the number of problems in living, psychiatric services would not be available for all who experience the crisis of bereavement. He suggested that training in grief work should be given to auxiliary workers, such as paraprofessionals and ministers, in order to expand the possible number of caregivers. His seminal research provided a foundation for the later investigation of crisis intervention, psychological support services for victims of disasters, and grief and loss counseling.

Although Lindemann is recognized as the initiator of crisis theory, Hans Selye is in some sense the originator of not only the biopsychology of stress but also its relationship to the person-environment fit. Ignoring the chiding of his medical colleagues, Selye made the bold move to shift the focus of his scientific investigations from ovarian endocrinology to a new body of research. This new focus would ultimately employ empirical techniques to clearly demonstrate physiological manifestations of psychosocial stress. One of the first individuals to recognize the chemical intricacies of the mind-body connection, Selye described the General Adaptation Syndrome (GAS).

http://columbine.free2host.net/victim/surviving.html

General Adaptation Syndrome (GAS)

According to Selye, stress physiology occurs in three distinct stages: the alarm reaction, which is a short, nonsustainable chemical burst; resistance, which is the body's protective line of defense against the chemical attack caused by the alarm reaction; and finally (if the stress is not alleviated), exhaustion, which is a total physiological depletion that at its most extreme may result even in the death of the organism. The GAS can be compared with the experience of exercising on a treadmill. The first few minutes are awkward and difficult (alarm reaction); then there is a general adaptation to the constant speed of the machine and the stride necessary to meet its demands (resistance); and finally, the realization that the activity must be stopped, for even one more step would be physically impossible (exhaustion).

Selye studied physiological changes in stress responses across a wide variety of occupations and many interesting and uniquely diverse environmental conditions, such as overcrowding, social and cultural differences, simple daily hassles, and far-reaching ecological conditions including meteorological changes (Selye, 1976). Through these studies, he demonstrated that individual perceptions of the environment can have a significant physiological consequence. Selye was able to replicate his findings across many populations and thus concluded that humans meet all perceived forms of psychological stress with the same adaptive defense mechanisms (GAS). He further determined this mechanism can be studied in specific physical and chemical terms, including through the changes in the structure of certain organs and the production of certain hormones. He believed, in light of these findings, that people could be taught to combat disease by bolstering the body's defenses against stress (Selye, 1976). Just as "marriage" and "the holiday season" appear on ratings scales as indicators of psychological stress (Holmes & Rahe, 1967, 1997), Selye recognized any situation requiring an individual to undergo a process of readaptation would produce the GAS response (Selye, 1974). Therefore, working to improve the individual's ability to mitigate that response could promote increased mental and physical health.

Timing of Intervention

Lindemann's model of grief work is a form of tertiary prevention for persons who are already experiencing the crisis of bereavement. Selye's GAS construct stems directly from the medical model, in that it identifies the physiological by-products of stress. In later works, Selye made some attempts to suggest coping mechanisms that might reduce the intrapsychic turmoil and physiological toxicity of the GAS (Selye, 1976). Although these theorists laid a critical foundation for understanding the impacts and potential mediations for crises, it should be noted that both models work from a clinical rather than a community viewpoint. Their constructs posit mechanisms for managing stress reactions only after they have already occurred.

As mentioned in Chapter 1, Dohrenwend (1978) took the most practical approach to crisis theory. In similarity to Erikson's developmental stage theory, she noted persons experiencing a crisis can either grow to a new level of competency on the basis of successful resolution of the conflict, regress into a self-perpetuated pattern of psychopathology, or return to their previous level of functioning once the stressful situation has passed. Perhaps the beauty of this particular theory is in its practical simplicity. The resolution of any situation implies that things will get better, get worse, or remain the same. In labeling these obvious components, Dohrenwend helped turn our attention toward predicting which intervention points can result in the most positive of the three possible outcomes.

Dohrenwend recognized that most strategies for working with crisis situations were indicated or at best selected forms of psychopathology prevention. Realizing that two out of the three potential outcomes to crisis situations were not harmful to the individual and that psychological services were focusing on only one outcome, it made sense that the timing of the intervention could make a significant difference in outcome. Interventions that aid individuals only after they have experienced significant problems in functioning are poorly timed. Dohrenwend posits that the best way to inoculate individuals against stress-induced psychopathology is to attend to crisis situations at the earliest possible entry point, moving prevention efforts as close to the primary level as possible. As a result, Dohrenwend developed a community-based model of the stress process to demonstrate that through political action support networks and education, crisis intervention could be offered to entire communities before undesirable events occurred, or at the very least before they were likely to result in lasting problems for the individual.

Kobasa's Approach to Crisis Intervention

Kobasa agreed with Dohrenwend's approach, recognizing that life events have a serious impact on the individual and that this impact can impair physical health and psychological functioning. She also concurred that the best methods for navigating through situational stress involve either preventing crisis situations or using them as a catalyst for human development. Kobasa (1979, 1993) sought to determine the type of individuals that were most likely to leverage life stressors to their best advantage.

Through her landmark study of successful utility executives who experienced high levels of life stress and disproportionately low levels of illness, Kobasa identified a series of character traits that are common to individuals best able to weather difficult circumstances. Identified as "hardy personality types," these individuals exhibit a clear sense of direction; an internal locus of control; commitment to self and to a personal value system; and a special level of "vigorousness" rather than "vegitativeness," in viewing situations as challenging rather than problematic.

Perhaps what was most significant about Kobasa's research was the notion that successful psychological interventions could be achieved by focusing on personal competencies and replicating them, rather than targeting individuals on the basis of their weaknesses. Kobasa suggested the development of programs to cultivate these adaptive characteristics, or stress management skills. In this sense, she joined Dohrenwend in proposing the application of preventive, competency-increasing, community-oriented services. Individuals who do not exhibit these hardy traits and therefore find themselves in a state of disequilibrium can still maximize turning-point situations. These individuals can be taught the life skills needed to maximize these situations. Community mental health practitioners can put programs in place that teach problem solving and coping skills before crises occur. This preventive approach would render individuals better prepared to handle the inevitable realities of life.

Stress Management Stages

Perhaps the best approach to managing stress is to intervene during the early stages, in order to prevent it from reaching crisis level. According to Rahe and Arthur (1968), there are six stages through which stress passes toward illness:

1. *Perception of the situation.* The individual realizes the threat of a stressor.
2. *Psychological responses.* The individual employs psychological defense mechanisms (repression, intellectualization, denial, reaction formation, rationalization, etc.) to reduce the level of stress.
3. *Physiological responses.* The "fight or flight" response is activated.
4. *Protective behavior.* The individual attempts to appropriately manage the situation.
5. *Signs of illness.* The individual develops physical symptoms in response to the stress.
6. *Frank disease.* A physician determines that the individual is in fact physically ill.

Rahe and Arthur (1968) stated that stress-related illness can be easily prevented if effective coping strategies are implemented during the first four stages. As the stress level moves into the fifth and final stage, the process is much more difficult to reverse.

Intervention strategies appear to help prevent stress from developing into chronic conditions and may also help people function at an improved level afterward (Kaslow, 2004). The interaction between psychological and situational mediators is complex at best. However, some general skills appear to be important. First, people can be taught how to develop a personal philosophy of life when they are confronted with stressful situations. They can also be taught to change cognitive perceptions and to view problems as challenges rather than threats. Community approaches can foster social skills such that individuals have strong networks in place when they are needed. Also, nurturing self-esteem, a sense of perceived control, and beliefs in one's ability to problem solve will all help an individual to function more effectively during a crisis. Finally, teaching people which particular coping skills to use in various situations as well as encouraging the development of personal coping styles goes a long way in preparing them to deal with adversity. By teaching these skills to the public in schools and programs to the public, or by making them goals in therapy, psychologists can not only intervene in crisis but also prevent problems and improve psychological health.

Crisis Theory

The actual operationalization of what constitutes a crisis situation is somewhat subjective. Allowing for personal differences in coping styles, it is fair to say that any situation or combination of life occurrences that tax an individual beyond his or her typical ability to function can be viewed as a crisis (Levine & Perkins, 1996). Levine and Perkins (1987) explain "crisis" as a time when "a person enters a state of crisis because attachments are threatened and he or she lacks the immediate resources to respond adaptively" (p. 174).

TABLE 5.1   Social Readjustment Rating Scale

Item	Life Change Units	Check Changes in the Past Year
1. Marriage	50	_____
2. Trouble with boss	23	_____
3. Detention in jail or other institution	63	_____
4. Death of spouse	100	_____
5. Major change in sleeping habits	16	_____
6. Death of a close family member	63	_____
7. Major change in eating habits	15	_____
8. Foreclosure of mortgage or loan	30	_____
9. Revision of personal habits	24	_____
10. Death of close friend	37	_____

Item	Life Change Units	Check Changes in the Past Year
11. Minor violations of the law	11	_____
12. Outstanding personal achievement	28	_____
13. Pregnancy	40	_____
14. Minor change in health or behavior of family member	44	_____
15. Sexual difficulties	39	_____
16. In-law troubles	29	_____
17. Change in family get-togethers	15	_____
18. Change in financial state	38	_____
19. New family member	39	_____
20. Change in address or residence	20	_____
21. Son or daughter leaving home	29	_____
22. Marital separation	65	_____
23. Change in church activities	19	_____
24. Marital reconciliation	45	_____
25. Being fired	47	_____
26. Divorcing	73	_____
27. Changing line of work	36	_____
28. Change in arguments with spouse	35	_____
29. Change in responsibilities at work	29	_____
30. Beginning or ceasing work	26	_____
31. Change in working hours or conditions	20	_____
32. Change in recreation	19	_____
33. Taking mortgage greater than $10,000	31	_____
34. Taking loan less than $10,000	17	_____
35. Major personal injury or illness	53	_____
36. Major business readjustment	39	_____
37. Change in social activities	18	_____
38. Change in living conditions	25	_____
39. Retirement	45	_____
40. Vacation	13	_____
41. Changing schools	20	_____
42. Beginning or ceasing formal schooling	26	_____

Source: Holmes & Rahe, 1967.

A score of 0–149 describes no life crisis, 150–199 describes a mild life crisis, 200–299 describes a moderate life crisis, and 300 or more describes a major life crisis.

Compare your score to these categories. If your score is high, are there ways in which you could reduce the adaptational requirements of your life pattern? Are there anticipated changes you could postpone to prevent your score from rising further?

If all of the members of your class complete this scale, it may be informative to calculate an average score and the range of scores. It may also be interesting to have each student (anonymously, of course) indicate whether he or she has experienced some major illness in the past year. Are those students with high life change scores more likely to report a recent illness? What other factors might account for differences in results reported by the students?

Lazarus (1991, 1998) pointed out it is not the externally perceived stressfulness of a situation that causes a state of disequilibrium, but rather the manner in which persons internally appraise events that dictates whether or not they can muster the internal resources to manage them. Although some individuals react to a hangnail the way others react to a house fire, both occurrences are valid crisis situations if they present challenges that are above and beyond the emotional and/or cognitive resources of the particular person at a particular moment.

Having made some individual and contextual allowances for what constitutes a crisis situation, we can turn to Golan (1978, pp. 7–9), who consolidates the theories postulated by Lindemann, Caplan, and other experts in the field to offer ten key points that embody this important paradigm for understanding and assisting with problems in living:

1. Crises occur throughout the normal life span of individuals and groupings of individuals. They are usually initiated by a hazardous or an unexpected event, or a series of smaller issues that, when taken together, form a cumulative stressful circumstance. For example; the loss of a job followed closely by a move to a less expensive home in a new neighborhood can be conceived of as a crisis in some circumstances.

2. The impact of a crisis makes those who experience it feel off balance, placing afflicted persons in a state of vulnerability. The strong desire to return to a more even keel forces the vulnerable parties to pass through a series of predictable stages. At first, there is an attempt to utilize familiar coping mechanisms to deal with the extraordinary circumstances. When the usual or more familiar defenses do not work, stress levels increase, and individuals will struggle even more intensely to relieve their feelings of discomfort.

3. If the problem cannot be resolved through these techniques, tension climbs to an acute level, and the individual experiences a loss of control and a state of disequilibrium and disorganization, known as the active crisis state.

4. As the crisis builds toward the active state, individuals view the event as a distinct threat to their well-being or as a challenge to survival, development, and achievement.

5. Each aspect of the crisis seems to have corresponding emotions that the individual will likely experience. For example, the individual's perception of feeling threatened typically manifests itself in feelings of increased anxiety, while the challenge aspect of the crisis stimulates a combination of anxiety mixed with hope and expectations. People react to a crisis in different ways and at varying levels of intensity, on the basis of their own subjective interpretation of the experience.

6. Crises in and of themselves are not pathological situations. They reflect the normal struggles of an individual in the face of difficult circumstances. Sometimes however, crisis situations unearth earlier, unresolved issues, which can make the afflicted respond in an exaggerated fashion. For example, the unexpected death of a household pet may force the owner to confront unresolved feelings surrounding the earlier loss of a grandparent.

7. As mentioned before, most crises can be categorized as following a particular and predictable pattern of stages and responses. Determining where the individual has become "stuck," or where the working-through process has failed, can provide important clues in helping the person master the present situation.

8. The duration of the active phase of the crisis situation usually lasts between four and six weeks.

9. Having experienced the inadequacy of their usual defenses in meeting the current challenges, those who are in a crisis state tend to be particularly amenable to assistance from others. Brief interventions can have more dramatic results than more extensive therapies might if the person was not experiencing an intense crisis. Drawing from a medical example, a patient may be more likely to heed a doctor's warning to cut back on cholesterol intake following a mild heart attack.

10. Individuals who successfully mobilize new resources to master a crisis will typically retain and integrate their newfound coping mechanisms, moving to a higher level of personal hardiness. Those who do not receive the necessary assistance during this pivotal period may develop maladaptive patterns of coping that can result in an inability to address future stressful situations. In other words, the agoraphobic who successfully uses systematic desensitization or other anxiety-reducing techniques to complete a shopping trip to the mall is likely to venture out on another day, whereas the person who has an anxiety attack in the parking lot and immediately drives home may in the future avoid the mall entirely.

Crisis Intervention Designed by Community Mental Health Practitioners

Golan's (1978) ten principles successfully frame the body of literature that defines crisis theory, offering the most important strategies to bear in mind as we design relevant, timely, and context-specific interventions.

Adaptation and Support

As Golan's (1978) review of the research on crisis theory mentioned, individuals in a crisis state tend to be particularly amenable to assistance from others. Who should provide assistance in a crisis situation? How can we make sure that help is provided in those early, critical moments when the person is most likely to derive lasting benefits? What helps the individual to manage life stress without experiencing a pathological outcome? Early intervention is perhaps the best predictor of a successful resolution of a stressful or crisis situation. However, many individuals are unaware of the crisis intervention services available in their area. For example, the United Way Agency has branches in communities throughout the United States, and many have a 24-hour information and referral service called Infoline. Persons in crisis or in need of support services can call Infoline and be directed to programs appropriate for their needs.

Even though crisis is sometimes inevitable, having the ability to manage stress is an effective strategy to prevent stress from becoming a crisis. There is evidence to suggest that people can reduce their vulnerability to life stress by utilizing social supports and by developing the types of coping skills that Kobasa mentioned as being intrinsic to some individuals (Levine & Perkins, 1987, 1996).

Anna Freud's construct of defense mechanisms (1966) provides one venue for looking at adaptation and coping. Valliant (1977) divided the classical defense mechanisms into a four-tiered hierarchy of adaptation and coping, demonstrating how certain ego-preserving mechanisms can either facilitate or obstruct the individual's ability to manage psychosocial stressors. That hierarchy is as follows:

For Valliant, it was not so much the availability of social supports and interventions that assist the individual in a crisis situation; rather, it is the individual's intrinsic ability to internalize those supports and opt for the more productive coping mechanisms available on his or her unconscious palettes. Community mental health practitioners, on the other hand, believe these coping skills can be nurtured and that the family provides members with their first experiences in accepting these supports and forming more mature and productive strategies for managing stressful life events.

Caplan (1976) posited the notion that the "ideal family" scenario (elaborated upon in the following chapter) provides the most powerful example of the supports necessary to turn a crisis situation into a developmental experience. He noted that families serve the function of collecting and disseminating important information about the world, perhaps even helping individuals choose appropriate defense mechanisms to employ when mitigating stressful situations. Ideal families also provide feedback and advisement, which can help shape an individual's beliefs, values, behaviors, and level of personal empowerment. Family members help each other to problem solve, and often they provide material necessities that might lend crucial relief in a crisis situation, for example, a place to stay after a home fire. As Robert Frost so eloquently stated, "home is where they have to take you in." Family members also assist each other with emotional mastery (Tugade & Fredrickson, 2004) and the development of components that comprise personal identity. One component related to coping is the concept of resilience: the ability to withstand and rebound from crisis and adversity. However, Walsh (1996) suggests that because resilience involves organizational patterns, communication and problem solving processes, community resources, and affirming belief systems, it may be less genetic and more learned. She acknowledges that resilience may be an interaction between nature and nurture, but that the family should be considered a potential source of resilience. For example, Riolli, Savicki, and Cepani (2002) found that survivors of the Kosovo crisis in 1999 who possessed higher levels of optimism,

TABLE 5.2

Level I	Projective Defenses (i.e., distortion and denial)
Level II	Immature Defenses (such as fantasizing and acting out)
Level III	Neurotic Defenses (repression and displacement, for example)
Level IV	Mature Defenses (characterized by altruism, humor, sublimation. etc.)

extroversion, openness to experience, conscientiousness, and control coping paired with lower neuroticism showed fewer signs of maladjustment than those with reduced optimism and reduced control coping. Riolli et al. believe that such resilience, whether genetically acquired or learned, may decrease the effects of stressful events and may lead to a more healthful adjustment to crisis.

In the work *Broaden and Build Theory*, Fredrickson (2001) holds that positive emotions foster personal resources needed to effectively manage crises. These personal resources include physical resources (physical skills, health, longevity), social resources (friendships, social support networks), intellectual resources (knowledge, abstract thinking ability), and psychological resources (resilience, creativity, optimism). Fredrickson, Tugade, Waugh, and Larkin (2003) indicate that crisis and the resultant depression are best arrested by trait resilience, which is characterized by positive emotions. They found that persons who scored high on trait resilience also had low levels of neuroticism, high levels of extraversion, and high levels of openness, which result in a generally positive affect. Although these psychologists report such resilience is likely to benefit an individual in crisis, it is also likely to contribute to overall quality of life in the absence of crisis.

In a study of college students conducted by Fredrickson et al. (2001) after the September 11 attack on New York City, findings indicated a negative correlation between depressive symptoms and resilience. Not only did those with higher resilience suffer fewer psychological difficulties after the terrorist attack, but they even reported more frequent experiences of gratitude, love, and appreciation of others. It seems that resilience not only results from experiencing crisis but also protects individuals from extreme psychological symptoms after a crisis.

It is important to remember that problems in living dictate that all individuals must learn to manage stressful situations in an effective manner. Our emotional and physical health is affected by the manner in which we appraise and deal with our daily trials and tribulations. Community mental health practitioners have the unique opportunity to design primary prevention programs that lessen overall problems in living, while empowering individuals and designing networks of support to help transform turning point situations into human triumphs.

Coping and Self-Help

The ability to lessen overall problems in living is often a result of the extent to which one is able to cope with stress. Since both eustress (excitement, anticipation, or positive stress) and distress are unavoidable, the following section provides various life skills that can enable an individual to become better able to cope with stressful situations and problems in living. The skills discussed are useful to the reader, both in managing personal stress and in designing community prevention interventions to help others cope more successfully.

> I feel determined to strive to use whatever power I have to change the unpleasant stresses of life that I can change, to dislike but realistically accept those I cannot change, and to have the wisdom to know the difference between the two. (Albert Ellis, 1979)

In the preceding words of Ellis, there are two types of stressful situations in life; those that can be changed and those that cannot be changed. In this section, coping strategies that help us to change stressful situations are examined, as well as methods for reducing the effects of unchangeable stressful situations.

Cognitive

As discussed previously, an individual's interpretation or cognitive appraisal of an event is often the determining factor in whether or not it is perceived as stressful. For example, a student may view a final examination as an obstacle he is unlikely to overcome successfully, the result being a failing grade. On the other hand, he may see the same exam as an opportunity to demonstrate to the professor the knowledge that he has acquired in the course. In the first case, he is likely to become anxious, and thus taking the test will be quite stressful. In the second case, he is likely to be excited rather than anxious, and instead of being distressed, he'll experience eustress. Clearly, the final exam occurs in both cases, but the appraisal of the event determines the emotional response.

Perhaps then the first step toward effective coping is to be aware of the subjective interpretation of stressful situations. As Ellis (1969, 2003) stated, people for the most part disturb themselves. If stress or anxiety is related to one's thoughts, then positive thinking will reduce stress. Using the example of the student who fears taking an exam, the following steps would allow him to change his response to the test:

1. *Evaluate self-talk (statements an individual tells himself/herself about the event or about himself/herself), and analyze distorted thinking.* The student is probably telling himself this:

   I'm a lousy student.
   That professor gives unfair tests.
   My parents will be so mad when I fail.
   There's no point in studying because I'm going to fail anyway.

2. *Challenge negative thinking.* For example, the student could dispute his negative self-statements by telling himself this:

   Maybe I'm not a straight-A student, but that doesn't mean I'm an awful person.
   I know this professor gives hard tests, so I'll set aside extra study time to prepare for them.
   Even if I do poorly and my parents are disappointed, it won't be the end of the world.

3. *Exchange negative with positive self-statements.* For example, the student could use statements such as these:

   I've done well in the past on other exams.
   Because I know this will be a difficult exam, I'll prepare myself as well as I can so that I'll be confident about doing well.
   My parents will be pleased when my GPA is higher this semester.

As Epictetus (A.D. c. 55–135) taught us long ago, people are disturbed not by things themselves, but by the views they take of these things. Very often we cause ourselves stress through distortions in thinking. Following is a list of common distortions and definitions outlined by O'Keefe and Berger (1993), and a psychotherapeutic intervention. Rational Emotive Behavior Therapy is used to treat such distortions and is presented in the brief therapeutic interventions section of this chapter.

1. *Filtering*. Focusing on the negative aspects of a situation and ignoring the positive aspects.

    Example: I would really enjoy going away to college, but the exams make the whole experience horrible.

2. *Polarized Thinking*. People or things are viewed as all good or all bad. Situations are seen as all or none, black or white. There is no gray area or middle ground.

    Example: If you truly loved me, you would love even my negative qualities.

3. *Overgeneralizing*. Conclusions from a single event are applied to all related events or situations.

    Example: I know that all my relationships with men will end in disaster because my boyfriend broke up with me.

4. *Catastrophizing*. Disappointments or problems are "snowballed" into major crises.

    Example: If I fail this exam, I will fail the course, get kicked out of college, and never get a job. I'll be forced to depend on others for financial support for the rest of my life.

5. *Shoulds*. You have a set of unchangeable beliefs about how life or people should or must be.

    Example: Life is supposed to be fair, so I should not have to be enduring this difficult situation.

As illustrated in these examples, negative thinking will produce anxiety or stress. Disappointments and unpleasant situations will occur in each of our lives, but the way one views or thinks about these situations will influence the level of stress one experiences in relation to them.

The importance of positive thinking cannot be overstated in the successful management of stress. Perhaps a case in point is the influence of religious beliefs on coping. According to McIntosh, Silver, and Wortman (1993), along with the social support provided by religious affiliation, religious belief systems may enable individuals to cope more effectively with crisis.

In a study of 257 parents who had lost an infant to SIDS (Sudden Infant Death Syndrome), parents who were part of a religious community handled their bereavement with less distress, and those with greater religious participation experienced less depression and loneliness (McIntosh et al., 1993). Although social support provided by the religious community was an important factor, the religious schemas about death were found to facilitate cognitive processing, resulting in lower levels of experienced stress. In addition, religious beliefs about the meaning of death were found to aid in the process of coping with bereavement. Parents with religious convictions were more likely to trust God (or their Creator) with the life of the lost child and to find meaning in what could be perceived as a senseless loss. Such perception aids in the transition from grief work to resuming daily living. Therefore, one cannot understate the importance of cognitive processes and beliefs in effective coping and the management of stress (Bonanno, Wortman, Lehman, Tweed, Haring, Sonnega, Carr, & Nesse, 2002).

Mental Preparation

Even though stress can be reduced by positive cognitive appraisals, there are times when stress is unavoidable, and the most successful coping strategy in this case is mental preparation. Mental preparation involves acknowledging the fear associated with an anticipated event and mentally rehearsing possible outcomes. Janis studied patients before and after surgery, and found that those who coped with the fear by working out solutions to whatever might result from the surgery recovered more successfully (Kasschau, 1995). He concluded that the more the patient was prepared for the possible outcomes, the less anxiety was experienced.

The fear of the unknown is often a major stressor in crisis situations. Mental preparation enables individuals to cope with such fear by acknowledging it and preparing for how they will deal with both the event and its consequences. Simply imagining oneself successfully coping with a particular crisis will lay the groundwork for developing an appropriate strategy. Before being able to overcome an obstacle, a person must first be able to picture himself or herself doing so (Ellis, 1969). Having an appropriate plan does not change the fact that the event will occur, but it allows individuals to be confident in their ability to manage it.

Reframing

In addition to positive thinking and mental preparation, reframing a negative situation allows an individual to handle it more easily. Reframing involves focusing on any positive outcomes of a crisis. As discussed earlier in this chapter, reframing is a way to go about viewing a crisis as an opportunity rather than a disaster.

In the previous example of the student who feared taking the final exam, the situation could be reframed as an opportunity to develop better study skills and time-management skills. By placing a "positive spin" on a negative event, an individual will not only reduce anxiety but will also develop better personal skills and self-confidence relating to the ability to cope with academic challenges.

Most, if not all, crises have at least some positive outcomes. By reframing an event as something that has beneficial aspects, it will become less frightening. If nothing else, the event can be reframed as a learning experience by which one can expand his or her repertoire of coping techniques. The more coping strategies an individual has used successfully, the more resources the person will have available to draw upon in order to handle future crises.

Social Skills Training

Stress is often a result of difficulty with interpersonal relationships. Poor communication skills and an inability to behave assertively can cause individuals to be misunderstood by others. One of the best methods for overcoming these tendencies is to learn to interact more appropriately, by developing better social skills. In addition to reducing stress, this ability will increase self-confidence, decrease interpersonal conflict, and provide the tools for social support networking (Longo & Bisconer, 2003). An added bonus to having good interpersonal skills is that they are valued in the workplace and are viewed favorably by prospective employers. Those who are successful in leadership positions invariably possess well-developed social skills, including listening and communication skills.

Relaxation

Relaxation, it is well known, is incompatible with stress; one cannot be tense and relaxed at the same time. Therefore, methods for relaxation can be used to counteract anxiety and manage stress. By "turning on" a relaxed state, an individual can "turn off" negative sensations and emotions (O'Keefe & Berger, 1999). Relaxation is most effective when done systematically and practiced regularly.

In a quantitative review of recent studies that evaluated the effects of abbreviated progressive muscle relaxation training (APRT) as a treatment for psychophysiological and stress-related disorders, Carlson and Hoyle (1993) found that APRT is an effective treatment for a variety of disorders. The use of progressive relaxation resulted in a decrease in the signs and symptoms of clinical disorders. Among the most effective means of achieving a relaxed state is through the use of audiotapes. (Carlson & Hoyle, 1993).

Following are two methods for achieving a relaxed state, as described by Davis, Eshelman, and McKay (1988).

Deep Breathing Relaxation
1. Sit or stand up straight.
2. Inhale and exhale through the nose.
3. Fill the lower portion of the lungs while inhaling by pushing the abdomen outward and allowing the chest to move slightly forward. Then, fill the upper part of the lungs by raising the chest and pulling in the abdomen a bit.
4. Hold your breath for a few seconds.
5. Exhale slowly, and pull in the abdomen a bit more.

Progressive Relaxation
1. Clench both fists, tightening the forearms and biceps in a sort of "muscleman" pose. Hold for five seconds. Then, release the tension, and relax the muscles for twenty seconds. Repeat this procedure two times.
2. Close your eyes tightly. Wrinkle the forehead. Press your head as far back as possible, rotate it clockwise, and then counterclockwise once. Relax. Repeat two times.
3. Arch the back and shoulders, take a deep breath, and hold it for five seconds. Exhale, and let the back and shoulders slump forward. Repeat two times.
4. While seated, straighten and lift the legs. Bend the toes toward your face, and tighten the thighs and buttocks. Hold this position for five seconds, and then release the tension, and place the feet back on the floor. Repeat two times.

Meditation

Another method for achieving a relaxed state is through meditation (Seeman, Dubin, & Seeman, 2003). According to Janowiak and Hackman (1994), meditation training has been used successfully by clinicians to enable college students to control stress, anxiety, depression, and somatic distress associated with the rigors of educational requirements.

Meditation involves practices and techniques designed to train attention and bring various mental processes under greater voluntary control. Much like Maslow's (1971) concept of self-actualization, meditation is intended to foster higher states of personal integration, whereby the individual has a clear and an accurate perception of self. This realistic perception enables the individual to more fully actualize his/her potential, develop talents, and live more purposefully.

Maslow and Eastern philosophers have provided constructs for personal development, but those same constructs involve applying relaxation techniques, which decrease stress and increase systematic relaxed behavior (Janowiak & Hackman, 1994).

Support Groups

Social support and shared experience play a tremendous role in reducing stress. Chapter 6 deals with the effectiveness of a social network in more depth, but the coping strategy deserves mention here as well. Stressful situations are exacerbated when an individual feels isolated and alone in attempting to deal with a crisis. A support group allows the individual to recognize that she or he is not alone, that others share similar circumstances, and that there are people who understand the pain because "they've been there." The support group also provides an arena for sharing coping strategies, which benefits all members. In addition, each individual is empowered by the process of helping others by sharing his or her own experience.

Winkel and Vrij (1993), Schwartzberg (1993), Zeidner and Hammer (1992), Blatter and Jacobson (1993), and Bonanno, Wortman, and Nesse (2004) all concluded that people use both problem- and emotion-focused responses to help them cope. Support groups provide the opportunity for members to explore and experience both responses. Some people may need to come to terms with a crisis emotionally before they are also able to assess the situation and take action. There are two main problems within a crisis: managing internal emotions like anxiety and anger, and taking appropriate steps to resolve the crisis. Support groups offer a continuum of care over the crisis stages.

Training

Along with mental preparation as discussed before, behavioral approaches are also effective in coping with stress. For example, if a pregnant woman learns that her child will be born physically handicapped, she will surely become distressed. Enrolling in a class on how to address the special needs of handicapped children will enable her to be more prepared to deal with the situation.

Stress in the Workplace

Stress was once considered "just part of the job." However, it is recently getting more attention as a costly workplace hazard. Studies on the health dangers of stress and employers' liability have many employers scrambling for preventive approaches. Paul Rosch (1994), president of the American Institute of Stress, warns that employers are being increasingly held responsible for job stress and must "do something." The American Institute of Stress and the American Psychological Association have estimated that employee turnover, unscheduled absenteeism, and declining morale all impact the bottom line. Problems related to stress cost companies an estimated $200 billion or more annually (United Nations International Labor Organization, 1993).

Although stress is part of many jobs, specific jobs routinely expose individuals to stress and trauma. For example, public safety and emergency responders, including law-enforcement officers, hospital emergency personnel, and other emergency workers often suffer from vicarious traumatization or compassion fatigue (Kinzel & Nanson, 2000).

Tips on How to Beat Job Stress
- Be sure that job responsibilities are clearly spelled out and that your role is clearly defined.
- Find a job that fits your skills and abilities, and that you enjoy.
- Use labor or employee organizations to help improve the working environment.
- Utilize time-management skills and stress-management techniques.
- Believe in your role in making the organization successful.
- Exercise and eat properly.

Job pressures vary, and some of the most high-stress occupations include these:

- Secretaries
- Waitresses
- Medical Interns
- Middle Managers
- Police Officers
- Editors

Books, videos, and other educational materials are available to provide training in a wide variety of issues. Direct experience is another way to prepare. Examples of this could be volunteering at a local nursing home in preparation for becoming the caretaker of an ailing parent, or taking a public-speaking course, if giving oral presentations causes anxiety. Practicing the stressful situation allows the individual to become familiar with it in such a way that it is no longer as foreign or anxiety provoking. The benefits of training are twofold. First, exposure to the stressor in a relatively sage environment enables the individual to gain skills and experience; and second, it promotes confidence in one's coping ability (Kasschau, 1995). The effectiveness of stress management and of coping-skills-training workshops is discussed further in the chapter on prevention.

Attending to Physical Health

Stress has both emotional and physical components, which interact and influence each other. When an individual is physically exhausted, his or her ability to manage emotional distress may be compromised. For this reason, people often tell each other to "sleep on it, things will look better in the morning." When one is in crisis, the emotional strain can take a toll on the body.

In terms of prevention, maintaining physical health (daily exercise, proper nutrition, and adequate sleep) places the individual in a better position to adjust and adapt to stress. Since mind and body are interactive, physical health influences "frame of mind." A fatigued or hungry individual is generally more irritable and anxious.

Coping with anxiety can be achieved through physical methods other than relaxation. For example, exercise can reduce negative emotions, since physical exertion releases mood-elevating hormones (O'Keefe & Berger, 1999). Exercise allows an individual to "work it off" and become relaxed as a result.

Avoidance

In certain cases—those that inevitably cause stress and become crisis situations—the best strategy may be avoidance. Certainly, avoidance should be used as a last resort and not as a way of life. However, there are some situations that cannot (or perhaps should not) be managed by other techniques. For example, association with a person who is abusive and who refuses to change is most effectively coped with by severing the relationship with that person. Whenever a stressful situation can be avoided without compromising personal growth, doing so becomes the appropriate strategy.

As mentioned, there are stresses in life that can be changed simply by changing the way we perceive them, yet there are also situations that are inherently stressful and must be adapted to. As Ellis's remark quoted earlier in the chapter suggests, perhaps the wisdom is in knowing the difference between the two situations. Life experience and personal development are the avenues through which we acquire such insight; and as we live, learn, and grow, the wisdom that comes from having done so will help us to know how and when to cope. More importantly, such wisdom will teach us that we truly can cope with whatever comes into our lives. Community mental health practitioners can teach these coping skills and perspectives that can go a long way in helping people adapt successfully to crises.

Professional Help: Brief Therapeutic Interventions

Brief psychotherapeutic intervention, or brief treatment (consisting of six or less sessions), was born of the evolution of the practice of psychology, the increased number of individuals seeking assistance, and the demands of a managed-care system's requirement for treatment options that were both effective and cost-efficient. According to Levenson and Davidovitz (2000), 89% of APA Clinical Psychology and Psychotherapy Divisions members spend half of their practice time using brief therapies, and yet half of those practicing reported taking no courses in brief therapy in graduate school. Further investigation by Levenson and Davidovitz (2000) found that only 60% of APA-approved graduate programs in psychology offer classes in brief treatment.

Because brief treatment is not merely a shortened version of longer-term treatment, appropriate training is necessary to generate efficient and effective therapeutic outcomes. The goals of treatment are the same as those for longer-term traditional therapies: to clarify perspective, to reduce psychological suffering, and to assist the individual in making positive changes in his or her life. Such personal growth should be promoted as rapidly and durably as possible (Lazarus, 1989). However, the presenting problems of today's clients may not be the same. Sperry and Carlson (1996) indicate that qualitatively and quantitatively, the disturbances of today's patients are more severe, raising the question of whether time-limited approaches are effective. A general overview and several brief treatment interventions will be presented next, followed by the results of their attendant effectiveness studies.

General Characteristics of Brief Treatment

According to Bitter and Nicoll (2000), five components characterize the systematic, integrative, comprehensive framework of brief treatment. These are time limitation, focus, counselor directiveness, and the assignment of behavioral tasks, or homework. These characteristics are not utilized equally in brief treatments; some approaches may focus more on one characteristic than on another, and individual therapists may favor one more highly than the others.

Arnold Lazarus (1989) also recognized the importance of therapists as a factor in therapeutic outcomes. Therapy is facilitated by therapists' flexibility, versatility, and knowledge about and application of performance-based methods. Their ability to recognize "what works best for whom and under which particular circumstances" (Lazarus, 1989, p. 5) is a critical factor in successfully treating individuals in a time-limited manner.

Multimodal Therapy (MMT)

Established by Arnold Lazarus in 1971, Multimodal Therapy (MMT) evolved from the notion that cognitive behavioral therapy (which targets both cognitive and behavioral problems) would be enhanced by a *broad spectrum* approach that expanded the modalities of human experience to include affect, sensation, imagery, interpersonal relationships, and physiological influences. Lazarus developed the "BASIC ID" framework (Behavior, Affect, Sensation, Imagery, Cognition, Interpersonal Relationships, and D to account for drugs taken or biological functions) for assessment and treatment. "By assessing each individual through each of these specific modalities, and then examining the salient interactions among them, one is better able to achieve a thorough and holistic understanding of the person and his social environment," wrote Lazarus (1989, p. 13).

MMT is based on the belief that problems in living have elements in each of the modalities, and that to reduce psychological suffering rapidly and durably the clinician must assess and treat the multifaceted nature of problems. For example, a graduate student who is overwhelmed by the demands of her education may have procrastination or time-management issues (B), may experience anxiety (A) that leads to butterflies in her stomach (S), may imagine herself becoming homeless because she fails out of school and cannot get a job (I), and may think she cannot meet the demands of the program or may believe she is inadequate (C). She may also experience difficulties in her relationships with others because her mood is poor and she is cranky (I), and she may have difficulty sleeping as a result of the distress (D).

To treat our graduate student comprehensively, MMT would involve first addressing the modality that seemed to trigger the chain of experiences. For example, an MMT therapist is likely to challenge the client's belief about her inadequacy but would also help her to reduce procrastination and manage her time more effectively to enable the student to be more successful academically. This method would provide evidence that she can, in fact, manage the work. The change in her thinking would in turn eliminate the anxiety and attendant sensations. Her more successful school experience would improve her mood, reducing conflict with others, and she would likely be able to sleep more peacefully. In addition, the images or mental pictures of being homeless would disappear as she renewed the belief in her ability to be academically and professionally successful.

For Lazarus, the systematic nature of assessment followed by the comprehensive approach to treatment (considering each modality individually and then treating the interactions) leads to sustained change. The MMT approach also generates self-awareness, so the client is better able to recognize the chain (called a firing order) that results in problems. MMT proposes that individuals have typical patterns of behavior that are fairly consistent over time. An example of a typical pattern or firing order is C—A—B, which means that particular irrational thoughts or beliefs trigger negative affect (feelings) and result in maladaptive behavior. If the individual is able to change his/her cognition (the trigger) to more effective thinking, he/she can interrupt the firing order. However, sometimes changing behavior is the most efficient means of changing one's thoughts. For example, if one believes that she is an inadequate student, her therapist may suggest that she act as if she were a good student (go to class regularly, complete assignments on time, study seriously, etc.), and to simply "fake it 'til she makes it." If she behaves (B) as if she is a good student, she will earn good grades, and such success should change her beliefs about herself as a student (C).

Lazarus (1989) does not adhere to a particular theory of cure; instead, he considers what works best for whom and under what conditions. Therefore, MMT is not a specific "treatment," but rather an orientation or approach to treatment. Lazarus advises clinicians to base therapeutic intervention on empirical support for the effectiveness of a particular treatment for a specific type of patient. He calls this "therapeutic pluralism," and indicates that the approach is technically eclectic because it uses interventions based on their effectiveness rather than any adherence to a particular school of thought or psychological theory. Simply stated, the MMT clinician is able to use a behavioral technique as well as a humanistic technique to help an individual, if each has been deemed effective in treating the type of problem from which the individual suffers.

Rational-Emotive Behavior Therapy (REBT)

Rational-Emotive Therapy (RET), founded by Albert Ellis in the mid-1950s, became (REBT) in 1999. It is based on the premise that negative emotion is a result of faulty thinking and erroneous beliefs. Ellis claims that "men disturb themselves" by choosing to interpret experience in rigid, absolutistic ways that support their irrational thinking. According to Ellis (1979), individuals can learn to be rational, self-preserving, authentic, and self-actualizing during childhood, or they can develop magical, faulty, nonempirically based, or irrational thinking. The factors that most often determine which mode of thinking is developed are parental influence and sociocultural institutions. Therefore, irrational belief systems are learned in early childhood, are reinforced by the individual's tendency to erroneously find "evidence" to support those beliefs, and are difficult to change even though they result in unhappiness and distress.

Ellis (1974, p. 329) also stated the following:

> [There is an] immense amount of evidence from historical, anthropological, religious, psychological, and biological sources that virtually all humans, individually and in groups, at all times and places have been exceptionally irrational and self-defeating in much of their behaviors and that, in all probability, they have inborn, as well as environmentally acquired, tendencies to behave this way.

On the other hand, Ellis (1979) claimed people have a tremendous propensity toward self-actualization and can, simply by choosing to do so, change their thinking to be more congruent with their ideal self. REBT is directed toward assisting individuals in changing their irrational beliefs to more self-actualizing thinking. Ellis developed a model of assessment (A, B, and C) and treatment (D and E) used in his Institute in New York City:

A	activating event
B	beliefs about activating event
C	consequences (positive or negative) of beliefs
D	dispute irrational belief
E	eliminate irrational belief and exchange with rational belief

Effective New Perspective

Similar to most therapeutic approaches, REBT involves building rapport with the client, problem identification (including clarifying the chief complaint or identifying the areas where the client is most distressed), and setting the goal of therapy. The goal of REBT is always to change irrational beliefs by assisting clients in realizing that these erroneous beliefs lead to maladaptive behavior and destructive emotions. Although the cognitive modality is prime, Ellis (1999) stresses the importance of attending to the affective or emotive and behavioral modalities as well.

Critical to the success of REBT is clients' recognition that not only are they responsible for their thoughts but also they alone sustain their disturbance by continuing to think irrationally (Capuzzi & Gross, 1995). The therapist disputes the client's irrational beliefs by demonstrating the lack of evidence for such beliefs. For example, a

A (activating event) = failing test grade

B (belief about failing grade)

= I'm a terrible student.
= I'm a disappointment to my family.
= I'm a loser.
= I'll never get a job.

C (consequences) = negative emotion (distress)

D (dispute) = show evidence to the contrary of irrational beliefs.

E (exchange irrational for rational beliefs)

= It is unlikely that everyone passes every test taken. Even good students like me can expect less than perfect performance sometimes. Besides, perfection itself is irrational.
= Even if my family IS disappointed in me, that doesn't make me a bad person or a loser.
= I WILL get a job because I will complete this program even though I may fail a test every once in a while.

graduate student may be extremely distressed because she failed a midterm exam. She may be telling herself, "I should have passed that test. I'm such a terrible student I'm going to fail out of grad school. My family will be so disappointed, and on top of it all, I'll never get a job. I'm such a loser." The therapist would then challenge the statements made: "How can you be a terrible student? You're in grad school. In order to be here, you must have passed more tests than you failed." The therapist would also explore the notion that the family's disappointment makes her a loser. In reality, disappointment on the part of others may be uncomfortable but does not automatically make one a loser. However, if an individual continues to believe he or she is a loser, that individual will likely feel depressed and behave accordingly.

After learning more about how their own thinking and interpretation of events causes them to become distressed, clients can then begin to assess commonly held societal beliefs that lead to disturbance. These are often referred to by Ellis (1989) as "musts," "shoulds," and "oughts." Here, are some examples:

"Since I'm a good person, life should treat me fairly. I should get what I deserve, and no ill should befall me."
"I must be loved by my family."
"If I want to be respected at work, I ought to do my job perfectly, or I am inadequate."

Ellis would suggest that even though each of the preceding is a nice thought, believing it must be so will cause distress for the individual because life is not always "fair," and sometimes we're not loved by all those around us, and perfection is an impossibility. A more realistic view would be this:

"The universe is indiscriminate; misfortune is visited upon saints as well as sinners."
"I would like it best if my family loved and admired me, but if they don't, I'll be OK. I can choose to fill my life with friends who will love and admire me."
"I am committed to excellent job performance that reflects a work ethic for which I am proud. If others respect my work, I will be pleased; however, I don't need the approval of my coworkers."

According to Ellis, people have the choice of whether they hold their desires about life as wishes (life-enhancing) or whether they allow them to become demands and perceived entitlements (destructive). Far more self-helping, says Ellis (1999), is to realize that our wishes are simply preferences, and although we strive to realize our preferences, we are not devastated if they do not come to fruition. Fundamental to REBT is the idea that much human disturbance comes from making self-actualizing, psychologically healthy wishes for accomplishment, approval, and happiness into absolutistic, rigid shoulds, musts, and oughts.

It is important to note that Ellis (1999) also recognizes the fact that the term "rational" indicates "empirical and logical," which may be erroneous in and of itself, since "rational" is often subjective. There is no absolute standard for rationality; what is considered rational by some may not be so by others. Ellis (1999) defines rational as "cognition that is effective or self-helping, not merely cognition that is empirically and logically valid" (p. 154).

In addition to the techniques used in treatment to help clients change irrational beliefs, REBT therapists use homework assignments to reinforce learning and sustain change. Simply understanding how one's thinking impacts behavior and feelings is not sufficient; practicing new critical thinking skills, applying rational thought to interpretations of experience, and changing behavior to be congruent with new beliefs is necessary for meaningful change to occur. Such practice is considered by Ellis (1999) to engage patients in active participation in their own treatment, and to promote cognitive change by acting against self-defeating beliefs (Ellis, 1975). As Eleanor Roosevelt said, "You gain strength, courage and confidence by every experience in which you really stop to look fear in the face. You are able to say to yourself, 'I lived through this horror. I can take the next thing that comes along.' You must do the thing you think you cannot do." Ellis reflected the same belief: "The therapist encourages, persuades, cajoles, and occasionally even insists that the patient engage in some activity (such as doing something he is afraid of doing) which itself will serve as a forceful counter-propaganda agency against the nonsense he believes" (p. 95).

Solution Focused Brief Therapy

Solution Focused Brief Therapy (SFBT) is a relatively new approach to psychotherapy geared toward helping clients construct solutions rather than solve problems (Gingerich & Eisengart, 2000). Based on the work of Steve de Shazer, Insoo Kim Berg, and colleagues at the Family Therapy Center in Wisconsin in the early 1980s, SFBT is aimed at identifying the chief complaint or problem, and then attempting to find a solution by assessing the client's answers to the following questions:

"What is the complaint?"

"What solutions has the client attempted?"

"What is the client's goal?"

"What are the client's positions on the problem and treatment?" (Capuzzi and Gross, 1995, p. 450).

Given that the solutions attempted were unsuccessful, it is assumed these "solutions" may actually perpetuate the problem. Treatment is an attempt by the therapist to assist the client in finding and implementing more effective solutions. The therapist is relatively more directive than in other psychotherapeutic approaches. He or she determines a treatment strategy by answering the following questions:

1. What solution has been attempted?
2. What solution will bring the opposite result from the attempted solution?
3. What particular action needs to be taken to begin the implementation of a more beneficial solution?
4. Considering the client's perceptions about the problem, what can the therapist do or say to foster the client's buying into the new behavior as a solution to the problem?
5. What is the indicator the client will report signifying that the solution has been successful?

According to Gingerich and Eisengart (2000), the main objective of treatment is to encourage clients to imagine how they would like the problem to change and then to recognize the steps needed to initiate that change. Weiner-Davis, deShazer, and Gingerich (1987) indicated that clients, at least on some level, are already attempting some version of the solution when they come into treatment. Hence, therapy in this context is really a process through which the solution is fine-tuned or modified so that it can be more successfully implemented.

It is interesting that SFBT clinicians often use what is called a "miracle question," in that they ask the client this question: "if a miracle were to occur and the perfect solution to this problem were to appear, what would it be?" The client's response can either provide information about the best possible solution or inform the clinician about the client's reality testing.

Another note about SFBT is the relatively small amount of emphasis placed on diagnosis and the origins of the problem. In general, this type of therapy focuses on the here and now and the client's current willingness to change. The client's previous inability to effect change is viewed simply as a lack of realization in terms of how to go about resolving the problem effectively, and not some form of resistance or sustenance of secondary gain from the perpetuation of the problem.

Systematic Desensitization

In 1958, Joseph Wolpe wedded classical and operant conditioning to form systematic desensitization, which is still considered one of the best behavioral therapy techniques used in practice today (Goodwin, 1999). On the basis of the work of Mary Cover

Jones, Wolpe believed that anxiety and relaxation were incompatible responses and could not occur simultaneously. Therefore, he endeavored to reduce anxiety by pairing the anxiety-producing stimulus with relaxation. He was also influenced by Edmund Jacobson (1929), who developed progressive relaxation, and he used Jacobson's approach to create a relaxed state in the patient in order to begin introducing the feared stimulus. The feared stimulus is introduced in small doses or at lower-level intensity while the patient is relaxed, and as tolerance for the stimulus increases, the intensity of stimulus is increased. Wolpe called this process an "anxiety hierarchy." The anxiety hierarchy is created by the patient, who identifies a list of approximately ten situations related to the feared stimulus that produce anxiety. He or she is then asked to rank-order the situations in relation to the degree of anxiety each produces. For example, a patient who has a phobic reaction to snakes may identify the simple thought of seeing a snake while weeding her garden as a low-level anxiety situation. On the other hand, she may report that having a snake sitting on her lap would generate a much higher level of anxiety.

Systematic desensitization is highly process oriented, and it is important for the therapist to be skilled in its use. One must use caution in ensuring that the patient is adequately relaxed before introducing the feared stimulus, in order to prevent traumatizing the patient. After the patient is adequately relaxed, the therapist introduces the lowest level of anxiety situation for a short period of time. The stimulus is then removed, and the patient is returned to a relaxed state and given verbal reinforcement for remaining calm. The verbal reinforcement used is similar to challenging erroneous beliefs and cognitive restructuring. Patients learn to pair relaxation with the previously feared stimulus while the therapist helps them to change their perceptions about the stimulus. The anxiety response is considered to be a learned or conditioned response, and Wolpe found that a conditioned response could be counterconditioned. However, Lazarus and Abramovitz (2004) reported that the success of systematic desensitization is largely dependent on the extent to which clients are able to change their beliefs about the stimulus.

Adlerian Brief Therapy

Adlerian Brief Therapy is based on Alfred Adler's Individual Psychology, developed in the early 1900s. Adler believed that understanding the individual's lifestyle or subjectively socially constructed pattern of living (Bitter & Nicoll, 2000) is necessary when attempting to enable the individual to live more purposefully. Ellis (Capuzzi & Gross, 1995) claimed that Adler attempted to understand people's behavior as a product of their thoughts and beliefs. Applying the approach developed in Individual Psychology to Adlerian Brief Therapy, therapists construct treatment around the understanding of the clients' goals and attendant behavior in relation to their interpretation of themselves, others, and the world (their worldview). Adler (Capuzzi & Gross, 1995) considered his orientation to be teleological, in that his approach focused on the here and now, as a springboard toward the client's intended future! The past is viewed as a provider of information about how or why current behavior developed.

According to Bitter and Nicoll (2000), Adlerian brief therapists strive to support clients in identifying and implementing functional solutions to problems, to increase the number and types of choices available to clients, and to capitalize on previously underutilized resources. Adlerian Brief Therapy consists of the typical components of therapy. First the therapist gathers information about the client, either from a phone call with the client or from other sources. From this, the therapist begins to formulate hypotheses about the client and his presenting problems. These hypotheses "jump start" the treatment process by enabling the therapist to save time by formulating educated guesses about the client based upon the data collected. Further, the hypotheses can be discarded or modified if upon meeting the client, they are found to be erroneous or in need of refinement.

The initial contact with the client is focused on identification of chief complaints and on the development of a therapeutic relationship between the client and the therapist. As in traditional Adlerian therapy, valuing of the client is fundamental to positive therapeutic outcomes. Such valuing is demonstrated by therapist validation of the clients' feelings, assisting clients in the telling of their stories, showing genuine interest in the client and his or her experience, and recognizing the client as the "expert" on his or her own life (Anderson & Goolishian, 1992). Bitter and Nicoll (2000) also suggest that therapy is enhanced when the clients perceive the therapist as competent and completely present for them. Therapy then commences with the therapist attempting to determine how clients' behavioral patterns reflect their beliefs about themselves, others, and their place in the world. Furthermore, the therapist attempts to determine how such behavioral patterns contribute to the chief complaints presented in the initial interview. Adler posed the questions "What would you be doing if you didn't have these symptoms or problems?" or "How would your life be different if you didn't have these issues, concerns, or problems?" The answers directed the course of treatment. If the answer was "nothing, except that the problem or symptom would not exist," then the problem would likely be biological. When the problem or symptom serves to enable the client to avoid some necessary human task (Bitter & Nicoll, 2000) or is a defense against some psychological discomfort, treatment must address this avoidance such that the client learns to resolve rather than avoid the problem.

When chief complaints or presenting problems have been addressed and the client is in the process of resolving them, the client is better able to begin assessing his or her lifestyle more holistically. Adlerian Brief Therapists call such lifestyle assessments an "objective interview." The components of the objective interview are similar to a bio-psycho-social evaluation, including the history of the problem, medical history, use of medicines (past and present), social history, education and training, family history, and the patient's motivation for treatment.

Effectiveness Studies

What factors determine the effectiveness of brief treatments? Levenson and Burg (2000) indicate brief therapy as the treatment of choice for many clients, but questions remain about what makes brief treatment any more effective than longer-term treatment. Is it the directive nature of the approaches, or as Blatt, Pilkonis, Quinlan, and

Zuroff (1996) suggest, the interpersonal dimensions of the therapeutic process? Perhaps brief interventions can serve as stand-alone treatment for those with less severe symptoms, or a first-step intervention for those with more significant problems (Breslin, Sdao-Jarvie, Li, Tupker, & Ittig-Deland, 2002).

Gingerich and Eisengart (2000) compared the outcome results of various studies of SFBT and found that current studies fail to meet research standards to establish efficacy, but they do provide initial support for the belief that this type of therapy is beneficial. Perhaps more rigorous evaluation should be conducted in an effort to establish brief treatments as efficacious treatments of choice. The following are summaries of studies conducted on various brief treatments.

Students with Emotional and Behavioral Difficulties.   In a study conducted by Thorne and Ivens (1999), students were able to maintain or improve their behavior in school through a short-term intervention focused on strengthening problem resolution skills and increasing effective communication ability. Specifically, the intervention involved allowing students, their teachers, staff, and parent(s) to assess the students' problem behavior and its significance. Then each party offered solutions to the problem from his or her own perspective. The most appropriate solution was identified, and a process for implementation was developed. Finally, a system by which the new behavior would be reinforced and strengthened was determined. In general, the entire process took four meetings. Follow-up studies conducted one month after intervention found that the behavior change had been sustained.

Adults in Treatment for Marijuana Use.   Stephens, Roffman, and Curtin (2000) compared brief substance abuse treatment outcomes of three groups: one receiving 14-session cognitive-behavioral group treatment called relapse prevention support group (RPSG); a second receiving a 2-session individual treatment using motivational interviewing called individualized assessment and intervention (IAI); and the third, the control group, receiving a 4-month delayed treatment condition (DTC). Researchers found a significant difference among the treatment groups' marijuana use 4 months after the start of treatment compared with that of the control. The RPSG and IAI group reduced their pretreatment use by 70%, whereas the DTC group reduced use by only 30%. Treatment for the RPSG group involved learning to recognize risky situations or triggers for use, and preparing to quit using altogether. The IAI group developed plans for quitting in the first session. Both treatments were cognitive-behaviorally based, and no significant differences were found in treatment outcomes between these two groups. The study suggests that a 2-session cognitive-behavioral intervention is just as effective as a 14-session intervention for marijuana use.

Generalized Anxiety in Older Adults.   Wetherell, Gatz, and Craske (2003) compared treatment outcomes for older adults (average age of 67.1 years) suffering from generalized anxiety disorder. Participants were randomly assigned to cognitive-behavior therapy (CBT), a discussion group (DG) to process anxiety-generating issues, and a waiting list. Both brief treatment approaches were effective, although CBT participants showed more improvement immediately after treatment on more measures than DG participants. However, in most cases, improvement was not significantly different from that of the DG participants, and at 6 month follow-up, there were no significant differences in improvement between the groups. The researchers concluded that brief treatment was effective in the treatment of older adults with generalized anxiety disorder.

Treatment for Phobias in Youth.   Children ages 7 through 17 who met the diagnostic criteria for specific phobias were randomly assigned to a 1-session exposure treatment alone group, a 1-session treatment with parent present, or a wait-list control group for four weeks. The researchers, Ost, Svensson, Hellstrom, and Lindwall (2001) measured emotional and behavioral symptoms pre, post, and at 1-year follow-up, and found that both treatment groups showed significant improvement compared with the control group. Further, each treatment group's improvement was comparable to the other. The improvements were also sustained at the 1-year follow-up, indicating that 1-session exposure treatment was effective for specific phobias in children.

Conclusion

In conclusion, although crisis is part and parcel of living, negative effects can be moderated by intervening as soon as possible with empirically demonstrated treatments, in an effort to enable the individual to manage the crisis effectively. As Helen Keller said, "Although the world is full of suffering, it is full also of the overcoming of it."

DISCUSSION QUESTIONS

1. How does one's perception about a situation impact the extent to which it becomes a crisis? How does one's resilience contribute to problem resolution? What are some other pivotal constructs that affect the outcome of this process?

2. If a community mental health practitioner is asked to consult on the development of a crisis intervention program, what strategies to strengthen coping skills might he or she build into the program?

3. Suppose you were completing your graduate internship in a college counseling center and you had a client who was using alcohol to reduce stress. How would you go about assessing the severity of the client's problem? What treatment would you use, and why?

4. What are some types of distortions in thinking that can affect stress responses? Give specific examples of each type, and techniques that might help counter the negative thinking prevalent in each example.

5. What are some practical coping strategies that can be used to deal with stress? Which of these strategies would be most practical and useful in dealing with stressful situations encountered in your own life?

Setting and System Focus: Social Support and Self-Help

OBJECTIVES

This chapter is designed to enable the reader to:

- Understand the importance and benefits of social support.
- Describe the elements that are necessary to foster a sense of community.
- Describe the functional aspects of a social network and variables that affect them.
- Explain how a proper balance of social support is essential to well-being.
- Understand the concept of vulnerability and its importance to determining needed social support.
- Understand why timing is critical in terms of support.
- Explain how skill building can reduce stress and can strengthen social support networks.
- Define the four elements of a physical and psychological sense of community.
- Understand how Caplan's ideal family model relates to social support.
- Identify different social networks that correspond to life cycles.
- Understand the link between social support and self-help.
- Describe aspects of self-help groups.
- Identify advantages and disadvantages of Internet support groups.
- Understand difficulties inherent in research on self-help groups.
- Become familiar with ethical issues involving professionals and self-help groups.

"We may have come on different ships but we're all in the same boat now."
Martin Luther King, Jr.

We've all heard the saying "misery loves company," and many of us interpret it to mean that people enjoy sitting around wallowing in their troubles. Others of us believe that unhappy people like to spread their misery by making others unhappy as well. But what if we reframe the statement such that sharing misery with others experiencing similar problems is therapeutic? Then misery would indeed love company, as it would be a means toward relief.

Perhaps the sharing of experience and the realization that one is not alone is the single most important benefit of social support networks. According to Levine and Perkins (1987), an individual is more likely to enter a state of crisis when personal coping strategies are poor and social support is unavailable or inadequate. Social support is highly valued by mental health practitioners; data support its effectiveness in protecting against physical and psychological difficulties. In addition, it serves as an important intervention for assisting individuals in their efforts to cope with and manage the effects of traumatic life experiences (Hoff, 1984). Social support can include friends, relatives, peer support groups, clergy, family physicians, and professional therapists. Each of these groups provides different types of support, and knowing when and whom to ask for help is an important factor in reaping the benefits of social support. In addition, social support is often influential in the self-help process.

This chapter focuses on the benefits of social support and its influence on mental health. Social support is considered in relation to each stage of the life cycle and in relation to changing needs for social support over the life span. Implications for a variety of interventions regarding these changing needs are also discussed.

Social Support

Psychological Sense of Community (PSC)

Social support can best be described as a physical and psychological sense of community (PSC). But what constitutes a "sense of community"? McMillan and Chavis (1986) integrate both the geographic or location-based elements with the social or relational-based aspects to formulate their definition of community. McMillan and Chavis, as well as Obsr, Smith, and Zinkiewicz (2002) postulate that a community is composed of four dynamic and interactive elements: membership, influence, integration and fulfillment of needs, and shared emotional connection.

Membership is a sense of belonging and is accompanied by a personal investment to achieve and maintain that commitment. Bidirectional expectations serve to unite individuals and to instill loyalty and a sense of privilege regarding membership in the community.

The *influence* of the community is closely related to the bidirectional expectations. Members are more likely to conform to group practices if they perceive that their feelings are validated and supported by the group. Taylor, Peplau, and Sears (1997) indicate that a positive relationship exists between group cohesiveness and the influence to conform. The level of influence is indicative of the strength of the ties between the group and its individual members.

Integration and fulfillment of needs can be equated to the behavioral concept of reinforcement. Simply stated, members must perceive membership in the community to be rewarding. A common reinforcement is that of shared values. Shared philosophies imply similar goals and a desire to work together to achieve those goals. A strong community is able to meet group and individual needs, thus creating another reinforcement of membership.

A *shared emotional connection* involves the extent to which members "share a history" or have similar past experiences. Members tend to be more emotionally connected when the quality and the quantity of their interactions are greater and when their shared history has greater personal significance. A spiritual bond can also increase the level of shared emotional connection.

In a later revision of this theory, McMillan (1996) renamed the four elements of community: spirit, trust, trade, and art, respectively. His reasoning was that membership focuses on friendship and connection between the members and that the "spirit" of their interactions is the commitment to truth, which is the primary means of ensuring emotional safety.

Trust involves the equitable allocation of power within the community and replaces McMillan's previous concept of influence. The establishment of group norms, decision-making processes, and group and individual roles help in the development of an authority structure based on shared values. McMillan suggests that a social economy arises out of a spirit of trust within the community, and in turn promotes *trade* of members' needs and resources.

Trade, then, is the give-and-take process of self-disclosure—the trading of feelings, understanding, and support among members.

Art refers to the equity of trading that transcends scorekeeping and embraces giving for the joy of giving. Art represents the symbolism of a community's shared history, the expression of shared values, and the level of spirit experienced by members.

In effect, McMillan's theory of community encompasses the importance and the benefits of social support. Human beings establish social networks to provide themselves with a physical and psychological sense of community. Those aspects of community deemed most important to its members are emotional support and instrumental support.

Functional Aspects of Social Networks

The functional aspects of a social network are the ways a network operates to provide social support. These include social feedback, information access, companionship, emotional support, and crisis mobilization (Mitchell & Trickett, 1980; Pines, Ben-Ari, Utasi, & Larson, 2002). Material or tangible support such as child care or help when one is ill can also be provided by the network.

Social feedback refers to the response one is given by members of the network regarding feelings, thoughts, and behaviors. It is the "reality check" provided by family, friends, coworkers, and the like, on the perceived appropriateness of the individual's functioning. Social feedback can be either positive or negative and can help the individual reevaluate a stressful situation and his or her reaction to it.

Information access is any information given to the individual by members of the network such as advice, coping strategies used by the network member, or the helpful hints traded among network members as they help each other to manage a particular situation.

Companionship includes friendship, spending time with members, and any other social interaction that reduces the members' sense of being alone.

Emotional support is the expression of feelings among members of the network that allows them to believe that others are concerned about their well-being. This type of support promotes positive self-esteem by validating the individual's feelings and by acknowledging that although the person's circumstances or problems may be labeled "bad," the individual himself or herself is not intrinsically "bad." In addition, emotional support contributes to members' experience of being emotionally connected to others who care about them.

Crisis mobilization is the rallying around an individual to provide any needed support in a crisis event. This involves gathering resources that will help the individual to minimize the stress and problems associated with the crisis. Crisis mobilization usually includes ensuring that the member has companionship, emotional esteem, and informational support, social feedback, and material or tangible support.

Material support, sometimes referred to as tangible or instrumental support, includes specific items or services given to the individual. Examples of services that constitute material support are child care and transportation. Some examples of material support involving tangible items might include lending a neighbor a lawn mower when his is broken, giving an expectant mother an infant car seat, bringing a meal to a sick friend, or giving a student financial assistance with tuition.

The functional aspects of the social network depend on its structure, meaning that the number of contacts available to the individual and the frequency of contact with those individuals. For example, Lounsbury and DeNeui (1996) found that college students who lived on campus reported higher levels of PSC than those who lived off campus. Presumably, students living on campus would interact with other members of the college community more frequently and thus would be more likely to engage in activities that promote PSC. However, the functional aspects of a social network also depend on the larger social environment and the individual's willingness to ask for help. Davidson et al. (2004) found that in many cases, a social network will not readily respond to an individual's call for help when calls for help are excessive and responses do not meet the individual's expectations. For example, a family may give a deaf ear to a member who frequently "cries wolf." Thus, it can be concluded that the functioning of the social network is also influenced by the frequency and severity of the individual's needs and the extent to which the relationships comprising it are balanced. In addition, Day and Livingstone (2003) found that when undergraduate college students were given scenarios to rate for perceived stressfulness, women were more than twice as likely to perceive a scenario as stressful compared with men. However, the researchers also found women were more likely to seek social support when distressed than men.

The functions of social networks are critical factors in the individual's well-being. Friendship networks have been found to reduce psychological disorders and job strain. Kaslow (2004) found that married persons have more positive feelings of well-being, and according to Bloom (1984), the death of a spouse is one of life's greatest stressors. Although marital cohesion reduces alcoholism, depression, and psychiatric relapse, single close relationships may be essential (even if not completely sufficient on their own) for overall emotional well-being. Overall emotional well-being depends on the availability of a wide range of resources and various types of support, which are unlikely to be found within one single close relationship.

Factors Affecting the Effectiveness of Social Support

As with many things in life, too much "support" is not necessarily a good thing. The degree and the type of support must be balanced with fostering the well-being of the individual. Simply stated, the extent to which a person's needs are matched with an environment responsive to those needs influences the effectiveness of social support. As was mentioned earlier in the Introduction of this text and in Chapter 5, crises can be seen as opportunities for personal growth or challenges with the potential to produce new or improved coping skills when managed effectively. For example, close relationships offering high levels of support are helpful in the crisis stage but not in the transition stage, when the individual needs to "try out his/her wings." Microsystems composed of too-close relationships such as family can actually reduce independence, as is sometimes seen in college students' adjustments to being away at college. The ancient wisdom postulating that if you give a man fish, you feed him for the day, but if you teach him how to fish, you feed him for a lifetime, can be applied to social support as well.

Attachment styles also impact an individual's perception of social support. Collins and Feeney (2004) found that anxious and avoidant individuals viewed their spouse's support in stressful tasks as negative, and that these individuals performed much worse at their task even when given genuinely supportive messages by their spouse.

As illustrated, the appropriate type and level of support depend on the individual and the particular situation. Although sometimes difficult to determine, the following guidelines should be considered: support should be perceived by the individual as stable, reliable, available, and adequate. The person's expectations of the support network are highly correlated with the perception of being helped when those expectations are realized by the network.

A person's level of vulnerability at a given time was identified by Levine and Perkins (1987) as an important consideration regarding needed support. Vulnerability is determined by factors such as genetic inheritance and prior coping ability, as well as environmental factors including social support. Vulnerability can fluctuate over time and is impacted by the overall life situation at the time of crisis. Levine and Perkins's (1987) vulnerability model connects life events with Dohrenwend's model (Chapter 1). According to this model, stress is everywhere; dysfunction is not a character trait in that everyone will become stressed at some time and will need help coping with that stress. Adaptive functioning is more likely to occur in times of stress when social support is adequate and/or complements treatment, whereas maladaptive functioning is predicted by an inadequate support network or one that undermines treatment (Gottlieb, 1985).

Timing of Support

The timing of support is also an important factor in its effectiveness. Different types of support are emphasized at varying time periods after a crisis in order to meet the changing needs of an individual. The hierarchical-compensatory model holds that immediately following a crisis, family is usually most important to the provision of emotional support, after which friends provide informational support to the individual throughout the transitional stage. When the crisis includes a deficit stage such as illness, instrumental (or tangible) support is needed as well. For example, when first diagnosed as having a serious illness, an individual needs the emotional support that family can provide. The greatest need, initially, is for reassurance. Later, when learning about various treatments and the way that others have endured the same or a similar ordeal becomes important, friends might provide valuable information. Finally, as an illness becomes chronic and the person is unable to take care of routine tasks, tangible assistance is most needed. A friend offering to walk the dog or a neighbor providing a cooked meal to raise the individual's spirits might help meet this need. At a given time over the course of a crisis, certain specific needs become more significant, and types of social support that compensate for the greatest current need at that stage are most beneficial. The perception of support also mediates the long-term effects of stress or exposure to trauma (Norris & Kaniasty, 1996).

In a study conducted by Crockenberg (1988) involving teenage mothers and their perceptions of social support, the researchers found that 75% of the mothers indicated they would like additional advice regarding parenting skills and the availability of organized neighborhood support groups as well as contact with visiting public health nurses. The mothers especially needed these types of support when the children were infants, suggesting that the timing of such support is a critical factor in its effectiveness. Further, Crockenberg and Leerkes (2004) found that maternal support was correlated with reductions in infant negative affect.

On the basis of Kobasa and Maddi's (1985) theoretical framework indicating that well-timed social support can enhance personal hardiness, Harrisson, Loiselle, Duquette, and Semenic (2002) evaluated the relationship between hardiness, work support, and psychological distress. Personal hardiness describes stress-resistant personalities characterized by social skills, commitment (versus alienation), control (versus powerlessness), and challenge (versus threat) orientation. Such hardiness, enhanced through social support and exercise, was found to increase resistance to illness and to be a significant mediator between work support and psychological distress. In this example, the qualities of the relationships (environmental factors) interact with the individual personality factors of the network members to positively impact health and well-being.

Critical Incident Stress Management

One particular social support strategy for reducing potential stress-related illness is Critical Incident Stress Management (CISM). This highly structured intervention was first designed to assist military combat veterans and then for civilian first responders such as police, fire, and emergency personnel. It has since been adapted for use whenever traumatic incidents occur. The purpose of CISM is to support individuals involved in a critical incident in expressing their emotions about the experience, sharing the experience with others, and learning about traumatic symptoms and possible reactions to the incident. CISM includes the following interventions:

- *Pre-Crisis Education* involves a plan for crisis response within an organization. Such a plan is generally articulated in the employees' handbook, or in a "policies and procedures" manual.
- *Debriefing* is the process by which individuals gather together to discuss the critical incident and express their emotional reaction to the incident. The debriefing is typically facilitated by a team of crisis intervention specialists and should take place between 24 and 72 hours after the incident.
- *Defusing* is a shorter, less formal intervention conducted immediately after the incident has occurred. The purpose of defusing is simply to educate those involved in the critical incident about possible stress reactions and to stabilize them before they return to their normal activities. Debriefing may also be needed after defusing.
- *Grief and Loss Session* is a facilitated group or individual session that enables people to process their emotional reactions to death. The process is therapeutic in two ways; first, it allows for emotional expression, and second, it fosters healthful exploration of and dialogue about the concept and experience of death.
- *Crisis Management Briefing* occurs within a large group setting before, during, and after a crisis. The purpose of such a briefing is to keep those involved informed about the progress of the situation. In addition, coping skills may be presented, and other support services may be recommended.

Although CISM is not a magic bullet, it can be an effective strategy to keep healthy people strong and a good management technique for taking care of emergency personnel. It achieves these goals by providing well-timed support that can reduce the likelihood of becoming ill.

Networks, Support, Health, and Illness

Networks can be a source of stress as well as support. A function of social support is to provide feedback on the individual's behaviors, opinions, and attitudes, and distorted or inadequate feedback can result in deviant behavior, stress, or poor adaptation. Social networks can also inhibit positive change. For example, many parents fear their child's involvement with what they consider to be "the wrong crowd." In these cases, social contact does not necessarily imply positive emotional support. Catalano, Haggerty, Oesterle, Fleming, and Hawkins (2004) present evidence that such youth bonding with groups involved in violence, delinquency, and drug use negatively impact academic competence. Therefore, they stress the importance of bonding to school to reduce deviant behavior.

Cohen and Willis's (1985) mediational model suggests that even though social support may be helpful to health in general, for some it is helpful only in the presence of stress. In other words, since social support benefits some individuals by reducing the intensity of the stressor, in the absence of a stressor, social support itself will have little effect on mental health. Additionally, social networks reinforce normal behavior that contributes to mental and physical health, but illness tends to reduce social contact. For this reason, the link between social support and health is often described as an interactive spiral; illness, divorce, unemployment, and other stressors reduce support, which in turn increases stress, illness, and vice versa. From this perspective, community mental health practitioners target special needs for support in planning interventions in order to break the spiral. In addition, Riessman and Banks (2001) propose the infusion of social support principles into the health care and human service systems, as well as a more cooperative relationship between self-help groups and professionals.

Social support was found to be an important factor in Cherniss and Herzog's (1996) study of the health of pregnant teens and their babies. Teen mothers of low socioeconomic status benefited from social support in that they were more likely to complete high school, delay future pregnancies, meet the basic needs of their infants, and become financially independent. Teen mothers of low socioeconomic status were aided particularly by the support they received from their family. Support appeared to have a stress-buffering interactive effect, meaning that support was most helpful when stress was present.

Many studies have identified the need for specialized social support for patients and their significant others following serious illnesses. Mastectomy patients studied were experiencing feelings of isolation and rejection and were in need of coping skills. Cancer patients in their acute phase of the illness reported poorer quality of life (Sprangers & de Haes, 2002). Davison, Pennebaker, and Dickerson (2000) reported that social support had a positive influence on the health of individuals suffering from stigmatized diseases (AIDS, alcoholism, breast and prostate cancer). Stewart, Cianfrini, and Walker (2005) found that health status was improved among HIV-positive individuals when social isolation, life stressors, and adequate housing issues were addressed. Minkler (1985) reported that social support had a positive influence on health in the elderly during bereavement, retirement, relocation, and the loss of autonomy. Long-term studies in Alameda County, California, and Tecumeh, Michigan, support Minkler's findings by revealing that persons who had more ties to the community tend to live longer (Salzinger, 1992). Caretakers and spouses of mentally ill persons are under severe stress and are also in need of support.

The psychological well-being of individuals with mental illness was found to be related to reduced isolation and social connectedness in a study conducted by Ryan and Solky (1996). It was argued that social supports and social contacts that foster autonomy also enhance psychological well-being, since these components fulfill the basic psychological needs for autonomy, relatedness, and competence, which in turn enhance self-regard, self-management, vitality, and a feeling of connectedness with others. In addition, Perese (1997) found that a lack of connectedness through friendship and social support negatively affected the physical and psychological health of mentally ill individuals.

The families of mentally ill or learning-disabled individuals also benefit from social support. In a study of mothers of adult children with developmental disabilities, Ben-Zur, Duvdevany, and Lury (2005) found a relationship between social resources and mental health. Those mothers with support had fewer and less-severe symptoms of stress than those without social support.

The preceding are examples of stressful life events that cause a greater need for social support. Community mental health practitioners plan interventions around both anticipated life-stage and accidental life events, and have found that participation in peer support groups has a positive influence on health during such stressful life events.

Implications for Intervention

People who are able to rely on others tend to have good social ties, and community mental health practitioners can easily strengthen those ties by teaching interpersonal skills and a variety of communication skills techniques. Material caregivers (nurses, teachers, clergy, etc.) can be taught listening and empathy skills in order to be able to help others as well as being able to help themselves. Welfare agents and counselors often serve as social support for the lonely, and although the type of care is different, bolstering social skills adds to the multiplexity of their functioning as supporters.

On the basis of the research indicating that social ties change the context of stress, community mental health practitioners can develop programs reflecting the notion that stress is "normal." This development helps reduce the long-term effects of stress, since it removes the stigma of being labeled "bad" or "sick" or "maladjusted." For example, rather than labeling individuals as "withdrawn," they can instead be considered as lacking in social support. Thus, interventions are focused on helping them to develop social networks. This can be achieved by teaching individuals interpersonal and coping skills that attract social support systems and combine to reduce stress.

Community programs that focus on skills-building related to employment and support for working mothers, for example, are beneficial in reducing stress. In a study of low-income families who were either current or former welfare recipients, perceived support was not related to quality of employment but reduced the likelihood of living in poverty (Henly, Danziger, & Offer, 2005). It seems that social support can be an important factor in coping with lack of employment, since it provides emotional, instrumental, and informational assistance that enables individuals to better their circumstances.

Certain life events, such as the suicide of a family member, have unique aspects that must be addressed by community mental health practitioners when developing interventions and appropriate support. The grief process surrounding a suicide is different from the grief process common when a family member dies as a result of external causes. Families of suicide victims experience painful soul-searching regarding motives for the suicide. If motives are discovered, they are often very difficult for the family to accept, and members tend to go through a period of blaming themselves for not recognizing that their relative was in psychological and physical danger. These and many other dynamics unique to those affected by suicide must be examined in providing helpful support. Specifically, Dyregrov (2004) identified "social ineptitude" on the part of members of a social network and explained that members are often unable to effectively communicate support because there is a lack of social norms about how to best assist others at such a difficult time.

Caplan's Ideal Family

Caplan's (1976) ideal family model is often used by community mental health practitioners to replicate the functions of traditional families. The ideal family supports its members by the following:

- Collecting and disseminating information about the world;
- Providing a system for feedback and guidance about the individual within the context of the social environment; among other things, such feedback helps the individual to understand the reactions of others and acts as a point of reference for the individual.
- Presenting a belief system based on values and codes of good behavior—a reality check, if you will;
- Serving as guides and mediators in problem solving;
- Providing material and concrete service to members;
- Acting as a haven for rest and recuperation—a safe place to go when the outside world is a tough place to be in;
- Providing emotional love, affection, and comfort, and allowing the individual to regroup; and
- Reviving personal identity by reminding the member of precrisis strengths and achievements.

The need for the diverse type of support provided by ideal families is especially relevant today. The apparent breakdown of family and traditional social groups such as church groups as well as the greater anonymity in society has resulted in less social support. When rebuilding this support, community mental health practitioners need to consider the functions the family used to serve and attempt to replace them with available resources.

Support Networks in the Life Cycle

Throughout the course of a lifetime, individuals benefit from different types of support. The various kinds of support needed at any given stage dictate the types of networks in which individuals participate. One factor that influences one's choice of network is the commonality of shared experience. For example, individuals often gravitate toward other individuals who are in the same situation or are at a similar life stage as themselves. Some specific networks corresponding to life-cycle stages are discussed next.

Parental Social Networks

The quality of support available to mothers has a great influence on child development. Parental social network factors such as child-rearing sanctions, access to information and ideas, emotional support, motivation and modeling affect the child's attachment, independence, perceptual and cognitive functioning and understanding of social roles. Maternal stress was found to reduce mothers' sensitivity to babies' cues, and the perception of satisfactory social support among mothers with chronically ill children was found to positively impact adjustment (Horton & Wallander, 2001).

The type of social feedback was an important factor in child maltreatment. Good parenting was related to mothers' having stable, open networks characterized by long-term frequent contact with friends and periodic contact with relatives. The stability of a network refers to the extent to which the network is in equilibrium, or in other words, how well the network is balanced in terms of give-and-take among the members. The openness of a network relates to whether or not new people are able to join the network. A closed network is one in which outsiders are kept from becoming part of the network. Salzinger, Kaplan, and Artemyoff (1983) found that child neglect was correlated with mothers' having stable, closed networks of frequent contact with relatives but infrequent, short-term contact with friends. Unstable, open networks comprised of short-term friends and frequent contact with friends and relatives were also related to child maltreatment.

Children's and Adolescents' Networks

The immediate family generally provides to children their first experience with social networks, and kin contact is usually stable from infancy through adolescence. The size and salience of peer networks increase with age. Adult contact affected toddlers' comprehensible speech, labeling, and naming, whereas peer contact affected expressive speech.

DuBois et al (2002) found social support to be an important resource in fostering positive adjustment in early adolescence. In a longitudinal study, the researchers found fewer emotional and behavioral problems among adolescents who had higher levels of self-esteem and social support. Furthermore, evidence indicated that a balance of peer and parental support was most desirable and predictive of psychosocial adjustment during adolescence.

Adult Networks

The presence of children facilitates adults' development of functional and communicative ties in the community. Many adult networks are made up of their children's teachers, coaches, and other parents whose children are all involved in the same activities.

Coping with stress is facilitated by multidimensional friendships, defined as networks with less dense boundaries between family and friends. This arrangement allows for separation of family and nonfamily roles and activities. Coping is less successful when networks have high density, or are as clinicians term them, "enmeshed."

Enmeshed refers to excessive interdependence among members. For example, when family members insist on accompanying an individual on social outings intended to be shared with friends, or when family members demand to be included in every aspect of the individual's life, the network is considered to be high density, or enmeshed.

Warren (1983) found that optimum PAHN (Problem Anchored Helping Network) consisted of three or four different types of help such as support, information, role models, guidance, etc. In a study of successful adaptation to divorce, Wilcox (1981) learned that women adjusted to a lesser extent when networks were composed primarily of family members. Divorced individuals were less likely to have a confidant, were lonelier, and had smaller, more homogeneous networks compared with their married counterparts.

Social Networks and Aging

Typically, the capacity for self-sufficiency decreases with age, and social networks also decrease as friends die and younger friends either move away or are unavailable due to the demands of their own lives. This tendency, coupled with the rise of nuclear families, results in the need for the elderly to find new support resources. It is interesting that loneliness was found to decrease with age, but loneliness was also affected by recent changes in social relationships. Many elderly find themselves forced to rely on informal rather than formal or institutional support systems. Informal support systems are those that include members of the community who have contact with the individual but are considered acquaintances, such as the local grocer or letter carrier.

Gurung, Taylor, and Seeman (2003) also found a gender difference in social support among older adults. Men received more social support from their wives, whereas women sought emotional support from their friends, relatives, and children.

Social Networks and Mental Health

Psychosocial factors, especially during social disorganization, affect susceptibility to mental illness by introducing distortions or inaccuracies in feedback provided on behavior. Networks of mentally ill persons are half the size of those of persons considered to be mentally healthy, have more family, and have higher density that limits access to others (Schoenfeld et al., 1986). Furthermore, Erickson, Beiser, and Iacono (1998) found that support from families of schizophrenics did not predict adaptive functioning five years after the first schizophrenic episode, but social support from nonfamily members did predict this outcome.

Having a close confidant was found to reduce mental illness in general and depression, particularly in women. Schizophrenics received more support than they were able to provide to others in their networks, thus suggesting that peer support groups may be more appropriate for support over time. This conclusion is drawn from the evidence previously discussed in this chapter relating to the need for reciprocal support among members of a highly functioning network. Schoenfeld et al. (1986)

found that adding community members and professionals to mentally ill persons' networks reduced hospitalization.

In most cases, mentally ill or distressed persons cope more effectively when networks provide symmetrical support and when contact is with a greater number of persons. Battered women, for example, cope better when they have many contacts independent of their spouse.

Social networks play a role in adaptation, and structural factors of networks affect members' adjustments. Optimal personal networks change over the life cycle, and the relationship between the social network and adaptation is not static. Different attributes are needed in stress versus nonstress conditions. In light of this fact, one can conclude then that although each place in the life cycle produces the need for specific types of support, the need for support is universal and is important throughout one's lifetime.

Self-Help Through Social Support

In the coping and self-help section of the previous chapter, many techniques for helping oneself through the stress of everyday living and that of crisis situations were presented. These methods can be used for prevention of problems, the development of intervention strategies when problems do arise, or the reduction of consequences that arise as a result of the original problem. Although such methods are very effective, in some cases individuals experience a sense of isolation in dealing with particular difficulties.

The concepts of social support networks and self-help are closely linked in community mental health. Although there are many techniques by which persons are able to "help themselves," most are more effective when accompanied by social support. The support of other individuals who have experienced or are experiencing similar difficulties is particularly important when one is in the process of managing a crisis situation. Given the skyrocketing cost of psychological care, the decline in traditional support groups such as family or church groups, changing societal values, and increased mobility, self-help groups provide therapeutic social support at low cost. From the community mental health perspective discussed in the Introduction, there are simply too few professionals to help all those who are distressed, and the development of self-help groups promotes empowerment and allows individuals to help themselves while helping others in the process.

Powell (1993) explained the benefit of reframing self-help organizations as forums for people to tell their stories. This arrangement helps to get away from the stigmatizing implication that members of self-help groups are needier or less competent than those who are dealing with difficulties "on their own" or that the comparison standard is professional treatment. Rappaport (1993) also took the view that persons choosing to join self-help groups are not looking for treatment but are seeking to define their personal identity. Both researchers conclude that these perspectives remove the medical model orientation from self-help and replace it with an ideology focused on quality-of-life improvement. This ideology is consistent with the belief that stress and problems in living are normal and that managing crisis is part of living. According to Rappaport (1993), people participate in mutual help organizations as a way of joining and living within a community that provides support in a variety of ways.

How To Locate Self-Help Groups

National Self-Help Clearinghouse (NSHC)
Graduate School and University Center of the City University of New York
365 5th Avenue, Suite 3300
New York, NY 10016
Phone: (212) 817–1822

National Self-Help Clearinghouse

The National Self-Help Clearinghouse was established to centralize information about the more than 4,000 self-help organizations in the nation, many having multiple chapters. The Clearinghouse acts as an interface between self-helpers and the professional community by providing information and referrals, assistance in forming self-help groups, and support of the existence of groups by providing problem-solving expertise, education, and training for groups. It also acts to educate the community about the benefits of participation in self-help groups.

The National Self-Help Clearinghouse is a centralized point for information and referrals, and supports an information telephone line that is listed in telephone directories nationally. The line is staffed during business hours, and a recorded message is played after hours. Callers are asked to define the problem with which they need assistance, and then appropriate referrals are made. The Clearinghouse database is divided by location and topic, and callers are given names, telephone numbers, and a short description of the group. If no group exists in the caller's area, the Clearinghouse looks for state or national "model" groups, and if there are none of these, the Clearinghouse asks the caller if he or she wishes to start a group. If so, the caller is given free telephone consultation on how to begin and how to recruit the three or four members typically needed to start a group. Follow-up letters and materials regarding practical considerations such as where to meet, transportation, and information about the development of groups are provided. On-going support is available as the group is formed. Other members can contact the Clearinghouse, and in some cases a consultant may visit the group as an observer of the group process dynamics. The consultant may also provide education and training, teach leadership and communication skills, and even offer scholarships for training.

FIGURE 6.1

Sarbin (1970) noted that members of self-help groups assume a valued, achieved status role. Instead of having the ascribed role of cancer victim, a veteran member becomes a provider of support or a mentor to a new participant. Therefore, the ascribed role, defined as a role that is assigned to the individual and is often a negative "label," becomes an achieved role that is one the individual has earned and is valued for. As was described previously, an individual can become "involved" in an achieved role, and this step gives meaning to life and a positive self-identity, qualities that bolster personal hardiness. Ascribed roles, on the other hand, are stigmatizing and isolating, and they increase vulnerability.

Aspects of Self-Help Groups

According to Sagarin (1969), there are two types of self-help groups. The first is designed to reduce members' deviant behavior by socially reinforcing desired or appropriate behavior. An example of this kind of group is Alcoholics Anonymous (AA). Humphreys, Finney, and Moos (1994) found in a longitudinal study of alcoholics involved in AA that participation in this self-help group was a significant predictor of more active cognitive coping and less avoidant behaviors at three years. In addition, AA involvement was highly correlated with friend support, including intensive ties at three years. The researchers concluded that this type of self-help group provides universal human needs such as friendship, social support, and identity formation.

The second type of self-help group discussed by Sagarin (1969) redefines social norms to make behavior more acceptable in the larger community. These groups are social action groups in nature and unite to bring about attitude change by advocating for the civil rights of underrepresented groups in society. An example of this type of group is Gay Rights, which is active in promoting education about homosexuality and was instrumental in removing homosexuality from the DSM. When social stigmas related to the behavior are removed and the behavior becomes more acceptable in the larger community, the individual is able to seek social support without the previously associated shame and embarrassment.

Membership in Self-Help Groups

"Ordinary people with a common problem come together in settings they own and control, share their problems, and learn from one another without need of professionals" (Lieberman & Snowden, 1993, p. 178).

There are many factors affecting membership in self-help groups. Luke, Roberts, and Rappaport (1993) theorized that individual evaluation and group gatekeeping are determining factors in whether or not an individual will choose to become a member of a self-help group. Individual evaluation was explained as the process used by potential members to decide whether or not the group will be worthwhile for them, and group gatekeeping was defined as the process by which members either exclude or include a new member. The authors suggested that existing groups should be aware of the appearance of the group to newcomers and should recognize the way the group reacts to new members. They also suggest being clear about whom the group is for and to be sure that this fact is communicated to all members. Any potential new members should be asked why they wish to join, not as an interrogation but as a means to welcome them and establish rapport.

There are many ways of categorizing self-help groups. One way is to focus on the different types of individuals that comprise the membership of the groups. According to Levine and Perkins (1987), self-help groups include (a) those uniting individuals who have a stigmatizing condition, (b) relatives of a victim of a specific illness, (c) groups with common ethnic or religious identities, or (d) groups formed for common political interests.

In general, people join self-help groups to unite around a common condition or a shared goal. They are often those whose condition disqualifies them from being "normal." Frequently, there are social stigmas associated with their condition, such as in the cases of addicts, cancer patients, and homosexuals. The relatives of individuals with stigmatizing conditions may also seek self-help group support to assist them in coping with various stressors related to their relative's condition. For example, Al Anon focuses on the experience of living and/or dealing with a relative's alcoholism and the associated problems.

Some individuals who join support groups are socially isolated as a result of a particular condition but are not necessarily stigmatized. These groups include spouses or parents of cancer victims who unite to discuss emotional experiences related to their condition and to share coping strategies. In addition, groups may be formed for the purpose of sharing information about a certain condition. An example of this type of group includes those groups studied by Nash and Kramer (1993), which comprised African Americans affected by sickle cell anemia.

Fraternal organizations are another type of group that can provide social support and mutual assistance, and in this case membership is based on religious or ethnic commonalties. For example, the Knights of Columbus is a fraternal organization of Catholic men that enhances social support by fostering brotherhood among its members.

For other self-help groups, sociopolitical issues are the basis of membership. Members gather to advocate for a particular special interest, such as in taxpayers' associations and Right to Life groups. Members of these quasi-political, civic groups may be personally affected by the issues that they are fighting for or may simply share similar political views with the other members.

Clearly, there is overlap among the various types of memberships of self-help groups, and many groups could fit into more than one category. However, common to all self-help groups is the philosophical orientation toward empowerment: the belief that members are not victims, but survivors. Lieberman and Snowden (1993) found that those who seek help from support groups tend to seek help from multiple service delivery modalities as well. Thus, self-help group support is often combined with visits to therapists or other mental health professionals.

Functions of Self-Help Groups

There are many functions that self-help groups serve for their members. These include companionship, cognitive restructuring, emotional expression, insight, role models, and coping strategies.

Self-help groups promote a psychological sense of community and a social network for the members, and they also provide an ideology that can overcome maladaptive beliefs. Different groups frequently have opposing ideologies, and yet it is the presence of any principles in which members can believe that contributes to the success of these groups. For example, Antze (1976) discussed the differences in philosophical orientation between AA and Recovery groups. Alcoholics must feel less control over their illness as compared with those recovering from drug addiction, who must feel more control in order to manage their crisis situation. The belief that alcoholics cannot control their drinking is the basis for total abstinence from that behavior. In contrast, those in Recovery must believe that they are in control of their illness in order to promote the empowerment necessary for psychological well-being. It is likely that the process of believing in a wellness principle is more important than the content of the belief.

The self-help group also provides opportunities for confession and catharsis. Rappaport (1993) concluded that one can learn and grow through the insight gleaned from experience, and that others listening to the personal narratives given at group meetings can benefit from vicarious learning. Often, the empathic response from others who "have been there" allows an individual to deal with the emotional effects of the condition. This result not only helps the individual but also encourages other members to take on a helper or therapist role, which aids in their own recovery process. The "helpers" in the group provide role models to the individual who is in more immediate crisis. The realization that they are admired and respected reinforces the helpers' commitment to recovery. Thus, a reciprocal relationship exists among the members. This reciprocal relationship is characterized by Matano, Yalom, and Schwartz (1997) as the basis of interpersonal learning and is an important factor in the therapeutic effectiveness of self-help groups.

The nature and functioning of the self-help group is much like Caplan's ideal family situation. Within this network, members receive information and coping strategies for daily living with their condition, peer feedback, concrete aid, and positive reinforcement. Taken together, these allow for the formation or development of personal identity, while also reducing vulnerability and minimizing stress.

Self-Help and Ecological Concepts

Within the self-help group, the individual is able to change behavior. The group provides resources and a niche that establishes a better person-environment fit (Lewin, 1935). Social support is dependent upon the fit between the person and the environment, and self-help groups provide a place where individuals can experience a sense of belonging. Traditional psychotherapy is considered most appropriate for YAVIS (young, attractive, verbal, intelligent, successful), clients, whereas Knight et al. (1980) found that the average member of major self-help groups is middle-aged, has a low to moderate income, and does not have a college education. However, Meissen, Warren, and Kendall (1996) found that college students used some form of self-help group at a higher rate than that predicted by key informants. Specifically, college students were more willing to use self-help groups for difficulties related to physical handicap, sexual assault, childhood abuse, AIDS, and drug abuse, but not for relationship issues. In addition, females were more likely to use self-help groups than males, and previous involvement with self-help groups predicted future participation.

Lewin's student, Roger Barker (1964), postulated that the group is an alternative setting with standing behavior rules incompatible with former behavior. AA, for example, promotes abstinence from alcohol consumption, which is obviously incompatible with the members' former drinking behavior. Using Moos's (1973) social climate approach, self-help groups in general emphasize a high relationship, social, and personal development orientation.

Maton (1993) takes an ecological approach to evaluating the relative benefits of self-help by considering the multidimensional variables involved, such as group ideology, climate, structure, helping mechanisms, and the group focal problem. According to Maton, ecological assessment is necessary to determine the inevitable variance of group characteristics and their influence on members' well-being. Rappaport (1993) also pointed out that this approach ties self-help support group functioning with cross-disciplinary research in areas such as cognitive psychology, sociology, anthropology, and literary analysis, since these fields are focused on the stories people tell and the cultural settings in which they are told.

Social Support and the Internet

Social Support in the Internet Age

The broad societal impact of the Internet cannot be overlooked, and it has certainly added a new dimension to the concept of self-help. According to the National Telecommunications and Information Administration, (NTIA) (2002), the majority of American households are now online. As a result, the average American has access to a wealth of resources literally at his or her fingertips.

Computer technology is altering the way people interact, allowing access with privacy from the comfort of home. In a press release by the Pew Internet & American Life Project (Horrigan, Rainie, & Fox, 2001), it was reported that 84% of Internet users, or about 90 million Americans, have contacted an online support group. Of these, 43% use Internet groups to mange day-to-day responsibilities including medical conditions.

It has been generally noted that increasing numbers of people are using the Internet as a tool for their health care needs, and as an extension of this trend, there have been major changes in the nature of support-seeking behavior and information exchange. Online support groups can serve various functions. For some they are just one component of a comprehensive mental health treatment, whereas for others they serve as the sole support system. Groups may be led by either professionals or nonprofessionals; there are few existing guidelines at this point. Because of this, the legal and ethical ramifications regarding online support groups are a topic of concern among professional groups (Gary & Remolino, 2000).

Findings of a study conducted by the Healthcare Information and Management Systems Society, indicated that whereas over 55% of online support group members surveyed liked to attend online chats with health experts about their condition, almost 90% preferred to participate in e-mail-based discussion about their condition with other patients. In addition, almost all the respondents claimed to enjoy giving online support to other patients with the same condition. Nearly 90% of those surveyed reported being satisfied with the amount of support they received online from other patients and stated that they would like to meet more people online with the same condition. Whereas only 33% reported that their health had improved as a result of advice from online experts, almost 78% trusted the online advice of "expert patients."

Advantages of Online Support Groups

As outlined next, Internet-based support has several advantages:

Access.   Because of rapid advances in communication technology, we are living in a global environment that transcends physical boundaries. Online groups can foster a sense of community and help alleviate feelings of alienation and isolation (Suler & Phillips, 1998, 1996).

The Internet can allow those who are simply unable to attend a face-to-face meeting access to valuable coping resources. Online interaction can offer much-needed support and emotional connection to physically or geographically isolated individuals and can provide a sense of belonging and community to those stigmatized by their illness. The participatory nature of the online environment itself can foster a feeling of involvement or engagement (NTIA, 2002).

Anonymity.   One of the major attractions of online meetings is the ability to remain anonymous if desired. Some individuals may be discouraged from utilizing traditional support groups because of anxiety or other issues, such as privacy. Online support might provide a feasible alternative. Additionally, the greater discretion allowed in terms of personal disclosure might allow a further measure of comfort. For example, some group members simply "lurk," meaning that they observe exchanges without actually participating. The lack of physical proximity might also allow for more comfortable and honest expression, particularly among shy individuals. Online support groups can help alleviate the fear of social stigma attached to support group use (Suler & Phillips, 1998).

Disadvantages

Despite the positive aspects, there are several concerns associated with the use of online support groups that must be addressed in order to promote a safe and productive Internet environment.

Credibility.   Credibility issues are always a concern when dealing with people via the Internet. It is relatively easy to impersonate or misrepresent oneself from behind the safety of a computer screen.

Social Context Cues.   There is the potential to "misread" a person's intent because of the lack of subtle behavioral cues, a risk inherent in text-based communication (Suler & Phillips, 1998). Some people are frustrated by the absence of these interpersonal cues and avoid online support as a result (Galinsky, Schopler, & Abell, 1997). Technological advances may eventually make online support groups comparable to face-to-face support groups through the use of videos, while continuing to avoid issues related to geographical restrictions. However, some of the benefits of privacy and anonymity could be compromised as a result (Gary & Remolino, 2000).

Accuracy of Information.   The quality of information available through the Internet is questionable at times, and the search for reliability can be reminiscent of looking for a proverbial needle in the haystack. To complicate this issue, it is all too easy for well-meaning but misinformed group members to unwittingly pass along inaccurate information.

Hoaxes and Scams.   There is no shortage of scams and hoaxes popping up on the Internet, most being perpetuated by individuals with questionable integrity and a desire to make a quick dollar or simply to cause trouble. It is important to be wary of "miracle cures" or "magic pills." These are at best ineffective and usually expensive. These schemes are often designed to take advantage of the most vulnerable individuals and thus may target Internet support groups in particular.

Confidentiality and Privacy Issues.   New ethical issues are always a concern as the use of the Internet becomes more widespread, particularly issues regarding privacy. Support groups are no exception. The confidentiality of personal information disclosed in a group context may vary greatly by group. Guidelines should be established regarding the dissemination and distribution of personal information, particularly if a support group is moderated by a professional practitioner (Internet Healthcare Coalition, 2000).

In conclusion, the Internet can certainly be a valuable resource for support and social contact related to difficulties in living or illnesses. However, the use of this and other emerging technology should always be accompanied by a sense of caution and skepticism, particularly when dealing with information that seems too good to be true.

Effectiveness of Self-Help Groups

It is often difficult for community mental health practitioners to study the effectiveness of self-help groups, because research is not a goal and anonymity is an important feature of these groups. Since participation is voluntary, members enter and exit groups at will, and attendance is often irregular; on an as-needed basis, it is difficult to track members over time, especially those who drop out. Each self-help group is unique, and there is little standardization, and as a result, comparison is limited. As group structure and functioning fluctuates, control of the research design is minimal, thus negatively influencing reliability, validity, and generalizability. Finally, one of the usual criteria of the effectiveness of treatment, the number of sessions needed before termination, is meaningless, since self-help groups are essentially free of any costs and members can continue to participate for as long as they desire.

However limited, there are some conclusions that have been established. AA has been found to be the single most effective intervention for alcoholism (Polich, Armor, & Braiker, 1981), since it includes all natural processes for recovery: substitute dependency, new constraints on drinking, increased spiritual involvement, and focused social support (Valliant, 1983). AA reaches twice as many alcoholics as all clinics, hospitals, and physicians combined, and treatment duration is much longer, providing lifelong support.

A study by Gillick (1977) that evaluated Al Anon for spouses of alcoholics and found that six-week involvement resulted in better family relationships and positive change in community adaptation. In addition, spouses benefited from adopting the AA ideologies of "living one day at a time" and "learning to let go."

In a study conducted by McKay, Alterman, and McLellan (1994), alcohol- or cocaine-dependent male patients were placed in a hospital day treatment program. The treatment goals of the program were overcoming denial, psychoeducation regarding addiction and warning signs of relapse, and encouraging self-help group participation. Those who participated in self-help groups after completing the hospital day treatment program had significantly better outcomes than those who did not.

Since the empowerment of individuals is an important factor in the effectiveness of self-help groups, although development of groups can be facilitated by professionals, the structure and functioning of the group are primarily the responsibility of the members. Professionals may refer clients to the group and may be consulted for specific assistance such as identifying common concerns of the group or teaching certain skills to members, but must leave its operation to the members themselves. Participants attending The Dutchess County, New York Outreach Center Conference in 1985 warned psychologists that attending group meetings might change the nature of meetings and often negatively affect groups' activities. However, community mental health practitioners can be helpful by consulting with the group leader on competence building, developing cognitive antidotes for "why me?" attitudes, relabeling shame to constructive anger and advocacy, and developing group ideology. Such consultation was found to increase the probability that the group would be successful and durable over time.

One of the authors (JS) found an innovative way of assisting self-help group functioning by sponsoring a self-help group for leaders of such groups. In this forum, participants shared their experiences of facilitating self-help groups. As members disclosed problems encountered by their groups, others were able to describe solutions that they attempted in dealing with similar issues and the degree to which these solutions succeeded. Leaders of long-lasting groups helped facilitators of novice groups to overcome the difficulties of establishing groups. The recipients of this assistance helped the "veteran" leaders with ideas for enhancing members' enthusiasm, which apparently decreases in the more established groups. Members also provided emotional support for each other in this leaders' group. Thus, professionals can play an important role assisting the functioning of self-help groups without compromising the efficacy or sense of empowerment of the members.

More research is needed to determine which factors contribute to self-help group effectiveness. Christensen and Jacobson (1994) suggested that psychotherapy outcome research should shift away from comparisons of different professional therapies and instead compare nonprofessional therapies with professional therapies for effectiveness. Nonprofessional psychological treatment includes self-administered materials and self-help groups, which studies have shown to have positive effects. They suggest that research indicates paraprofessionals usually produce effects that are greater than outcomes for control conditions and comparable to those for professional therapist treatment. Additionally, research is needed to investigate the value-added effect of participation in self-help groups as a supplement to professional treatment.

The need to examine such issues as facilitator credentials, structured versus unstructured meeting styles, and the many different types of self-help and nonprofessional resources available to people is apparent when evaluating effectiveness. The length of time one participates in a group, as well as the demographic variables such as gender, race, age, marital status, education, income, and employment status, all need to be researched in relation to their influence on group involvement outcome.

Ethical Concerns Regarding Professional Recommendations of Self-Help Groups

Although the effectiveness of self-help groups is influenced by many factors, some of which are listed previously, there are particular factors that must be assessed by a professional before recommending a self-help group to a client. As with all forms of treatment, clinicians are bound by ethical principles ensuring that therapy will "do no harm."

The ethical issues related to self-help groups include, but are not limited to the following:

- Training and competency of group leadership (some self-help groups are led by participants who may have no training);
- Group adherence to confidentiality standards;
- Availability of training for group members (i.e., appropriate training from national organizations); and
- Evaluation of group participation outcomes, including follow-up assessment of effectiveness.

The professional is ethically obligated to make referrals only to those self-help groups that are effective and therapeutic. One of the resources available that professionals and clients may contact to get information on self-help groups is the local United Way, which keeps lists of the various services as well as self-help groups offered in the area. There is a United Way office in nearly every community in the United States. Another resource is the National Self-Help Clearinghouse, which provides information regarding where particular groups are offered throughout the country and whom to contact for additional information.

Social support in general and self-help groups in particular can help individuals encountering difficulties in living to cope with their concerns. Enhancing the quality of such support decreases the likelihood that these persons will succumb to their stress. Community mental health practitioners can improve the quality of mental health in society by intervening to provide greater access to social networks when such support is lacking.

DISCUSSION QUESTIONS

1. Consider the functional aspects of a social network. How could an individual who, for example, has lost his or her job because of alcoholism utilize these types of social supports successfully? What might prevent such an individual from achieving a favorable outcome in this type of situation?

2. How can the need for social supports change, and what types of events can cause these changes? How do individual and environmental factors affect the type and degree of social support needed in a given situation? In what ways can a social support network have a negative impact on well-being?

3. What makes a community dynamic? What are some examples of bidirectional influences?

4. Do you feel that in modern times, individuals in general have less adequate social support? If so, why? How can this problem be addressed? Why is it important to do so? Who should be responsible for addressing these concerns?

5. What are some of the advantages of self-help groups? What are some disadvantages? What are some reasons that a person might join such a group? What are some ways in which these groups can provide support?

Cultural Competence

OBJECTIVES

This chapter is designed to enable the reader to:

- Understand the importance and implications of diversity.
- Understand key dimensions of cultural identity.
- Determine knowledge, skills, and attitudes that professionals need in order to become culturally competent.
- Define culture and understand the way it influences what people perceive, believe, and do.
- Identify important issues related to culture.
- Understand why it is important to view behaviors from a cultural context.
- Explain how cultural sensitivity impacts the design of an appropriate intervention program.
- Understand the importance of differences in cultural learning and communication styles within an educational context.
- Understand the subjective nature of behavior interpretation.
- Understand how work-related factors can be culture-sensitive.
- Understand the impact of family relationships as an important variable when interacting with people from different cultures.
- Understand how traditional cultural beliefs about mental illness can affect treatment.

Diversity is the one true thing we all have in common. Celebrate it every day.

Anonymous

I do not want my house to be walled in on all sides and my windows to be stuffed. I want the cultures of all the lands to be blown about my house as freely as possible. But I refuse to be blown off my feet by any.

Mahatma Gandhi (1869–1948)

According to Juliene G. Lipson, Professor of Community Health Systems at the School of Medicine at the University of California, "The people of the world can be seen as a tapestry woven of many different strands. Those strands differ in size, shape, color, intensity and place of origin; yet each strand is integral to the whole" (Lipson, Dibble, & Minarik, 1996, p. 7). Each strand adds strength, texture, and beauty. Some strands respond better to stretching, some to light, others to heat, and each has its own built-in fragilities. The color one sees when looking at the tapestry is just a small part of that which makes it strong, warm, and durable. Diversity is just like that. It's not only about race, or religion or the color of one's skin; it's about the unique worldview each person brings to his or her interactions with others and to the interpretations of his or her experiences. It's about relationships and recognizing and responding to gross as well as subtler points of human differences. It's about people's strengths and about their frailties, none of which can be known by looking solely at a person's skin color or knowing where he or she was born.

In a society where one can communicate with someone from across the globe with the ease of a few keystrokes and where collaboration across geographic and cultural boundaries is the norm, it is becoming increasingly critical for people to develop a sensitivity to and understanding of the worldview of others. It's no longer enough to acknowledge that people think differently, all the while believing that one's own worldview is really the only one that makes any sense. Such parochialism is not a good strategy for the future. The time has come to develop a set of skills and beliefs that allows one not only to look at the world through the eyes of others but also to begin to value and appreciate what one sees through those eyes.

The following chapter is designed to help the reader understand some of the key dimensions of people's cultural identity and to determine the knowledge, skills and attitudes that professionals need to bring to their work in order to be effective with the varied people they will encounter. The author acknowledges that cultural competency cannot be learned by reading a chapter in a textbook. Like riding a bike, one must go out and practice it. The more often one steps out of one's comfort zone and sits on that wobbly bike, the better one will get at riding it. In the same vein, the more diligent one is about seeking out culturally varied experiences, the more culturally competent one will become.

Overview and Definitions

The current U.S. Census reveals that people of minority groups make up over 30% of the total U. S. population and are projected to become greater than 50% in the year 2060 (U.S. Bureau of the Census, 2000). These demographic data suggest that within the professional "lifetime" of students graduating during this decade, they will inevitably come into contact with students/clients/consumers from cultural backgrounds other than their own. In some districts in California (and elsewhere), teachers and mental health professionals have been interacting with clients and students from as many as 10 different cultures speaking 50 different languages and dialects for over 10 years (Lynch & Hanson, 1992).

To understand cultural competency, it is important to look at what is meant by culture. One of many definitions of culture is this: "A system of symbols that is learned, shared and passed on by people of a particular social group. Culture influences what people perceive, believe and do. It guides our interactions with each other and shapes our world view and communication patterns" (Lipson, Dibbler, & Minarik, 1996, p. 8). Each formal and informal group, each family, and each organization has a unique culture, and that culture has a significant impact on the behaviors and attitudes of its members. In order to be culturally competent, one must first become sensitive to the numerous issues related to culture, among them being economic factors, level of education, gender, geographic origin, sexual orientation, race, and social class (Meleis, Isenberg, Koerner, & Stern, 1995).

There are a number of phrases used to refer to health and mental health care that are tailored to sociocultural characteristics of a particular client or client group, such as culturally compatible, culturally appropriate, culturally sensitive, culturally responsive, and culturally informed. Regardless of the exact phraseology used, all of these terms refer to the knowledge, attitudes, and skills a practitioner brings to his or her interaction with someone from another culture (Lipson, Dibbler, & Minarik, 1996). Cultural knowledge is acquired by deliberately seeking out various worldviews and explanatory models of health, wellness, and disease (Campinha-Bacote, 1994). Having a culturally supportive attitude refers to appreciating and accepting differences. Some of the key cultural skills needed are the following:

- The ability to culturally assess a client, client group, or environment, and to avoid relying only on written "facts";
- Being able to explain the issue from the client's perspective and not the practitioner's;
- Knowing how to reduce resistance and defensiveness based on cross-cultural misunderstandings and barriers to communication; and
- Being humble enough to let go of the security of stereotypes and remain open to the individuality of each client (Tervalon & Murray-Garcia, 1998, p. 121).

The degree to which one can understand and appreciate the beliefs of those who are different from oneself is affected by the variety of one's own cross-cultural experiences and personal attributes, such as flexibility, empathy and language facilities. Thus, in addition to being knowledgeable about the theories and principles of the mental health field, one must also study cultural variation and acquire as much knowledge as possible about how clients identify with and express their cultural background, and must then incorporate these beliefs into one's plan of intervention. Rather than being insulted by another culture's perspective, culturally competent providers welcome collaboration and cooperation. For example, a culturally competent psychiatrist working with a Native American family might notice the wife is depressed. During their sessions, the wife might slowly reveal that her uncle had sexually assaulted her when she was young. The less culturally sensitive provider might start the wife on antidepressants and provide psychotherapy. Even if this helps, it may not resolve the underlying problems as seen by the woman and her family. A culturally competent provider would spend time learning about this family's culture and might find out the family believes the woman has acquired a bad spirit because of the incest. In addition to the more typical methods of treating depression, such a provider might consult with a Native American medicine man and participate in a traditional purification ceremony to release the woman of the spirit and thus help speed her recovery from depression. One way to begin acquiring some of the sensitivity, skill, and attitudes needed for cultural competency is by examining the various dimensions of culture and the way they may manifest themselves in behavior.

The Dimensions of Culture

It should not be surprising that there is no universally agreed upon list of cultural dimensions. However, academic work from as early as the 1960s up through the early 1990s has proposed a number of possible dimensions that would allow one to start thinking about the vast areas in which people differ. These differences can't necessarily be seen when one first meets a person. Rather, they are not directly tied to a person's race or skin color, although people with a similar religion and ethnic, geographic, and socioeconomic backgrounds are more likely to exhibit similar beliefs and values. However, within each culture, there are people who have assimilated the dominant cultural beliefs to a greater or lesser degree, and the individual differences are often more emphasized than the similarities. It would be easy but totally misleading to typecast people using the dimensions that follow. They are discussed here not to serve as an academically acceptable way of stereotyping but instead are offered up as a framework for checking out what people believe so as to better understand them and thus better serve them. Kluckhohn and Stodtbeck (1961) were among the first to propose a set of five cultural dimensions based on people's value orientations.

Human nature.   The first dimension deals with a person's basic belief about human nature. Are humans basically good, evil, or a combination of both? It is common for Western society to see people as a mixture of good and evil; however, some cultures lean more toward one than the other. Religious teachings, regional pride, and personal experiences, among other things, influence this dimension. Regardless of its origin, it can easily be seen how such a fundamental view impacts the relationships a person has, the degree to which one trusts others, and the way one reacts when meeting new people. For example, Finnish people are very modest. They have a saying: "Modesty makes beautiful." If a Finn is praised a lot, he or she becomes suspicious and cautious. It is also common and accepted practice among many Finns to expect the worst, since when one expects the worst, one can't be disappointed (Levo-Henrikson, 1994). When a child whose family holds these beliefs is placed in the highly positive, reward-based environment of the local elementary school, he or she experiences a great deal of discomfort. The teacher becomes frustrated by the child's undesirable response to positive reinforcement and thinks the child has a problem. In actuality, the problem that exists is the teacher's lack of knowledge and sensitivity to the worldview of the child and his or her family. Knowing a student's or client's inclination may allow the helping professional to develop interventions that are more easily accepted and thus followed.

The goal of being culturally sensitive and knowledgeable is not to change the person but to use that information to develop more effective interventions.

Relationship of Man to Nature.   A second dimension suggested by Kluckhohn and Stodtbeck focuses on a person's relationship to nature. Does the person believe humans are to be subjugated to nature, live in harmony with nature, or strive for mastery over nature? It is a commonly held belief that Native Americans value their collaboration with nature and strive toward harmony with the natural world, whereas people of European descent look to master the physical environment around them. Such a generalization may hold true in some circumstances but should not keep one from seeing the young white woman from Maine who strives to achieve harmony with nature and the Native American in Brooklyn who wants to become the master of his entire universe. It is more productive to see value in both perspectives and then bring in a more holistic view of illness and wellness to the provider-client relationship. At this point, one can collaborate with alternative forms of treatment such as meditation, spiritual healing, and purification ceremonies when they are warranted.

Temporal Focus of Human Life.   The third dimension, which has a significant impact on the provider-client relationship, is a person's orientation to time. Is the client tradition-bound (focused on the past), situational-bound (focused on the present), or goal-oriented (focused on the future). In past-oriented cultures, the customs and traditions represent the wisdom of society. Innovation and change must be justified according to past experiences. Change that is made for the sake of change or in order to create a better future is not as compelling as change that can be traced back as a natural evolution of what has been valued in the past. Future-oriented societies pay less attention to the past, and innovation and change are justified according to the future benefit they will yield. Present-focused cultures have a short-term horizon—they focus on the benefits of the here and now (Iivonen, Sonnenwald, & Parma, 1998). It is easy to see how a highly goal-oriented, future-focused provider can be ineffective and frustrating to a highly tradition-bound client. The challenge of being culturally competent lies in the fact that those very things most highly prized in the society of the provider, such as having a list of concrete and measurable goals and objectives and working to achieve them, may have significantly less value in the culture of the client.

Orientation toward time can also be seen in terms of a person's understanding of time as being either monochronic or polychronic. According to Hall, "time is one of the most fundamental bases on which all cultures rest and around which all activities revolve. Understanding the difference between monochronic time and polychronic time is essential for success" (Hall, 1990, p. 179). Hall found a cluster of characteristics are linked to how one perceives time. According to him, members belonging to monochronic societies are more likely to have a linear time perception. They generally do one thing at a time and are very comfortable adhering to strict time commitments, such as deadlines or schedules. This sense of time being linear also carries over into a person's working world. Monochronic cultures place a great deal of value on work and take their duties very seriously. They tend to have a high capacity for focused concentration, and often, interpersonal relationships suffer under this job commitment. In addition, it has been found that monochronic people are concerned about having privacy and not disturbing others. Germany can be seen as a typical example for a monochronic culture. Many Germans follow strict rules of privacy and show great respect for private property, and as such, they generally are not very comfortable with borrowing and lending things.

On the other hand, polychronic societies do not have a linear but have instead a cyclic perception of time. They are very comfortable with doing several things simultaneously and do not see deadlines and schedules as rigid or fixed. Polychronic people can be characterized by their great involvement with people and human relationships. They change plans often and easily on the basis of the needs of those close to them. And since they are more concerned and engaged with those around them, they do not put as much emphasis on privacy or ownership. For example, in many Brazilian cultures time is subordinate to personal and social relationships. Meetings often start when certain people arrive rather than at an appointed hour. It would be very rude for a provider to start a meeting at a given time if the most respected elder was not yet present—for example, to discuss a child's circumstances with a young parent if the grandfather was not in the room (Lipson, Dibble & Minarik, 1996).

Modality of human activity.   The importance a person places on being versus doing versus becoming is at the core of the fourth dimension discussed here. Does the person stress expressing one's emotion (being), or is the focus on inner development (becoming)? In one's worldview, is action of ultimate value, or does true change come only after lengthy contemplation? One of the most important values in the Finnish culture is the appreciation of work. A person is respected if he or she is a hard worker or "doer." Work is the measure of success and the basis of self-esteem (Iivonen, Sonnenwald, & Parma, 1998). Most Sami people—the indigenous people of the Scandinavian Peninsula—on the other hand, are also always doing something, but they are not very driven. Life goes on, and days are filled with everyday tasks. Sami people, for the most part, just want to achieve a state of happiness. Collecting wealth and possessions has little appeal for them (Iivonen, Sonnenwald, & Parma, 1998). This dimension is at the core of what people find motivating, and psychologists must be able to touch the individual's values if they wish to effect change. In addition, this dimension deals with expressing emotions, and serious misunderstandings can arise between a mental health worker who values and encourages the expression of emotions and a client who sees emotional restraint as critical to inner development. Finally, this dimension has many implications about the cause of illness. For example, many Chinese and Vietnamese people believe in the traditional Chinese philosophy of balance between yin and yang. Yin and yang represent all the opposite principles that are in the universe. Under yang are the principles of maleness—the sun, creation, heat, light, heaven, dominance, and so on; and under yin are the principles of femaleness—the moon, completion, cold, darkness, material forms, submission, and so on (Hooker, 1996). According to this philosophy, mental illness is caused by an imbalance between yin and yang, and only by bringing one's inner self back into balance can one expect to be cured (Gold, 1992). Therefore, telling a person to start jogging to release some of the anxiety he or she is feeling would be much more effective if combined with sending the person to work with a healer who can help balance the yin and the yang.

Relational orientation.   The fifth dimension deals with peoples' social relations. Are the client's social relationships marked by linearity (authoritarian decision making), collaterality (collective decisions), or individualism (equal rights) (Kluckhohn & Strodtbeck, 1961)? Individualists use personal characteristics and achievements to define themselves, and they value individual welfare. They believe in the rights of each person to do what is in the person's own best interest, and they understand when someone defies group norms in an attempt to do what is best for oneself. In other cultures, people are group oriented and define themselves as members of groups. In these cultures, people consider common goals and the group's welfare most important (Adler, 1997). People who are seen as striving for self-expression and individual fulfillment are viewed as being selfish and ungrateful. In yet other societies, obedience is stressed and rewarded above all else. For example, Samoan society stresses politeness and deference to those in perceived positions of authority. This often takes the form of silence, agreement, or attempted compliance to requests. All suggestions are taken as orders, and people strive to obey (Macpherson & Macpherson, 1990). To a provider with limited cultural knowledge, a person whose social relationships are collateral may appear to be unable to make a decision and may seem too dependent upon his or her significant others. The provider may consider this behavior the root cause of the person's difficulty in living, when in reality it is just a cultural difference, and the real causes of difficulty lie elsewhere.

In addition to people's social relations, their sense of *personal space* also differs greatly. In many cases, the way in which a person greets a stranger can provide a clue about his or her need for personal space. It has been said that Americans generally require more personal space than many of their brothers and sisters across the globe and that they feel most comfortable at a distance of about an arm's length away from others. Thus, the common greeting among Americans is shaking hands, with both parties providing an outstretched arm. Many other cultures routinely greet strangers with hugs and kisses. For the most part, Central Americans are considered very friendly people who often touch and kiss in nonintimate situations (Glittenberg, 1994). Filipinos smile a lot, and their elderly people are shown respect by kissing their hands, forehead, or cheeks (Espiritu, 1995). Hindus often press palms together in the front of their chest. Many traditional Muslims take the palm of a person's right hand and press it to their forehead, and then they bow down slightly (Patil, 1996). By being unaware of a person's personal space preferences and gestures, one can easily make someone else feel very uncomfortable by standing too close or seeming to be cold and uncaring by keeping too much distance.

In addition to the five dimensions just discussed, Edward Hall added another meaningful dimension to the list. He referred to culture as "man's medium," and according to him, there is not a single aspect of human life that is not altered or at least touched by culture. It determines how people express themselves (including shows of emotion), the way they think, how they move, how problems are solved. . . . "It is the least studied aspect of culture that influences behavior in the deepest and most subtle ways" (Hall, 1977, p. 14). He focused much of his attention on communication styles, and he coined the term "high versus low context societies". In this situation, "context" deals with nonverbal communication and information management. It refers to the amount of information a person can comfortably manage. In high-context cultures, information is more likely transmitted in nonverbal and indirect ways. Gestures are very important and often supersede the actual words that are being spoken; therefore, listeners have to carefully pay attention. The most important facts often need to be interpreted by reading in between the lines. In such societies, information passes spontaneously and in wide networks, and people tend to be informed on many subjects. Much nonverbal decoding is necessary to make sure one understands another person, and it takes time to understand the internalized messages and reserved reactions of people. According to Hall, Arab countries as well as France are high-context cultures. On the other hand, he believes that the United States, the United Kingdom, and Germany are low-context cultures. In these societies, information is communicated in a very direct way. People convey what they mean by using precise words and sending explicit messages. In such cultures, a person's reaction to another is usually visible, and emotions can be read relatively easily. As a result, people tend to be less observant and less aware of subtle, nonverbal communication. Hall also found that they tend to be less informed on subjects outside their own interests. Again, it is not hard to see how a teacher or therapist from one culture can easily misunderstand a client or child from another culture.

Michelle K. Hosp and John L. Hosp (2001) studied the behavioral differences between African American and Caucasian students. Using what they refer to as the African American Behavioral Style (AABS) and the Caucasian Behavioral Style (CBS), they compared the behaviors of students in three interrelated areas: orientation, physicality, and communication style. These researchers found that the orientation of the AABS is generally considered to revolve around people and that of the CBS around objects (Castenell & Castenell, 1988). That is, students operating in the AABS are generally more attuned to social cues such as facial expressions or body language (high context). Also, they appear to be more influenced by signals such as an "open" posture or indications of status or authority (e.g., being well-dressed, giving other people directions). According to Hosp and Hosp, CBS students, on the other hand, are more likely to look to objects for the context of their experience instead of to people. For example, one student who is not sure about how to do an assignment might look for written directions on the board or in the textbook (object-oriented), whereas another student (person-oriented) might ask a classmate or the teacher what to do (Hosp & Hosp, 2001).

Another aspect of a people orientation is a strong inclination for cooperation and a higher need for social interaction. According to Hosp and Hosp, students operating in the AABS are more likely to prefer working with others rather than working alone. Instead of focusing on competition and individual achievement, these students prefer sharing the task with others (collectivism). By contrast, students with an object-orientation (a predominantly white, middle-class value) are more likely to prefer working on tasks independently, focusing on individual achievement and thriving on competition with others. This tendency has significant implications in the academic success of African American and Caucasian students. As discussed earlier in this book, an environment that promotes one orientation over the other will give one group of students a distinct advantage over the other.

The second area studied by Hosp and Hosp is called physicality, which refers to the physical aspects of behavior. Almanza and Mosley (1980) reported that Caucasian students exhibit passive behaviors (e.g., standing still) 60% of the time, whereas African American students exhibit these behaviors 26% of the time. It seems that students acting in the AABS are more likely to get up and move around or fidget in their seats. Unfortunately, this higher need for physical movement is often associated with younger children or students with emotional or behavioral disorders. Physicality also refers to contact with objects and people, and has a number of implications for our education system. AABS is more inclined to a "hands-on" style of learning, because these students usually prefer to participate in projects or activities rather than reading or passively listening.

Hosp and Hosp proposed that having a people orientation and a high degree of physicality forms the basis for the AABS communication style. In the AABS, the listener is very much an active participant in a conversation (Bennett, 1989). In addition to reading social cues from the speaker, the listener is also sending cues. The listener interacts with both the speaker and the topic. The listener may be touching the speaker or giving verbal response such as "You are so right about that" and "That's what I'm talking about." When this communication style extends to the classroom, where rather than sitting passively listening to a lecture (as is often expected, either explicitly or implicitly), the student may be inclined to get up and walk around, ask questions without raising his hand, or verbally support the teacher (i.e., interact with the speaker) by responding. If the teacher does not understand the origin of these behaviors and is not able to appreciate the value of such diversity, these behaviors may be considered disruptive and may lead to disciplinary action.

Behavior differences in themselves are not problematic. It is the observer's perceptions of the behavior of others that can lead to problems. People interpret the behavior of others through their own personal experiences and expectations. When someone acts consistently with the dominant expectations for a certain situation, that behavior is interpreted as "good." Behaviors that conflict with the dominant expectations are often seen as "bad." In addition to the lack of congruence between expected and observed behaviors, the intent of behaviors is often misinterpreted when the cultural knowledge and expectations of the individual are limited. For example, the student who says "That's right" while the teacher is giving directions may be trying to support the teacher, but the teacher may erroneously believe the student is being disrespectful, and thus the teacher may respond in a negative way.

Up until now, this chapter has looked at some of the cultural preferences students may encounter in their professional lives. The following paragraphs look at cultural differences from the perspective of interacting with coworkers, supervisors, and subordinates who bring with them their own cultural uniqueness. Hofstede (1984) added four work-related values to the list of cultural dimensions. He proposed that the way people react at work is closely linked to four cultural dimensions that were largely ignored by Kluckhohn and Stodtbeck. "These four dimensions are power distance, the degree to which hierarchies and pecking order are seen as an irreducible fact of life;

uncertainty avoidance, the aversion to ambiguity and the need for formal rules; individualism/collectivism, where the former is the concern for self as opposed to the rules and priorities of the group; and masculinity/femininity" (Hofstede, 1984, p. 4). Hofstede uses the term "masculinity" to represent a focus on assertiveness and achieving work goals such as earning money, power, and advancements. He uses the term "femininity" to encapsulate nurturance and the attainment of more personal goals, such as working to create a friendly atmosphere and striving to get along with the boss and others. In addition, Hofstede suggested that "masculine" societies also define gender roles more rigidly.

Trompenaars (1993) proposed eight additional dimensions, many of which overlapped significantly with the work of those before him, so they will not be discussed here. The three areas that were new are the dimensions of obligation evaluations, status legitimization, and power distance. Obligation evaluation looks at where a person's ultimate alliances lie. Those who believe in universalism will be guided by societal rules, whereas people who believe in particularism will define the world in relation to their current, personal circumstances, and will act accordingly. Status legitimization refers to how people acquire status within a culture, either through personal achievement or through ascription. And last, power distance gets at the core of how much control people believe they have over their lives. It looks at the degree to which the average person is removed from the source of power. In cultures in which it is believed that each person is in control of his or her own destiny, the power distance is short, for all the power that is needed lies within each person. On the other hand, in cultures in which control resides with a chosen few or in the hands of the spirits, the distance is significantly larger. Asking a person who believes that power lies with a chosen few, to find the strength to change destructive behaviors from within may be impossible. Encouraging the same person to ask someone who is perceived to have power to give one the strength to change the destructive behavior may be much more productive.

These twelve dimensions of culture are by no means all encompassing but are included here simply to increase awareness of some of the many points of difference among people. Although a number of these differences are linked to religion, race, and place of origin, none of these demographic characteristics are flawless predictors of how a person perceives the world around him or her. The only way to know for certain is to ask.

Culture and Family Relationships

Community mental health professionals are among the first to acknowledge that individuals cannot be separated from the families with which they reside. This section will take a brief look at some of the basic structure, decision-making, and gender issues among Native Americans, Brazilians, Cubans, Haitians, Japanese Americans, Russians, Mexican Americans, African Americans, and other ethnic cultures in the United States. The intent is not to have the reader memorize and then apply this knowledge in a rote manner to all people from these cultures, but only to help foster an understanding of how varied these elements of family life can actually be.

In many cultures, the extended family plays a very significant role in shaping the dynamics of the family. For example, it is quite common for Arab Americans to have aunts, uncles, and grandparents live in the same household (Meleis, Isenberg, Koerner, & Stern, 1995). Many Brazilians include a child's godparents when making decisions dealing with the child's welfare (Lipson, Dibble, & Minarik, 1996), and Gypsy households routinely have at least three, and more often four to five, generations living in one household (Sutherland, 1992). In many Korean families, a person's self-esteem is gained through family identification and the degree to which the family is held in high regard within the community (Kim, 1995). Ethiopians characteristically introduce childhood friends and other close friends as siblings, and it is not unusual for them to have their friends live with them (Beyene, 1992). In traditional South Asian communities, a woman is expected to move in with her husband's family after marriage (Rajwani, 1996). In Eritrean communities elders play a major role in raising and disciplining grandchildren (Beyene, 1992). The decision-making power within a family also varies greatly from the traditional patriarchal society of many of the Caribbean islands to the more matriarchal society of the Haitians. Mexican Americans usually bring the entire family to the table when major decisions are made, whereas in Iran the thoughts of the eldest male member of the nuclear and extended family of the household are the only ones that matter (Lipson, Dibble, & Minarik, 1996). It does not matter which of these structures a provider encounters, what matters is that the health care provider should be aware of the predominant structure and act accordingly.

It is often difficult for people from different cultures to accept help from predominantly white, middle-class social organizations. Instead of imposing such an agency-based solution onto a family, a culturally sensitive professional may be able to use information about the family's culture to help strengthen the family. For example, a study done by Jarrett and Burton (1999) explored the impact of various aspects of family structure on the health and well-being of poor African American families. Burton and Jarrett identified four dimensions of family structure that are important for understanding African American families: extended family networks, the socioeconomic structure of extended family networks, the pace of change in family structure, and the age structure of family members. Each of these dimensions had an enhancing or constraining impact on the family and its ability to cope with challenges in living.

Burton and Jarrett found that in female-headed households lacking extended kin, women have a more difficult time maintaining domestic and child-care tasks, whereas in similar households with support from extended kin, women can satisfactorily manage despite living in a challenging environment. They also found that if all members of the extended family are poor, they were able to assist one another with basic survival needs, but their support did not alter the life chances of individual family members. On the other hand, if some family members were to achieve a level of economic security, they would be able to assist poorer family members with mobility-enhancing activities, such as access to better schools, mentoring relationships, and job networks. Their economic support could change the life chances of individual family members. Burton and Jarrett's research further showed families that experienced consistent change were depleted of family energy, thus making it difficult for them to perform basic child and youth monitoring tasks. And finally, these authors found that if the age distance between generations within a family was broad (18 years or more), the family exhibited more age-appropriate behaviors and a clearer family role.

Such information can be invaluable to the culturally aware provider who can now craft interventions that impact each of these four dimensions. By doing so, the counselor will strengthen the natural family network and have a much better chance of having long-term impact on the health and well-being of the various family members. Given the previously cited information, it may be much more effective to connect a single mother without family nearby to an older woman and her family and then to provide that unit with access to resources, rather than to pressure the young mother to go through the paper-driven process of filing for support from various social service programs.

Culture and People's Beliefs About Physical and Psychological Health and Illness

This final section addresses some common beliefs about illness, mental illness, problems in living, and psychological interventions among different cultures. For example, for many American Indians, mental illness is perceived as the result of ghosts or spirits invading the body, as the consequences of having broken taboos, or because one was no longer in harmony with one's environment. In such cultures, healing often includes a combination of Western medicine and the use of a spiritual healer (Kramer, 1996). In some Arabic communities, mental illness is believed to result from having experienced a sudden fright, pretending to be ill to manipulate the family, or experiencing the wrath of God. It is also believed that mental illness can be controlled by the individual, so it is not unusual for the family to avoid seeking treatment (Meleis et al., 1995). Many African Americans believe that mental illness results from a lack of spiritual balance, and drug therapy is often viewed with skepticism (Height, 1989). Some Russians believe that mental illness is caused by stress and moving into a new environment and that it is the family's responsibility to take care of the ill person with home and folk remedies. Such families have a tendency to avoid professionals and are very reluctant to take drugs (Evanikoff, 1996). Again, these examples are included to offer the reader a glimpse into the diversity of feelings, thoughts, and behaviors likely to be encountered, and to encourage more sensitivity about exploring these issues before intervention strategies are developed.

Principles in Cultural Competency

McPhatter (1997) suggested adopting what she called the Cultural Competence Attainment Model for moving a professional toward cultural competency. This model assumes achieving competence is developmental and that learning may take place in thinking, feeling, sensing, and behaving dimensions. The Cultural Competency

Attainment Model is made up of three components. The first component, "grounded knowledge base," includes a critical analysis of the major gaps and weaknesses in a person's knowledge base and an understanding of the new knowledge needed to become more culturally component. The second component, "enlightened consciousness," involves reordering a person's worldview and a shifting of consciousness, thinking differently about what is seen and about what is "real." The third component, "cumulative skill proficiency," is an ongoing process of skill development, growing to value another's worldview, and moving toward accepting and engaging a culturally diverse client population. This component also involves the use of cross-cultural communication skills.

Unfortunately, there is no definite rule as to what skills, knowledge, and attitudes are needed for someone to be a culturally competent mental health care provider. There are, however, a number of general principles that appear to make sense. Evelyn Lee, the Executive Director of RAMS (Richmond Area Multi-Services, Inc.) (Lee, 1999) has published such a list of principles. Her list is included here to provide a way to start assessing one's degree of cultural competency and to develop a plan for acquiring more knowledge or skills if needed.

Knowledge
- Clinician's self-understanding of race, ethnicity, and power.
- Understanding of the historical factors that may have impacted the health and well-being of the client, such as racism and immigration patterns.
- Understanding of any particular psychosocial stressors relevant to the client. These include war trauma, migration, acculturation stress, and socioeconomic status.
- Understanding of the common cultural dimensions expressed by the clients and their social network.
- Understanding of the client within a family life cycle and intergenerational conceptual framework, in addition to a personal developmental network.
- Understanding of the differences between "culturally acceptable" behaviors and psychopathological characteristics in the client's community/culture.
- Understanding indigenous healing practices and the role of religion in the treatment of the client.

- Understanding of the cultural beliefs of health and help-seeking patterns of the client.
- Understanding of the health service resources for the client.
- Understanding of the public health policies and their impact on the client and his or her community.

Skills
- Ability to interview and assess the clients on the basis of a psychological/social/biological/cultural/political/spiritual model appropriate to their culture.
- Ability to communicate effectively using cross-cultural interpreters if necessary.
- Ability to diagnose clients with an understanding of cultural differences in pathology.
- Ability to avoid underdiagnosis or overdiagnosis.
- Ability to formulate treatment plans that are culturally sensitive to the clients and their families' concept of health and illness.
- Ability to utilize community resources within the client's own community (church,

Community-Based Organization, self-help groups).

■ Ability to provide therapeutic and pharmacological interventions, with an understanding of the cultural differences in treatment expectations and biological response to medication.

■ Ability to ask for consultation.

Attitudes

■ Respect the "survival merits" of immigrants and refugees.

■ Respect the importance of cultural forces.

■ Respect the holistic view of health and illness.

■ Respect the importance of spiritual beliefs.

■ Respect and appreciate the skills and contributions of other professional and paraprofessional disciplines.

■ Be aware of transference and countertransference issues.

The need to understand cultural differences is obvious. The world is smaller than it used to be. New technology makes it easy to cross previous boundaries and to collaborate and communicate with people from across the globe. However, the new technology does nothing to assure that when one communicates, one hears and understands, and that what is shared actually has meaning and is not just a bunch of words. It is up to each person to leave behind outdated ethnocentric beliefs and to educate one's self to become culturally sophisticated and effective in this multicultural world.

DISCUSSION QUESTIONS

1. What are some ways in which a mental health professional can become a culturally competent practitioner? Give an example of a situation requiring cultural sensitivity that you might encounter while practicing psychology in the community and the way that you would address the issue, using some of the skills described in this chapter.

2. How much of mental illness diagnosis do you feel is culturally based? What is an example of a "mental illness" in one culture that may not be considered as such in another context? How does this relate to the person/environment fit covered in previous chapters?

3. How do different conceptions of time affect an individual's worldview? Why is this consideration important to a mental health practitioner? What is an example of a problem that might arise if a mental health professional does not understand the time orientation of a client? What should he or she do if such a problem arises?

4. What are some individually oriented cultures? What are some group-oriented cultures? What are some differences in values that might exist between the two? How might these value differences lead to confusion if misunderstood?

5. Why is it important to be sensitive to culturally different communication styles in the classroom? What are some exercises that could be used inclusively with different cultural styles of learning in the same classroom? Be creative.

Empowerment and Ethical Issues in Community Mental Health

OBJECTIVES

This chapter is designed to enable the reader to:

- Define empowerment as it relates to community mental health.
- Understand how empowerment manifests at the individual level of treatment.
- Recognize barriers to recovery.
- Describe psychological empowerment (PE) and the way it contributes to individual recovery.
- Understand how the ACT program contributes to empowerment goals.
- Understand the contribution of the mental health professional to client empowerment.
- Describe ways in which empowering organizations benefit members or clients.
- Understand the elements that make an organization empowering.
- Explain the purpose of using multiple criteria to evaluate objectives.
- Identify factors that contribute to an empowered community.
- Understand the importance of ethics to mental health care and how standards are developed.
- Understand the importance for mental health professionals to be familiar with ethics and standards.
- Consider real-life examples of ethical issues arising in the mental health field, and alternative solutions to these issues.
- Identify ethical issues and interventionist responsibilities related to primary prevention programs.

> *Reading about ethics is about as likely to improve one's behavior as reading about sports is to make one into an athlete.*
>
> *Mason Cooley (b. 1927), U.S. aphorist.*
> City Aphorisms, *Fifth Selection, New York (1988).*

> *Ethics, too, are nothing but reverence for life. That is what gives me the fundamental principle of morality, namely, that good consists in maintaining, promoting, and enhancing life, and that destroying, injuring, and limiting life are evil.*
>
> *Albert Schweitzer (1875–1965)*

Community mental health professionals need to be well-grounded in a philosophy of helping that enhances client empowerment, respects the rights of consumers to make decisions regarding their lives, and ensures their safety and well-being in as normalized a setting as possible. In order to give substance to this philosophy, two topics of interest are described in this chapter. The first concerns empowerment, or the process by which consumers gain mastery over their lives. The second topic involves the unique ethical considerations that mental health professionals typically encounter when helping consumers in the community.

Change as Seen Through Empowerment

Empowerment is a concept that has long been associated with caregivers. In many regards, empowerment can be considered as a values orientation. The value orientation, as Zimmerman (2000) points out, "suggests goals, aims and strategies for implementing change." Community mental health professionals will act as change agents and raise questions as a result. Should community mental health practitioners, as social scientists, be value free? Some believe applied science necessitates a completely neutral investigation of the issues. Community mental health practioners conceptualize social problems as resulting from a poor fit between people and settings. They design interventions to alter the highest feasible level of the social system. In a system analysis, the factors affecting behavior can be categorized according to levels of complexity ranging from individual, group, and organizational, to institutional and societal. Simple factors are more narrow and micro level, whereas complex factors are more broad and macro level. Traditional psychology studies individual-level factors such as genetic makeup, biochemical imbalance, and types of psychopathology, whereas community psychology investigates higher-level factors such as family dynamics, sense of belonging in social networks, participation in communal decision-making, and availability and accessibility of resources and services in the community. Systems analysts believe that by altering the more complex factors, the individual-level factors change accordingly or become less important.

A review of the empowerment concept from these various perspectives will be illustrative, and therefore the concept can be seen from an individual, a group, and a society perspective. Rappaport (1984) expresses this view in a definition of empowerment: "Empowerment is viewed as a process: the mechanism by which people, organizations and communities gain mastery over their lives." Empowerment, then, is construed as more than an interaction at the individual level. Included are empowerment concepts related to group perception toward goal setting as well as improving organizational effectiveness. In addition, empowerment may be construed as either a value or a theoretical construct (Zimmerman, 2000). It would seem that community mental health professionals need to have the understanding of and accepting of empowerment as a valued goal that would direct behaviors in a positive fashion to those in need.

Individual

Underlying the concept of empowerment at the individual level is an emphasis on enhancing wellness and focusing on the strengths, not the weakness or disabilities, of individuals. Over time there has been a shift to this conceptualization as evidenced by a change in terminology. Not long ago, those who were receiving mental health services were referred to as "patients" (most likely reflecting the "inpatient" hospital experience). This term implies, of course, that one needs "attending to" and is admitted to "receive" services. Today, the implication that a person is dependent on others for help in order to impact a positive health change has shifted dramatically. Individuals receiving services are referred to as clients, constituents, or consumers. It has even become more prevalent among those engaged in treatment to refer to themselves as "recovering." This carries a strong implication that these individuals are overcoming the disabling aspects of their condition. In addition, it implies that similar to recovery from alcohol or drug abuse, the process is a lifelong endeavor. Much of the shift from a dependent position to one of more independence has roots in the "independent living movement" (Deegan, 1992). This movement is led by people with disabilities and espouses a philosophy of treatment based on the member's own personal experiences. As Fisher (1994) points out, it includes a recognition that barriers to recovery rest not exclusively in the individual but rather in the attitudinal and physical environment as well. Fisher (1994) states it is vital to have ". . . an emphasis on choice in and control of services by the people who are receiving them and an assertion that it is possible to be a whole, self determining person and still have a disability." This independent movement has also reached out and established linkages and networks with agencies that provide advocacy services. Zimmerman (2000) refers to this force at the individual level as psychological empowerment (PE). He goes on to indicate the PE construct integrates perception of personal control, participation with others to achieve goals, and an awareness of factors that facilitate or hinder a person's ability to exert control. The value of PE is the resulting belief system: providing an approach or attitude toward one's own competence and functioning. Freund (1993) states that empowerment, like the word "love," expresses a fundamental human need. Unlike love, however, empowerment ". . . refers to society's relationships to the individual (not one individual's relationship with another) and to the role that individual performs in society." Cnann, Blankertz, Messinger, and Gardner (1989) discuss creating safe and healthy environments to help individuals to grow and become competent. These environments need to work with individual needs to create a good "fit." The person becomes partner or player in this fit, and is no longer seen as a disabled person but rather as someone in the process of "enabling" him or herself in the current environment/context. Much of this discussion is essential to understanding and implementing psychiatric rehabilitation. Anthony (1989) describes psychiatric rehabilitation as a technology for helping mentally ill persons develop the skills and environmental supports to become more successful and satisfied in their living, learning, and working environment.

In a recent effort to incorporate the value of empowerment and recovery into new program development, the New York State Office of Mental Health (NYSOMH) developed statewide training for implementation of Assertive Community Treatment (ACT). As mentioned previously, ACT is a current evidenced-based practice for the treatment of the severely mentally ill. Generally thought of as an advanced outreach case management program, NYSOMH has undertaken a process to incorporate other evidenced-based practices into the ACT program (Carpinello, Rosenberg, Stone, Schwager & Felton, 2002). Most significantly, NYSOMH has openly and directly indicated that ACT has a core value, namely an empowerment and a recovery approach to treatment. Training was consistent with implementing that approach and emphasized aspects of personal empowerment. This focus on personal empowerment includes encouraging consumers to actively manage psychiatric symptoms and to make choices not only about treatment (as seen in treatment plans) but also about aspects of community life. These choices, it is reasoned, will produce a positive self-image. In effect, consumers are now challenged to take responsibility for their life (to the greatest extent possible) and to manage any personal barriers that prevent them from leading a fuller and more satisfying life. Professionals are seen as collaborators in this process, guiding but not prescribing. It is also important to note this is not currently the trained role of mental health professionals. Most mental health professionals (psychologists, psychiatrists, mental health counselors, and social workers) are trained in certain skills areas, meaning that they generally give, prescribe, or offer treatment to those in need. The awareness of where the responsibility for wellness lies, with the consumer, is an essential value orientation in the empowering process and in personal recovery. This construct may cause role conflict for mental health professionals in whose clinical judgment the consumer's psychiatric disabilities may negatively impact his or her cognitive functioning.

Organizational

Zimmerman (2000) defines an empowering organization as one that provides opportunities for people to gain control over their lives. Such an organization provides members with an opportunity to develop skills and a sense of control. In the mental health field, as in other disability fields, self-help groups have often been seen as a valuable asset and recovery resource for those with disabilities. The positive impact of Alcoholics Anonymous (AA), for example, has generated a number of similar programs. There is, however, little research on the overall effectiveness of self-help groups (Chamberlain & Rogers, 1996). Although these groups are often loosely organized and have very high turnover, they often serve as an essential component to recovery from mental illness. An understanding of the elements that make an organization empowering is more crucial than focusing on individual details.

Maton and Salem (1995) describe four key elements to an empowering organization:

- A culture of growth and community building;
- Opportunities for others to take on meaningful and multiple roles;
- A peer-based support system that helps members develop a social identity; and
- Shared leadership with commitment to both members and the organization.

In a study by Chamberlain and Rogers (1996) that reported on a survey of 64 self-help groups for those recovering from mental illness, it was found that involved individuals reported a salutary effect on their quality of life, their self-esteem, and their social lives. Carpinello, Knight, and Jatules (1992) reported positive effects of self-help groups on self-concept, well-being, social functioning, decision making, and in achieving educational and career goals. Although the specific structure of such groups and their operational components are elusive, Chamberlain and Rogers (1996) reported that in their study of 64 groups, all contained the following criteria: groups are local; they control their own budget and staffing; the group philosophy is developed by group members; membership and participation are voluntary; there is no set program to follow; members are described as mental health clients (usually consumer, ex-patient, etc.); and the group is participatory. It should be noted that the ingredients that Maton and Salem (1995) found for empowering organizations can also be found within these criteria.

Community

An empowered community is one that will work collaboratively to improve the common good. It is all-inclusive and not biased against disability groups. Zimmerman (2000) stated that "an empowered community is expected to comprise well-connected organizations (i.e. coalitions) that are both empowered and empowering." From this perspective, it is unfortunate that with regard to the mentally ill, empowered communities are the exception rather than the rule. Morrissey, Tausig, and Lindsay (1986) studied mental health system referrals in two communities and found little evidence for coordinated systems of services. To make matters worse, coordination was reviewed for mental health agencies and did not include areas such as recreation and housing.

As part of the ACT implementation, staff are encouraged to learn the community and begin to develop linkages and activities both within the typical mental health system and outside the system.

For example, ACT workers will follow clients (consumers) through all mental health system components including hospital stays. In typical case management fashion, they will ensure clients get the services they need. In effect, ACT members create a subsystem of a mental health network based on client preference. In a similar fashion, ACT members will work with existing community resources such as landlords, YMCA, and so on, to develop relationships in which a consumer, if interested, could participate.

Ethical Considerations in Community Mental Health

When counseling and advocating for clients in the community mental health system, practitioners are likely to encounter many situations in which the well-being of the consumer is at risk. Most service providers belong to one or more professional associations, and these organizations publish codes of ethical and professional behavior. All who belong to these groups are expected to abide by their standards. When learning of a violation, the appropriate organization conducts a hearing, and if the violation is judged to be founded, the individual may be sanctioned or even expelled from the group. It is also possible that the counselor may be legally penalized as well. Consistent with the proactive orientation of this text, understanding the ethical principles and utilizing them as guides for actions in the mental health field prevents violations from occurring. It is necessary to learn the principles and standards of the relevant professional association and to periodically review them to keep abreast of changes in the codes as the mental health system evolves.

The ethics statement of various organizations can be found online as follows:

- American Counseling Association — www.counseling.org/site/pageserver?pagename+resources_ethics
- American Psychological Association — www.apa.org/ethics/code2002.html
- National Association of Social Workers — www.naswdc.org/pubs/code/code.asp
- National Board of Certified Counselors — www.nbcc.org/depts/ethicsmain.htm

These ethical codes provide both guiding principles and specific standards that are applicable to most situations. However, practitioners consulting to agencies affecting client well-being need to reflect on value issues that go beyond the professional association guidelines. Frequently, systems-level policies are at issue, whereas most of the professional association guidelines concern the individual counselor-counselee relationship. The value of empowerment is often an overriding criterion when making ethical decisions. What follows are some situations that some of the authors of this book have encountered. Each situation is presented along with some guiding principles. The reader might reflect on alternative ways in which these situations might be dealt with appropriately.

Case Studies of Situations Involving Ethical Dilemmas

Developmental Disabilities and Sexuality

How should a residential agency assisting adults with developmental disabilities deal with the issue of sexuality and sexual behavior? Some adult consumers invariably engage in sexual intercourse. Should the agency passively ignore the behavior, prohibit it, or even encourage it? Since the consumers have a developmental disability, is each one able to give consent to the activity? If the client is intellectually unable to do so, can the other party be charged with rape? Assuming the activity is consensual and condoned by the agency, performing sexual intercourse in the community residence might be disturbing to other residents in the home. What principles should guide the agency in making its decision?

The Board of Directors and staff of a private, nonreligiously affiliated agency recognized the need to balance opposing values of clients' having rights to choose how to behave and the agency's having a mission statement to encourage as normalized a lifestyle as possible on the one hand, while ensuring the safety of consumers and verifying the ability to freely consent to sexual activity on the other. In addition, some Board members were concerned about the reputation of the agency in the community. A few members of the Board were amazed that the issue ever surfaced. They recalled that prior to 1970, many people with a developmental disability, mental illness, or criminal history were forced to be sterilized to prevent others from being born with the same condition (Quinn, 2003). After all the arguments were expressed, the agency developed a policy that required that consumers, prior to sexual activity, participate in a lengthy social skills training program that included issues of relationship, sexuality, pregnancy, child care, and other related concerns. At the completion of the program, a mental health professional interviewed those who wanted to engage in sexual relationships to determine their understanding of the issues involved and their ability to freely consent. Also, the agency announced that its group homes were not capable of having married residents or residents with infants or children, and that the agency would attempt to help consumers find a new residence if the consumer(s) decided to get married.

Consider how this situation would be different if the agency were sponsored by a religious organization that considered abortion, homosexuality, sexual behavior outside of marriage, and/or artificial means of birth control as immoral. Should the social skills training program include the moral teachings of the religious organization? Again, how would the outcome change if a staff member who professed to be a member of that religious organization were asked to provide the relationship training program? On the one hand, counselors should not impose their moral or religious views on consumers. On the other hand, counselors should not be forced to act contrary to their religious beliefs, but should be prepared to act in accordance with those of the agency. Suppose this issue arises in an agency that offers an alternative to incarceration for 18 to 21-year-old offenders. What rights must be safeguarded? What limitations are appropriate? Those who value retributive justice accept many limitations on freedom as justifiable punishment. Others view the limitation as a necessary component of treatment, and still others accept restrictions on movement and behavior as a protection for the rest of the community. There are opposing views, and debate continues. In many cases, legislation establishes acceptable policy. For example, some disciplinary actions by staff against juveniles is considered to be abusive in child-care agencies but acceptable punishment in programs that are alternatives to incarceration.

A similar problem occurs with those agencies that serve the elderly. Assisted living residences and nursing homes are developing policies regarding sexual relationships between spouses and also between unrelated residents in the facility. The issue is when an individual who is suffering from Alzheimers Disease or other forms of dementia loses the ability to consent to sexual activity. If the agency sponsoring the residence chooses not to become involved in these private matters, who will advocate for the cognitively impaired consumer? Where there are gray areas, Boards of Trustees set policy, and mental health professionals are frequently asked for their advice. Indeed, mental health practitioners often serve on these Boards and sometimes see as part of their role the education of other Board members who represent the financial or legal resources of the community.

Behavioral Problems on Community Outings

How should staff who take consumers with autism on outings deal with concerned citizens who observe the staff restraining a consumer in tantrum? Occasionally, some consumers act inappropriately when they participate in community activities. Although agencies provide social skills training to the consumers prior to such outings, activities such as standing in line to enter a movie theater or waiting to be served in a crowded restaurant can result in a sudden tantrum. A staff member accompanying the consumer may need to use reasonable restraints or perhaps to allow the tantrum to continue if there is no threat of injury to the individual or to others. A concerned citizen might interpret that the adult companion is abusive or neglectful to the consumer and may intervene. The citizen's action, although well intentioned, is likely to be inappropriate and counterproductive.

The agency needed to balance the value of the behavioral objective (to take consumers to various community activities even though they might occasionally need to be restrained or segregated) against the effect the outings might have on others in the community. The agency chose to develop a small identification card which stated that the staff person is a trained professional hired by an agency that deals with consumers who have special needs. The card included an agency hotline number the citizen could call to discuss what was observed. The card did not indicate the client was autistic, because doing this would violate the consumer's right to confidentiality. Staff members could distribute the card to passersby who wanted to intervene to protect the consumer.

Community Volunteerism

In a similar situation, how should a residential agency serving individuals suffering from mental illness deal with the offer of volunteers to take clients on community outings? Many agencies have volunteer programs that encourage those in the community to develop relationships with consumers. The agency needed to balance the value of encouraging altruistic individuals to provide normalizing experiences for consumers and the agency's responsibility to ensure the safety of the consumers. Volunteers need to be taught not to offer the consumers food or beverages that might interfere with medications. Similarly, the community activity should not adversely affect treatment objectives.

The agency developed a policy for volunteer-related outings. A parental/advocate release form was constructed describing the particulars of each outing. The form included what relevant information regarding medications, and even in some cases, those aspects of the consumer's diagnosis that might be shared with the volunteer. The volunteer was trained regarding how to deal with unusual behaviors. The appropriate staff member was required to review the projected itinerary to certify that the outing was consistent with the consumer's behavioral plan. The policy required that staff would note any injuries the consumer may have encountered while on the outing. Liability issues were also addressed, but these are not primarily based on ethical concerns.

Consumers' Rights and Agency Policy

There are issues of consumers' voting in public elections, attending religious services, using public transportation, receiving counseling regarding birth control and abortion, and maintaining privacy regarding diagnosis. Each agency should establish policies that are within the law, consistent with the ethical codes of the relevant professional associations, fair and equitably applied.

Ethical Issues for Graduate Students

Ethical issues are frequently encountered by graduate students performing their field experience as part of a mental health counseling training program. Consider the following dilemma. On internship, a doctoral candidate is treating a 6-year-old boy who is one of 5 siblings. All 5 children have been placed together in foster care because their mother is an active crack cocaine addict. The boy came to a counseling session with a large, shoe-shaped bruise on his face, and he indicated his foster mother "slapped him with a shoe for sassing her." It is important to note that although the psychologist-in-training is a mandated reporter, in this child's culture, physical discipline is an acceptable way of teaching children to behave appropriately.

The psychologist-in-training is conflicted about whether or not to report this incident, so she decides to follow the ethical guidelines of the APA, which require her to seek supervision in making her decision. She discusses the situation with her supervisor and is advised that her dilemma is even more complicated than previously thought. Her supervisor indicates that a report of abuse on the part of the foster mother may result in removal of the children from the home. At the time, this was the only home approved for the care of 5 children. If the children were removed, they would be separated from each other.

What is in the best interest of the child? What is the ethical responsibility of the psychologist-in-training? How does the supervisor's opinion about what should be done factor into the decision? If the supervisor recommends that the student not report the alleged abuse but the student disagrees, to whom can she appeal?

Internet Guidelines

Offering mental health services using the Internet is becoming more common, and professional associations have begun to develop guidelines to deal with challenging situations arising from this process. Principles such as offering service within one's range of competence and ensuring client privacy must be upheld. In addition, consider the dilemma faced by a professional who participates in a support group for depressed individuals. Assuming the professional has established a helping role in the group, what happens if a group member expresses a clear and specific suicidal intent? The professional is responsible to do all in his or her power to stop the intended suicide. Consider how this dilemma is magnified if the professional knows only the member's e-mail address and first name. Suppose the group member is participating from a state in which the professional is not licensed. Would this factor affect the required or ethical response of the professional? Extending on the same example, note that if the professional and client were interacting in the same room, the helper would have a limited ability to observe nonverbal cues concerning the client's emotional state and determination to commit suicide. Such observation is not easily done on the Internet, even with the increasing use of emoticons when sending electronic messages.

Preventive Interventions

Most of the preceding ethical examples concern situations arising from treating individuals and groups. Consider also that there are ethical concerns when performing preventive interventions in the community. Some primary prevention programs are conducted on a large scale, and it is not always possible to inform individuals that they will be subject to an intervention. Neither students nor parents are told that a social problem-solving workshop is to be integrated into a lesson on literature. Similarly, it is difficult to pinpoint which community leader has the authority to give the informed consent of the population when a radio station decides to air a drug-abuse prevention program. Finally, some programs have unplanned and unhealthy consequences. For example, the federal government mandated that all automobiles built after 1996 must have dual front seat air bags as a measure to reduce auto fatalities. From 1990 to 1998, air bags have saved over 2,600 lives. However, 87 individuals have been killed because of their sitting too close to the air bag when it was deployed (National Highway Traffic Safety Administration, 1998).

Pope (1990) presented several areas of ethical concerns regarding primary prevention programs. These include the following:

- The interventionist should make certain that the program harms no one. Although harm is never intended, there may be aversive secondary effects of the program. Participants who do not achieve the desired goal might perceive themselves as failures. The individual providing the treatment is responsible to assess and then remedy such potential harmful effects.
- It is important to "practice with competence." Before a preventive program is implemented on a large scale, it should be tested on a smaller sample, and the consequences should be examined. The interventionist needs to ensure that all components of the program are implemented as planned. Of course, one is never certain that even a well-researched program will work with a new population or in a new setting, yet it is important to reduce any risks of failure or harmful effects beforehand.
- The participants must not be exploited for the interventionist's self-gain. The program should be designed to benefit the targeted individuals and not the mental health professional. The primary purpose is not to advance one's career or social status, but to provide an opportunity for participants to change their lives for the better.

- Treat participants with respect and dignity. Interact with them as human beings, and do not attempt to unnecessarily restrict their freedom or right to decide their future.

- Maintain confidentiality. Both in implementing the program and in any evaluation of it, the anonymity of participants is to be preserved. Interventionists have a social responsibility to evaluate programs and to disseminate effective primary prevention programs, but they should do so without divulging personal characteristics that could identify specific individuals.

- Act only with informed consent. This is a challenging requirement, as was mentioned previously. Whenever possible, inform potential participants in advance, and fully disclose both what is expected of them and what they can expect the potential consequences to be. Ask for voluntary involvement. The right of the person to refuse treatment and opt out of the program at any time must be maintained. Individuals should not be coerced by threats to withhold a needed service if they refuse to participate. In community-wide interventions, consult in advance as many civic leaders, public officials, and clergy members as is possible, and revise the program on the basis of their advice. In a school-based program, the administrator and ultimately the school board are the legitimate authorities, and their permission is needed prior to implementing a program, even if a classroom teacher approves the plan.

- The program should be designed to promote equity and justice. Primary prevention should enhance access to resources for those unable to obtain them. In addition, the mental health professional should be sensitive to cultural differences and should respect the values and traditions of the targeted population. The program should not be seen as a method of imposing the values of the dominant culture on minority groups.

The interventionist is ethically accountable for all effects of the program. Unanswered questions must be investigated fully and remedies found for any undesirable consequences that may have occurred.

Conclusion

As the community mental health system evolves and grows, it is expected that the current ethical codes will need revision to deal with situations not considered previously. Each of the preceding vignettes has at least some component that could be debated on the basis of today's ethical guidelines. Readers might consider discussing the preceding recommendations and developing alternative solutions. This is a beneficial process; as you navigate through the community mental health system, discuss challenging ethical dilemmas with colleagues to obtain a variety of valuable perspectives.

DISCUSSION QUESTIONS

1. How does individual responsibility affect the course of treatment for mental illness? How does the role of the practitioner shift when a recovering client begins to internalize the concepts of empow-

erment and responsibility? Give examples of how a person living with schizophrenia might make positive changes as a result of accepting the concepts of empowerment and responsibility, and how a mental health practitioner might facilitate this shift.

2. How does advocating empowerment differ from the current role of most mental health professionals, and what might help to change this? Why might mental health professionals be reluctant to adopt the new paradigm? How can these concerns be realistically addressed?

3. Give an example of an empowering organization that exists in your community. List five ways that this organization assists clients in overcoming the ramifications of their illness. Can you think of any other ways that such an organization might help a mentally ill person gain control over his or her life? What are they?

4. How are ethical standards and guidelines developed? Who develops them? What happens if a mental health professional violates these standards? Whose responsibility is it to be familiar with ethical standards and practices? Where can one review these guidelines? How should mental health professionals address issues that go above and beyond specific guidelines?

5. What are some logical ways to balance the pros and cons of a sensitive situation? When client and public needs and rights clash, which should take priority? How are these issues situation-dependent? What are the overlaps and distinctions between ethical and liability issues? Use some of the examples outlined in the chapter as a starting point for discussion.

OBJECTIVES

This chapter is designed to enable the reader to:

- Understand the benefits of consultation.
- Identify the different types of consultation.
- Identify various tasks performed by consultants.
- Identify reasons why consultants are hired.
- Gain an understanding of the consultative process.
- Identify some of the challenges inherent in the consultative process and some possible ways of counteracting these challenges.
- Understand why it is important to view behaviors from a cultural context.
- Explain how to assess the effectiveness of consultative services.
- Understand how consultation fits into the ecological perspective.
- Understand the importance of community-wide collaboration.
- Understand why consultation is economically feasible and viable.
- Explain how managed care can impact the ability to pursue mental health treatment, and why consultation can help alleviate some of the associated difficulties.
- Identify ways in which consultation can be cost-effective as well as functionally effective.
- Describe different phases of the consultation process, from initiation to implementation and beyond.

> *"The greatest good you can do for another is not just to share your riches but to reveal to him his own."*
>
> *Benjamin Disraeli*

> *"What you always do before you make a decision is consult. The best public policy is made when you are listening to people who are going to be impacted. Then, once a policy is determined, you call on them to help you sell it."*
>
> *Elizabeth H. Dole*

In 1969, George Miller, in his Presidential Address at the American Psychological Association Annual Convention, encouraged his audience to "give psychology away." At that time, the suggestion that psychologists actually offer their services not only directly to clients experiencing difficulties in living but also to clergy, teachers, medical doctors, police, lawyers, and other professionals in the community was a novel and radical idea. Miller proposed that these community leaders, though typically not trained in psychology, are experts in their own fields. They frequently come in contact with many community members who are experiencing crises; thus, developing a consultative relationship with such professionals will help all of us work more effectively with those in need.

On the basis of this belief, this chapter will discuss the various reasons, both altruistic or "other-serving," as well as the more self-serving reasons, why community mental health professionals should seek out opportunities to share their services via the consultative process. The following pages will explore the why and what of consultation, identifying the different types of consultation, the various tasks commonly performed by consultants, and the reasons why people, organizations, and institutions hire consultants. This discussion will be followed by a brief outline of who hires consultants, the consultative process, some of the most common challenges inherent in this process, and some possible ways of counteracting these challenges, and will conclude with a few words on how to assess the effectiveness of consultative services. This chapter is intended to give the reader a good sense of the need for consultation, the consultative process, and the value that can be added by embracing the concept of consultation. Much good can be accomplished by developing a mindset of sharing all that the field of psychology has to offer with educators, law enforcement officials, grassroot organizations, and community leaders. Consultation is indeed a viable and much needed process, and one by which we can enhance the quality of life in our communities.

Why "Give Psychology Away?"

Many mental health practitioners in training might wonder about the value of providing consultation to members of other professions. Perhaps they might fear that doing so will reduce the likelihood of their obtaining employment in the future. Ultimately, consultation is beneficial, not only to the client and community but also to the provider (A. Dohrenwend, 1996, personal communication). Let's begin by looking at some of the more altruistic reasons for providing consultative services and sharing psychology.

Volume of Services

Consultation can help to accommodate the volume of services needed. It has been made clear in earlier chapters that there are not enough mental health care workers to reach all those who need assistance. Recall the statistics presented in the introductory chapter of this book; problems in living are the norm, and many people encounter serious challenges in living. Those who are more severely incapacitated require intensive and extensive therapy. Given the number of providers and the financial resources available for delivering mental health services, it is not possible to effectively treat the severely disturbed and at the same time help those encountering less severe difficulties.

Increased Access to Sound Interventions

Consultation can provide increased access to psychologically sound interventions by increasing the immediacy of the intervention; decreasing the stigma associated with such interventions, and reducing the cost.

Mental health professionals do not have access to everyone who needs psychological assistance, and even when an individual in need can see a therapist, the waiting periods are often long and services relatively expensive. Often, this is not the case with the professionals with whom psychologists and social workers consult (called "consultees"). In many cases, these consultees are "on the front lines" when a crisis occurs. Police officers respond in minutes to calls involving domestic disputes, robberies, and assaults. Nurses are on the scene when someone's loved one dies in a hospital. Bereaved parishioners are more likely to call a priest, minister, or rabbi than a social worker or psychologist. Funeral directors will encounter depressed and bewildered individuals within hours of a relative's dying. Access to these professionals is nearly immediate, and with the necessary training, they can provide an effective resource in the community. As cited earlier in the book, providing such resources quickly can help to ensure that victims will be better able to resolve crises effectively and to emerge from the situation as healthy and productive citizens.

In addition to the immediacy of the "front line" workers' response, seeking assistance from these individuals can circumvent some of the stigma still associated with getting help from a social worker, psychologist, or psychiatrist. A study done by Patrick Corrigan (as cited by Levin, 2001) suggests that mass media has tended to misrepresent persons with psychiatric disability, and as a result, persons seeking support from a psychologist or psychiatrist suffer societal scorn and discrimination. This kind of social rebuff frequently leads to diminished self-esteem, fear of pursuing one's goals, and loss of social opportunities. Persons suffering from mental illness have limited options. They can either hide their mental health experience from the public and suffer a private shame, or be publicly labeled as mentally ill and suffer societal scorn. Working with professionals who are not part of the psychological community gives them a third option, as long as those professionals have the tools and skills to help the individuals. Community mental health practitioners can work to assure such skill transfer.

Along the same lines, the norms surrounding mental health and mental illness make seeking mental health services from teachers, doctors, spiritual leaders, and so on less threatening than going to a psychologist and psychiatrist. Despite laws having been passed enhancing the acceptance of mental illness and more people having been educated on the nature of mental illness and the value of psychological interventions, seeing a mental health worker still erroneously signals to the world that there is something wrong. In some cultures this tendency is more prominent than in others, but in all cultures these invalid perceptions still keep people from seeking the help they need. In 1999, a study conducted by Nabors, Reynolds, and Weist (2000) found that high school students are very much aware the "stigma of being crazy" associated with getting treatment significantly impedes student participation in therapy and school-based mental health programs. According to a 1,000-person survey conducted by John Fetto (2002), many Americans still fear the social ramifications they could face if others found out they were undergoing psychotherapy. Fetto found that 15% of the respondents cited this as one of the main factors that either had inhibited or would inhibit them from seeing a psychotherapist. Ironically, typically fearless members of Generation Y were most afraid of being judged. Almost a third (29%) of 18- to 24-year-olds, compared with half as many adults age 25 and older, shun therapy for fear of being found out.

Finally, in addition to being less stigmatizing, less threatening, and more immediate when delivered by other professionals and paraprofessionals, such psychological interventions are often less expensive and thus more affordable. Fetto's 2002 survey fund that regardless of what people say, more of them would likely be in therapy today were it not for the perceived *cost*. A third of the respondents (32%) admit they have avoided therapy in the past or will not seek the advice of a therapist in the future because they don't think they can afford the counseling. This perception is especially high in the Midwest and the West, where 37% of residents in both regions say that *cost* is a major factor keeping them from the therapist's couch, compared with only 29% of Northeasterners and 27% of those in the South who say the same. On the other hand, people do not think of cost when contemplating speaking with teachers, priests, or staff at local community organizations. Parents can get valuable insight into the needs and issues impacting their children at a given development stage from their teachers. Couples will go to their clergy for marriage counseling, and grieving widowers are more likely to go to a community organization such as Hospice to get information, social support, and acceptance. All of these services are free or relatively inexpensive, and if they utilize empirically tested, psychological methods, they can be very effective.

Consultation from the Ecological Perspective

Consultation brings the ecological perspective, which is fundamental to prevention, to schools, neighborhoods, community-based collaborations, churches, and so on. By sharing psychology, more residents are able to maintain themselves in the community. Mental health practitioners can train medical personnel in brief crisis intervention strategies and can provide information about local community resources and support groups available to their clients and their families. School psychologists and counselors can work with teachers to help students who encounter typical life crises and transitions. Industrial psychologists can train personnel managers to help employees manage job-related stress, plan for retirement, and ease the hardship of layoffs. All of these interventions can help to widen the "niche-breadth" of patients, students, and workers, and thus these individuals are better able to maintain themselves in the community. If such interventions are not available or if they are ineffective, tremendous disruption occurs, and it is likely that the distressed individual may require intensive therapy and possibly institutionalization.

Even when problems are not so severe as to require institutionalization, failure to consult teachers and those occupying other key roles will reduce the quality of life in the community. Students unprepared for challenging transitions are likely to experience reduced academic motivation and performance (Eccles et al., 1993). This situation can lead to many difficulties that impact not only the students but also their families, schools, and the entire community as well. Problems such as teen aggression, drug use, vandalism, school dropouts, and unemployment can be linked to poor academic performance (Allen, Chinsky, Larcen, Lockman, & Selinger, 1976; Scileppi, 1988). Preventing the occurrence of such snowballing problems through consultation and other methods makes sense from political, economic, and psychological perspectives.

High-Level Interventions

Consultation allows community psychologists and social workers to intervene at higher levels of the social system and to impact the macrosystem. Whereas traditional counseling strategies help distressed persons one at the time, changing the dynamics of the system can eliminate the social causes of the problem, thereby preventing many persons from encountering the crisis in the first place. Consultations to schools, local government, law enforcement, and not for profits can change systems and thus impact the masses. Such a strategy is cost-effective. Using system analysis (Hearn, 1969; Murrell, 1973) and Kelly's (1966) principle of interdependence, community mental health professionals can predict how a particular change in one sector will impact other aspects of a community.

For example, many have realized that no single government entity, organization, or program can fix complex social issues such as teen pregnancy, juvenile crime, domestic violence. One strategy that has gained momentum in the late 1990s and into the twenty-first century is the development and funding of local coalitions whose mission is to explore interventions that cross systems, channel the efforts of the local health and human service workers, and engage nonprofessionals in the solution-finding process. Such coalitions are often successful at developing and implementing multilevel interventions that make a real difference in their communities. This approach and the funders' inclination to support such efforts are not only effective but also ripe for consultants who can bring the numerous tools of community mental health to the table. A 2001 article in the American Journal of Community Psychology reported that community coalitions and other forms of community collaboration (e.g., partnerships and networks) are among the most defining approaches to social problem-solving over the last decade. Collaboration has become an essential requirement for government and foundation support (Chavis, 2001). Without cooperation among community groups, funding is becoming more and more difficult to secure.

There are numerous examples of successful collaborations in most communities. One such community collaboration is the Dutchess County Children's Service Council (DCCSC), which was established in Dutchess County, New York, in 1999. The DCCSC's mission is to improve the lives of the children, youth, and families living in Dutchess County. This small group of people (about 35 to 40), which brought together consumers and providers of health and human services providers, professionals and paraprofessionals, and legislators and concerned citizens, was able to do the following:

- Attract over 2 million dollars in funding over a three-year period;
- Implement changes in the way local government agencies interacted and communicated with each other; and
- Align the efforts of various public and private programs and agencies.

At various points over the coalition's life span, the group hired consultants to develop a countywide needs assessment; conduct a survey on tobacco use among local youth; assess the local outcomes of various research-based prevention initiatives; and develop a local report card to share with key community leaders, political leaders, service providers, and the general public. Such coalitions are being formed all across the country in every state and in an untold number of communities. Each can benefit from the information, expertise, skills, and resources that a consultant can bring.

This is just one way community practitioners can impact the higher levels of Bronfenbrenner's macrosystem. By consulting with legislators and other political leaders to produce laws and modify regulations, replace programs that "sound like a good idea" with those that can demonstrate outcomes, and help direct funders to wisely invest their limited health and human service dollars, then community psychologists and social workers can impact the lives of thousands, even tens of thousands of people.

As can be seen in the preceding reasons for giving psychology away, there are many effective and productive roles consultants can assume in order to enhance mental health in the community. There are also some more self-serving reasons for "giving away" psychology: although mental health professionals are often inclined to act in altruistic ways, they must also make a living and thus preserve their livelihood.

Building Relationships

Consultation helps practitioners build significant relationships in the community that enhance their ability to advocate for their clients and thus be better mental health professionals. Psychologists and social workers who know the key players in the community and who have an awareness of the social systems in which their clients operate as well as the effects on those client groups, are more likely to suggest effective interventions that will be accepted and implemented. Consulting in one's local community keeps one current on these issues. Consultants need to have a clear understanding of the various resources that are available in a given community, information that is also critical when working in a more traditional therapeutic setting.

The Implications of Managed Care

Consultation can help a practitioner remain viable in the current filter model of care (managed care) environment. Managed care has limited the ability of individuals to receive insurance-reimbursed psychotherapy. In addition, the requirement to select a provider from a participating provider list can add to the fear that patient-therapist confidentiality might be breached, and an emphasis on cost containment, accountability, and outcome assessment are among the issues associated with managed care.

Across the nation, health maintenance organizations (HMOs) and managed-care-oriented insurance companies are utilizing a filter model (Goldberg and Huxley, 1980) approach to the providing of care. Through this model, which originated in Great Britain, a person must first see a primary care provider (usually a medical doctor) who must refer patients to mental health services before the insurance company will pay for therapeutic sessions with a mental health specialist.

Pathway to care models, are designed with inherent obstacles to the provision of psychological treatment. First, the individual experiencing difficulties in living must realize that he or she has a treatable problem. Then the individual must overcome the fear that discussing psychological symptoms with the primary care provider could be embarrassing. The individual must then make an appointment to see a primary care physician where he or she must articulate the problem sufficiently to convince the primary care provider that a problem exists.

After that, the care provider has four general strategies from which to choose:

1. Discount the significance of the problem, and tell the patient to return if the symptoms worsen;
2. Prescribe drugs to alleviate the symptoms;
3. Attempt to counsel without adequate training; and
4. Refer the patient to a specialist.

This complex process will in all likelihood limit the number of people referred to the mental health services. Although it is difficult to determine the exact number of people who could benefit from mental health services but who do not receive them because of the HMO process, Orford's (1987) research found that at least in the area of treatment for alcoholism, the assumption that many do not get treatment holds true. Orford estimated that in a community of 250,000 people, some 7,500 have an observable problem linked to their drinking behavior. Of these, only 125 individuals, or 1 in 60, sufferers actually receive specialized treatment. The other 59 out of 60 have been "filtered out" of the care system. Goldberg and Huxley (1980) conducted a parallel study for mental illness and estimated that only 1 in 15 persons with an identifiable mental disorder actually receive treatment. David Mechanic (2001) found that of 1,792 study participants, 32% (571) perceived a need for professional help in a 12-month period and that only 147 people actually received services from a mental heath professional. Although these estimates may vary across diagnoses, this fact remains: in a filter model, not all who suffer some form of mental illness are treated.

Education

Consultants can play an important role in enhancing the proportion of persons receiving help for their problems, and at the same time reducing the stigma associated with seeking such help. Consultants can educate the public about the signs of mental disorders. This education can occur by using the mass media, or it can be provided through talks at the workplace or at meetings of social organizations. In addition, consultants can educate primary care providers and encourage them to utilize assessment tools to screen for mental disorders. Consultants might also work for client advocacy groups such as the National Alliance for Mental Illness (NAMI) to persuade managed-care companies to eliminate policies that discourage primary providers from referring patients to mental health specialists.

Cost-Effectiveness

Funding for traditional mental health service is becoming more and more difficult to attain. Employing consultative strategies focusing on preventing episodes of mental illness in large groups of people can be viewed as cost-effective. Many businesses, health care facilities, and governmental entities offer seminars on problem-solving, stress management, anger management, and similar skill areas in the workplace. For example, the Department of Veteran Administration has adopted a competency-based training model that recognizes "personal mastery" (being able to handle stress, anger, and other psychological and emotional issues) is critical to developing an effective, an efficient, and a satisfied workforce. As a result, the agency is willing to release employees during the workday to attend workshops and classes, and to invest training funds to address such issues. It seems that consultation is here to stay, and many mental health specialists trained in individual psychotherapy are performing consultative activities. Bernstein, Forrest, and Golston (1994) surveyed college and university counseling-psychology faculty regarding their involvement in school consultation. Over 40% of those responding to this national study had applied their learning in K–12 school settings, and 14% spent over half their consultation time in the schools. In addition, over 20% of supervised graduate students consulted in the schools. Some faculty chose not to become involved because they feared that such activities infringed on the territory of school psychologists or of their university colleagues; however, consultative activities are becoming more common, and these barriers are falling. In order to enhance the quality of mental health in the schools or in the community, it is worthwhile for mental health practitioners to learn the various methods of consultation.

Caplan's Types of Consultation

Caplan (1970) presented one of the most significant systems for understanding the categories of consultation. Although some authors have modified Caplan's typology, his categories have guided the literature for the past 35 years. Although it is not essential or even particularly useful to attempt to divide consultative services into hard-and-fast categories, since many activities fall into more than one category, using Caplan's types of consultation does help the consultant to conceive of alternative approaches to helping a consultee.

According to Caplan, consultation is neither therapy nor education nor advocacy, but is a service aimed at lending expertise to assist the consultee to provide better service. As the quote at the beginning of the chapter suggests, the greatest good you can do for someone is to help that person to find his or her own riches. Consultants, by the very nature of the tasks they perform, spend a relatively short time with the client, the agency, or the program, and they must make sure to leave something of value behind. Categorizing the consultative process as being either client-centered, consultee-centered, or program-centered can help determine who or what the target of the "riches" should be.

Client-Centered Case Consultation

In client-centered case consultation, the consultant is called in to deal with a specific client. The consultant assesses the client's problem and makes recommendations to the consultee regarding how to handle the problem. Client-centered consultation can occur in a variety of settings. For example, a teacher might ask a school psychologist how to reduce a particular student's disruptive behavior. The consulting school psychologist might sit in on the class to observe the student's behavior, and then meet with the teacher and suggest some strategies for helping the student. In another example, the house manager of a group home might ask a consultant to help a resident whose behavior is inappropriate. The consultant might assess the client's problem and develop an individual behavior plan for the staff to consider implementing.

The consultee need not be a mental health worker. A shopkeeper, police officer, or clergy member might ask a consultant to help with a former patient who is loitering in a public area.

Consultee-Centered Case Consultation

Although similar in many respects to the first category, consultee-centered case consultation focuses on the consultee's difficulty in helping a group of similar clients. A consultee might have problems helping minority clients, and a consultant might be hired to recommend strategies to incorporate the culture of these clients into the services provided to them. In another situation, the consultee might have a bias against drug-addicted clients or abusive parents that inhibits the consultee from effectively helping them. The consultant helps to build up the consultee's abilities to deal with these concerns. Typically, the consultant doesn't rely on psychotherapy, favoring instead a more behaviorally oriented approach of suggesting strategies for the consultee to consider.

In the first category, client-centered consultation, the emphasis is placed on the consultant's assessing and improving the client's functioning; in this category, the focus is on improving the consultee's functioning. In many situations, the consultant does both simultaneously. Another difference lies in the intended level of intervention. In the client-centered approach, the consultant is making recommendations to the consultee regarding how to help a particular client (e.g., a specific acting-out student). In the consultee-centered approach, the intervention is geared toward a specific target population or a group of similar clients (e.g., all hyperactive children in class). Whenever possible, it is more cost-effective to help the consultee deal with categories of clients, since this approach impacts more people and has the added benefit of leaving behind a set of recommendations/tools that can be generalized to other clients in the future.

The following are some examples of client- and consultee-centered consultations in the schools. Graham (1993) provided an example of client-centered consultation to help educators be more sensitive to diagnosing, preventing, and treating child abuse in the schools. He found that a consultant can be very effective in training and working with school staff to help them plan relevant curricular activities for preventing child abuse and also to help develop support systems for abused children and their families. Babinski and Rogers (1998) from the University of North Carolina at Chapel Hill found that "new teachers are often unprepared for the emotional, physical, social, and psychological demands of teaching and that traditional staff development models may not be well suited to meet the needs of these teachers." They proposed that school psychologists and counselors, on the other hand, were in an excellent position to facilitate the professional and problem-solving skills of new teachers, and to provide them with a sense of community and support and a forum for discussing their work in a safe and supportive environment.

Program-Centered Consultation

In program-centered consultation, the focus is on program planning, evaluation, or administration. Consultants can help in all stages of program development and implementation. In this category, a program administrator might hire a consultant to perform an outcome assessment to determine the effectiveness of an existing program. The consultant might utilize the principles outlined in Barker's behavior settings model (discussed in the second chapter) to ensure a program's activities are consistent with its goals and that all components of the program are operating efficiently and effectively.

The focus of this type of consultation can also involve program administration and management. Consultants can be employed to establish personnel polices regarding hiring, promoting, and firing workers. Also, they might suggest changes in program structure, leadership style, and role description. If a consultee complains the staff is not working well together, a consultant might suggest interpersonal communication or team-building in-service training. The consultant should be prepared either to provide expertise in filling any gaps in the administrator's ability to run the program or to locate an expert who can do so. In program-centered consultation, the consultant works cooperatively with the consultee to improve program functioning.

If done right, all three types of consultation should be capacity building. Consultation should help solve an existing, specific problem, as well as increase knowledge and strengthen skills such that the client, program, or agency can resolve future issues without the use of a consultant.

Tasks Commonly Performed by Consultants

As has been indicated throughout this chapter, the type of things a consultant can do are varied and limited only by the level of expertise and creativity of the consultant. A consultant's clients can come from any sector of the community, as well as from any agency, program, or government entity. Clients can be individual people, groups of people, or groups of agencies. A consultant can work directly with grassroots groups functioning as community organizers and can empower members of nearly any under-represented group to band together around a common political or social cause, or the consultant can be hired by agents of the social system. In addition, a consultant can be hired by local governmental agencies to plan and/or evaluate programs for targeted populations.

The types of tasks undertaken by consultants are extremely varied. What follows are some of the most common types of consultative activities that take place in a typical community, the Mid-Hudson Valley region of New York State.:

1. *Conducting needs assessments for a whole community or a target population.* The United Way of Dutchess County hires a consultant every three years to help them conduct the County-Wide Needs Assessment, a document that guided health and human service funding decisions for more than four funding streams.
2. *Providing community education.* Each year the Dutchess County Children's Service Council (DCCSC) conducts a one-day retreat for youth and youth workers where a consultant is hired to discuss an issue relevant to this population. After an introductory lecture, the consultant runs workshops for the teachers, social workers, and other youth workers, as well as for the students. In many cases, some follow-up work is then done by the DCCSC or the consultant.
3. *Team building.* The VA Hudson Valley Health Care System hires a number of consultants each year to work with their leadership and management teams on using effective communication, assessing the different personality styles of the team members, and helping them develop consensus-reaching and conflict-resolution skills.
4. *Helping collaborating agencies and grassroots groups to develop effective goals and/or to evaluate their effectiveness.* The New York State Office of Children and Family Services set aside over $1 million dollars to hire a variety of consultants to help 15 local coalitions establish their mission, set their goals, and evaluate the effectiveness of their efforts after the grant period expired.
5. *Conducting program evaluations.* More and more funders insist that up to 15% of a grant be set aside for an independent, third-party outcome evaluation. Each year the Dutchess County HIV Health Services Planning Council sets aside up to 10% of its large Ryan White Title I grant to hire a consultant to do an outcome evaluation for all of the programs funded under that grant.
6. *Bringing mental wellness, interpersonal effectiveness, and personal development programs into the workplace.* Each year many local schools, hospitals, and businesses hire consultants to conduct workshops on the Myers Briggs Type Indicator (Myers, 1962), personal goal-setting, and other topics.

The list can go on and on, and for each of these tasks, the community psychologists and social workers are the ideal candidates, since they possess the theoretical framework, skills, and expertise to serve as change-agent or broker of social action, to conduct research, and to assess systems as well as individuals. As the former senior vice president of the United Way of Dutchess County, this author was involved in selecting, funding, and evaluating many of the previously mentioned initiatives and consultative services.

Why Do People Hire Consultants?

The reasons for hiring an outside consultant vary from lack of knowledge, skill, self-confidence, or objectivity (Caplan, 1970) to mandated third-party program evaluation, to the creative management of limited resources. In order to "leave something behind," consultants need to be clear as to why they were hired and to tailor their interventions to deal with the relevant difficulties or concerns. At times, consultees lack knowledge about the client's problems. A police officer, bartender, or hairdresser might benefit from learning about information and referral services available for homeless persons. As was mentioned earlier, a teacher might need to know the signs of child abuse, or an agency administrator might request ideas on new programs to deal more effectively with a particular client population.

At other times, consultees lack the skill to make good use of knowledge. Key community leaders may need instruction on how to interact with a homeless person, or the teachers might need to know the steps to take when child abuse is suspected. Program heads might need help in starting a new program. Along the same line, staff, frequently those who are still new to the field, lack the self-confidence that they can use the knowledge and skills correctly. Frequently, new mental health workers feel more comfortable if they have access to a consultant with whom they can freely review how an incident was handled and can discuss how to improve their techniques. Often those who staff telephone crisis "hot lines" are reassured to know that a consultant is on call should a difficult emergency arise. Also, at times, a consultant might increase the consultee's self-confidence merely by validating what the consultee is already doing correctly. Such feedback from an outside expert is a useful support for novice workers.

In some cases, a consultee might lack objectivity in perceiving a client or in judging his or her probable prognosis. The consultee might have preconceived attitudes regarding gender, race, or age, and this outlook could limit his or her ability to work fairly with all clients. For example: a consultee might believe welfare recipients or drug addicts can never change and that it is fruitless to try to help them. A counselor who was abused as a child might find it too emotionally distressing to listen to a child who is currently being abused. In all these cases, the consultees' attitudes, beliefs, or feelings have become obstacles preventing them from providing a needed service. The consultees' clinical supervisor (consultant) must point out the biases and transferential issues to the consultees.

This is probably one of the more difficult consultant tasks, because the consultant needs to be very careful when confronting the consultee's lack of objectivity. In most cases, the consultee is not aware that a loss of objectivity is causing some of the difficulties experienced. If this problem is deep-seated, the consultee might reject the consultant's recommendations and terminate the relationship. It is better to address problems of lack of knowledge, skill, and self-confidence first, and to allow trust, rapport, and respect to build before attempting to deal with lack of objectivity.

Less sensitive and increasingly more common reasons for hiring a consultant are the need for third-party validation of a program's outcomes and limited, short-term funding commitments. In today's limited funding environment, government funders, foundations, and private funders want some assurance that their investment does indeed have an impact. In the interest of cost efficiency, many funders require independent evaluations to validate the agency/program has done what it promised to do. For that reason, consultants are frequently hired to do needs assessment, conduct program evaluations, and develop and interpret client surveys. From 1999 to 2002, the United Way of Dutchess County was able to secure over $600,000 to support the evidence-based FAST program (Families And Schools Together), and each of the funders required an independent evaluator to be part of the implementation team. The more than $1 million dollars set aside by the County Executive for the Dutchess County Children's' Services Health Initiative provided numerous grants for youth-smoking cessation and education programs. Each of these grants also required an independent evaluator, and 10% of the annual grant was set aside to pay for this service.

Along the same line, many funded positions are task-specific and very short-term, reducing the likelihood that agencies will hire full-time staff, knowing that the grant is limited to only 6 months or a year. This is very similar to the outsourcing trend that has become very popular in the private as well as the government sector. It is cheaper to hire someone with a very specific skill on an as-needed basis to perform a required service than to take on a full-time staff member. For the most part, agencies can't afford to pay for the level of knowledge they may need on a full-time basis. They hire college professors, psychologists, or researchers to consult for them, thus providing them with resources that they could not otherwise afford.

The Consultative Process

Few mental-health professionals are sufficiently trained in the process of consultation, and it is useful to explore the characteristics of the process and the steps involved. It is important to remember that the consultee has hired the consultant to provide a service—generally to assist the consultee in performing his or her work more effectively. The consultant must recognize that the consultee is also a trained professional. A school psychologist who views a teacher as inferior is destined to fail, and it is likely that the teacher will never request a second consult. Caplan (1970) coined the phrase "one-downmanship" to describe the preferred attitude the consultant should take when communicating with a consultee. Drisko (1993) noted that teachers often see a referral to the consultant as an indication of failure. The consultant must reduce this perception by creating a productive relationship built upon mutual respect, acceptance, and the sense of equality. Of course, the consultant should present views in a confident and an assertive manner and defend the value of the recommendation made. Yet ultimately, the recommendations are advisory in nature, and the consultee is responsible for deciding on their implementation. The consultant's influence is based on persuasion, and the suggestions presented are not mandates to the consultee.

Sax (1999) outlined the phases of the consultative process as follows: creating the work agreement; defining key issue and solution ideas; gaining commitment for recommendations; and implementing solutions and follow-up. Each of these phases is fraught with challenges that need to be addressed if the consultants want to leave behind their riches and have any long-term impact.

Creating the Work Agreement

This phase is made up of three specific steps: gaining an understanding of the client's business, establishing credibility, and confirming and communicating the work agreement. The more the consultant knows about the consultee's situation, the more comfortable and focused the initial interactions will be. Consultants should have a basic understanding of the type of consultation they will be doing, the reason why they were hired, and the specific skills, tools, and expertise that the consultee wants to continue once the consultation has come to an end.

The prospective consultant must also consider the interpersonal aspects of the consultation process. To be successful, the consultant needs the support of both the formal and the informal leaders of the organization, and the agency staff needs to believe the consultant is credible. If the consultant is external to the agency, credibility depends on expertise based on appropriate training and a demonstrated successful track record elsewhere, as well as on the way the consultant treats the staff. In each new consultative relationship, respect must be earned, and it will be given only if the consultant can demonstrate respect for the professionals already working in the agency. Early (1992) observed that in order to be seen as credible, an education consultant needs to become integrated into the work group of the school as a member of equal status intent on cooperating to provide service to students. The relationship should be reciprocal and collegial, and should involve a two-way exchange of information. The teacher has knowledge of the student and educational methods, and the consultant has specialized expertise in areas relating to psychology or learning disabilities. If an outside consultant is seen as an outsider who lacks intimate knowledge of the agency, the staff may view the recommendations as impractical or unrealistic and thus fail, or worse yet, refuse to implement them. In order to be successful, the consultant needs to prove otherwise and to dispel any other mistrust that the consultee may feel.

In addition to developing a rapport that will lead to trust, a critical task in phase one is to confirm and communicate the work agreement. Although most consultations begin with an informal and a general sharing of ideas, eventually the specific scope of services, including the responsibilities, rights, and authority of each participant in the process, needs to be spelled out formally in writing. Both the consultant and the consultee have "mental pictures" of what is to be accomplished, but the views may not be consistent; therefore, specifying these activities in the contract clarifies any ambiguity. The relationships among key personnel and their responsibilities should also be

alzheimer's association
AGREEMENT between the
Fulton County Office for Aging and
Northeastern New York Alzheimer's Association
ATTACHMENT A

In compliance with the Agreement signed between Fulton County Office for Aging (OFA) and Northeastern New York Alzheimer's Association (ASSOCIATION), the ASSOCIATION will provide an environmental assessment of all living and recreational space used by persons with Alzheimer's and/or related dementias. Each assessment will be conducted within a two month period from start to finish and culminate in a list of recommendations on environmental modifications that will improve the functionality of the space, assure the clients' safety, and support the management of behavioral issues.

The ASSOCIATION will respond to any written requests for OFA for services within 5 business days by contacting the head of the agency requesting services to set up an initial interview. At that interview,

1. A timeline for the delivery of service will be established.
2. The agency will be asked to identify a Project Leader who will be working directly with the ASSOCIATION and an Implementation Team who will be responsible for implementing all approved recommendations.
3. A date or dates for training all staff will be set up.

During the actual assessment the ASSOCIATION will need to have access to all staff, clients and records to get a sense of any unique behavioral issues that need to be addressed.

The ASSOCIATION will provide the head of the agency, the Implementation Team and the Project Leader with a draft of its recommendations no less than two weeks before the final report is released. During that two week period, a meeting of all parties will be held to openly discuss the feasibility and barriers of implementing the recommendations and any changes that may need to be made to make this report as useful as possible.

The ASSOCIATION will submit the final report to the head of the agency, the Implementation Team and the Project Leader and provide a formal presentation to any governing body agreed to by the head of the agency and the ASSOCIATION staff.

The ASSOCIATION will make itself available for phone consultations for up to six months after the final report has been delivered.

FIGURE 9.1   A typical consultant contract

detailed. It is important to know whether decisions are made in a hierarchical or a collaborative manner, as well as how, when, and to whom to communicate progress. Who will be responsible for approving and for implementing the final recommendations? Key decision-makers need to be identified and included in the process in order for the consultation to be effective, and the consultant needs to know where his or her authority begins and ends. If the consultative activity is a program evaluation, the contract should also address issues such as who is responsible for the accuracy of the data being reported and collected, and what, if anything, the consultant may be able to publish. Finally, the consultant also needs to know what resources will be committed to implementation and maintenance of the solution, because that information will impact the type of interventions to be recommended. If there is a staff person designated to perpetuate the effort started by the consultant, the consultant can proceed in a different manner than if no one and no recourses can be set aside for the venture once the consultative relationship commences. If this phase is not completed thoroughly and formally, miscommunication will abound, and disappointment will prevail.

Defining Key Issues and Solution Ideas

The second phase of the consultative process focuses on operationally defining the problem and developing solution options. This is perhaps the most significant step in consultation, and care should be taken to avoid overly quick diagnosis, which might focus on symptoms rather than on the source of the difficulty. The way the problem is defined and who defines it affect the nature of the remedies taken to solve the problem. It is therefore essential to gather input from a variety of sources and not to rely on one person or group of persons. If the person who hires the consultant is the main source of information, the consultant may develop a narrow and limited view of the problem that will result in an equally limited solution.

In order to have long-lasting impact, the consultant must make every effort to look at the problem and then develop solutions that intervene at the highest possible level of the system (Lachenmeyer, 1992). Frequently, the consultee sees the problem at a lower level. The consultee is likely to report that a student is lazy, a client is uncooperative, or an employee is not working effectively. The consultant and consultee need to negotiate and collaborate to develop agreement regarding understanding the problem as multifaceted. Treating it at many levels can lead to a more successful intervention. One way to make sure the consultant has enough data to reach such conclusions is to gather the data from clients, staff, and community leaders as well as from the competitor, that is, other agencies serving the same client population or trying to impact the same problem.

Levine and Perkins (1987) noted that defining the problem is essentially a political activity. For example, a teacher might complain that students of color are not learning well in class. If the problem is perceived as residing in the children, the consultation becomes case-centered and the solutions include labeling and placing the students in a track for slow learners. If the problem is seen as a symptom of a classroom problem or school-level problem, the consultation becomes more consultee-centered, and solutions include adding cultural amplifiers to the curriculum.

Before presenting alternative solutions, the consultant must investigate what remedies the consultee has already tried. It is critical not only to know that a previous solution failed but also why it failed. Was it the wrong alternative, or was it a good strategy but poorly implemented? When presenting the plausible alternatives, the consultant needs to outline the advantages and disadvantages of each and then to guide the consultee through the process of weighing the value of the alternatives. Ideally, the consultant should not apply too much pressure favoring one alternative over others. At times, a consultee may realize that a particular solution is the best one, but might be reluctant to accept it because it is seen as difficult to implement or politically challenging. The consultant needs to encourage the consultee to express these concerns, so that by working together, creative approaches to minimize potential drawbacks can be discussed. Ultimately, the consultee must decide on which recommendation to adopt because he or she must then commit the agency to its implementation.

The specific aspects of the intervention depend on the nature of the problem addressed and on the type of consultation involved. Case-centered consultations deal with more individually oriented problems, and the resulting interventions tend to be simple. The consulting activity is typically brief but may need to be repeated with each new case. Program-centered consultations, on the other hand, tend to be more complex and multifaceted, and they are likely to continue over a period of many months. In either case, the intervention should be implemented according to an agreed-upon plan and modified only by a consensus decision.

Gaining Commitment for the Recommendations

In order to increase the likelihood that implementation is successful, the consultant must gain commitment to the implementation plan from as many people as possible. One step in assuring such commitment is to clearly outline the resources that will be necessary and the time needed to reach the desired outcomes. If these resources are not readily available, a plan must be developed for securing the resources, and a skilled consultant will include this part of the process in the work agreement. It may be necessary to secure a grant, hire staff, and develop a working agreement with another agency or set of agencies. If no plan exists for how this will be done, any brilliant solution brought forth by the consultant may in all likelihood remain a vision without ever being fully realized.

One way of stacking the odds in favor of successful implementation is to make sure there is a change champion on staff who is committed to implementing the solution. A change champion is a person, or more ideally a group of persons, who

- Truly believe the recommendation(s) will have a real impact on the problem;
- Have a personal stake in seeing the problem successfully resolved;
- Are given the time and resources to see the implantation plan through; and
- Have enough formal or informal power to drive the needed change within the organization.

Without a change champion, it is highly likely that some, if not all, of the recommendations will never be fully implemented and the problem only partially addressed. The consultant-consultee relationship is by its very nature a time-limited relationship, and real solutions to complex problems usually take a great deal of time and involve many segments of the community.

Once the plan has been developed, the resources secured, and the change agent identified, the intervention procedures should be monitored on a regular basis to ensure that all activities are taking place as planned. This formative or process evaluation has two purposes. First, if certain components are not being carried out as planned, errors can be corrected early enough to get the project back on course. Second, this process evaluation can aid in the interpretation of the outcome evaluation to be conducted at the end of the consultation. That is, if the intervention was not implemented properly and the outcome data show that the original problem was not remedied, the fault might be due to the plan's not being carried out as designed.

The consultant and consultee should communicate regularly throughout the process to confront problems as they occur and to correct any misperceptions or rumors. As will be discussed in the chapter on change, interventions cause flux in the system, and in transitional situations, some participants benefit, whereas others are harmed in some way. Through good communication, the consultant and consultee become aware of such adverse effects early on and can plan strategies to reduce these consequences.

Despite the need for all to keep involved, the consultation must formally end at a specified time, and the process, the timing of termination, and the form of the final report should be clearly stated in the work agreement. The consultant also needs to be clear as to who has the final authority of deeming the work product acceptable. Is it the Executive Director of the agency, the Board of Directors, or the leadership team of the coalition? Must the entire voting body approve, and so on? Once approval has been attained, a clear plan for follow-up should be made. With whom will the consultant follow up? At what time? And for what purpose?

Implementing Solutions and Follow-Up

In this final phase, the consultant develops the implementation map. This is a document that is more detailed than the work agreement and includes specific steps for the following:

- Determining and increasing readiness;
- Outlining the roll-out activities;
- Identifying and planning for reinforcement activities; and
- Establishing the follow-up process and schedule.

At this point it is critical to involve the change agent(s) and clearly outline the roles each person will play. Intervention procedures should be monitored on a regular basis to ensure that all activities are taking place as planned. The coordination, orchestration, and sharing of information are critical to the outcome, and at this point, midcourse adjustments and unexpected obstacles are common and should be expected and planned for.

Finally, the most important activity to perform just prior to termination is the evaluation of the consultative intervention. Although the evaluation is implemented at this time, the process for evaluation should have been designed when the intervention was being planned.

Why Evaluate?

Since consultation in community mental health is the result of a merger between social scientific research and mental health models, it is important to evaluate the effectiveness of any intervention. There are three types of benefits to performing this activity:

- Program evaluation provides the consultee with a fairly objective measurement to determine whether the original problem was solved, and to what degree.
- Program evaluation helps the consultant determine whether the intervention was successful. If it was not fully successful, the consultant can suggest strategies to fine-tune the process, which the consultee may perform either in-house or with further assistance.
- Program evaluation allows us to disseminate the results of the psychological intervention to others so that consultees experiencing similar problems can adopt some or all of the effective intervention(s). Although this step can be very helpful, there are some limitations to the value of dissemination.

Ethically, such dissemination must follow the rules governing consultant-consultee confidentiality. Opposing criteria, such as maintaining the privacy and the reputation of the consultee's agency versus the consulting psychologist's responsibility to share the fruits of action-oriented research, must be balanced. Guidelines regarding any public disclosure of the consultative activity should be clearly stated in the work agreement. The second significant limitation to dissemination is more technical in nature. Few, if any, interventions can be replicated exactly and applied to a new setting. That is, viewed from the ecological perspective described in Chapter 3, each agency consists of a different pattern of factors, has a unique physical, social, and political setting, and has different staff and clients. Thus, the conditions in which the intervention(s) will be applied will always be different, yet the principles upon which an effective intervention is based can be tailored and then applied to a broad array of consultees or programs. In effect, the strategy for designing an appropriate intervention can be generalized to similar programs experiencing similar difficulties, even if the details need to be tailored to the individual situation.

The Characteristics of a Good Evaluation

The best evaluations are multifaceted, collect diverse types of data from a variety of sources, monitor both process and outcome measures, and include intermediate criterion of success. The evaluation should be as multidimensional as the intervention. For example, if an agency hires a consultant to reduce unemployment among former psychiatric patients, and the consulting psychologist develops an intervention consisting of both job training and job placement, then both services need to be monitored. If the program were to fail, it would be helpful to know whether the problem was caused by too few patients being adequately trained or the placement service's inability to find jobs for the trained individuals. The outcome measure (the increase in the number of working former patients) needs to be related to the process monitoring that should have started during the intervention itself. If staff provided only half the agreed-upon number of training sessions, poor outcome might be explained by the failure to carry out the intervention as designed.

Along the same line, diverse types of data need to be collected from a variety of sources. In addition to utilizing the process and ultimate outcome measures, the effectiveness of a consultation can be assessed using intermediate criteria as was described in the prevention chapter. These are measures that are available earlier than the outcome data, and they are tied either logically or empirically to the final outcome. For example, the work skills and abilities of the former patients can be assessed more quickly than the number of jobs these individuals obtain. These intermediate criteria serve as markers along the way to predict the effectiveness of the intervention, and are called initial outcomes.

Included in the evaluation package should be measures of both quantitative and qualitative data. Quantitative data are observable and objective. How many individuals obtained employment, and what was their average salary? Qualitative data are more subjective and consist of attitude measures. Were former patients satisfied with the training and placement programs, and were they more confident that they could get and keep a job? Such data should be collected from a variety of sources, using a variety of tools. In the preceding example, questionnaires measuring perceived program effectiveness need to be administered not only to the former patients but also to their employers and to the training agency staff. Even the quantitative evidence should be collected from many sources since participants, employers, and staff may disagree regarding the number of jobs actually obtained.

Evaluations of actual consultations are considered applied research because they are often not as precise as research conducted in artificial laboratory settings. Many uncontrollable factors affect the outcome and its measurement in these real-world studies. Measurements of actual interventions may be biased by those reporting the data. Training agency staff might overestimate the number of participants who found jobs, whereas employers fearing public disfavor may underreport the number of former patients they hired. Almost any job-training program can succeed in times of very low employment, for example, and yet an excellent program can fail during an economic recession. By monitoring many factors collected from a variety of sources, the quality of the intervention can be more precisely assessed. If it is determined that participants did learn job skills adequately, it is likely that many will be employed when the economy improves, and the intervention will eventually succeed. If on the other hand, the participants did not learn required skills, a program's current failure will probably continue even when the economy becomes healthier.

Consistent with the preceding, Rossi, Freeman, & Wright (1978) suggested that a series of small studies, each with its own advantages and design flaws, is more convincing than depending on the results of a single large study. If all (or even most) of the individual measures point to the same conclusion, a researcher can expect that the experimental design flaws have canceled each other out, and can trust that the evaluation is more accurately a reflection of the intervention's effectiveness. The conclusion of a single study is less credible, since it is open to plausible rival interpretation (Campbell and Stanley, 1963). This method of generating many small evaluation instruments, each utilizing different designs, is called "triangulation," named after the method of locating a radio transmitter by positioning receivers in geographically different locations. Although each receiver can determine the direction from which the signal is coming, no one receiver can pinpoint the exact location of the source. A number of receivers, each from a different perspective, must all point to the source in order to locate it precisely (Scileppi, 1988).

How Effective Is Consultation?

Since consultations are individually tailored to the needs of the consultee in specific settings, it is difficult to determine whether a specific consultation will be effective when applied to a new agency. Yet it is possible to study whether consultations in general are effective. To investigate this question, some authors have relied on meta-analysis. In a meta-analysis, the results of a large number of studies are grouped together to determine whether the treatment yielded more positive outcomes than the nontreatment controls. Medway and Updyke (1985) performed such a meta-analysis on 54 consultation evaluation studies, most of which occurred in school settings. They measured effect size, which is an index of the magnitude of the difference in outcomes between the consultation and no-consultation groups. Medway and Updyke found that following the intervention, the average consultee improved more fully than 70% of those who did not receive consultation. In a similar study, Gibson and Chard (1994) reviewed 1,643 consultation outcomes cited in the research literature. They found that such interventions produced an 11% greater improvement in consultee and organizational functioning, which they interpreted as very substantial evidence of the effectiveness of consultation. In a final meta-analysis, Wilson, Lipsey, and Derzon (2003) reviewed 334 studies of interventions to reduce school violence. They compared the pretest-posttest changes in student aggression and found that after the intervention, approximately half the number of students engaged in physical fighting on school grounds as before the intervention. The control-group students showed no difference in posttest compared with pretest aggressive behavior. The authors noted that the 1999 Youth Risk Behavior Survey conducted by the Center for Disease Control (Wilson, Lipsey & Derzon 2003) found that 15% of students report involvement in a physical fight at school during a 12-month period. If these consultative interventions were to be applied nationally, only 8% of the students would be aggressive. However, most of the studies included in this meta-analysis were demonstration programs in which the conditions for program implementation are carefully controlled. Wilson, Lipsey, and Derzon (2003) caution that effectiveness would probably be reduced if the programs became full-scale, routine practice in the schools.

The results of meta-analysis studies need to be interpreted with caution. Journal editors typically publish only the reports of those research projects in which statistically significant outcome differences are found. The rationale for this policy is that journals have limited space and can print only a small number of the research studies submitted. Editors believe that readers want to learn about those interventions that truly had an impact on client or agency functioning. In addition, nonsignificant results are difficult to interpret. Such results can be due to any of the following reasons:

- The treatment had no observable effect;
- The instrument used to measure the effects was not valid or reliable;
- The statistical test used was not sufficiently powerful to detect a difference; or
- Other extraneous factors (error variance) were not adequately controlled to allow for detecting the effect of the treatment.

On the other hand, published research might underestimate the impact of consultation. Many successful interventions are not submitted for publication because the consultant either did not believe disseminating the results was a sufficiently worthwhile activity or thought confidentiality would be compromised by doing so. In conclusion, meta-analyses have value as indices of the effect of consultations, but such studies do not precisely measure the actual outcome of all consultation attempts.

Other researchers investigated the types of school-based consultation studies that are cited in the literature. Fuchs, Fuchs, Dulan, and Roberts (1992) reviewed 119 published studies and an additional 59 doctoral dissertations, and found that most of the consultative interventions (67%) targeted groups rather than individuals. Some form of student or teacher behavior was the dependent variable or outcome measure in 80% of the studies, and student achievement was assessed in 25% of the research reports. This finding suggests school consultation projects are being evaluated and the results disseminated. Since most consultations in the schools aim ultimately to enhance student achievement, this outcome should be reported more frequently.

Conclusion

As can be seen, there is a large and growing body of research investigating the diverse effects of consultation, and empirical evidence indicates that consultative activities are effective. The key to the degree to which a consultative process results in achieving its outcomes depends in large part on the manner in which the consultant navigates the four phases of the process. At each phase, the consultant will be faced with challenges and resistance from one or more entities involved, and the more prepared the consultant is for each of these challenges, the more likely that the interventions will have a significant impact. In conclusion, if done correctly, consultation is a worthwhile activity that can effectively and efficiently impact the quality of mental health in the community.

DISCUSSION QUESTIONS

1. What are some issues that a mental health professional involved in the consultation process should be mindful of? List some examples of individuals who do not work directly in the mental health field

who could be trained to participate in this process, as well as a few potential advantages and disadvantages for each.

2. What are some factors that prevent individuals from seeking treatment? How can consultation help ameliorate some of these concerns? List some specific problems and alternatives.

3. Identify specific elements of a good consultation evaluation. What might some special considerations be when evaluating a workplace program? An educational program? A community-wide prevention program? A targeted intervention?

4. What is the aim of consultation? What are the different categories of consultation, and do you feel that categorization is valuable? How does consultation fit with the preventative model of mental health? How can the consultation process positively affect the community as a whole?

5. Name some specific ways in which consultants could help reduce the stigma attached to mental illness. Which consultants might be the most successful when addressing grief? Substance abuse? An anxiety disorder? In what forums could these issues be addressed with the least social discomfort to the person in need?

6. Consider the adage "you can give a man a fish and he will eat for a day, but teach a man to fish and he will eat for a lifetime." How does this analogy apply to the consultation process?

OBJECTIVES

This chapter is designed to enable the reader to:

- Identify reasons why and ways in which applied research should be conducted.
- Understand the politics of program evaluation.
- Understand critical statistical concepts related to program evaluation.
- Identify needs assessment techniques.
- Understand the differences between experimental research and program evaluation.
- Understand the importance of a systems approach to program evaluation.
- Identify different types of program evaluations.
- Understand the development of program outcomes and indicators.
- Explain the purpose of using multiple criteria to evaluate objectives.
- Identify factors that can jeopardize the results of a program evaluation.
- Identify specific diagnostic procedures used for needs assessment.
- Understand the use of cost-benefit analysis.
- Identify factors that can affect the utilization of assessment results.
- Explain CQI, its techniques, and its themes.

> *"Do not put your faith in what statistics say until you have carefully considered what they do not say."*
>
> *William W. Watt*

Program evaluation is a type of applied research in which program characteristics are systematically and explicitly related to a set of values such as program goals, objectives, and costs. The purpose of program evaluation is to provide information that can be used to improve management decision making. Along with community mental health practitioners, businesses, schools, human service agencies, hospitals, and government agencies implement new programs, and the effectiveness of these programs must be measured.

Program evaluation and other applied research in the community is a challenging activity, since it is nearly impossible to control all factors. Findings are scrutinized by those who have vested interest in the program. In this chapter, information regarding the "whys" and "hows" of conducting applied research is presented. The politics of program evaluation, along with relevant terminology and an introduction to critical statistical concepts, are considered first. Then, since good program evaluation must first show that a need existed that was met by the intervention, needs assessment techniques are discussed. Finally, client satisfaction measures and the continuous quality improvement perspective are included in a section on qualitative evaluation.

Historical Overview

The need to evaluate programs first became apparent in the fields of education and public health (Rossi & Freeman, 1993). Prior to World War I, assessments focused on the effects of educational programs on literacy and occupational training, and on the influence of public health initiatives on mortality and morbidity from infectious disease. In the mid 1800s, Dorothea Dix became famous for her evaluations of health care programs administered in hospitals by conducting qualitative reviews of services related to patient satisfaction. In 1867, the Office of Education conducted a study to determine the number of Americans who were illiterate, in order to develop programs to address this condition. Similarly, between 1907 and 1927, surveys assessing needs found that one-third of homeless persons in New York City were former mental patients, thus allowing social workers to create programs that enabled these former patients to live within the community in residences. Today, similar studies such as the Support and Family Education (SAFE) Program evaluation (Sherman, 2003) are being conducted to evaluate the impact of serious mental illness on the family.

In the 1930s, as many programs were developed to help individuals cope with the effects of the Depression, the need to evaluate those programs became increasingly important. After World War II, insurance companies were required to pay for various treatment programs which gave rise to their demand for assessment of these programs. The human rights movement of the 1960s was also influential in the evolution of program evaluation, as the sociopolitical climate of the country focused on ensuring commitment to serving the needs of historically underserved and underrepresented individuals. In the 1980s and 1990s, a primary component of program evaluation was the cost-effectiveness of service provision.

Mental health care has become primarily focused on accountability and quality determined by the measurement of treatment outcomes (Sperry, Brill, Howard, & Grissom, 1996). Over time, the need to evaluate programs has grown, and today, most programs are planned with monitoring strategies built into the design. In addition, the agencies that fund various programs usually require evaluation of the effectiveness and need for the program or service. Whenever possible, evaluators utilize experimental methods to assess programs; however, some programs must be evaluated through applied or quasi-experimental methods. Salyers, Bond, Teague, Cox, Smith, Hicks, and Koop (2003) assert that there are too few established standards for the evaluation of community-based programs, particularly assessment of program implementation. Furthermore, Mervis (2004) points out that the 2001 education reform bill—the *No Child Left Behind Act*—requires schools to offer empirically based programs (described at the end of this chapter), but that there are few programs that meet this standard because of a lack of rigorous scientific evaluation or empirical research of programs.

Differences Between Experimental Research and Program Evaluation

One of the more important issues in understanding the process and function of program evaluation is identifying the ways in which program evaluation differs from experimental research. Program evaluation is applied research, in that evaluations lack the rigorous control of traditional research. In addition, the purpose, orientation, design, generalizability, and accountability differ depending on whether one is conducting experimental research or program evaluation. The differences are listed in Table 10.1.

Although experimental research is sometimes considered "the research of choice" by scientists, others, such as social researchers and community mental health practitioners, realize the limits of experimental designs for the evaluation of human services programs. For example, random assignment, or selecting a representative sample of the general population, is impossible in evaluation because subjects are chosen

	Research	Program Evaluation
Orientation	Increasing knowledge	Decision making
Purpose	Establishing causal relationships, support theories	Resolving administrative questions
Design	Experimental, with control groups	Quasi-experimental, continuous monitoring
Generalizability	Of effect to other populations, or settings	Of measurement methods to other programs
Accountability	To scientists	To administrators

TABLE 10.1 A Comparison Between Laboratory Research and Program Evaluation

from those who are recipients of particular services or participants in certain programs. In addition, many experimental designs involve assigning subjects to a control group that does not receive treatment or intervention. However, failing to treat or offer services to individuals in need is unethical. Also, as many evaluations are conducted on educational programs and the subjects are chosen because of their assignment to a particular class, it is difficult to divide an intact class into two groups.

Another consideration in program evaluation is that it includes monitoring continuous change, which varies from client to client. When the evaluation concerns an educational program, teachers are likely to change over the course of the evaluation, and the difference in teachers becomes a confounding variable in the study. For example, if a two-year reading proficiency program is implemented for students in the first and second grades, the skill or enthusiasm of the first-grade teacher may be different from that of the second-grade teacher. This difference may account for the change in students' reading level and may not be attributable to the reading program itself.

In program evaluation, there is by definition a lack of proven reliability and validity, since the assessment is limited to a particular program at a particular time. Program participants change and may not be similar to other groups that have been involved in the program. In addition, staff changes affect program delivery, and programs necessarily evolve over time. According to Dr. James Smith, formerly Director of Quality Assurance at Rockland Psychiatric Center in New York (personal communication, 1994), these factors contribute to a lack of validity and reliability and add "slop" to research.

In experimental research, environments and interventions are carefully controlled, but because programs are a "package deal," it is difficult to identify which part of the intervention is responsible for the main effect. The fluidity of programs also contributes to the problem of isolating particular effects. Therefore, a systems approach must be utilized in program evaluation. In other words, while an outcome measurement system can provide reasonably reliable information on the benefit of a particular program for its participants, it does not, in general, indicate that the program *alone* caused the outcomes.

There are also political and ethical considerations in comparing various programs related to the selection of subjects. For example, if a mental health services agency is attempting to determine the effectiveness of behavioral treatment compared with psychoanalytic treatment and random assignment of subjects is used, a mental health professional may assess a subject as more appropriate for a particular approach. It is likely to be difficult for the mental health professionals to randomly assign a treatment when he or she believes the subject would be better served by a particular treatment approach.

It is important to understand the differences between experimental research and program evaluation in order to conceptualize the differences in methodology used in each process. In simple terms, traditional research measures the effects of explicit interventions given under controlled conditions, and program evaluation assesses the effects of a system on an individual or a group of individuals. However, in the field of evaluation today, researchers strive to utilize experimental designs whenever possible. Durlak and Wells (1997) recommend that the next generation of research should

Using Experimental Designs in Program Evaluation

The following is an example of how researchers used an experimental design in an effort to control for contamination of results by extraneous variables.

Project C.A.R.E. Substance Abuse Prevention Program for High-Risk Youth: A Longitudinal Evaluation of Program Effectiveness.

Using a pretest, posttest experimental research design, Hostetler and Fisher (1997) studied the effects of Project C.A.R.E. on the behavior of three cohorts of at-risk fourth-graders and their families. The program activities were to increase protective factors and decrease risk factors relating to substance abuse through school, family, and extracurricular activities. The program objectives were to decrease substance abuse, negative behaviors, intent to use substances, school suspensions and absences; and to increase alternative or positive activities, family communication, academic grades, and consistency of family behavior control and rules.

After the program was completed, a posttest was administered, and the results were compared with those of a control group. In addition, program participants were assessed again one year after completion of the program. The results were as follows:

- At posttest, participants (Ps) grades were higher than those of the control group.
- At posttest, more Ps were involved in community activities.
- Compared with controls, Ps increased participation in alternative activities from pretest to posttest and did not increase their school suspension to the same degree.
- At one-year follow-up, controls were more willing to use substances than Ps.
- The most impact was found with the third cohort of students and with black students.
- Ps with low participation tended to have the worst outcomes, often worse than that of the controls.

---

increase the precision of theory, design, and program evaluation. To ensure a more complete and useful database for analysis, experimental designs should be utilized. In addition, evaluability assessment, a process described by Thurston, Graham, and Hatfield (2003) and designed to improve evaluation via the use of a logic model, is suggested. The logic model was used to show the progression from objectives to activities to program outcomes. This process allowed researchers to assess the extent to which activities led to outcomes and also whether or not appropriate process and outcome measures were being used. And finally, through the process, the project goals were clarified and synthesized to better reflect the project capacity.

Types of Program Evaluation

There are three general types of program evaluation: program planning, program implementation and monitoring, and program outcome (Rossi & Freeman, 1993; Sperry, Brill, Howard, & Grissom, 1996). Program planning is based on needs assessment and involves conceptualization and design of the intervention program. Program planning evaluations are often referred to as "front-end analyses," because the focus is on developing new programs based on needs or gaps in services. They may also be created as preventive approaches to existing problems. Program planning includes deciding what resources will be dedicated to or consumed by the program. Such resources are often referred to as inputs; some examples are money, staff, and equipment.

Program implementation and monitoring evaluations are process or formative assessments. These assessments evaluate how the program utilizes inputs in relation to program activities. For example, if the program goal is to enable participants to gain employment, the activities may include job training, and monitoring evaluation would assess how staff and curricula were used to provide the job training. Outputs, or the direct products of program activities, such as the number of classes taught, would be measured as well.

Program monitoring assessments also measure the extent to which programs are conducted as planned and are often focused on cost-benefit analysis. A primary consideration is whether or not programs can be administered for reduced cost without compromising the program outcome.

Program outcome evaluations study the impact of a given program (Weiss, 1998). The questions being asked are "did the program do any good?" or "did the program meet the desired goals or objectives?" Outcomes then, are the benefits clients received as a result of participating in the program. These benefits are calculated by measuring the change in the participant from when he or she began the program (pretest) to when the program was completed (posttest). In addition, outcomes are compared with other programs to ensure that participants are receiving the same or better benefits than participants of similar programs. Outcome evaluations also have the potential to identify effects that occurred, other than those that were expected (Posavac & Carey, 2003).

TABLE 10.2   Program: Chemical Dependency Treatment

Inputs	Activities	Outputs	Outcomes
Agency provides: • mental health practitioner who is a certified alcohol and substance abuse counselor (CASAC); • best practices treatment protocols; and • other teaching materials	Program provides Cognitive Behavioral Group Therapy designed to improve insight, knowledge, and coping skills. Regular drug testing referrals to adjunctive therapies.	Clients attend group three times per week.	Reduced Substance use, increased knowledge regarding substance abuse, and improved awareness of precipitating feelings, thoughts, and behaviors (triggers of use).

The Politics of Evaluation

Regardless of the type of evaluation being conducted, there are political considerations that must be addressed. There are always a variety of stakeholders with differing perspectives and agendas that are influential in the process of program evaluation. For example, "quality of a program" is defined differently by stakeholders, depending on their interest in the program. For the evaluator, quality is defined by meeting the clients' expectations. Therefore, it is critical for the evaluator to identify the clients and stakeholders and then to assess the expectations of both. The best approach to managing the politics of evaluation is to be able to relate to several stakeholders and to effectively communicate with the various groups involved.

To become familiar with the differing perspectives of stakeholders takes experience, but a few of the more common opposing forces are provided here. When evaluating a program, there are almost always stakeholders from the community who have agendas different from those within the program administration itself. Some of the groups or individuals with opposing views are the funding agency versus the program director, the community at large versus the program director, advocacy groups versus the line staff, and the program's competitors versus clients or consumers of services (Weiss, 1998).

The political pressures on evaluators that can be negative factors in the assessment process include the fearful attitudes of those being evaluated. The sense of "being graded," fear of change, anxiety related to the possibility of increased work, and disagreement about measuring effectiveness are generally experienced by staff of the program. It is also common for staff to perceive the evaluator as an outsider who does not understand their program, and in fact, the staff and the evaluator do come to the evaluation from different vantage points. The staff are committed to the program, whereas the evaluator is objective and hasn't "bought into" the effectiveness of the program yet.

The need of the administrator to have the evaluation conducted is also an issue of concern to program staff. Often the motivation of the administration is questioned in terms of hidden agendas. Staff fear the evaluation may provide evidence that a particular program should be discontinued and that the administration is simply seeking the proof to support a previously made decision to cut the program—that the evaluation results will give administration an excuse, so to speak. These concerns are likely to cause program staff to react defensively to the evaluator and thus lessen cooperation. In the experience of one author (ET), staff resistance was exemplified in the refusal to make clients' charts available. The staff said that because the evaluator was not a "clinical person," she should not be able to read the charts because doing so would be a breach of confidentiality.

In some cases, there is political pressure to report outcomes consistent with the expectations of powerful contingencies within an institution or organization. Posavac and Carey (2003) suggest the best approach for managing such pressure is to confront it head-on, by having an expert or consultant approve of the evaluation methodology in an effort to ensure credibility.

Although the politics of evaluation usually create barriers to the process, these barriers are to be expected and can be overcome in most cases if the evaluator addresses them with sensitivity. The best approach to minimizing resistance is to foster staff interest in the evaluation or to get staff to buy into the process by showing them how it can benefit both staff and clients. This is done by communicating to staff that the evaluator recognizes their expertise and that their firsthand knowledge is critical to the accuracy of the evaluation. Explaining the benefits of evaluation, such as using the results to acquire additional funding, generating program improvement strategies, and providing concrete evidence of the success of a program, is another way to gain staff cooperation. In addition, the evaluator can develop an aura of scientific study which often appeals to staff. Evaluators working with human service agencies should remember that they are mental health practitioners first and that they may use their clinical/counseling skills to foster an attitude of mutual need between the evaluator and the agency staff and to help staff feel less threatened by the evaluation process.

Tailoring Evaluations

The considerations previously discussed are part and parcel of all evaluations, but each study must also be tailored to the particular program involved. Since programs are unique and have individual characteristics, program outcomes must be assessed from that perspective. Program outcomes are the benefits to participants as a result of participating in the program.

Defining Program Outcomes and Indicators

When the purpose of the evaluation is to develop a program, broad outcomes are preferable to narrow outcomes (Rossi & Freeman, 1993). For example, improving job skills for alcoholics is more attainable than a narrowly defined outcome such as assembly-line skills for alcoholics. If the goal is to provide alcoholics with employment skills, then this global goal must be broken down into measurable outcomes such as measuring the improvement in alcoholics occupational skill level. Outcomes must be developed that can be measured by indicators defined by consensus panels of service providers, consumers of services, and quality-assurance staff. The involvement of these groups is important because converting broad goals into measurable outcomes requires value judgments that should be made by all who will be affected.

To promote continued evaluation of programs, outcomes need to be ones that can be measured practically. For example, if measuring an outcome or monitoring progress requires a complicated process, staff are less likely to track it, which usually results in a failure to achieve the desired result. For example, avoid complex processes that involve double-barreled assessments, which evaluate more than one outcome at a time. Generally, outcomes should be measured separately.

There are a variety of issues to consider when selecting outcome measures and the indicators that signal the outcome has been achieved:

- The content area to be evaluated and operationally define the outcome that will be assessed;
- Who will be responsible for supplying the data (therapist, teacher, parent, independent observer, etc.);
- The appropriate statistics, such as those that are most reliable and valid; and
- Miscellaneous factors such as cost, training required, time involved, usefulness of repeated measures (parallel forms), and the level of ease or difficulty in scoring should be considered.

Whenever possible, multiple criteria should be used to evaluate outcomes. For example, if the outcome is to improve clients' occupational skills, measurement of the change in clients' skills needed for employment must be measured, as well as the number of clients who gain employment. The purpose of multiple criteria is to satisfy different stakeholders and to obtain confirming data. Utilizing different methodologies to assess outcomes is called "triangulation," named after the process of locating a radio transmitter by positioning receivers in geographically different locations. Although each receiver can determine the direction from which the signal is coming, no one receiver can pinpoint the exact location of the source. A number of receivers, each from a different perspective, must all point to the source in order to locate it precisely (Scileppi, 1988).

In addition to using multiple criteria, a control group that is similar to the group of individuals who are being evaluated but who do not participate in the program should be used for comparison with the experimental group. This technique allows the evaluator to be more confident that the effects found in the experimental group are a result of the program. The control group receives the traditional service and will be given the intervention (if found to be effective) after the study is completed.

Factors That Jeopardize Results

Once the outcomes and indicators have been defined and the program is ready for assessment, several factors must be considered in the actual evaluation and analysis of the results (Campbell & Stanley, 1963). These factors, called confounding or extraneous variables, include history, maturation, selection bias, testing effects, and mortality. Each of these factors, if not accounted for, could lead to plausible rival hypotheses which could explain the results of the evaluation. Stakeholders who are unhappy with the results could focus on one of these factors and question the validity of the evaluation.

History

History is the effect of something else that happened during the evaluation period that accounts for the change found. For example, the local economy weakened, thereby reducing the number of program participants who found jobs.

Maturation

Maturation refers to change which would have occurred because of personal growth or the passage of time, regardless of program participation. For example, a 2-year program designed to foster self-esteem may appear to be successful when the outcome may instead be a result of participants' growing up and becoming more comfortable with themselves.

Selection Bias

Selection bias may result in findings that may be unique to a particular group if the experimental group is not representative of the program population. This situation could occur if a school implementing a new reading program delivers the program to students who are more successful academically than the average student. If the results are interpreted as an indication that the program is superior to others, on the basis of its outcome with these students, such a conclusion may be erroneous because the outcome may simply reflect the academic ability of this particular group of students.

Testing

Testing a subject more than once sensitizes the individual to what is expected. The resulting improved performance may be due to a testing effect rather than a program effect. Simply stated, the participant becomes more familiar with the test and is likely to score higher the second time around. For this reason, students often take SATs and GREs more than once.

Mortality

Mortality occurs when individuals drop out of the evaluation for any reason, causing a change in the makeup of the group that is being evaluated such that it is no longer the same as it was at the start of the evaluation. It is important to find out why individuals dropped out of the program in order to determine how mortality affects the results. For example, those who may have been helped by the program may leave prior to completion because they no longer need the treatment. Their departure leaves the group being composed of the less successful participants, thus skewing the outcome data since the more successful clients are not part of the outcome measurement data.

The actual measurement process is often complicated when more than one person is involved. The problems associated with interrater reliability, or achieving the same result from several evaluators, is minimized by training raters on the measurement procedures. Whenever possible, only the best raters should be used to administer a scale. A larger number of comparable items on a scale also increases reliability. Another way to increase reliability is to have more than one rater administer a scale and then to compute the mean of the raters' results.

The Meaning, Not the Mechanics of Statistics

Statistics often make the budding mental health professionals break out in a cold sweat, but a general understanding of what statistics are all about is important nonetheless. The most significant statistical factors including sample size, alpha level, strength of effect, and power are discussed in order to provide the basics for determining the statistical outcome of an experiment.

The size of the sample of any given population must be adequate to ensure representation of the population. If the sample size is too small, randomization loses its effect, and representativeness can no longer be certain. If the sample size is too large, a minute difference between groups can be statistically significant, yet it might not provide any meaningful assistance in decision making. The level of significance (alpha) is the probability that the result is due to chance. This means that at a .01 level, one in one hundred times the result will occur for reasons other than the effect of the program. Therefore, the alpha selected influences whether or not a difference will be found. For example, at the .01 level, it is more difficult to find a difference considered statistically significant than at the .05 level. The strength of the effect is the degree of difference found. For example, if a new medication is being tested and the first three recipients break out in a rash, obviously the researcher need not continue in order to determine that the medication is harmful. The power refers to the probability that an effect will be found if one exists (Dr. James Smith, personal communication, 1994). Some statistical tests have greater power than others. Consult a statistics textbook when deciding which test to use to analyze data.

Once a statistical test is chosen, only three of the four factors just described must be controlled for; if the sample size, alpha level, and strength of effect are appropriate, then power is determined mathematically. It is also wise to be aware that statistical significance does not always have real or practical significance.

Errors of Inference

There are two types of error of inference: Type I (false positive) and Type II (false negative). A Type I error is finding a statistically significant difference when there is none, or determining that a program has an effect when it does not. The probability of a Type I error is the alpha level. A Type II error is NOT finding a difference when there in fact is a statistically significant difference, or failing to find an actual program effect when there is one. The probability for making a Type II error, called the beta level, is unknown (Fitz-Gibbon & Morris, 1987).

Needs Assessment

Human service programs are developed in response to real or perceived need. In this section, the methodology of assessing need is discussed. Terminology is provided, as are the specific diagnostic procedures for conducting an evaluation of needs or gaps in services.

A needs assessment is the systematic study of the severity and scope of a particular problem. It is a way of determining what individuals need related to human services. The design of a needs assessment identifies targets, incidence, and prevalence; develops operational definitions; and outlines diagnostic procedures. A needs assessment is a planning tool to be used in the development or initiation of service programs. Planning is most successful if the assessed need is the basis for program development, outcome, and immediate goals (Posavac & Carey, 2003).

Definitions

Targets refer to the individuals, groups, or communities that will be assessed in relation to the problem in question. Broad-based targets, meaning inclusion of anyone affected by the problem, are preferable to limiting the assessment to those individuals who have the problem. For example, a needs assessment conducted in Dutchess County, New York (Teed, 1996), appraised the HIV health service needs of individuals infected and affected by the virus. HIV "needs" were defined as both the services required to treat the infected individuals and the services needed by those affected, such as the children and caretakers of those individuals. This broad-based target allowed Dutchess County to develop programs that both directly and indirectly impact infected individuals, to provide more comprehensive care.

Operational definitions are the specific identifications of problems based on clearly delineated parameters. For example, the problem of illiteracy must be operationally defined in terms of what constitutes "illiteracy." If adults can read at a third-grade level, are they illiterate? These definitions can be rather difficult to construct, may require much deliberation, and should be reached by the consensus of those responsible for the assessment and those who will use the assessment results.

As discussed in the chapter on prevention, incidence is the number of new cases within a particular period of time and is usually presented as a percentage of the number of new cases divided by the number of persons at risk. For example, if 2,000 individuals lose their jobs in one year in a population of 100,000 employed persons, the incidence of unemployment would be 2%. Prevalence is the number of people who have a given condition divided by the total population. The importance of incidence and prevalence in needs assessments is that if one underestimates the number of people in need of a service, the staff will be overwhelmed when the program starts. If need is overestimated, limited resources will be wasted. Unfortunately, the more precise estimates of need are usually costly and require rather complex methods of measurement.

Diagnostic procedures are the methods that will be used to carry out the needs assessment. The best strategy should be selected given the limits of time and funding for the project. The evaluator must consider demand as it differs from need—the squeaky wheel gets the grease, so to speak. The evaluator must also recognize that human service needs are complex and interrelated. For example, a person's homelessness may be related to illiteracy. As in program evaluation, all good strategies have high stakeholder involvement.

The purpose of needs assessments is to evaluate need for services such that programs can be offered to address those needs. This is always value laden, since decisions must be made about which needs should be met with limited dollars.

Specific Diagnostic Procedures

The methods of assessing need, termed "diagnostic procedures," are performed through the use of key informants, community forums, rates under treatment, social indicators, nominal group, Delphi technique, and survey. Each of these techniques or groups provides different perspectives that, when combined, create a real and an accurate picture of the scope and extent of a problem.

The use of key informants or experts in the field involves gathering data from community members who have knowledge about the particular problem or the individuals in related programs. Key informants are often service providers, medical doctors, teachers, or clergy.

Community forums are gatherings of diverse groups of community members in which participants can discuss and offer opinions about the need or problem. The evaluator acts as a group facilitator and collects information provided by the participants.

"Rates under treatment" refers to using data from other agencies or existing providers to assess need. This technique allows the researcher to make predictions or extrapolate data to another area. For example, if one knows how many individuals received services in 2001 and 2002, estimates can be made about how many people will need services in 2003; or if one knows the extent of need in a particular area, predictions can be made about need in a related area. In the case of alcoholism, if there is a high incidence of alcohol abuse, one could predict the need for a program designed for children of alcoholics.

Social indicators are the findings of epidemiological studies that characterize the disorder. Often more-stressed areas have higher needs. For example, poverty, unemployment, single-parent households, driving while intoxicated (DWI) rates, and other environmental factors are correlated with human service needs. Police reports and census data from the National Institute of Mental Health (NIMH) provide information from which such inferences can be made. In addition, existing data can be used to extrapolate information that may be difficult to collect otherwise. For example, if 1% of alcoholics commit suicide each year, finding the number of alcohol-related suicides will allow the researcher to calculate how many alcoholics there are in the total population.

Nominal groups are structured group workshops created to reach consensus about a particular need. The participants have little interaction with each other and are merely asked to narrow need categories until decisions about the priority level of a need can be established.

The Delphi technique is similar to the nominal group, but the participants are experts in the field who are sent a questionnaire by mail asking them to rank needs. After responses are returned, the researcher totals the results and sends another questionnaire with only the top-ranked needs of the first round listed, and asks the participants to rank-order those top priorities. Consensus of the highest priority needs is reached though this process.

The survey is the most scientific approach to needs assessment. A random sample of the population is drawn, and those individuals are interviewed by telephone, in writing, or in person to assess perception of need. The specific methodology for designing and administering a survey is discussed in *Survey Research Methods* (Babbie, 1990).

Qualitative Evaluation

Qualitative evaluation is a type of assessment that focuses more on the depth of a program and its effects than on the breadth or quantitative aspects of the program (Weiss, 1998). The programs that are best suited for this type of evaluation are those in which quality transcends quantity. For example, the Red Cross offers assistance to individuals or families victimized by disaster. The quality of this kind of program is determined by the perception of the recipients and by the scope of assistance received by the client(s) in need, more so than the actual number of clients served. Also, the kind and level of aid provided is determined by the particular crisis, so outcomes vary among clients. A victim of a serious house fire has different needs compared with a victim of domestic violence, yet both are given assistance.

Because individual needs vary, program outcomes can be measured only on a case-by-case basis. Data collection and evaluation are also conducted on a case-by-case basis. Three data collection techniques are used to evaluate the quality of a given program. These are (a) in-depth, open-ended interviews; (b) direct observation by an outsider or by a participant observer such as a decoy acting as a client sent in to evaluate the program; and (c) examination of written documentation, such as charts and staff work schedules. The validity of qualitative evaluation depends upon the skill of the observer (Lincoln & Guba, 1985; Posavac & Carey, 2003).

Qualitative evaluations are naturalistic inquiries that require inductive logic and a holistic or systems approach to program assessment. They are characterized by a dynamic developmental perspective, and they utilize individual case studies to determine program effectiveness. Qualitative evaluations are conducted when stakeholders want an in-depth assessment and when outcomes for clients are qualitatively different. They are also done when stakeholders are looking for unusual successes or failures or when no quantitative measurements exist. Qualitative research can also provide insights into the processes occurring within a client group, whereas quantitative research focuses more narrowly on outcomes. Evaluation designs often incorporate both qualitative and quantitative measures in order to provide a more comprehensive assessment of the program.

Client Satisfaction

Client satisfaction is the evaluation of the participants' perspectives on a program and is usually part of both qualitative and quantitative evaluations. Client satisfaction has good face validity because program participants appreciate being asked for feedback on their experience in a program. In programs in which participation is voluntary, satisfaction is often favorably inflated because those who are dissatisfied with the program usually do not return, and in addition, if a participant doesn't like the program, he or

Community Psychology Values and the Culture of Graduate Training: A Self-Study

Using quantitative and qualitative methods, the evaluator, a graduate student in the program, studied the training goals of an MA program in community mental health in relation to the values of collaboration, empowerment, and diversity. The evaluator cooperated with a stakeholder committee, other students, staff, and faculty members of the program to determine the evaluation methods and to interpret the findings. Although the converging sources of data indicated that the program was meeting its process goals, there were some areas that needed improvement. These areas included the culture of training, such as the community, and a supportive learning environment. Alcalde and Walsh-Bowers (1996) interpret these findings in terms of the impact of the university system and patriarchal norms on training in community mental health.

---

she may be afraid to say so (Denzin & Lincoln, 2000; Fetterman, Kaftarian, & Mandersman, 1996). There is also a strong halo effect, in that if clients like a therapist, they often gloss over other, less positive aspects of the program.

Quality Assurance

One of the most common systems for assuring the quality of a program is Continuous Quality Improvement (CQI). This system is based on the belief that programs are consumer driven, which means that quality is defined by what the consumer wants from the program. The system focuses on evaluating the process and not the staff of a program. This empowers staff and fosters input "from the trenches." Program management must be committed to the philosophy that continuous improvement can occur only if the frontline staff, those who administer the program, are considered experts who are encouraged to suggest ways of improving the program. Deming (1986) employed this system in his attempt to drive the fear out of an automobile manufacturing organization, and the result was the development of the extremely successful Japanese car industry.

A technique used in CQI to get staff involved in pinpointing problem areas is creating flowcharts of the program process. Through this approach, workers uncover the problem areas or bad processes in a faulty system. From there, an Ishikawa, or fishbone chart, can be developed. An Ishikawa is a chart that looks like the skeleton of a fish, and the problem or issue is written on the horizontal "bone." The back-slanted bones are used to list process issues that lead up to the problem. This approach involves brainstorming to find out what is wrong with a process that is causing the identified problem. This approach was utilized by one author (ET) in a quality assurance evaluation of case management services provided by several agencies that collaborated to form one program. In gathering all case managers involved in the program together for a discussion about service duplication, the process for assigning clients to a case manager was found to be faulty, and it was discovered that many clients had several case managers. The case managers were asked to brainstorm possible solutions, and the result was the development of a centralized case management system. In addition to resolving the problem of service duplication, case managers reported feeling empowered by the process itself.

Fiscal Evaluation, or Cost-Benefit Analysis

A component of most evaluations is a comparison between the cost and the benefits of a program or service. This type of assessment is called a fiscal evaluation, or cost-benefit analysis. The relationship between costs and outcomes is defined in monetary terms and is the basis for decision making about effectiveness (Rossi & Freeman, 1993). When decisions are being made about the effectiveness of a program, administrators often rely on information about the cost of the program relative to the effectiveness (in dollars) of the objective measures of outcomes. The purpose of the analysis is to minimize the cost per stated outcome (find the cheapest way to provide treatment) or to maximize the outcome per stated cost (find the best way to get the biggest "bang for the buck"). For more detailed information, *Evaluation: A Systematic Approach* (Rossi & Freeman, 1993) is an excellent reference on the methods of cost-benefit analysis.

Dissemination and Utilization of Evaluation Results

The how, when, and to whom of reporting evaluation results are critical factors in determining the extent to which the results will be utilized. Each of these factors must be carefully considered by the evaluator in order to ensure that the assessment is as meaningful as possible.

Factors That Contribute to Failure to Utilize Evaluation Results

There are four factors that influence utilization. These are poor communication, dissemination, organizational factors, and outside influences. Poor communication during the planning phase of the evaluation includes misunderstanding of how the evaluation is relevant to stakeholders. An evaluator should never design an evaluation process "in a vacuum." The stakeholders' input must be included in the design to enable the evaluator to develop valid or credible evaluation measures. Also, as stakeholders' issues vary, the result is divergent information that must be looked at separately and then in relation to all other information. Addressing different issues and then bringing them all together at the conclusion of the evaluation is called creating converging information.

The dissemination of the results involves timeliness, format, and presentation. Timeliness means making certain that program directors receive evaluation results before decisions need to be made. Clearly, if a decision is related to funding and there is a budget approval deadline and the director does not have the evaluation results in time, they cannot be considered in the decision-making process. This situation could lead to inappropriate choices because of lack of information. Another timing issue is to ensure that those responsible are given the evaluation outcomes before the formal presentation of those results. No one appreciates being caught off-guard, and when people are put in that position, a defensive reaction may lead to the entire evaluation being discounted.

The presentation of the material is at least as important as the information itself. The explanation of the results should be appropriate for the particular audience and should not be jargon-laden. It helps to present the major findings first and to limit the presentation to the critical or significant findings. Clarity can be added to written reports and presentations by the inclusion of simple, self-explanatory graphs, so that data can be viewed as well as heard or read. The more understandable the results are, the more likely they will be utilized. All researchers must be extremely careful about what information is provided to the press. The way the "facts are publicly reported is extremely influential in the public's perception of a program. One would be wise to limit the possibility of any distortion of data that may occur.

The organizational factors that impact utilization of results are the degree to which findings confirm expectations and conservatism, or inertia. If the results fail to support expectations, they are less likely to be utilized and more likely to be dismissed. Conservatism, or inertia, refers to a fear of change, and organizations are often resistant to changing programs that have been in place for a long time. The status quo is sometimes viewed more favorably than new initiatives that bring new problems and new challenges. Results that counter prevailing beliefs must be dramatic and very credible to have any effect. In a sense, they must have "intraocular validity," by hitting the reader "right between the eyes."

Outside influences may also determine whether or not evaluation results are utilized. For example, the national Drug Awareness and Resistance Education (D.A.R.E.) program has been found to be ineffective in reducing drug use by teenagers. However, this program is well liked by teachers and parents, and has been

In Dutchess County, New York, an exemplary program, Families and Schools Together (FAST) was implemented as a violence-prevention program for children from disenfranchised or marginalized families. According to Catalano and Hawkins (1992), students who are actively involved in their school community are less likely to behave in maladaptive ways. During the course of this program, student participation in school activities increased by 36%, and parental involvement in their children's education also increased by 31%. Outcome measurement of the 2003 FAST was also impressive in that 53% of parents reported being more involved in their community after participation in FAST. In addition, 42% of parents reported increased social support from peers, and all participants indicated that communication within their family had at least moderately improved since participation. Taken together, these data showed the FAST program demonstrated quantitative improvements in family functioning and students' academic performance, and qualitative satisfaction with the program and participants' perception of program effectiveness.

maintained in most communities despite negative evaluations (Dr. James Smith, personal communication, 1994).

Evidence-Based Interventions

The field of human services has evolved to the point of delivering evidence-based programs and interventions whenever possible. Evidence-based programs are those that have been studied extensively and found to be effective for the prevention or treatment of a particular issue. That is, after a service need is identified, programming is selected for implementation on the basis of evidence of its effectiveness. In many requests for proposals (RFP) and grant-funding opportunities, funders require the use of an evidence-based program. Some other names for evidence-based programs are data-driven programs, research-based programs, exemplary programs, empirically supported intervention, model programs, and best practices; however, each has one thing in common: its outcomes have been studied and found to be effective.

Most evidence-based interventions are described in some type of publication, often an implementation manual, which provides information about the target population for which the program has been deemed effective, as well as the specific steps for carrying out the program. It also articulates the particular resources needed for program implementation. Any available evaluation tools are usually included, as well as how and when the evaluation should be conducted. If an agency chooses a particular "model program" and implements it according to design and with the appropriate population, expected outcomes should result.

It is important for agencies to implement model programs according to design, to ensure that outcomes will be similar to those expected. "Deviation from the model" is the phrase used to describe when exemplary programs are not carried out according to design. Such infidelity often results in less than satisfactory outcomes.

Studies are continually being conducted to determine the "latest and greatest" in the field, and new evidence-based programs are being identified regularly. The following are some sources where a community mental health practitioner can find information about these programs:

- *The Together Foundation and UN-Habitat:* Best Practices Database
- *CDC:* Best Practices of Youth Violence Prevention: A Sourcebook for Community Action
- *U.S. Department of Health and Human Services:* Best Practices Initiative

Conclusion

As discussed in this chapter, there are a variety of program evaluation methods, and it is the responsibility of the evaluator to determine which is most appropriate for a given program, and which most accurately assesses the issues of interest to the stakeholders. In closing, the authors learned the following through experience in conducting evaluations. First, much data already exists, and a researcher need not re-create the wheel.

Second, data are powerful and often define solutions. Third, the way data are presented to management is critical. Fourth, solutions are often more simple and less expensive than anticipated. Fifth, nearly every systems analysis has at least one surprising finding that makes this type of work interesting. Last, CQI is actually a lot of fun if one works with staff as a team to find and implement a solution to a problem, and seeing the result of teamwork in an improved process is rewarding.

DISCUSSION QUESTIONS

1. How does program evaluation differ from experimental research? Why are outcome evaluations important? How are program benefits calculated? How can these results be utilized?

2. How do politics affect program evaluations? What are some steps an evaluator can take to minimize difficulties that stem from the politics of evaluation? Give an example of an evaluation situation that might be affected by differing agendas and some possible solutions.

3. Explain the importance of selecting appropriate outcome measures and their indicators. Why is it important that these measurement procedures be clearly defined? What are some good general guidelines for developing program outcome measures?

4. What are the factors that contribute to failure of an administration to utilize program evaluation results? How would these variables manifest, for example, in the evaluation of a program that is aimed at helping those living with schizophrenia to reintegrate into the community?

5. Name the various groups from whom data should be collected in a needs assessment.

6. Why are control groups important? Is there an ethical way to use control groups, since the controls will not receive treatment? Give an example of how this issue might be resolved.

Leading and Managing Institutional and Organizational Change

OBJECTIVES

This chapter is designed to enable the reader to:

- Understand how the concept of change applies to community mental health, in a broad sense.
- Identify political, organizational, and personal aspects of change.
- Identify various steps in the change process.
- Understand challenges that arise during the change process and provide possible solutions.
- Define and contrast transformational and transactional types of change.
- Develop an awareness of the different conceptions of social problems.
- Understand how and why vested interests affect research.
- Understand how politics impact the dynamics of change in a community.
- Describe the role and responsibility of the community mental health professional in change situations.
- Understand the role of a community organizer in affecting change.
- Describe ways to measure and assess the effectiveness of a change.
- Define and understand methods of organizational change.
- Understand the link between community mental health and organizational psychology in the context of change initiation.
- Explain the diagnostic-prescriptive model of organizational change.
- Identify characteristics of business-oriented change agents.
- Understand how principles and values affect organizational change.

"Change is inevitable, except from the vending machine."
Found on a sign above a broken soda machine

"The art of progress is to preserve order amid change and to preserve change amid order."

Alfred North Whitehead

In the preceding chapters, the principles of the community mental health paradigm, along with the research demonstrating the effectiveness of many programs derived from this model, have been discussed. In this chapter the key principles of community and organizational change are presented. As social conditions evolve and environmental situations change, each community, each agency, and each program must adapt in order to continue to meet the needs of its citizens/clients.

As a community agency or program strives to meet the emerging needs of a new population, the power, resources, and focus shift. Thus, as one intervention helps some groups, it will inevitably harm others. In a sense, this represents a community concept analogous to Newton's third law of motion in physics: "For every action, there is a reaction." In terms of Kelly's ecological perspective, the principle of succession is operative. Change is never neutral. It disrupts the status quo, and in turn, those who benefit from the status quo.

According to Webster's *New Riverside Dictionary*, change means "to make or become different." "Change" is a small, seemingly benign word that carries with it tremendous political, social, and personal significance. This chapter considers some of the political, organizational, and personal aspects of change; explores the various steps of the change process; and identifies challenges that need to be addressed to successfully navigate each of these steps.

Types of Change

Scholars and practitioners currently use numerous dichotomies to discuss change such as revolutionary versus evolutionary; discontinuous versus continuous; episodic versus continuing flow; and strategic versus operation. Despite such abundance in language, there are only two basic types of change: transformational and transactional (Burke, 2002). The first is punctuated by a sudden event—a jolt to the system. As a result of transformational change, nothing will ever be the same again. This type of change usually requires that a large part of the organization, system, or community changes. It requires the attention of many and is inevitably met with much resistance. The second type of change, transactional change, is much slower and more evolutionary. It is defined by small adjustments, improvements, and incremental progress. Transactional change is often associated with programs, community-based agencies, and individual organizations. It is estimated that 95% of all change is transactional (Burke, 2002).

Rappaport (1977) also differentiated between individual and organizational change on the one hand, and institutional or societal change on the other. He focused on the point of intervention, noting that whereas the former are effective in modifying an individual's behavior or helping an agency become more efficient in meeting its goals, the latter changes the goals of the social system and rearranges the status relationships among groups in the community. The latter then makes such change very political in nature. The first part of this chapter will focus on institutional change. It will look at the challenges inherent in defining the problem, exploring alternative solutions, developing the vision, communicating the vision, implementing the plan, and evaluating the outcomes. It will also look at the values of community mental health professionals as they apply to each of these steps.

Change and the Community Mental Health Perspective

Defining the Problem

Social problems are not viewed in the same way by all. The way in which an issue is defined affects the people, organization, and systems that become involved; the point of intervention that is perused; and the type of solutions that are considered and are ultimately chosen. Levine and Perkins (1987) presented a strong case for conceiving of social problems not as absolute truths, but as relative interpretations of reality. Diverse publics have opposing vested interests in how a community problem is approached, and these constituencies advocate for opposing solutions.

For example, in the field of criminal justice, the issue of providing prison inmates with the opportunity to earn a college education has been debated for more than 25 years. Those who believe crime is deterred more effectively by ensuring that convicted felons receive harsh punishment see the offering of college courses in correctional facilities as counterproductive and a waste of taxpayers' money. They further believe it is unjust to give lawbreakers easier access to educational resources than what is available for those who obey the law. Others, however, believe convicted felons commit crimes because they have acquired an illegal pattern of behavior and because they have not learned sufficient job-related skills. In addition, inmates are far more likely to come from impoverished neighborhoods where access to educational and other resources is extremely limited. Proponents of this viewpoint see great value in providing higher educational opportunities in prison. They perceive such programs as providing the tools to break the cycle of criminal behavior and poverty and as such, to increase the likelihood that an ex-offender will lead a productive and law-abiding life.

The resolution of the debate depends on which set of values is more salient in the eyes of the public at any given time. As the political realities of the community and/or the decision makers shift, so do the desirability of various solutions. If providing a college education in prison is perceived as creating a "country club atmosphere" at taxpayers' expense and as rewarding inmates for breaking the law, citizens will urge their legislative representatives to end such programs. If the issue is viewed from the standpoint of rehabilitating the inmate and changing his or her direction in life by providing alternatives to a career of crime, citizens will perceive such programs as cost-effective methods to reduce further crime.

Another example is the issue of deinstitutionalization. Deinstitutionalization has significant political and economic overtones, and the values of more vocal members of the community influence how those diagnosed with psychiatric disorders are treated. If the public focuses on the fear that former patients living in the community could scare away customers, perpetrate crimes, or lower property values, states will alter their deinstitutionalization policies, and fewer individuals will be released into the community. Also, law-enforcing agencies, local politicians, and business people will become involved in designing a solution to the problem of "the mentally ill." If the problem is interpreted from the standpoint of client advocacy, other issues become more salient. Unnecessary and involuntary institutionalization with inadequate treatment will be seen as unlawful incarceration, and clients' rights to live in a normalized, least restrictive (but appropriate) environment will be supported. Therefore, deciding who "frames" the problem is a critical first step in determining what approach is taken to solving it.

Unfortunately, mental health professionals frequently interpret their role narrowly: to provide individually oriented psychological services specifically requested by the community. In some instances, this position has merit. On a larger level, however, it may be more useful for psychologists and social workers to advocate for new programs and to attempt to persuade the public to understand social issues from the perspective of the client group. If a problem is inaccurately defined, an intervention that focuses on solving the wrong problem may be designed. For example, if one student is performing poorly, a teacher might analyze the problem as occurring at the level of the individual and have the child referred for a battery of tests to determine the nature of the learning disability. As a result of the testing, appropriate counseling or instructional supports could be given to enable the child to fit better within the system. If a number of children are performing poorly, the problem might be more correctly understood as falling at the interpersonal or group level of complexity. Perhaps the problem is that the school staff is not sufficiently flexible in their response to the needs of these students. An appropriate intervention might address either the teaching methodology of the school or its ability to adapt to individual differences. If the students are not learning well because the values of the school conflict with those of the community, the change agent might design an institutional-level intervention targeting the school's value system. The change agent might perceive that a particular group of students is not doing well academically because they are members of an underrepresented group that may be discriminated against in the community. These students might have lowered self-confidence, little expectation for academic success, and no hope that working hard in school will have any effect on their lives because of the social discrimination. In this case, the interventionist might analyze the problem as existing at the societal level of complexity and realize that the values of the community itself need to be modified. The change agent would then seek a more equitable set of power and status relationships in the community and would advocate for a more equal distribution of resources. The change program would consist of social action, community organizing, and the development of new alternative institutional structures.

The failure to design an intervention at the level appropriate to the problem can lead to ineffective or counterproductive programs. If the preceding problem resulted from social discrimination, an intervention consisting of the placement of a minority child in a special education class will only increase the child's lack of self-esteem and reinforce the notion that the child's cultural background is deficient. As William Ryan (1971) noted, those in power tend to "blame the victims" of discrimination for their own plight. Viewing the problem from the wrong perspective or level of complexity will increase this tendency. The preceding example can be used to illustrate that not only individual level intervention ineffectiveness will result, but worse problems as well. The educational system might interpret the failure of the intervention as proof that such children cannot learn and are truly hopeless, academically. The school then absolves itself of all responsibility in searching for the solution (or even the real problem). With their prejudice validated, the staff might criticize the child's family and cultural background as being responsible for the learning failure. If a problem is defined at the wrong level, the resulting solutions will always miss the mark in a "game without end" (Watzlawick et al., 1974).

In many situations, it may require a community mental health professional to persuade the public that a problem needs to be reformulated before any effective solution can be designed or implemented. If community psychologists and social workers do not participate in the process of defining social problems, others in society will fill that leadership vacuum. As a result, the way in which the problem is understood might not be in the best interest of the client population. Issues such as cost, preservation of the status quo, fear of change, and prejudice could take precedence over the value of serving the clients and facilitating their development.

Exploring Alternative Solutions

The types of solutions considered for solving a problem are directly linked to what is salient at any given time. Although many people hold to the myth that scientists and research studies are value free, in actuality, all scientists hold values and incorporate their beliefs in their research. No matter how objective scientists try to be, scientific research involves vested interest. Most applied research projects require extensive funding, and researchers who agree with the values of the funding agency are more likely to receive the resources needed to conduct the research. Consider the following example. A major controversy that has been debated for over 40 years involves the issue of whether television violence causes viewers to become more aggressive (Hughes & Hasbrouck, 1997). If so, should the government restrict broadcasts that contain violent content? Parents and other concerned citizen groups believe that violence and sexual exploitation on TV contribute to increased aggression and criminal behavior in the community. Media network executives believe that such action-packed shows increase the number of viewers, and advertisers pay more to present their products on shows that have higher Nielson ratings. The issue pits the values of free speech and the right to make a profit against the responsibility of legislators to preserve the common good.

Social scientific research could provide a means to resolve the issue, and legislators might cite studies that support their views. Will studies be conducted that fairly represent the effect of TV violence on aggression? Each side has a vested interest. Citizen groups hire researchers to demonstrate that TV violence does increase aggression, whereas media networks fund those who attempt to show the opposite. Large-scale research in the community is costly, and the ability of each side to fund studies affects the proportion of empirical projects that are conducted.

Even when research is funded in a balanced manner, the way the findings are presented to the public is not always fair. One of the authors (JS) learned of a study commissioned by New York State in the 1970s to investigate welfare fraud and eligibility errors in the state. The researchers found that some individuals were receiving aid they were not entitled to receive, whereas others who met the qualifications did not receive it. When the study was completed, one political party paid for large-scale advertisements that highlighted only half of the findings (that some were receiving aid illegally). The opposing side lacked the funds to present the other findings. The researchers attempted to disseminate the results in a balanced way, but without adequate funding and a place to air their analysis, they were unable to do so. Furthermore, the public at that time wanted to hear only one side and so accepted the biased reports in an uncritical manner.

In many ways, society "stacks the deck" regarding which research is to be conducted, what data will be collected, and which findings will be disseminated. This is the case in the biological as well as the social sciences. The federal government, through the National Institutes of Health, differentially supports research projects investigating genetic versus environmental causes of cancer, depending on the prevailing beliefs of the time. Similarly, the National Institutes of Justice fund either more crime-prevention or more law-enforcement projects, depending on the political views of the majority of voters. In addition, scientific journal editors, mass media gatekeepers, university faculty, and the public itself restrict the types of studies funded, conducted, and published.

As a result, even if solutions that are explored are all research-based, and the research was conducted in a credible way upholding the appropriate scientific methodology, bias is still inevitable. The way in which the problem is defined determines who becomes involved. Who becomes involved determines what research will be funded and commissioned, and which results will be reported. The results that become accepted by the public as "the truth" will determine what actions a community will take. For example, if a group of homeless families are building a tent city on a vacant lot in the middle of town, it may be seen as a health and human service problem and interpreted as a group of poor, unemployed, and possibly mentally ill people who need some sort of help. As a result of this interpretation, human service agencies would become involved. On the other hand, if it is seen as an economic issue in which these people are impacting tourism and business at local stores and restaurants, local government and the business community would become involved. If it is seen as a safety issue, the police will become involved. Each constituency will have its own preferred solutions and varying amounts and types of resources available to advocate for a particular solution.

Community mental health professionals can have a real impact by taking on a political role. Gary Melton (2000) challenges community psychologists and others to explore ways of matching legal institutions and political agendas to the needs of the community. In doing so, they will assist in the creation of new legal settings that can facilitate the resolution of disputes and enhance perceived justice. He further proposes that psychologists and community mental health practitioners must view the legal and political system as a series of opportunities for empowering individuals and groups. Since changes at the higher levels of the system have greater impact, becoming involved in the political process can alter societal level factors and produce true institutional change. By passing a new law, such as the Americans with Disabilities Act of 1991, which prohibited certain forms of employment discrimination, the relationship between persons with disabilities and employers was significantly changed. Through this act, those with disabilities experience a greater sense of empowerment and a more favorable economic outlook. Consider how many individual therapeutic sessions would have been needed to produce as much growth in self-esteem for members of this group as the passage of this one bill.

Politicians must answer to many competing constituents in order to remain in office, and the perspective of those in need is not always heard. Either in office or consulting to a legislator, a community mental health professional could advocate well for a disenfranchised group or possibly reduce the inequity among various interest groups. At other times, legislators might have a sincere desire to help but are uncertain regarding how to do so most effectively. Again, a consultant with an understanding of community psychology could recommend cost-effective strategies to produce real change. Consider the impact this could have on issues such as health care reform, welfare, and the funding of primary prevention programs.

Developing the Vision

Once the problem has been defined and an appropriate solution (intervening at the highest possible level) has been decided upon, the community mental health practitioners have an opportunity and obligation to help develop a vision of the strategy. Theoretical principles must be translated into a compelling vision before a community can be mobilized to take action. According to John P. Kotter, the core pattern associated with successful change is see-feel-change. If people can be helped to see a problem through the creation of a dramatic, eye-catching and compelling situation, they will be able to visualize and connect with the situation and the people involved in the situation. This visualization will awaken feelings that support and facilitate change, such as a sense of urgency, optimism, and faith in an achievable solution. "Seeing" hits people at a deeper level and can evoke a visceral response that can, in turn, drive a change in behavior. Ultimately, change cannot take hold if people are unwilling to change their behavior (Kotter & Cohen, 2002).

Inexperienced or unaware change agents may not always capitalize on people's emotions and may instead try to use the analysis-think-change model. They may gather information, write reports, and make presentations in an attempt to change people's thinking and thus bank on the notion that new thinking will lead to new behaviors. For some people, this model is effective, and careful data gathering, analysis, and presentation are important. However, "often change launched through feelings creates a radically better approach to analysis" (Kotter & Cohen, 2002, p. 12). Politicians and experienced community activists know and often use the see-feel-change method to achieve their outcomes.

One nonviolent example of promoting true social change is described by Alinsky (1972). Alinsky emphasized that if community organizers can get a group of people passionate about change, a new politically active core group can emerge and shift the power base away from the status quo group. He further proposed that once passions have been aroused, specific policy changes come about as a by-product of more significant modifications in the social structure.

Using this approach, the community organizer works for one group or a number of disenfranchised groups within a community and uses the group's "people power" to overcome those whose status is based on "money power." Instantaneous change is not expected; the organizer assists the group in realizing that they must struggle to gain power and community resources rather than be given them. In this manner, Alinsky's approach represents true second-order change, since the structure of society itself is altered and the status relationships between the dominant and the minority groups become more equitable.

The goals of the community organizer are to gather a group together, to assist the group in attaining power, and to use the power for the benefit of the community. According to Alinsky, the organizer should possess the following traits: a curious and questioning approach to the values of society; an ability to take the irreverent stance that nothing is sacred; a willingness to attack any institution, corporation, or bureaucrat; and a good imagination, both to use creative means of organizing the group and to identify with the sufferings of people. In summary, a community organizer must be able to create a compelling vision.

Alinsky believed that an organizer should have a blurred, nondogmatic view of a better society and should never become a "true believer" of any political cause. This outlook allows the change agent to compromise with the system after the client group has attained equal status with the formerly dominant group. Similarly, Alinsky believed that a nondogmatic organizer has more leeway in assisting a group to attain its goals. He reasoned that a group with no power should fight for total control and then flexibly compromise to attain half of its demands. The group would then exist as a significant force in the community, and the members of the group would feel less helpless, because they would possess political power. In addition, the group and its grassroots leaders could continue the process of change through negotiation with the heads of institutions long after their organizer leaves. A change agent who is too dogmatic or idealistic is not able to compromise later on, and if this outcome occurs, a group might not realize any of its goals. In addition, a change agent should have personal characteristics such as an open mind, a good sense of humor, and a high tolerance for ambiguity. The change agent must not desire to lead but must strive to be a catalyst, organizing the group to use its own "people power" to obtain social change.

In order to describe his method more fully, Alinsky (1972) provided the organizers with a large number of principles and tactics to use when achieving change. Some of these "rules for radicals" and successful tactics in applying these principles are presented next:

- *Never go outside the experience of your friendly audience, but baffle your opponents by devising tactics outside of their experience.* For example, in order to obtain some employment concessions from the mayor of Chicago, Alinsky threatened to mobilize "people power" to occupy all the restroom facilities at O'Hare International Airport with jobless members of his group. The city swiftly conceded, since they realized that Chicago would suffer greatly. Business leaders might be less inclined to hold conventions in the city, and airlines might, as a result, choose other airports to schedule connecting flights and layovers. In addition, Chicago police would not be able to arrest the protesters, since no laws specify the length of time a person can spend using public facilities.

■ *Create the belief that change is both possible and probable.* This is not an easy process. Oppressed people perceive that they are powerless and that any activity to create change is futile. Generally, oppressed persons experience learned helplessness (Peterson, Maier, & Seligman, 1993) and refrain from getting involved in efforts to improve their condition. Alinsky engineered situations in which the group could win an easy battle initially, to foster faith in the power of community organizing. For example, he scheduled a large group meeting in a public park and arranged for the necessary public permit. After securing the bureaucrat's permission and after being told that such permits require 24 hours to process, Alinsky went back to the group, indicating that the city was stalling regarding issuing the permit. The group, then, decided to picket city hall on the following day, demanding that they be allowed their right to gather. The officials, confused about the supposed communication mix-up and seeking to avoid a confrontation, presented the group leaders with a permit. The leaders believed that the city conceded because of their efforts, and thus the group members felt that ultimate victory was very likely if the group organized itself fully. However, it goes without saying that change plans should be free of duplicity for ethical and practical reasons. If Alinsky's scheme had been uncovered, the group would have unified in their mistrust of the change agent.

■ *Organize diverse community groups by appealing to superordinate values and cultural truisms; approach people on a visceral level.* Alinsky assisted in gathering over 100 local social and religious groups in Rochester, New York, under a coordination group called FIGHT, which stood for Freedom, Integrity, God, Honor, Today. Nearly every minority organization in the city found some common positive cause with a group so named, and hence the group quickly gained thousands of supporters. Its leaders harnessed this "people power" to gain important job concessions for minorities from the Eastman Kodak Company, the largest industrial employer in the area. Notice that there was no collection of data, report writing, or formal presentation at the local Chamber of Commerce.

■ *Make the best use of "people power," particularly if the other side has "money power."* In the Rochester effort, Alinsky capitalized on the free classical music concerts that Kodak offered in the community. Typically, these concerts were attended by the company's executives and their spouses. The FIGHT organizers obtained a large number of tickets for the concert and distributed these tickets at a preconcert baked-beans party attended by the FIGHT members. Later on, the atmosphere at the concert was affected by those who attended the earlier cookout. The company executives quickly found that "people power" was a force to be recognized and negotiated with.

■ *Seize the moment; invent new creative tactics as presented by current events.* In a Midwestern city, Alinsky and his group were attempting to persuade the city council to pass rat-control laws, in order to encourage landlords to improve the living conditions in the poorer neighborhoods. The city administration was unsympathetic about the problem until the group leaders collected a large number of rats from the slum buildings and freed them in City Hall. The action, of course, was not illegal, because the city had no rat-control laws. Alinsky's group made their point, and the legislature swiftly passed the necessary bill.

With all these community-organizing tactics, Alinsky demonstrated that true social change is, in fact, possible and that minority groups can gain their fair share of institutional resources. However, as Alinsky found, the dominant society does not relinquish its power readily, and those who choose to organize minority groups in the community must be prepared for a long and difficult struggle. Despite this state of affairs, Alinsky's strategies of organizing minority groups to gain power and resources in the community are very powerful methods of altering the values and status relationships of the social system to create true change. These techniques emphasize the fact that, at times, the interventionist must revamp the entire social system to produce real change, since innovations at lower levels might be ineffective and counterproductive. Change attempted at these high levels will have a positive spiral resulting in positive community changes and individual growth, belonging, and a sense of empowerment for those who participate. The change agent must be aware of possible intervention strategies at all levels of the system in order to choose the appropriate type of innovation and to avoid being confined to a single approach.

Communicating the Vision

In successful change efforts, once the problem has been accurately identified, the alternative solutions explored, and the vision, strategies, and direction of change developed, the vision, strategy, and direction must then be widely communicated. It must be communicated for understanding, but even more important, for "buy-in." According to John P. Kotter, the goal of the fourth step in the change process is "to get as many people as possible acting to make the vision a reality" (Kotter & Cohen, 2002, p. 83). Good communication is not about data transfer; rather, good communication addresses people's anxieties, accepts their anger, and shows them a better way. It is therefore critical that the change agent or spokesperson of the change initiative is appropriate for this task.

Malcolm Gladwell (2000) provides a fascinating account of how society-level change occurs in his book called *The Tipping Point*. He brought the analogy of how a virus gradually spreads and at a certain point becomes an epidemic to the concept of social change. His notions are based on three principles: contagiousness, the fact that small causes can have big effects, and the fact that true change occurs at one dramatic moment when a critical mass has been reached (Burke, 2002). Change happens in large part because a few people spread the virus. For example, the fax machine sold 80,000 units in 1984, rose steadily until 1987 when a million machines were sold, and then exploded with over 2 million sold in 1989. The tipping point was 1987.

Gladwell proposes that the people who spread the virus are not ordinary people. He calls the people who spread the virus the connectors, the mavens, and the salespeople, all of whom are important when it comes to communicating the vision and spreading the change. Stanley Milgram (1967) first proposed the notion of "6 degrees of separation." He found that we are only 5 or 6 steps removed from any other person. That is, if 5 separate people are asked to do so, they connect any one randomly chosen individual to any other randomly chosen individual. Gladwell added to this line of thinking by suggesting that not all of these 6 degrees are equal. He believes that a few people are more highly connected than most. He calls them the "connectors" because they have a special gift for bringing people together. They are curious about and like people more than most, and they are able to successfully navigate many different worlds and subcultures. Connectors do not generally start the change initiative, but they are critical in facilitating the process and communicating the vision (Burke, 2002). The second group identified by Gladwell is the "mavens." They are the information brokers, who transmit the content of the change initiative from one person to the next as they share what they know and have learned. Finally, there are the "salespeople," who are persuasive and tune in to subtle, nonverbal cues and then use that information to relate, empathize, and influence others. The connectors provide wide access, the mavens spread the content of the change initiative, and the salespeople spread the emotional energy. All are critical for change to take hold. One final interesting aspect of Gladwell's work is the magic number 150. Reviewing the work of Daniel Wegner (as cited by Burke, 2002) on transactive memory (knowing people well enough so what they think of you makes a difference) and Robin Dunbar (as cited by Burke, 2002) on social channel capacity (the number of 2-way relations we can comfortably keep track of), he concluded, "150 people is the tipping point" (Burke, 2002, p. 77). Given this notion, if 150 people can be convinced at both an emotional and a logical level that change is necessary and the proposed vision for that change is desirable, the likelihood that the change initiative will succeed is high.

Implementing the Plan

The fifth step of the change process deals with the actual step involved in creating true second-order change. Kurt Lewin (1951) proposed a 3-step model for permanent change. According to him, successful change follows 3 steps: unfreezing the status quo, moving to the new state, and refreezing the new change. The status quo can be looked at as being in a state of equilibrium, and in order to move from this state, one must overcome individual resistance and group conformity. The latter half of this chapter will offer a number of suggestions as to how to accomplish this unfreezing. One critical aspect of this is to create a sense of urgency. Kotter (2002) proposed that increasing the urgency for change and creating a guiding team (as discussed in the previous section) are the first 2 steps toward successful large-scale change. Moving to a new state requires people to buy in to the change, be empowered to act, and achieve short-term wins to maintain momentum. The third of Lewin's steps, refreezing, involves establishing new norms, laws, systems, and infrastructure that can maintain the change over time.

Evaluating the Outcomes

Finally, one must evaluate the outcomes, both intentional and unintentional, that have resulted from the change. Human environments, and even more so, the capacities of human beings to adapt and restructure these environments, are so complex in their basic organization that they are not likely to be captured, let alone comprehended, through simplistic, unidimensional research models that make no provision for assessing ecological structure and variation (Bronfenbrenner, 1979). In order to assess the impact of a change initiative, a multidimensional evaluation strategy is needed. One must look at process as well as at client outcomes and use good system-focused evaluation tools. In order to know if a change intervention was effective, the change in people and their social status, as well the setting in which they find themselves, must be assessed and the results compared with the vision.

In conclusion, community mental health professionals are embedded within systems of values, language, time, culture, and power. According to Altman and Rogoff (1987), "we need to put aside, once and for all, our notion that we can be 'objective observers' of systems and events at the same time we participate in them . . . To try to be objective from these experiences is artificial and unnecessary" because there are multiple perspectives in defining a context, and one's perspective is limited by one's worldviews. Mental health professionals need to elicit the perspectives of various constituencies within communities and to reframe their roles as collaborators with communities rather than with experts. It is important to reassess the roles that community psychologists and social workers can play in community organizing and other social change efforts. By developing long-term relationships with community organizations, these professionals are also well positioned to contribute to critical analysis of the issues undertaken. Rather than operating as experts, community mental health professionals represent one set of stakeholders who can contribute particular skills and perspectives. By involving themselves in promoting social change goals, social scientists and community mental health practitioners can take a step toward bridging the gap between rhetoric and practice in community psychology (Tseng et al., 2002).

Organizational Change

Thus far in the book, various ideas have been presented regarding ways in which the community psychological/social systems approach could be applied to improve the abilities of groups of individuals to function more productively in their social setting and to change the setting to enhance the quality of life in the community. In the previous pages, many principles were described that would help community mental health practitioners formulate effective and useful interventions to achieve institutional-level change. In the last few pages of this chapter, the methods of organizational change are presented. After a brief overview of the change process, classical and contemporary strategies for encouraging organizational level interventions are described, and techniques for producing change are discussed.

Most of the principles for instituting innovation have come from industrial organizational psychologists working in business settings and from community mental health professionals and other social scientists consulting to human services agencies and grassroots groups. There has always been a strong tie between community psychology and organizational psychology. Authors such as Argyris (1964), Bennis (1966), and Katz and Kahn (1966) devised the basic principles of planned organizational change in large industrial establishments, and others such as Miles (1964) and Johnson (1970) applied these methods to education. Strategies that have worked in education are also likely to work in mental health and other areas of relevance to community mental health practitioners. Much of the material presented in this chapter regarding the contributions of industrial and social psychologists presented was taken from Johnson's review.

Diagnostic-Prescriptive Model

The industrial or organizational psychologists as a group believe that comprehensive change programs in a business or social system should be conducted within a diagnostic-prescriptive model. That is, the consultant or change agent should first determine what type of problem or deficiency is inhibiting the organization from growing or becoming more effective in achieving its goals. After the diagnosis is completed, a prescription or remedy for the deficits is proposed. The diagnostic stage should include an assessment of the overall organizational health of the system and an evaluation of the degree to which the institution is effective in meeting specific objectives relevant to the proposed intervention.

As a general rule, community mental health professionals, who view problems in living as issues of poor person-environment fit or as a lack of ability to access the resources necessary for positive adaptive change, would not advocate for the implementation of a diagnostic-prescriptive model applied to individuals. A diagnostic-prescriptive model applied to settings rather than an individual is quite different in nature and outcome. For example, diagnosing the communication problems detected at a particular work setting and prescribing techniques that will improve the problem will likely validate and relieve employees who feel the stress of the dysfunction in the operation, offering them an opportunity to work together toward true organizational change. In this regard, this type of labeling, whereby no one individual is singled out or made to feel defective but a larger setting-related issue is addressed, can have a positive impact on those who are experiencing difficulty.

The first step is the diagnosis. Johnson (1970) listed three areas to consider when determining an organization's well-being. These areas include task accomplishment, internal integration, and growth and change. In the task accomplishment area, the consultant should determine whether the goals of the institution are clear, appropriate, achievable, and accepted by all the members. In an agency, it is useful to survey the service providers and administrative staff, as well as the clients and the advocates, regarding how they see the goals of the agency at that time and what they would like the priorities to be. The change agent can then observe the effectiveness of the administrators in communicating policy to all involved. When considering the task-accomplishment aspect of the diagnosis, the consultant should observe the process by

The internal integration area consists of the degree to which human resources are fully utilized and the degree to which all members feel that they are part of a thriving organization. The goodness of fit between the person's personality and his or her position in the role structure should be assessed. It is particularly important to study the leader's fit. One means of evaluating the person-position fit is to apply Fiedler's (1967, 2002) contingency model of leadership, described in the chapter on ecology. Fiedler found that the relative effectiveness of leadership styles depends on the specific group situation. In those groups in which the leader's power, group morale, and the degree to which tasks are objective are either very high or very low, an authoritarian style of leadership is more effective. In groups, which are moderate in these characteristics, a socioemotional leader who is concerned about the members' feelings and interpersonal relationships is able to achieve greater productivity with the group. If the person-position fit is not good, it is possible to either adjust the role demands of the office or to alter the style that the leader uses in performing the role. A change agent who understands Fiedler's contingency model can monitor the group situation and recommend to the agency director the proper leadership style and how to implement it.

which the agency measures its success in achieving goals. Such measures should include both objective assessments, which can be used as baselines for evaluations of proposed innovations, and subjective opinion-oriented feedback mechanisms.

The final diagnostic area proposed by Johnson concerns the ability of the agency to grow and change. Every open system must interact with the social environment, and as the cultural context changes, so must the organization. A healthy institution adapts in a manner consistent with the society. Diagnostically, it is important to assess an agency's innovativeness (how well the organization monitors external changes), its planning process, and its willingness to respond to emerging needs. It is also useful to determine which structures, policies, or staff in the bureaucracy inhibits planned change. In addition, change frequently requires decision making and problem solving in a timely manner, so that the organization's abilities and strategies in these areas need to be studied.

After the diagnostic stage is completed, the change agent or consultant is in a position to prescribe a new policy or program to enhance the organization. Often, the change agent already has a program in mind, or at least a general idea of the factors that should be modified to remedy some deficiency. It is important to review the research literature to find out whether such a program has been attempted before, and if so, whether it was successful. Frequently, the specific program has not been established elsewhere, but research might indicate that certain variables, which could be operationalized in a proposed program, have affected client outcome. This literature review serves two purposes: to develop the program more fully so as to increase the probability of its success and to provide persuasive evidence for administrators to accept the innovation.

After the relevant literature has been reviewed, it is necessary to state the general goals and specific objectives of the intervention. It is also useful to describe a scenario or a conceptualization of the program. Often the scenario will assist the innovator to concretize the intervention, and it will help others to understand the type of innovation being suggested. The scenario is only one possibility; the change agent must be willing to modify this picture while keeping the basic goals and objectives fairly fixed.

How to Get "Buy-In"

In order for any change initiative to succeed, the change agent must develop a strategy for encouraging a mental health organization to accept the innovation. The more the staff "buy into" the new program, the more invested they will be in its success. The following seven methods or strategies for encouraging change are from a list of nine proposed by Johnson (1970) as being effective.

Decree from High Authority

One means of having a new program accepted by a system is by presenting it to the agency director and the board, and securing their support. Nearly all successful programs have been endorsed by the agency head, but the method is more effective if used in conjunction with additional strategies that convince others in the system of the value of the innovation. Leadership has to be a central force in any change initiative, and without strong support from the top, the change initiative is destined to fail (Kotter & Cohen, 2002). However, a decree from a high authority is not enough, and it can increase resistance on the part of the staff.

Replacement of Personnel

Another strategy to ensure that an organization will accept a new program is to replace those members who oppose the change with those who support it. This method is based on the belief that as the program changes, role requirements also change, and that the staff occupying those roles may not be able to adapt. Although this belief is true in some cases, it is contrary to the most central premise of human service institutions: that people—staff as well as clients—can adjust to new environmental demands if they are motivated and provided with necessary information, training, rewards, and reinforcement.

Presentation of Information

Providing information and empirical research evidence supporting an innovation will give advocates a credible rationale for the new program; however, if used alone, this strategy will rarely motivate persons opposed to the program to change their position. Often, change agents believe that appealing solely to reason will cause staff or administrators to "see the truth" and change their approach. This outcome is unlikely to occur, since individuals tend to hold beliefs for many nonrational reasons. These can include fear of the unknown, fear that the innovation might disrupt other useful activities, or even a concern that their status or other vested interest might be threatened.

In addition, the information presented will be processed through the target person's attitude filter or frame of reference, and the message received will not be identical to the message sent. Finally, information alone is not motivating, and the person's affect, or emotion, must be addressed.

Skill Training

In-service training programs for staff are effective means of insuring that a new innovation will be implemented properly; and this method can also help in motivating them to accept the new program. Moynahan (1981), for example, investigated the effect of staff development on implementing magnet school and other desegregation programs. In her review of 39 studies, Moynahan found that 10% of the programs failed because of the lack of in-service staff preparation. In the majority of studies in which the new programs were successful, this researcher found that in-service training helped to sensitize school staff to the interpersonal and attitudinal problems associated with desegregation. Moynahan suggested that staff preparation should be comprehensive and include not only a presentation of the technical details of the program but also training in human relations, multicultural issues, and community participation. Thus, staff training is critical in determining whether a new program will be successful. In-service training is a necessary but not a sufficient method on its own for inducing an agency to accept a new program. Similar to the method of presentation, this technique is most effective with staff who are motivated to accept the program or with staff who are at least neutral. Service providers and administrators, who are resistant to change, usually require some additional incentive to attend training sessions and to accept the new program.

Sensitivity Group Training and Team Building

Another technique for encouraging the members of a school or an agency organization to accept change is sensitivity training through T-groups. Although no longer as popular, T-groups were used extensively in the 1970s. Sensitivity training consists of groups of approximately 15 to 20 members of the staff who meet for an extended period of time to study themselves and the relationships among the participants. A facilitator encourages each participant to clarify and express feelings, thoughts, and experiences. The goal of sensitivity training is to provide a setting in which free, direct, intimate, and role-free communication can occur. As a result, the typical roles and norms of the organization are temporarily set aside, allowing for new communication patterns and decision-making processes to emerge. A technique similar in some respects to sensitivity training has been gaining prominence in organizational development and change. This technique, called team building (Boss, 1983; Dyer, 1977), seeks to develop a spirit of cooperation and interdependence among staff members. In business and industry, self-managed teams have been formed to reduce resistance to change, to support innovation, and to increase staff ownership. These teams have been found to be vehicles for increasing efficiency, effectiveness, and motivation at the worksite. Experts who advocate the use of teams to gain employee buy-in and owner-ship cite the following as reasons for its success:

- Those closest to the work know best how to perform and improve their jobs.
- Most employees want to feel they "own" their jobs and are making meaningful contributions to the effectiveness of their organizations.
- Teams provide possibilities for empowerment that are not available to individual employees (Maeroff, 1993).

Survey Feedback Method

Yet another way to encourage staff members to participate in the change process is to use the survey feedback method. In this intervention, a consultant asks the staff, and in some cases also the clients and members of the community, to indicate their concerns regarding the service agency's internal functioning and task performance. These concerns are then converted into questions for surveys. The surveys can be either specific to one part of the organization or global assessments. The questionnaires are then distributed to the staff, clients, and community members. The consultant tabulates the results (broken down by respondent group) without performing any extensive analysis or interpretation of the data. The results are then presented at an agencywide meeting. Each participant is able to see the extent of agreement among survey respondents as to which problems are the most significant, and then each person is encouraged to draw conclusions and implications from the data. In order to maximize free and open discussion, these group meetings are usually facilitated by a consultant who does not have any particular bias relevant to the agency. Typically, at the end of the meeting, a representative group of the participants is formed to make specific recommendations for change that are based on the survey data. The primary value of this method is that the staff and consumers of services who have a major role in all stages of the change process are more likely to accept the innovation as their own and participate cooperatively in its implementation. The consultant enters into a collaborative relationship with the organization and serves solely as a catalyst for gathering together the perspectives, concerns, and solutions of members of the entire system in an objective manner. In addition to developing a specific innovation, the staff learn the process of change and, in conjunction with administrators and the community, can continue to utilize this technique long after the consultant leaves.

Demonstration Projects

Among the most successful methods for decreasing resistance to change is to have the staff of the targeted agency visit a successful innovative program in operation. They can then observe the effective implementation of the new idea and can consult with the staff of the demonstration program regarding the new methods, in order to resolve any concerns they might have regarding the new program.

This approach is most effective in producing support for the new innovation if the staff perceive many similarities between the conditions present in the demonstration project and those in their own workplace. Thus, it is good to choose a demonstration project in which the type of client, size of the agency, and financial and human resources available are nearly identical to the target organization.

If it can be done, establishing a demonstration project in the target agency itself is often effective, since the conditions present in the project are then identical to those of the rest of the program. In the mental health field, Fairweather and Davidson (1986) found that psychiatric hospitals that accepted a small-scale demonstration project were more likely to adopt the full innovation later than those institutions that wanted only to review literature or talk with a consultant about the new program. The drawback in establishing a demonstration project is that there is a great likelihood of initial start-up problems that might produce some staff resistance to the program. This resistance might cause the demonstration project to become isolated within the agency, and the prevailing social structure of the rest of the system might force the project to be terminated prematurely. Assuming the initial problems are not great, an effective demonstration project is likely to produce greater acceptance.

The previous listed techniques of encouraging organizational change are not mutually exclusive, and the change agent should consider combining as many methods as is feasible to increase the likelihood that the change program will be accepted and that it will be implemented effectively.

Burke-Litwin Causal Model of Organization Performance

As mentioned before, the diagnostic perspective model of change is preferred by social scientists. It focuses on the problems and deficiencies within an organization, and proposes that the dissidence between what is and what should be is the driving force for change. The diagnostic-prescriptive model examines organizational functioning in the here and now to determine and correct deficits that help groups advance to the next level of functioning. The corporate world, on the other hand, often focuses on the organizational climate as the centerpiece of organizational behavior and thus organizational change. Business-oriented change agents such as Stephen Covey (1989, 1991); George Litwin (1992, 1996); Peter Senge (1994); and Maira and Scott-Morgan (1996) advocate future-focused strategies that require all members of an organization to examine not where they are but rather where they ultimately wish to be, in an ongoing process. Such proactive models involve determining an organization's philosophy, developing a group vision reflective of this philosophy, and operationalizing these shared concepts into strategy and action plans.

One such model is the Burke-Litwin Causal Model of Organization Performance and Change (1992). According to this model, changing an organization's climate is critical in initiating and sustaining change. Burke and Litwin define organizational climate as a set of psychological principles present in a work environment that are based on the collective perceptions of the people in that setting. Organizational climate is created by organizational variables such as the leadership style of the CEO, and the norms, values, policies, and procedures of the organization. The model argues that when trying to overhaul a company's business strategy, one must overhaul not only the organization's mission but also its leadership and culture. The culture has more influence on what will or will not happen in an organization than the organizational structure and management practices (Burke & Litwin, 1992). When looking at change from this perspective, it becomes critical to create an engaging vision, mission, and set of values that will impact an organization's culture, for without this, sustainable change is not possible.

Determining an Organization's Philosophy

Maira and Scott-Morgan (1997) note the importance of developing an organization's philosophy to serve as a secure and comfortable constant for all members of the organization. Reinforcing these common, guiding principles is particularly useful during times of organizational change when many are feeling disenfranchised. In developing an organization's philosophy, it is important to address three key elements: mission, values, and principles.

Much like the U.S. Constitution, the mission is simply the answer to the question "why do we exist?" (Senge, 1994). It is, as Covey (1989) points out, the focal point from which all activities derive their meaning. The mission addresses issues such as who makes up the organization, which markets or individuals are served, and which products or services are offered. For example, the mission of a human service organization might be this: "Helpful House is a vocational rehabilitation organization dedicated to providing the necessary job training and placement skills to ensure the success of consumers who are visually impaired." The manner in which the mission is executed depends largely on an organization's values and principles.

Principles are a set of declaratives—all or nothing statements that do not change under any circumstances. For example, one principle in a human service agency might be to respect consumers as individuals. This principle is a constant regardless of funding pressures, leadership changes, or advances in pharmacological interventions. Values, on the other hand, are ideas we prize more highly than other ideas. They can exist in varying degrees and are frequently adjusted by organizational circumstances. For example, an agency value might be to promote from within when a vacancy arises before hiring outside staff. An agency might have a very loyal employee who appears deserving of advancement to an executive position. However, if funding pressures are such that the agency needs to hire an individual with experience administering government grants, the agency may well suspend the value of promoting from within in this particular instance. The organization may also change the degree to which this value is employed by offering the inside candidate a raise for his or her loyalty or additional responsibilities that might enhance his or her application in the future.

A key element in an organization's ability to change is the underlying understanding of "what we are and what we want and value." (Covey, 1989). Given this, all members of an organization should participate in the development of its philosophy, and the process of developing these ideals is nearly as important as the product. Participation breeds a familiar buy-in that helps each member of the organization to feel a shared sense of responsibility and commitment.

Vision

Believing one is a member of an organization with a meaningful philosophy is not enough. Most innovations begin with a "dream," and a change agent needs to help the group begin to develop a platform for innovation by way of a shared vision. Hamel and Prahalad (1994) define vision, or "strategic intent," as the animating dream that provides the emotional and intellectual energy for the journey, implying a sense of direction, discovery, and destiny.

Time & Space Limited: Successfully Communicating an Organizational Vision

Time & Space Limited (TSL) is a small, nonprofit organization based in Hudson, New York, and a good example of how organizational growth and effectiveness can be fueled by the ability to communicate a vision. TSL seeks to build trust and rapport with and within the Hudson community through an innovative utilization of the arts. Art is an integral part of human expression and can be a powerful unifying tool, since it has the ability to transcend language and other barriers and to speak directly to people's hearts and souls. To realize its vision, TSL not only offers diverse arts-related programming but also serves as a safe and an open meeting-place for community members to engage in dialogue within a positive and creative environment.

Linda Mussmann and Claudia Bruce, the founders of the organization, at one time owned a Manhattan theater company. In 1991, the couple moved to the Hudson area with a dream, hoping to use artistic expression to enrich and unite their newly adopted community. As a result, TSL was born, and it continued to evolve along with its surroundings; the very nature of the organization allows it to grow according to the dynamic of the community. Programming includes film screenings, open forums, youth and community projects, theater performances, music and dance performances, literary readings, and art exhibitions. Yet of most importance, TSL functions primarily as a gathering space, and one that responds to the needs of those who attend. TSL thus reflects the intent of its founders to connect people to resources and opportunities, and thus plants the seeds for growth of both individual community members as well as the community as a whole.

Not only has TSL's overall vision allowed it to successfully meet the needs of the community, but also this same vision fuels the loyalty and enthusiasm of the staff who are at the very heart of the organization. The passion and enthusiasm of the people who comprise TSL are the keys to the organization's strength and effectiveness. TSL employees are not only involved in running its extensive programming but also actually help to shape the organization through a hands-on approach.

TSL exemplifies several community psychology principles, including a focus on prevention and the acknowledgment of the important dynamic relationship that exists between organization and community. None of this would have been possible in the absence of the innovative vision that drives this unique organization and has made TSL an integral and irreplaceable part of the Hudson community. (M. M. Wojtaszek, 2005)

http://www.timeandspace.org/tsl/

Direction comes from determining where an organization, as an entity, is trying to go. Discovery offers employees the enticing journey to a new destination; and destiny, which commands the respect and leadership of every employee, must be both distinctive and worthwhile.

In simpler terms, Senge (1994) defines vision as the answer to the single question "What do we want to create?" To Senge, group vision is similar to individual vision. Instead of carrying around individual images in our own heads, organizational vision involves the development of shared images that create a commonality, which gives coherence to diverse activities. A good vision statement should take into account the needs of all of the organization's stakeholders, in order to avoid fostering a state of compliance rather than commitment. In light of this, a change agent should work carefully to ensure that there is true bottom-up participation in the development of an organization's vision.

Strategy and Action Plans

According to Maira and Scott-Morgan (1996, p. 12), "To be truly effective, strategy must be a lot more than a neat construct. It must reflect the vision of the external world, the internal world, and the journey to realize the goal, and it must inspire the entire organization to take that journey."

They note that 5 elements must be present within the organization to establish change readiness:

- An understanding that change is necessary;
- Agreement that the proposed innovations are appropriate;
- The feeling that members have been acknowledged as individuals;
- The understanding that members have the skills to achieve the goals; and
- The knowledge that the organization supports the required changes.

In many respects, these newer methods of organizational change implicitly incorporate many of Johnson's strategies for facilitating change. The primary difference in this approach is the issue of labeling. In working together to develop shared philosophy, vision, and goals, an organization has an opportunity to focus on their competencies. There is a proactive attempt to look at where the group can go rather than the reactive position of trying to address what is currently wrong. In this sense, individuals have an opportunity to think outside of the box and create true innovation. This proactive approach empowers members of an organization through a collective sense of membership and power to effect creative and meaningful change, and continuous quality improvement.

Conclusion

In conclusion, every community mental health practitioner has ample opportunity to become involved in the initiation, support, and implementation of various change initiatives. In addition to having ample opportunity, this author also feels that community mental health practitioners, and all citizens for that matter, have a personal and professional obligation to support change that will positively impact the quality of life for the disenfranchised, the powerless, and those with limited access to the communities resources. Whether one is a staff person at a local health and human service agency, a psychologist or social worker with a private practice in the community, a program evaluator, a researcher, a college professor, a board member or a political advocate, one should use solid change management principles to help support the reforms that will most benefit the constituency one serves.

DISCUSSION QUESTIONS

1. What are the two types of change? Which is more common? Why do you think one is more common than the other? Describe an example of each type of change, as would be addressed through a community psychology program. Why is it important to enact change at the highest possible level?

2. What are some important considerations when defining social problems? How does perspective affect the solutions that are considered? What are some practical ways in which a community psychologist can address conflict between vested interests? What is the responsibility of a community psychologist in mediating between clients and the public to effect positive change?

3. How does society influence research? What are the ramifications of these practices? What, if anything, can be done about it? Can you describe ways to address the problem from an individual level? What about from a community level?

4. Does the community psychologist have a responsibility to facilitate change in the community? Why? If so, what are some roles and responsibilities that might be suited to a community psychologist? What traits would make someone an effective or ineffective change agent, respectively?

12 A Focus on Gerontology: Community Mental Health Services for the Growing Elderly Population

OBJECTIVES

This chapter is designed to enable the reader to:

- Identify important demographic trends that will impact the health care system.
- Understand the impact of deinstitutionalization on the elderly.
- Develop awareness of implications of an aging baby-boom cohort.
- Identify ways in which older individuals may be psychologically affected by economic situations.
- Identify important aspects of effective interventions targeted to the older generation.
- Identify specialized mental health service needs for the elderly.
- Identify reasons why older adults are less likely to utilize available mental health services in the community.
- Develop a familiarity with legislation affecting mental health needs of the elderly.
- Outline examples of programs in the community designed for older adults.
- Identify how ethnic and gender considerations impact the structure of elder care.
- Understand special needs of the chronically mentally ill elderly and their caregivers.
- Become familiar with the proposal of a voluntary self-insurance plan designed to address health care costs.
- Review examples of programs designed to provide quality-of-life improvement for residentially placed elders.
- Gain an overview of factors that affect life expectancy.
- Identify ways to promote good physical and mental health to the elderly in the community.

"With a little luck, there's no reason why you can't live to be one hundred. Once you've done that, you've got it made, because very few people die over one hundred."

George Burns

Introduction

Two major demographic trends have occurred in our society within the last 50 years. First, the average life span of older adults has increased dramatically. Second, the large baby boom cohort swelled the population numbers of those born in the mid-1900s. Both of these factors are expected to have a major impact on demands for health care in the near future. As our society ages, increasing numbers of elderly adults will need mental health services within the community. Governments, agencies, and the private sector will all be impacted by this increased demand for services.

This chapter begins by reviewing the historical perspective on growing community mental health needs for the elderly, as well as demographic changes and their effect on the community mental health system. Current mental health needs, barriers to service, and legislative responses to the growing mental health needs of the elderly are then covered. The next section of the chapter provides examples of various community mental health services and interventions for the elderly. Considerations of gender and culture as well as ways in which community services meet the needs of the chronically mentally ill and their caregivers are covered. Finally, the chapter concludes with the promotion of good health through community services, future trends in community mental health services for the elderly, and a model program that promotes successful aging and improves the quality of life of the elderly within the community.

Community Mental Health Services for the Elderly—The Historical Perspective

Major changes in mental health services for the elderly in our society have come about because of deinstitutionalization, as covered in Chapter 2. In brief review, because of the increased ability to control symptoms of schizophrenia through the use of psychoactive drugs, thousands of patients were discharged from psychiatric institutions into the communities. The communities were expected to provide the mental health services for these patients that the mental hospitals had been providing up until that point.

Recent studies have shown a number of complicating trends. First, outpatient facilities have not replaced inpatient hospitals, but both are increasing. Second, private psychiatric hospitals and general hospitals with psychiatric units have taken over responsibility for many of the services. Thus, there is a trend for the privatization of mental health services in this country (Gatz & Smyer, 1992; Simons, 1989).

One of the unintended consequences of deinstitutionalization of older patients was that large numbers were sent directly to nursing homes rather than into the community. The Omnibus Budget Reconciliation Act (OBRA, 1987) later addressed that problem by indicating that individuals seeking nursing home placement needed to be screened, and that those with mental problems but no physical problems had to be excluded from nursing home care (Freiman, Arons, Goldman, & Burns, 1990; Gatz & Smyer, 1992).

The community mental health centers in the 1980s also sought to reach the underserved elderly. According to Gatz and Smyer (1992), that goal has been only partially accomplished. Currently, slightly more than half of the mental health care for the elderly is provided through community mental health services. The rest is handled by primary care physicians who often fail to recognize mental health symptoms and therefore fail to refer patients to mental health facilities.

Population Changes—The Graying of America

In the year 1900, life expectancy was about 47.3 years. Today, it has reached 76.7 and is still increasing (National Center for Health Statistics, Centers for Disease Control, 2002). As this trend continues, the population within this country and around the world will become increasingly older, with the largest growth in the segment of the very old, aged over 85 (Vaupel, 1998). By the year 2030, 1 out of every 4 or 5 people will be over 65.

According to death and longevity statistics tabulated by the Centers for Disease Control and Prevention's National Health Statistics for 2001, life expectancy at birth in the United States for all races is 77.2 (79.8 for females and 74.4 for males). Whites, with an average life expectancy of 77.6 (80.2 for females and 75.0 for males), have a slightly higher expectancy than Blacks, who have an average life expectancy of 72.2 (75.5 for females and 68.6 for males) (Arias & Smith, 2003).

Much of the increase in life expectancy can be attributed to improved health care, reduction in deaths from disease, and improved hygiene and nutrition, as well as fewer deaths in childbirth (Lemme, 2002). Although people in modern society tend to connect illness to old age, it is a fairly new phenomenon. In the early 1900s, people were likely to die from acute diseases such as pneumonia and influenza. Today, deaths from these diseases are rare, and people are more likely to live longer but with chronic health care problems (Hooyman & Kiyak, 1993).

As life expectancy has increased over the last hundred years, family size has decreased. Instead of four or five children, families today typically contain one or two. Rather than two or three generations living within a household, there may be five. This demographic change in the structure of the family has gone from what Bengston calls a "pyramid" structure, in which few generations exist but with many members per generation, to more of a "bean pole," in which multiple generations exist but with fewer members within each generation (Giarrusso, Silverstein, & Bengston, 1996).

Demographics within the larger society have mirrored the changes within the family. The age structure in the middle of the last century also resembled a pyramid, with the majority of the population of 152 million at the base of the pyramid, consisting of the youngest. Subsequently higher levels on the pyramid, representing older and older age groups, became progressively smaller, with the eldest being represented at the tip of the pyramid. The median age in the 1950s was 30 years old. In contrast, the population age structure of our current 301 million people has recently grown much more rectangular, except for the bulge that represents the baby boom generation. The median age in today's society has climbed to 32.6. These changes, reflected in the fact that the median age has risen and so many older adults are living longer, are now referred to as the "graying of America" (Lemme, 2002, p. 5).

Changing Demographics Within the Community— The Baby Boom Generation Ages

Improved health care and nutrition continue to contribute to increased longevity of the elderly. Additionally, sheer numbers of currently middle-aged adults will enter the ranks of the elderly within the next few years. The large group of births after World War II, termed the "baby boom generation," is composed of 79 million individuals born between 1946 and 1964 (U.S. Bureau of the Census, 1995). This group will begin to hit the traditional retirement age of 62 in 2008. This generation, the largest in U.S. history, comprises a full third of the population.

Throughout the last 50 years, the baby boomers have exerted a major impact on our society. Products and services have emerged to fulfill the needs of this group at every developmental step, and this trend is expected to continue as they age. The impact of the baby boomers on health care will be significant, especially as a result of the fact that the generations that succeed them are significantly smaller in size.

The birth rate in subsequent cohorts has declined from 3 to less than 2. This decline means that the total proportion of younger people within our society will decrease as the numbers of boomers reach old age (Foos & Clark, 2003, p. 4). To the extent that large numbers of baby boomers become dependent on society for health care, financial support, and community resources, the burden will fall more heavily on the smaller numbers of individuals in younger cohorts.

Effect of Changing Age Demographics on Community Mental Health Services

Community mental health services will need to expand to meet the challenge of the aging baby boom cohort. Not only will the sheer numbers impact the health care system, but also smaller family sizes and increased mobility within society will result in fewer family supports for the infirm.

There are many questions that will need to be answered regarding financial security, public policies toward the aging, and health care concerns. According to James (2004), women will have a more difficult time resolving these issues than men because of their longer life span and the fact that public policies favor men. Women are therefore more likely to face serious declines in their standard of living as they become widows, and they are more likely to be afflicted with diseases such as dementia that are associated with advanced age. On the positive side, women may fare better than men in some ways because they are more likely to be able to ask for help (Krause & Shaw, 2002).

Declining income, lack of social supports, and health concerns can lead to mental stress and negativity. Furthermore, dependence on public assistance programs can erode self-esteem. Older adults who end up depending on public programs such as welfare and food stamps tend to resent their economic situation and may develop psychosocial problems as a result. Such programs can foster dependence and lead to depression, especially in a cohort of aging adults where financial security was a hallmark of success (Krause & Shaw, 2002).

Community services for individuals on public assistance can be especially helpful if they focus on both the lack of social supports and the autonomy needs of the participants. Special care should also be taken to minimize any stigma associated with an inability to maintain a former standard of living. Krause and Shaw (2002) stress that interventions should be devised to address these issues. They also highlight the fact that dependence on assistance programs may actually disrupt existing informal networks, and that interventions should attempt to reestablish such networks to improve the well-being of the participants. They caution that any intervention should target those who would benefit the most. Hence, they suggest that a first step would be to gear an intervention toward older men who receive welfare benefits, since they tend to have fewer informal social supports and had more negative interactions related to receiving public assistance.

Mental Health Service Needs of the Elderly—Current Needs

Toward and Ostwald (2002) have undertaken a comprehensive investigation of the mental health service needs of the elderly. At three separate times, they interviewed 41 experts from housing, psychosocial, service provider, and medical fields in order to determine both gaps in service and future needs of the elderly in Harris County, Texas. The surveys yielded needs in five separate clusters: mental illness, access needs, need for services, need for education, and need for funding.

- *Mental illness.* Mental illness interfered with self-care, leading to isolation and poor mental and physical health. Toward and Ostwald believed the problem could be helped with improved case management services, as well as improved transportation availability and a home care option.
- *Access needs.* Access to services were hampered by lack of education, threatening environments, and lack of transportation. Enhanced access could be obtained by improving those factors plus providing home care.

- *Service needs.* Postdischarge planning, support services, and home health services (housekeeping and other physical and medical services) were lacking. Also needed were incentives and assistance for caregivers. Transportation needs also emerged.
- *Education needs.* There is a significant need for service providers and health care workers to receive training in geriatric services and psychiatry. Public education was also deemed important.
- *Funding needs.* Respondents identified a need for increased funding for inpatient and outpatient psychiatric facilities that serve the elderly and additional family supports for those who keep an elderly mentally ill patient in the home.

This study was particularly helpful in highlighting some of the gaps in mental health services in the community for individuals over the age of 65.

Barriers to the Utilization of Mental Health Services

Older adults are less likely to utilize mental health services in the community than are younger age groups. Although the ranks of the elderly comprise almost 13% of the population, they use just 2% of private mental health services, 4–7% of community services, and 9% of inpatient care services (Hatfield, 1999; Robb, Haley, Becker, Polivka, & Chwa, 2003). The reasons for underutilization do not stem from lack of need; according to Wykle and Musil (1993), the percentage of elderly with mental health problems is almost 13% of the population. Why, then, do they not avail themselves of mental health services, and what can be done to improve their utilization of these services?

First, the elderly may physically not be able to get to community mental health services. If they are too old to drive or have disabilities that require a wheelchair, they may have to depend on sometimes very limited public transportation (Crispi, Vangel, & Wetter, 2003). Second, the current cohort of elderly may have a negative attitude about mental health care; they may consider the need for mental health care as a sign of weakness, or they may lack education regarding the value of mental health care (Robb, Haley, Becker, Polivka, & Chwa, 2003).

Robb and her colleagues conducted a survey of almost 500 adults over the age of 65, regarding attitudes about mental health care and service delivery. It was found that older adults were only half as likely to use mental health services as younger adults, and that they were less knowledgeable about the value of mental health care than the younger adults. On a positive note, the majority of elders responded that they wished they knew more about the services and they believed that good mental health care was very important and vital to physical health.

Both older and younger adults named insurance and financial reasons as barriers to mental health care. It is possible that part of the problem was lack of dissemination of mental health insurance information and confusion on the part of the elders, rather than actual lack of coverage, since most of the respondents had at least some coverage under Medicare. An effective intervention to address these needs might consist of programs that educate elders on the availability of mental health services within the community.

One of the most promising results from the study was the finding that the lack of utilization of mental health services in the community by the elderly was not due to any stigma against mental health care, but rather insufficient public information and education regarding Medicare coverage. These older persons were receptive to large-scale public education initiatives regarding costs and insurance coverage for mental health services. Finally, the study found that older persons prefer mental health services provided by clergy and doctoral level therapists, but would like their primary care physician involved as well.

Respondents to Kent's (1990) study of the challenges related to recruiting and maintaining elderly patients voiced similar reasons for reluctance to use community services, namely, large amounts of paperwork related to public reimbursement, reluctance of physicians to treat the elderly, and inability of home-bound and frail elders to get transportation to the clinics. The responses differed from Robb and her colleagues' research, however, in that the respondents also expressed concern about the stigma attached to mental illness.

Kent's (1990) research has provided some of the answers to questions regarding elder underutilization of community resources aimed at the promotion of mental health:

- *Who is most likely to refer an elderly patient to a community mental health center?* Usually, the elder does not come to a clinic of his or her own volition. Most likely the family, generally a child of the patient, will refer the individual. Other types of referrals come from community agency caseworkers, hospital psychiatric wards, or state psychiatric hospitals.
- *Why do elderly patients come to a community mental health center?* The main reason is usually that the family has had some kind of crisis with the elder patient. Some reasons for the crisis may include depression as a result of some kind of loss, cognitive problems, or changes in behavior or personality.
- *What types of treatments are available at community mental health centers?* After a thorough medical and psychological intake, the patient might be put into a number of treatment programs including therapy, day treatment, education classes, referral for additional assessment/treatment, information regarding community resources, medication management and information, and case management. These services can be provided in the center or may be home-based, depending on the program. Some centers also provide information and services related to such things as alcohol abuse and domestic violence.

According to the American Psychological Association (2003), a significant number of older adults with mental and behavioral health problems do not receive the care they need. The fact that they often present with physical rather than mental symptoms is exacerbated by the fact that many primary care physicians have not been trained to assess and treat mental problems in the elderly. Recommendations for improving access to mental health care for older Americans include the following:

- Because older adults may be more likely to utilize primary care services, it is imperative that appropriate training be provided to physicians and other health-care professionals to identify mental health concerns.

- It is important that these health care professionals be encouraged to collaborate with and refer to other health professionals who have expertise in mental and behavioral concerns.
- Providers from various disciplines who serve the older adult community must work together as an interdisciplinary health-care team to provide a collaborative model of care for older adults.
- In order to meet the mental health needs of older adults, it is essential that there be parity for mental health services under Medicare. Currently, Medicare reimburses only for 50% of outpatient mental health care as compared with 80% for medical care.
- Medicare limits need to be extended for inpatient mental health coverage in order to care for older adults with persistent mental disorders. Currently, Medicare allows for only 190 days of psychiatric hospitalization in one's lifetime.
- Medicaid coverage needs to be expanded to include older adults as a "categorically needy" group. Currently, over half of Medicaid-covered older persons are classified as optional. In addition, the 50% Medicare copayment is fully reimbursed by Medicaid in only a very limited number of states.
- Efforts need to be made to reduce the stigma that is often associated with mental disorders and treatment.
- The geriatric mental health workforce must be expanded to accommodate the growing number of older adults in need of services.
- Increased funding and support is necessary for basic and applied behavioral research and for the incorporation of empirically based interventions into clinical practice with older persons.

Changing Mental Health Needs of the Elderly—The Legislative Response

Since the passage of the Community Mental Health Act in 1963, the response to the treatment of the mentally ill has shifted from institutional, custodial-type care to active, community-based treatment. It was expected that individuals who were chronically ill could receive treatment in institutions when necessary, and when stabilized, could return to the less restrictive home environment for ongoing treatment. In order for the model to work effectively, the patients would need to access community mental health centers on a regular basis for both treatment and medication management.

This model enhances the self-efficacy and independence of the patients, since it places responsibility for treatment with the patients themselves. It can work effectively, but only if the patients accept the responsibility and avail themselves of the treatments and services afforded.

The Positive Aging Act of 2003 (United States Senate Bill 1456, United States House of Representative Bill 2241) is a high-priority piece of federal legislation designed to improve accessibility of mental health services for the elderly. This bill, introduced in July 2003, amends the Public Health Service Act in order to provide for mental health screenings, appropriate referrals, and utilization of proper empirically based treatment protocols for the elderly. It also makes provisions for grants to fund community mental health outreach teams that treat the elderly in medical settings, adult day care settings, assisted living facilities, and other locations where they receive social services. The act contains the following provisions:

- Offering competitive grants to projects that integrate multidisciplinary mental health programs into primary care settings and creating a collaborative health care model for older adults.
- Establishing competitive grants to reward public or private nonprofit community-based providers of multidisciplinary mental health services for older adults that deliver those services where older adults reside or spend time, such as in senior centers and assisted living communities.
- Designating a "Deputy Director for Older Adult Mental Health Services" within the Center for Mental Health Services in the Substance Abuse and Mental Health Services Administration (SAMHSA) responsible for the development and implementation of initiatives to address the mental health service needs of older adults.
- Reserving representative positions on the National Advisory Council of the Center for Mental Health Services for older Americans, their families, and mental health specialists with appropriate training and experience in the treatment of older adults (American Psychological Association, 2003).

The American Psychological Association has actively worked to ensure passage of the bill, which as of May 2004 was read twice and then referred to the Committee on Health, Education, Labor, and Pensions. Unfortunately, the 108th session of the U.S. Congress ended before final action could be taken, and thus the bill must be reintroduced in the current Congressional session in order for it to be passed.

Examples of Community Mental Health Services for the Elderly Population

Community-Based Interventions for Patients with Alzheimer's Disease

Community interventions for patients with Alzheimer's disease can be effective if they follow a design that takes into consideration both the progressive nature of the disease and the significant burden on the caregivers. It is not enough to treat the person with Alzheimer's; other family members who live with the patient need services as well for the intervention program to be effective. Zarit and Leitsch (2001) outlined three major considerations for any community-based intervention for Alzheimer's patients. First, successful interventions need to form the foundation upon which others can be built. Second, they must also account for the characteristics and progressive nature of the disease, with the understanding that social interventions can be effective, whereas programs to halt the disease will not. Finally, successful interventions should involve the caregivers as well as the patient.

Most importantly, intervention goals should be reasonable. Behavioral strategies cannot alter the course of the disease or resolve issues of loss experienced by the caregiver. Designers of interventions should aspire to modest goals such as preventing the situation from worsening, helping to alleviate caregiver stress, and engaging the caregiver in a dialogue to provide goals.

Once the program has been implemented, it is valuable to begin to evaluate the effectiveness of the program in meeting its goals. As Zarit and Leitsch (2001) point out, careful consideration should be taken to select appropriate outcome measures. Three issues that should be considered when selecting outcome measures include consideration of the population on which the measures were standardized, the sensitivity of the measures and the advantages/disadvantages of qualitative and quantitative measures.

Concerning the first issue, there is an advantage to using a measure that is standardized on the population being measured, in that the norms and psychometric properties are known. However, there are times when measures of other populations might be more appropriate. It is valuable when assessing caregivers, for example, to use measures that have been normed on a nonstressed population in order to compare relative stress levels (George, 1994; George & Gwyther, 1986). Consideration may also need to be taken regarding a phenomenon or population for which no normed measures are available; in such a case, it may be desirable to pretest new questions (Zarit & Leitsch, 2001).

The sensitivity of the employed measures is an additional consideration. Zarit and Leitsch (2001) cautioned against the use of measures with high test-retest reliability (stability) when measuring change. It might be more effective to locate measures with a larger range of choices than a 3- to 5-point Likert scale, or to use multiple measures over time.

With respect to choices as to the use of either qualitative or quantitative measures, open-ended, qualitative questions are considered most appropriate at the measurement construction stage and in interpreting quantitative information, whereas quantitative measures may be used when there exists a need for more objective answers. Students who have an interest in the research design and outcome evaluations of community-based interventions for individuals with Alzheimer's disease are referred to the work of Zarit and Leitsch (2001) for further details.

Older Victims of Domestic Violence

Older women are often hesitant to avail themselves of mental health services within the community, since they were raised to consider psychological problems as a weakness. Women who have a history of being abused by their husbands have a particularly difficult time seeking services; they have been socialized to be subservient.

Physicians may not routinely assess older women for domestic violence, especially if the woman is a widow or divorcee who is no longer in a relationship. It has been found that domestic violence affects up to 64% of women in outpatient clinics (Sato & Heiby, 1992). However, these studies tend to focus on younger women who are in abusive relationships at the time. What about older women who have experienced violence earlier in their lives? What are the long-range effects of such abuse, and how can mental health facilities address these needs?

In a study by Wolkenstein and Sterman (1998), investigators examined two clinical populations of older women: those who participated in a community mental health center with a gerontology division and those who attended an older-adult-centered private, nonprofit mental health clinic. The study found that an incredible 93% of the women in the community clinic had experienced abuse in their marriages, and that 85% of the women in the private clinic had experienced some sort of abuse in their lives as well, either in their family of origin or marriage. Other studies have shown similar results (Goodman, Johnson, Dutton, & Harris, 1997).

Historical information related to violence was not assessed in the formal intake at these clinics, but it tended to emerge later through discussions of current depression, anxiety, and psychosocial difficulties. The women who disclosed the information had been reluctant to share it with their children, and those in second marriages were fearful that disclosure would threaten their marriages. Therefore, these women tended to become isolated and fearful of negative consequences related to divulging the information.

Wolkenstein and Sterman (1998) emphasize that clinicians need to assess older women for evidence of prior domestic abuse, and they realize that such information may not be readily forthcoming because of the reluctance of this age group to discuss mental health issues, their fear of reprisal from family and current husband, and the long-term impact of the abuse itself. Clinicians, during the initial intake assessment, need to advise clients that such issues are common, that discussion is appropriate within the clinical setting, and that it will be held in confidence. Clinicians also need to be aware of risk factors that might indicate prior violence such as a former husband's alcohol abuse, abuse of the children, unsatisfactory relationships with adult children, and isolation/lack of a support system.

Interventions for elderly women who have experienced prior domestic abuse can include psychoeducation to help them to understand battered wife syndrome and related family dynamics, or group therapy to help overcome dysfunctional patterns that have occurred over a lifetime and to build more fully functioning relationships (Wolkenstein & Sterman, 1998).

Educational Interventions

Cusack, Thompson, and Rogers (2003) developed an eight-week training program to improve the mental health of individuals over 50 years old. Intensive workshops covered the following topics: goal setting, critical thinking, creativity, positive mental attitude, learning, memory, and speaking one's mind. The participants were trained to discard ageist biases and other barriers to learning, to set and meet meaningful goals, to think creatively, to turn negative thoughts into positive, to appreciate diversity, and to enjoy risk-taking. It was found that the program did indeed contribute to improved mental health in the participants and paved the way for future educational interventions of this type. Strong effects were noted in participants for mental fitness, confidence in mental abilities, goal attainment, memory, creativity, flexibility, and speaking one's mind.

Community Interventions—Preventative and Treatment Programs

As the numbers of elderly in our community swell, there will be a greater need for mental health interventions. Appropriately targeted programs can meet health care system challenges by preventing or delaying diseases, and thereby improving the quality of life for the elderly (Drewnowski, 2003; U.S. Department of Health and Human Services, 2000).

As was covered in Chapter 4, the Committee on Prevention of Mental Disorders, Institute of Medicine (Mrazek & Haggerty, 1994) recommended that interventions be categorized at the prevention, treatment, and maintenance levels. Prevention programs target individuals who do not yet have a mental disorder but may be at risk for development of symptoms; the goal of such programs is to reduce risk and promote protective factors. Prevention programs are categorized on the basis of type of program, targeted group, and level of risk. These categorizations include universal, selective, and indicated intervention categories.

Preretirement Planning: Universal Prevention

When individuals begin to think about retirement after careers that span 30 or 40 years, they often focus on financial considerations, expected leisure time pursuits, and physical health issues. Certainly these are important issues, and all impact the quality of retirement, but mental health issues are equally as important over the long run. Individuals who spend their entire adulthood or a large chunk of it in a career tend to incorporate elements of it into a personal identity. This can take the form of a concept of self as a function of the company/career, as a functioning member of society, and as a breadwinner/family provider. These elements of self must be preserved upon retirement to help prevent depression, loss of self-esteem, and to help individuals enjoy the maximum quality of life that retirement can provide.

Preretirement workshops, as examples of preventative mental health interventions, are ideal opportunities to assist individuals in the transition from worker to retiree and to preserve and enhance their sense of self-identity. Retirement is a developmental milestone that can lead to a renewed interest in attaining personal goals and satisfaction, or to depression and loss of identity. Therefore, the potential to prevent psychological difficulties in transition is great if the intervention can help individuals to focus on retirement as a challenge and opportunity to develop new interests and skills rather than a stressful disruption of one's life (Floyd, Haynes, et al., 1992).

Other studies have shown that retirement satisfaction is related to finding sufficient rewards that become sources of life satisfaction in the person's continuing development. This means replacing rewards the person achieved through work with alternative rewards from activities in retirement, in order to maintain a consistent reward ratio (Howard, 1982). Interventions at this level can not only educate potential retirees regarding continuing sources of life satisfaction but also can help them in becoming sensitized to the process so that they can begin to nurture sources prior to retirement.

Bereavement Support Groups: Selective Intervention

Adjusting to the death of a spouse can be a painful and difficult process that lasts for years (Lichtenstein, Gatz, Pedersen, Berg, & McClearn, 1996). Statistics have shown that men may have more difficulty adjusting to the death of a spouse than women, and men are at higher risk for stress, isolation, and depression. This discrepancy may be at least partially explained by the fact that widows tend to have more well-established, long-standing informal support networks that buffer them from stress and isolation. Similar social networks can be formed if recent at-risk widowers can be attracted to community support groups.

Caserta and Lund (1996) examined 144 widows and widowers over the age of 50 in 20 bereavement support groups. They were recruited from obituary ads in local newspapers and assigned to short-term groups (eight weekly sessions), long-term treatment (ten additional monthly meetings), or no treatment. The groups, hosted by facilitators, met in community gathering places such as libraries and common rooms of community residences.

The researchers found that the amount of social contact participants maintained outside the support group setting was related to lower levels of isolation and loneliness in the participants over time. Females and those who were slightly more lonely and depressed at baseline were somewhat more likely to foster contact and friendships with group members on their own time, even after the end of the intervention, independent of the length of the treatment. Although widows tended to make more outside contact with group members initially, the widowers also began to socialize in a similar way later in the program.

These findings have important implications for support groups of this type. Participants stated that group meetings were not adequate to keep them from feeling lonely and isolated, but that the connection with group members outside the program and after completion of the intervention were considered very valuable. In other words, during the intervention, group members developed an informal support network that buffered them against loneliness and isolation even after the completion of the program.

Coping with Menopause—Indicated Intervention

Indicated interventions are designed to help alleviate mild symptoms in groups that are at higher risk. Menopause itself is not an illness but can be accompanied by unpleasant medical and psychological symptoms that can be addressed before they progress to more serious problems. Women may react negatively to the changes that take place in their bodies; moreover, they may develop negative feelings about their body image and feel isolated from others. Cunningham (2002) devised a community intervention program for women who had trouble coping with menopause that was based on Roy's Adaptation Model (Roy & Andrews, 1999).

Roy's Adaptation Model views individuals as holistic, adaptive systems whose coping styles respond uniquely to environmental stressors. These coping styles operate both on physiological and cognitive/psychological levels. When individuals are confronted with environmental stimuli, they tend to respond in one of four adaptive modes: physiological/biological, self-concept, role function, or interdependence. If responses are adaptive to the situation, the individuals are able to meet the goals of situational mastery and developmental growth.

The goals of Cunningham's (2002) intervention were to identify response modes in women who were struggling with menopause and to turn less adaptive modes to more adaptive ones, in order to promote growth and mastery over difficulties. The intervention consisted of educational sessions to expose women to facts about menopause and to dispel myths, support group sessions, medical care for physical symptoms such as urinary incontinence, and introduction of relaxation techniques. At the conclusion of the program, the participants reported an increased sense of confidence and an enhanced ability to talk freely about menopause. They also believed the education helped them to understand and appreciate the changes that were occurring within their bodies.

Depression in Patients and Caregivers—Treatment Intervention

Depression in older individuals may be difficult to diagnose; they tend to exhibit somatic symptoms such as loss of appetite and energy, sleep disturbances, memory problems, and confusion. These are symptoms that overlap with other illness such as dementia (Peveler, Carson, & Rodin, 2002). Depression often exists concurrent with physical ailments such as heart disease, blood diseases, and musculoskeletal diseases, and may contribute to lower life expectancy (Huffstetler, 2001). For these reasons, primary care physicians may fail to recognize depression in older adults or, believing that it is warranted in older, sick individuals, neglect to treat it (Harman & Reynolds, 2000; Huffstetler, 2001).

Interventions targeting the family caregivers of depressed individuals may also be an effective treatment option. Many older adults with depression remain in their homes with the spouse or adult child as primary caregiver. Successful coping strategies of the caregiver can be related to successful outcome for the depressed patient.

Hinrichsen (1991) discussed Coyne's (1976) analysis of the complex interactions between caregivers and depressed patients, suggesting that caregivers try to assist the depressed person via a wide range of behaviors but that these are often not received as helpful by the patient. This outcome can lead to isolation and confusion on the part of the caregiver when attempts to care for the depressed relative do not lead to any improvement. He suggested that these families need assistance with strategies for patient care, as well as support and effective coping mechanisms for the caregivers. Psychoeducational interventions can teach family members more effective ways to manage the care of the depressed relative and can recommend more effective coping mechanisms.

Meeting the Needs of the Elderly—Ethnic and Gender Considerations

Demographic trends indicate that the number of minority elderly are growing at an even more rapid pace than the overall population of those over 65. By 2025, elderly Black and Hispanic elders will comprise 20% of the entire population (Drewnowski et al., 2003; U.S. Bureau of the Census, 2000). Minority groups, especially African Americans, have had a history of economic deprivation that results in lifelong limited access to health care facilities and that is often accompanied by increased levels of economic hardship and resultant psychological stress and distress (Drewnowski et al., 2003).

Surveys have shown that ethnic minorities are at a disadvantage when it comes to provision of mental health services within the community; they tend to be neglected in both public and private care networks. In one study, it was reported that less than one-third of community mental health centers had made an effort to reach ethnic minorities (Flemming et al., 1984). A study by Fellin and Powell (1988) found that funding and assistance programs for mental health services targeted to the elderly were less likely to reach minority populations in specific areas. Services that were available tended to exist in catchment areas with higher numbers of minorities, thus neglecting minorities who lived in outlying areas. This finding highlights a growing need for community mental health programs to include an outreach component, so that they can deliver services to minorities in more diverse ways and in more locations (for example, churches, schools, senior centers, and residences).

Aranda (1990) described a comprehensive community mental health center designed for elderly Latinos in California that included a robust outreach program. Services that the center provided included the following:

- *Outreach:* This was a strong effort, since Latino populations tend to underutilize mental health services even more than nonminority populations; Latino churches were thus involved in recruitment and education. Educational classes were provided, in both churches and community centers, and included materials and videos presented both in Spanish and in English. The center adhered to Latino tradition and as a result, earned the respect of the community. Many referrals came in after hearing of the program via informal word of mouth.
- *Individual and family psychotherapy:* Therapy was conducted with adherence to Latino customs and culture. It was recognized that an elder in therapy might be at a different level of enculturation than the younger generations. Latino core beliefs were acknowledged during therapy, including respect for family obligations and responsibility, inner importance of the individual (personalismo), respect, trust, and interdependence.
- *"El Espejo Familiar":* Families became involved in this specialized type of life review, which included cultural elements as it offered opportunities to explore beliefs about aging.
- *Cultural heritage programs:* Programs were offered that emphasized cultural heritage, including holidays, rituals, festivals, and spirituality.
- *Support groups:* The center offered group interaction based on cultural heritage, including a club for displaced older Cubans who could not speak English.
- *Peer counseling:* Volunteers from the Latino community provided supportive counseling, case management, advocacy, outreach, and education to the elderly mentally ill in their community and their families.
- *Bilingual Alzheimer's support group:* The center developed the first bilingual Alzheimer's family caregiver support group in the nation.

This community mental health center provided valuable mental health services to the elderly within their community with sensitivity to cultural values and language considerations. The need exists for the continued establishment of programs like this, especially with outreach components, in other minority communities.

With respect to gender, studies have found patterns of differences in the type of mental health care sought. Generally, males were more likely to utilize informal care systems such as family and neighbors, whereas women were more likely to use formal community-based care. Many reasons may account for these differences, including demographics (age, SES, health differences, and marital status), an increased female tendency to seek help, and traditional age differences within a marriage (Lee, Dwyer, & Coward, 1993). Many studies have shown that women are more likely to become caregivers than men and to maintain care within the home, whereas male caregivers are more likely to obtain outside formal assistance (Johnson & Catalano, 1983).

Mutchler and Bullers (1994) surveyed a nationally representative segment of the elderly population in the United States and found striking gender differences regarding use of formal care. Those most likely to need formal community-based assistance were likely to be older, unmarried, lower SES, African American females who either lived alone or lived with a nonspouse. It was stressed that formal care would be increasingly needed to supplement informal care in the near future, especially for these segments of the population.

In numerous ways, aging women have different priorities and mental health care needs than men. Community care for the elderly needs to address both male and female issues, in addition to issues that are not gender-based. Focus groups have indicated that women believe their physical health needs are met by community services but that their mental health needs are not adequately met. A recent study by Tannenbaum, Nasmith, and Mayo (2003) found women tended to lack a feeling of validation as an active participant in their health care relationship, and also believed the health care system neglected to adequately affirm their anxieties about aging (including fears of memory loss, illness, and suffering).

Meeting the Needs of the Elderly—The Chronically Mentally Ill and Their Caregivers

Much of the research on chronically ill older people has centered on those in hospitals or nursing homes, yet significant numbers of chronically mentally ill elders live in the community. In some cases these individuals receive adequate community services, but in many others, mental health needs are simply not being met.

Meeks and Murrell (1997) investigated the needs of chronically mentally ill elders living within the community in rural Kentucky. Research was conducted within a theological framework that considers mental illness as influenced by socioenvironmental as well as disease factors; conceptualizing illness in this way affords an opportunity to assess the protective and risk value of social, community, and economic factors when examining psychiatric severity. Furthermore, future illness can be predicted using this model. The study consisted of 346 chronically ill, middle-aged to elderly adults with severe mental illness (mean age = 54), recruited from lists of community mental health centers. Five questions were addressed that related to socioenvironmental resources (p. 298):

- What are the levels of general economic, health, and social resources available to these individuals?
- How do these resources differ from those of other older adults in the same region?
- What are the illness-related conditions and adjustments of the sample?
- How are socioeconomic factors related to diagnosis?
- How do the younger (middle-aged) and older cohorts of this sample differ?

The vast majority of the sample (88%) lived in either family-owned homes or apartments, and all but nine were able to identify a significant other with whom they lived or lived near. Their mean social network size was 25 members, with most of the network being family. Additionally, 87% of the sample visited community mental health facilities at least annually.

The study's sampling procedures helped to identify groups that were likely to be excluded or underrepresented in the public mental health system: the homeless, those who used private mental health facilities, current inpatients, those in nursing homes, and those who had not received any treatment in the prior five years. Socioeconomic resources also played a factor. Those who were underrepresented tended to be on public assistance with few financial resources and a history of unemployment or underemployment. These individuals also tended to have three or more physical ailments or some mild chronic physical disability (none of which they complained about or sought treatment for), fairly small social networks, little or no mental health services, and long-term psychiatric illness.

It was found that because of older age and impoverishment, these individuals with psychiatric illnesses were only marginally able to maintain independence within the community. The only support from the public mental health system tended to be medication management. It was concluded that more aggressive psychosocial treatment of psychiatric illnesses could lead to a better outcome for the individuals, their families, and the larger community (Meeks & Murrell, 1997).

An earlier study focused on a similar group of psychiatric patients who used community mental health centers primarily for medication. Despite long-term chronic mental illness, the subjects and their families did not feel the need for any additional services, even though they rated the services they received as insufficient. One of the possible reasons for this seemingly contradictory behavior is that the families did not receive sufficient information or education related to the services that were available and the value related to those services (Meeks, Carstensen, & Stafford, 1990).

Interventions can also target the family caregivers of elderly patients with chronic illness. Many research studies have indicated that family caregivers undergo stress related to caring for a chronically ill family member. For example, the literature contains a wealth of data that indicate the high level of stress and burden related to caring for a relative with dementia (Cook, McNally, Mulligan, Harrison, & Newman, 2001; Crispi, Schiaffino, & Berman, 1997; Zarit & Teri, 1991). Cook et al. (2001)

reviewed 40 studies of interventions aimed at improving the well-being of caregivers of dementia patients. Findings indicated that effective programs incorporated social supports either alone or in combination with cognitive supports.

An Innovative Proposal to Assist Family Caregivers

As was mentioned, interventions to help elderly persons with Alzheimer's Disease or other disabling conditions should also target those who provide care for these individuals. Caregivers who assist ailing relatives may report loss of income, since they often need to cut back on the hours they work. Many middle-aged helpers find themselves "sandwiched," since they must take care of both their children and their parents. Typically, the caregivers have received little or no training in assisting relatives with Alzheimer's. Programs need to be established that encourage others to volunteer to provide basic care in the home of ailing elderly individuals, allowing some needed respite for the family caregivers.

Ultimately, such programs need to be funded at least partially by the government. If relatives are unable to provide care, the ailing person must pay for needed home health and personal care out of their savings; once savings are exhausted, providing these services becomes the responsibility of the government.

In the United States, the need for home health and personal care services has risen dramatically in recent years. The cost for providing these services is borne largely by taxpayers, through various sponsored entitlement programs. As costs rise and the proportion of tax-paying workers relative to the number of recipients falls, these programs will be forced to cut back, and services will be sharply curtailed. The two programs involved in funding these services are Medicare and Medicaid. Home health care is provided through Medicare, and it is limited to those eligible participants who require skilled nursing or other therapeutic services in the home. Medicaid provides personal care services for eligible citizens who have a disabling condition and require some form of basic assistance in the home. Both home health care

and personal care services are provided, in order to enable individuals to continue living at home rather than being placed in a nursing care facility. As was stated previously, the costs of providing these services have gone up astronomically. The Medicare program spent $14.9 billion in 1995 for home health care, up from $3.3 billion 5 years earlier; this is a rate of growth that cannot continue, given current interest in balancing the federal budget (Meckler, 1997). This growth is caused by more elderly people's using home health care for extended periods of time. In 1995, twice as many people—3.5 million—were receiving twice as many home care visits—68 per year—than in 1990 (Meckler, 1997). Medicaid expenses for personal care services are also very high. In New York state alone, such assistance provided through Medicaid costs over $1 billion annually. As the tax burden for these programs becomes heavier, voters will be eager to curtail spending and to tighten eligibility requirements.

A method of reducing cost and yet increasing quality of care would be to establish a voluntary self-insurance plan (Scileppi, 1998, 1999). In this plan, healthy retired persons and other individuals with free time could provide some home care to elderly in need of such assistance. A program could be established in which the volunteer service providers "bank" the hours they provide care, and then draw on these hours when they themselves become in need of home care assistance. Alternatively, volunteers might be allowed to transfer their banked hours to be used by an ailing relative or friend who lives in a distant town or state. In addition, volunteers would receive free training in how to provide basic physical care and to help recipients cope with life problems. Basic-care training would include helping in areas such as bathing, dressing, toileting, ensuring that medication is taken

(continued)

on time, shopping, and merely being available should a need or crisis arise. Training in coping skills would include communication and social interaction, daily life needs, safety issues (Hornbrook et al., 1994), stress management (Lopez & Silber, 1991), and perhaps grief counseling. Volunteers could also be instructed regarding information and referral services, and they could be taught to recognize when the recipient needs more professional assistance. This self-insurance program could also credit those volunteers who have more specialized skills with more hours of service, if they utilize their background more fully. For example; accountants might assist with record keeping (such as paying bills and completing insurance forms), and those handy with tools might provide assistance in minor plumbing and appliance repair. Mental health professionals who specialize in gerontology could oversee the entire process of establishing the program. A more complete description of this proposal is available on line at www.academic.marist.edu/carebanking/

Setting up such a system would require an alteration in the way the nation views home care. Volunteers would provide some of the services currently provided by the workers. Since the need for this type of care is increasing so rapidly, it would be unlikely for paid workers to lose their jobs. Politically, however, the fear of lost jobs would need to be addressed; it is possible that experienced workers could be involved in supervising and training volunteers in basic health care. Companies currently providing home health care services could also perceive the new plan as detrimental to their business. A solution might involve companies' contracting with Medicare and Medicaid to coordinate the program on a regional level. These home health care corporations might extend the range of services they offer, using volunteers for those requiring basic care and professionals for more specialized care and in situations where volunteers are not available. It is also possible that those recipients who meet current Medicare/Medicaid eligibility requirements would continue to be served by paid workers, and those just outside the income or disability limits would be assisted by volunteers. The latter group might be required to pay for the administrative costs of selecting, training,

and supervising the volunteers—a fraction of the total expense for home care. Service agencies, social groups, and religious organizations that already utilize volunteers for a variety of community activities might fear that fewer individuals would participate in their programs, yet under certain conditions, those involved in the work of neighborhood centers might also be allowed to bank their hours in this self-insurance plan.

As outlined previously, any change in policy has effects on all components of the social system, and successful interventions must address all related sectors of the system. Both volunteers and recipients would have to alter their perceptions of home care. Healthy retired persons and other volunteers would need to see themselves as both service providers and persons likely to be in need of services in the future.

Community gerontologists can learn effective means of altering the public's perceptions from the marketing experience of insurance companies that presently sell long-term care policies to healthy older adults. There are many obstacles reducing the likelihood that potential service providers would volunteer to become part of this self-insurance plan, and these issues need to be addressed. Also, some family members are already providing services for their infirmed relatives; if these individuals were to join the system, their activities might be seen as less altruistic. Potential recipients might question the value of the services that they would receive as part of the plan. They would need to be assured that the assistance would be stable, reliable, available, and adequate. The recipients would need to feel confident that volunteers had been fully screened and sufficiently trained.

Politically, for this plan to be effective, the federal government must adopt it as part of the Medicare/Medicaid programs. Some voters and public officials might perceive the plan as "creeping socialism" or increasing bureaucratization, thus reducing the likelihood of acceptance. The value of the plan in providing better care while dramatically reducing costs on a long-term basis needs to be made salient in the minds of all citizens.

To do so, community mental health professionals would need to utilize the mass media in educating the public. It would also be advantageous to involve grassroots advocacy groups such as the American Association of Retired Persons (AARP) in developing, fine-tuning, supporting, and disseminating the plan. Public officials would need to be educated about the plan, to ensure their assistance in creating the needed political climate. As was described in the chapter on change, each stakeholder in the plan should be encouraged to give input in its development and implementation. Although it is expected that the plan ultimately adopted would be very different from that originally envisioned, community psychologists and other mental health practitioners would need to ensure that the basic values and goals were upheld throughout the process.

Perhaps the greatest immediate need is to publicize the plan and determine public reaction. So far, one study found strong support for the proposal. Austin and Botsford (2003) conducted a needs assessment of older adults for the Dutchess County (NY) Office for the Aging. A description of carebanking was added to one-third of the questionnaires distributed, and respondents were asked if they would consider using such a self-insurance service. Fully 80% replied that they either might or definitely would consider using such a program. Hence, preliminary data indicate that once the public becomes aware of the proposal, it is likely to be strongly supported.

There are many other activities that would be needed during the implementation of such a plan that would best be performed by those knowledgeable about community principles and methods. Community mental health professionals could become involved in coordinating a self-insurance system, and they could also recruit, screen, train, place, supervise, and monitor the volunteers. Other activities might include the following:

- *Locating possible recipients and assessing their needs for service.*
- *Publicizing the program among potential volunteers and encouraging them to apply.* By attending local social and religious groups and by utilizing radio, television, newspapers, and the Internet, community psychologists could reach potential recipients and volunteers simultaneously.
- *Screening those applying to be volunteers, ensuring that they will not exploit or abuse recipients.*

- *Assessing the types of services volunteers can offer and building on the strengths that applicants could utilize in helping the recipients.*
- *Training volunteers both initially and on a continual basis.* This involves the establishment of a general curriculum that can be fine-tuned for each volunteer-recipient pair. The curriculum might evolve as new primary prevention interventions are developed. Community psychologists can utilize the network of trained volunteers as part of a strategy for disseminating new programs.
- *Matching the needs of recipients and the skills and abilities of volunteers.* In seeking a good fit, community mental health practitioners who specialize in gerontology should consider not only service needs but also age, gender, hobbies, former careers, and personal and cultural preferences.
- *Continuously assessing the goodness of fit as the needs of the recipient change.* On the basis of monitoring, volunteers may need to be retrained or reassigned.
- *Evaluating the effectiveness of the program.* Such an evaluation study should assess the recipient's level of health, independence, quality of life and personal happiness, the volunteer's perceived life satisfaction, physical well-being and sense of community, and the cost of the service relative to more traditional treatment systems.

Community mental health professionals might perform the preceding activities, or they might teach paraprofessionals to perform them, in a type of "mental health quarterback model" (Rappaport, 1977).

Many community principles are applied in this plan. Kelly's ecological principle of cycling of resources is perhaps the central concept. The untapped resources of those who have time available can be utilized to the mutual benefit of the volunteer and recipient. Enhancing adaptation and increasing niche breadth occurs through the tangible support and companionship provided by the volunteer, and through the coping skills taught to both volunteers and recipients. By bolstering environmental resources and individual abilities, the recipients are able to live longer in the more normalized social setting of their own homes. The

(continued)

plan would be successful to the extent that all components of the system would be able to be modified synergistically, consistent with the new policy. This undertaking involves Kelly's principle of interdependence and Bronfenbrenner's nested system approach as family (of both volunteer and recipient), government (Medicare), private industry (home health care companies), social service agencies, and advocates (AARP) combine their activities in support of the plan. Kelly's principle of succession is evident, since current recipients eventually would require more care than what is available from volunteers and would need to be placed in nursing facilities. Succession would also apply to the volunteers, who in turn would become recipients and be replaced by new volunteers. Finally, succession would apply to the need for this assistance; as noted in the Caplan's "ideal family concept," discussed previously, relatives would have formerly supplied the services described in the proposal. Because of many societal changes (longer life expectancy, greater geographic mobility, increased number of 2-wage earner families, and heightened challenges facing the sandwiched generation), relatives are less able to provide for these needs. Thus, volunteers or paid caregivers must replace them in a type of succession. Matching recipients' needs and preferences with volunteers' ability to meet these needs is an application of goodness of fit. Recipients would be empowered, because they would play an active role in the matching process. The training

provided to volunteers would serve as a type of primary prevention, since the skills learned will help them cope both at that time and in the future. The volunteers would gain an achieved status as they become more involved in helping others. This achieved status, that of "volunteer helper," might also be primary preventive in nature, since a newly retired person or a parent confronting the "empty nest" family situation is likely to perceive a loss of meaning in life. Such individuals are at risk of experiencing emotional disorders in living and could fall into the ascribed status of patient. Finally, social support is enhanced for both volunteer and recipient, and each becomes an important part of the other's social network.

If the self-insurance plan is successfully implemented, the goal of providing more home health care for less money will have been achieved. It should be stressed that this plan is still only an idea. In order for it to be adopted and implemented, much work is needed. It is beyond the scope of this chapter, however, to discuss the issues of feasible change strategies, legal restrictions and labor union regulations, income tax waivers, volunteer liability and malpractice, transportation and personal safety needs, public accountability and community involvement, and many others. If the idea has merit and community and civic leaders join together to resolve practical concerns, the plan can eventually be transformed into a working program.

Two Interventions to Improve the Quality of Life of Individuals with Dementia

The author of this chapter (E.C.) had the opportunity to develop and implement two grant-funded interventions designed to improve the subjective quality of life of individuals with dementia. Both programs were implemented in nursing homes but were designed to be used by family members and other members of the support network in various settings.

The Visiting Kit Program

The visiting kit program was an activity-based intervention designed to improve the quality of life of residents in nursing homes by enhancing the quality of visits with family members. The author had observed that many family members were bewildered when they visited their relatives, finding themselves at a loss as to how to relate to them. This difficulty often resulted in no or very little verbal interaction on the part of these visitors, who instead spent their time talking with other caregivers. Visiting family members reported being bored, frustrated, and unsatisfied with their visits, and at the same time, opportunities to engage the relative were missed. The intervention provided these family members with an opportunity to use various types of "visiting kits" with their relative. These kits were theme-related and were designed to be used as part of a normal family visit between a caregiver and a resident suffering from mild to severe dementia. The families tested different activity kits over a period of 12 weeks and rated the different types of activities in the kits on their effectiveness in improving the quality of the visits. Kits contained activities related to reminiscence, physical activity, ability to soothe, correspondence, games from childhood, and verbal interaction. Activity kits that contained foam jigsaw puzzles or reminiscence themes utilizing sing-along audiotapes and questions relating to the past were found to be more helpful and enjoyable than kits that contained physical activities, card games, or audiotapes with sounds of the past (Crispi & Heitner, 2002).

The Buddy Program

The buddy program was designed to improve the well-being and subjective quality of life of individuals with dementia who lived in nursing homes. The program sought to develop and enhance informal social networks among residents with dementia, the family caregivers, and various nursing and ancillary staff within the facility. Staff members from both nursing and other nonmedical departments such as housekeeping, dietary, and the business office provided information to the program director regarding their personal talents and interests (e.g., shopping, baseball, needlework). At the same time, family members provided similar information concerning the residents, as well as background/historical data. Staff members were matched with residents on the basis of common backgrounds or interests, and were provided with two 15-minute slots of time per week for three months to visit with the resident with whom they had been matched. During that time, which was during the workday and not during scheduled breaks, the buddy pair could reminisce, look through magazines, play simple sports-related games such as catching a ball, or just socialize. Staff, families, and residents all expressed satisfaction with the program. Furthermore, one year later, most of the staff members continued to visit the residents (Crispi & Rokeach, 2003).

Promoting Good Physical and Mental Health Through Community Services

Although the overall life expectancy for individuals within our society has steadily grown in the past hundred years, there are still wide discrepancies in longevity, even within our own country. It is commonly understood that life expectancy differs for males and females, yet longevity statistics also differ by region. For example, life expectancy in Hawaii is 75.4 for men and 81.3 for women, whereas life expectancies in Louisiana are 69.1 and 76.9 respectively (Foos & Clark, 2003; Glatzer, 1999).

Certainly there are some factors beyond our control that account for these differences. Genes can affect us both directly and indirectly, leading to vulnerability for numerous diseases such as heart disease and cancer, as well as mental illnesses, including bipolar disorder and schizophrenia. Additionally, genetic factors may play a role in how we respond to stress and might influence certain personality characteristics such as risk-taking (Foos & Clark, 2003). However, there are many factors influencing longevity that are not beyond our control. Community interventions aimed at increasing longevity and promoting good physical and mental health in the elderly can focus on many of these factors, including exercise, diet, smoking cessation campaigns, stress reduction, and preventive mental and physical health care. Additionally, programs that promote social networks and supports can also influence life expectancy.

Programs that promote good physical health by providing education related to healthy eating, exercise, and other lifestyle factors help to improve mental health and quality of life. For example, nonsmokers and people who abstain from drinking or drink only in moderation tend to have better energy and self-regard. Healthier, more active people tend to be happier and relatively stress-free, which in itself contributes to better physical and mental health. Indeed, one of the most effective types of programs to promote positive mental health in the elderly is a stress-reduction intervention. Stress can adversely affect blood pressure and can lead to heart attack, stroke, or lowered immune function. Programs designed to reduce stress have the potential not only to ameliorate certain physical risks but to promote improved mental health as well.

Effective control strategies—coping techniques that have been successfully used by adults across the lifespan to reduce stress and to increase well-being—can be valuable to incorporate into stress-reduction programs. A study by Wrosch, Heckhausen, and Lachman (2000) delineated and analyzed the following three types of control strategies: persistence (a primary strategy aimed at attaining goals and overcoming obstacles); positive appraisal (a secondary strategy used to protect emotional and motivational resources); and lowering of aspirations. Results indicated that for older participants under significant financial or health-related stress, control strategies using positive appraisal were linked to enhanced well-being, whereas control strategies using persistence were related to well-being in younger adults. The "lowering of aspirations" strategy was shown to correlate with a lesser sense of well-being in both age groups.

As implied previously, well-conceived research studies yield valuable results, and these results can be used to devise community interventions aimed at stress reduction and improved well-being in older people. This is especially the case for those suffering from health-related stress. Wrosch and colleagues (2000) determined that teaching elders to reframe their health problems might be more effective than strategies aimed at helping them overcome obstacles related to their health. This outcome does not imply that elders should "give up" but instead suggests they should appraise their health situation realistically and learn to compensate for losses by emphasizing what they can do rather than what they are no longer able to do.

In an additional example of how reframing might relate to improved health, Glatzer (1999) hypothesized that one of the main reasons Hawaiians live longer than individuals in any other state is that they don't let little problems overwhelm them. This capacity would be considered a secondary coping strategy; rather than constantly trying to overcome problems, Hawaiians instead tend to change their appraisal of the importance of the problems.

Future Trends in Aging and Need for Community Mental Health Services

The demand for mental health services in the community is expected to increase in the near future simply because the number of elderly will increase. Hence, one of the primary goals of mental health services in the coming years should be to enhance successful aging and increase the quality of life along with the quantity of years. A comprehensive approach should incorporate support, indices of well-being and positive mental health, nutrition, physical health, and physical activity (Drewnowski, Monsen, et al., 2003).

Although mental health is known to contribute to overall quality of life, there are currently no direct measures of mental health status used in routine health screenings (Drewnowski et al., 2003). There is a known reciprocal influence between physical and mental health. Untreated psychological issues can lead to an increased need for physical health services and may contribute to future disability. This possibility, in turn, can place an increasingly large burden on the health care system in this country. It is therefore imperative that society address the mental health issues of the aging, including alcohol abuse, depression, dementia, stress, and suicide (Drewnowski et al., 2003). One way to address these issues is through improved screening; measures must go beyond functional and disease status to also address mental status.

Another way the mental health needs of the elderly can be addressed is through professional training in the areas of geropsychology and public health. As mentioned, many older adults with mental health problems visit only their primary care physicians, practitioners who are often inadequately trained to treat mental health problems in the aged (American Psychological Association, 2004). As a result, the APA's Public Policy Office has petitioned Congress to provide additional funding for graduate training opportunities in those areas (Smith, 2002). The scarcity of full-time geropsychologists has led Sara Honn Qualls, Director of the Center on Aging at the University of Colorado (as cited in Dittman, 2003) to emphasize the importance of continued training for nongeropsychology psychologists and the guidance of students on all levels toward internship experiences related to aging.

Studies have also shown eagerness to hire graduates with training in gerontology on the part of community agencies that serve the elderly. A community needs assessment conducted by Crispi, Vangel, and Wetter (2003) found that agencies would not only be more likely to hire graduates with such training but would also be willing to start them at higher salaries.

As a final note, it is predicted that there will be an increase in concern with chronic mental illness (Gatz & Smyer, 1992). Individuals with chronic mental illness are found in institutions and nursing homes, and among the ranks of the homeless.

Some gains have indeed been made in the care of the mentally ill elderly within the community; the level at which they utilize community mental health services has not declined. Both nursing home and mental health systems have recognized the need to serve this population. The Administration on Aging has requested funding for projects that link mental and physical care, and funding for Alzheimer's disease research has increased. In addition, the Medicare system has made mental health services more available to the elderly within the community (Gatz & Smyer, 1992).

Conclusion: A Model of Successful Aging and Improved Quality of Life

As increasingly larger numbers of individuals within the population reach retirement age and beyond and as baby boomers begin to avail themselves of health care services for the elderly, it is important to aspire to the goal of improving quality of life for the elderly in the community. This can be accomplished by incorporating into future programs a goal of enhancing the quality of mental health as well as physical health.

The terms "successful aging" or "optimal aging" (as opposed to normal or diseased aging) refer to those people who exhibit little or no loss of functioning and are able to age in developmentally healthy environs (Baltes & Baltes, 1990). One of the ways in which individuals achieve successful aging and improved quality of life is through what Baltes and Baltes describe as "optimization with compensation." Those who age successfully learn to compensate for losses and declines, and they are able to do so by selecting strategies that improve their chances for success and by altering their goals to make them reasonably attainable. One of the key elements in this model is that of primary control: the ability of the individuals to exert control over the course of their lives (Schulz, 1996).

DISCUSSION QUESTIONS

1. Why must a patient's family be addressed in an effective intervention? How is this step consistent with the community psychology perspective? What are some examples of family interventions involving elderly individuals?

2. What factors have contributed to an increase in life expectancy? What social changes have resulted? What are the economic implications of an increased life span?

3. What is the baby boom generation? Why is this generation of particular concern to gerontology and psychology?

4. Identify some current service gaps that exist in the treatment of elderly mental health patients. Why do these gaps exist? In addition, describe some barriers that prevent older adults from utilizing existing services less than younger patients. How can these problems be realistically addressed?

5. What are the primary goals regarding the future of psychological health care for the elderly? Are these goals realistic? If so, what are some practical ways to achieve these goals? If not, what types of goals would be realistic to aspire to?

13

Evolution/Revolution in Behavioral Managed Care: An Insider's Reflections

OBJECTIVES

This chapter is designed to enable the reader to:

- Understand how the wider forces of our age affect the field of psychology.
- Understand the nature of the current U.S. health care system.
- Identify four stages of evolution that led to the current state of the health care system.
- Identify reasons for health care cost inflation in the 1980s.
- Define managed care and relevant factors that led to its implementation.
- Explain how managed care initially impacted those suffering from mental illness.
- Relate the importance and use of evidence-based medicine to the health insurance industry.
- Describe important changes that occurred in standardization and quality of treatment.
- Understand the role of the employer in the development of managed care.
- Identify improvements made to the health care system, as well as problems that remained unaddressed.
- Identify consumer demands that affected the evolution of the managed care system.
- Understand the impact of an aging workforce on the quality of health care delivery.
- Describe proposed guidelines for health care delivery redesign.
- Explain the role and impact of prevention in the managed care context.
- Explain how patient variables can affect treatment.

God bless the physician who warms the speculum or holds your hand and looks into your eyes. Perhaps one subtext of the health care debate is a yen to be treated like a whole person, not just an eye, an ear, a nose or a throat. A yen to be human again, on the part of patient and doctor alike.

Anna Quindlen (b. 1952), U.S. journalist, columnist, author

A Note from One of the Authors (DW)

When I started in this field I thought that if I mastered the "science" of psychiatry I would in due course (honed in the fires of experience) become a wise and helpful practitioner. Either this was wide-eyed innocent naïveté or truly excessive hubris. First, the "science" seemed to continually expand beyond the obvious. Biology and biochemistry, psychology and psychiatry, nosology and epidemiology, nutrition, genetics, medicine, religion, human development, pharmacology, neurology, sociology, philosophy, and anthropology all began to demand a place at the table of understanding human behavior, "normal" development, and psychopathology. To get a grip on the "science" seemed to be an elusive and demanding goal. This perception became more obvious as the speed at which individual fields expanded their breakthroughs; discoveries and scope seemed to accelerate exponentially. The "decade of the brain," the genome project, new drugs, and crises in academic integrity added their own color. But more than anything else, it has been in coming to terms with how to turn knowledge into wisdom, facts into action, and trying to do something valuable that I have learned I was even more naïve about the role of certain variables. These included economics, politics, the whole psychology of health, what motivates us to act, where our loci of control are seated, under what circumstances people will even contemplate change, and of stages of readiness. In my initial hubris, I seemed to think I would turn up with my wisdom and that people and institutions would change or move because it was clearly apparent that to do so would be a good idea. First, I had to learn that maybe it wasn't always a good idea. I have also had to learn that cognitive conversion is certainly not the same as action. Although we all learn at some point how much of the practice of psychology is knowledge and how much is art, I hope that by the end of this chapter you will also appreciate how much the wider forces of our age (economic, political, and cultural) shape both the science and the art of the field. With this awareness, we are better equipped to cope with the frustrations of trying to practice successfully and to make the most of the unique opportunities that the particular challenges of our time present.

Introduction

There is no other country in the world where the nature of health care delivery has evolved in such a way that it has fallen to the employer to be the one who holds the prime responsibility for funding the health care of employees (and for the most part, their families as well). For the majority of American workers, this has become so expected that they feel inalienably entitled to have it be the case. However, since profitability is vital to survival and affects corporate share prices, and share prices in turn affect the capital available for development and investment, this accident of history presents very unique challenges. Participation in a global economy and international competition for the price of goods and services has become even more critical, and as a result, the cost of doing business has become even more significant. Health expenses are second only to payroll in most companies and are critical in determining the eventual profitability of the company. In this chapter, managed care will be described through four stages of evolution and their repercussions. These include the manner in which the development of managed care has affected the definition and design of health and mental health benefits, and the impact that this has had on the services offered and their availability.

The first of these stages involves the birth of managed care and the behavioral carve-out industry, the age of promise, and "low-hanging fruit." The second stage was ushered in by the backlash: attempts at standardization and growing concerns for quality. The third stage was brought about by a concern with the impact of total health costs (not just direct medical expense), the erosion of mental health services, and the growing awareness that managed care, in the form it had developed, was failing. Finally, during the fourth stage, double-digit health inflation returned, cost-shifting in the name of empowerment seemed like the only workable solution, and the awareness of total health costs developed into a full understanding of human asset management and human capital investment.

Before the Beginning

In the late 1980s, health benefit inflation suddenly escalated from 6.9% in 1987 to 18.6% in 1988, and then a further 16.7% in 1989. Such double-digit inflation clearly threatened profitability, share value, and global competitiveness. The majority of insurance was indemnity, and the system had very few checks and balances. If a physician or therapist thought more services might help a patient, there was little reason for moderation. If a service or procedure was thought to possibly confer some benefit regardless of strict scientific evidence or cost, it could always be a consideration. The patient had no reason to curb this approach, and the fact that the practitioner would be reimbursed for each service meant that efficiency was not necessarily a high priority. Patient satisfaction and perceived quality of service were given higher priority than the level of effectiveness and appropriateness of service. Of all the areas of endeavor that are particularly vulnerable to inappropriate use/abuse, mental health provided the greatest challenges. What constituted bona fide mental illness? What constituted legitimate treatment? What constituted success in treatment? Why was 28-day inpatient treatment the preferred approach to substance abuse treatment? Did the high use of psychoanalysis as a modality within the government-sponsored Civilian Health and Medical Program of the Uniformed Services (CHAMPUS) program predict better outcomes? Should marital issues be covered as a "medical" benefit? The environment was ripe for abuse. Emotional and behavioral distress was prevalent among all groups of people at a variety of levels, and there was little agreement defining what constituted a genuine illness. Conditions were deliberately miscoded because of patient concerns about stigma and prejudice. Many treatment modalities were used, and there was little evidence of effectiveness for most of them. As a result, the cost of treating mental illness was increasing at 2.5 times the rate of general inflation. Psychiatric and chemical dependency expenses, as measured by claims' costs, constituted an

Health Benefit Cost Inflation

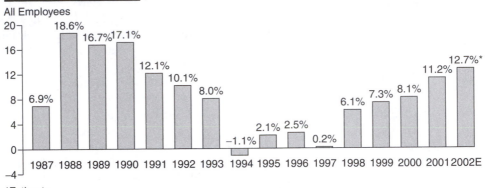

*Estimate

Source: Mercer/Foster-Higgins 2001

FIGURE 13.1

unparalleled 20 to 25% of benefit costs. Whereas medical inflation was at 18.6%, the mental health portion was increasing at a 27% rate of increase.

Another factor that shaped the health insurance policy response was a general feeling that psychiatry was less "scientific" than the rest of medicine. The business press was promoting the 28-day residential treatment for chemical dependence as a growth industry worth investing in. Psychiatric Institutes of America was publicly under scrutiny for practices in Texas. Some psychiatric hospitals were running ads in papers to coincide with the timing of report cards saying "Is your child underperforming? Maybe he or she is depressed? Checking into a psychiatric hospital could help diagnose the issues." Self-actualization was in demand, and the films of Woody Allen served as windows on psychoanalysis. Psychobabble was a source of humor to some, while the increasing expense of treatment for federal employees was causing considerable consternation elsewhere. Concerns that treatments for chemical dependency were ineffective fostered a moral attitude that viewed it more as a moral weakness than a legitimate disease. Detractors questioned whether substance abuse was deserving of funding and treatment, and added to voices decrying the blank-check mentality of paying for anything a provider wanted. Spending had to be curbed in an attempt to control a runaway process.

First Stage: The Birth of Managed Care

The definition of quality at this stage was focused on any process that would curb the overuse, misuse, and inappropriate use of services. Underutilization was part of the mantra, but the main concern was the waste and potential risks.

TABLE 13.1

Environment/ Drivers	Solutions	Quality	Providers/ Consumer
• Impression that psychiatry is less "scientific" than the rest of medicine • WSJ promoting 28d program as growth industry • PIA scandal in Texas • Moral attitude toward SA	• Benefit disparity • UM and UR • Carve-outs • Guidelines developed	• Focused on overuse and misuse/ abuse • Company specific	• Providers try to avoid • Consumers are not really incorporated • Focus on employer's concern as purchaser

Transition to Managed Care

The response was a feeling that mental health and substance abuse were far more vulnerable to subjectivity on the part of patient and provider, and that the most effective immediate control might be to subject these benefits to a greater level of copay (50% rather than the standard 20% on medical). This arrangement would mean people might think twice about frivolous uses of these benefits. There seemed to be minimal concern that this inequitable application of coverage unfairly penalized those whose illnesses happened to impact the mind rather than the body. Those with serious mental illness would have to battle not only stigma but also economic discrimination. Disparity was born. Utilization management and utilization review (UM/UR) were implemented as a further check on what appeared to be runaway processes. Before any benefit could be used, the provider would now have to explain the rationale for treatment, the diagnosis, the therapeutic plan, and the expected course of recovery or stabilization. In addition, such services would have to be "medically necessary," a term that suffered from a lack of definition in a way that made its application seem arbitrary and capricious at times. If the goal was to distinguish "self-actualizing" patients and those truly suffering from serious psychiatric symptoms, the lack of consensus in terms of nosology and effective treatment could easily lead to abuse on both sides. The patient became the unwitting victim in the middle. In addition, it soon became clear the medical surgical nurses who had been hired for these new UM/UR activities were frequently at a loss when it came to the ill-defined world of substance abuse and mental health. This led to the "carve-out" company, a company that exclusively employed clinicians with behavioral expertise/experience to engage in the UM/UR activities in this area.

The economic driver behind all this was to help the employer manage direct claims expense. The power of the managed care companies enabled them to control access to the employee's beneficiaries, since these beneficiaries could not access services without authorization. In the fights that quickly followed about "the practice of medicine," the insurers affirmed they never controlled clinical access, only the payment for services which it was their fiduciary responsibility to make sure were necessary and medically appropriate. The managed care companies' original intent was to use economic power to shape provider behavior for the best and to exclude abusers of the system. To help determine preferred/preferable clinical courses of action, appropriate treatments, and needed intensity of services, they established "clinical guidelines" and "levels of care." In a way, this was the beginning of the "evidence-based medicine" movement. The problem with these first attempts, however, was they frequently lacked the evidence base or clinical consensus needed to make them universally accepted. This situation was complicated by the fact that many individual companies saw these guidelines as the key to their uniqueness and thus were reluctant to share them. This attitude furthered the belief by many providers that these "clinical guidelines" were really just arbitrary internally developed rules with the sole aim of justifying the denial of care.

Although the managed care companies assumed that economic control would create economic competition and would drive the best providers their way, many excellent providers decided to have nothing to do with the new phenomenon and began to accept only "paying" patients. In contrast, a less successful provider having trouble filling his or her practice could make a contract with a managed care company. By being particularly cooperative (easy to deal with and not a high utilizer), the provider could gain a market share that clinical reputation alone might not have allowed. However, success and market share for the managed care company primarily came from keeping employers "happy," and initially this condition was defined by anything that could curb the double-digit annual rise in direct care health expenses that seemed to threaten economic viability.

And where were the patients in this? Without an economic card to play at this stage, they were merely passive recipients of the new manner of service delivery. Although the intention to limit abuse and misuse within the system made it a safer place for patients, those who truly suffered behavioral health illnesses, economic disparity, stigma, and now increased barriers to access treatment found the road to health more difficult to find. On the other hand, the increased oversight and evaluation of clinical effectiveness, along with a greater emphasis on treatment in the least restrictive setting, offered some potential for improvement in areas that really did matter to patients.

The first stage of the revolution had both positive and negative aspects. Costs did decrease, and markedly so. Although some of this decrease was due to the use of more appropriate services, some was due to frustration with the new hassles and barriers to access. These drove people either to seek help elsewhere or not to seek it at all. As the need arose to look at intensity of service issues, new approaches and clinical pathways were formed. Ambulatory detox and intensive outpatient substance-abuse treatment centers entered the field as alternatives to 28-day residential programs. Partial hospitalization programs were also constructed, the focus being on provision of more intensive services to either stave off a hospitalization or to allow for an earlier transition from an in-patient unit to home. Patterns of care changed, and the interest in guidelines from professional societies and expert consensus panels as well as more detailed outcomes from pharmaceutical companies added a real impetus to creating the evidence base and consensus necessary to help define "best practices."

On the down side, the birth of the carve-out helped lead to a major cost-accounting fallacy, namely that an employer's mental health and substance abuse expenses were now contained in the sum of money paid to the carve-out company. In fact, although 70% or so of all behavioral care continued to be provided through primary care, records of these services were rapidly going underground. One of the accelerators was the manner in which automatic claims adjudication systems were being set up. The system included rules that would automatically deny claims from non-mental-health practitioners for behavioral services. Practitioners, wanting to be reimbursed for services that had already been provided, recoded encounters in a way that was payable. The net result was that any attempt to look at claims by diagnosis on the medical side sorely underestimated the extent of services given. Furthermore, the distinction between mental and medical health drove a major barrier between the connection of mind and body in health. The focus at this point was on medical necessity and DSM credibility, and access to funds was contingent on meeting sickness guidelines. This practice ignored the whole realm of behavioral medicine, including patient response to chronic illness, problems with coping, and comorbidities that didn't reach the level of independent sickness in their own right. Also neglected were stress, general health psychology, and the relationship of behavior to chronic disease and treatment compliance. In the context of the narrowly defined sickness business, the patient was barely considered. There was also little focus on children or adolescents, since their health issues did not seem to have immediate impact for the employer except as a source of increased cost/expense. This view was, in fact, naïve. Studies have regularly shown the impact of dependents' health issues on the health of the other family members. For example, the impact of a child's or an adolescent's substance abuse, anorexia, or depression results in obvious stress in the parents and also leads to subsequent adaptive and maladaptive ways of coping, increased distraction at work, and possible physical health deterioration in the parents. Despite this likelihood, many employers at the time considered children and retirees as an expense whose improved health could do little to improve the bottom line, but whose escalating expenses could negatively impact the company as a whole.

The Second Stage: Emphasis on Standardization and Quality of Treatment

As inadequate solutions unfolded, they sowed the seeds of the next stage of evolution. The negatives became obvious, in part driven by a series of high-profile cases that drew attention to the lack of clarity around what was and what was not considered medically necessary. The questionable primacy of cost control over quality was brought front and center. The barriers to access, delays in treatment, denials of services that the average person expected to be covered, and the tales of families finding themselves liable for bills solely because they could not negotiate the system meant that whatever success the revolution might bring in terms of cost control threatened its acceptance by patients and providers alike. Continuous complaints, appeals, and problems, which embroiled benefit departments and human resource offices, had taken the glow off any gains. Since returning to the old system was not an option, a new set of solutions was needed.

Several other issues became apparent. Providers were responding in a much more cohesive fashion. Professional societies were taking public positions against managed care. Funds were being allocated to support political and legal campaigns against this "menace." The National Alliance for the Mentally Ill (NAMI), the National Mental Health Association (NMHA), and other consumer groups were mobilizing and beginning to provide their own "report cards." In the wake of these reactions, employers looked for answers that would provide clinical oversight while allowing them to continue the approach of "managing" care/benefits. From this reaction came initiatives from the Foundation for Accountability (FAACT), the National Committee for Quality Assurance (NCQA), the Health Plan Employer Data and Information Set (HEDIS), and the American Managed Behavioral Association (AMBHA) to create a common language and set of standards. This effort would assure employees their employers were concerned not just about cost but also about ensuring high-quality clinical access and supporting adequate oversight of the utilization management and review processes so that disputes would be handled quickly and employees would be handled with respect.

Although providers hoped the combined efforts of their initiatives plus consumer backlash and public sentiment might eradicate managed care for good, a report from the Institute of Medicine entitled "Crossing the Quality Chasm" (2001) was a reminder that misuse, inappropriate use, and abuse still lingered in the medical world despite all the accreditations, including the Joint Commission on Accreditation of Healthcare Organizations (JCAHO).

For managed care companies, the purchaser of services (the employer) was king. These companies embraced the concerns as outlined and agreed that although "bad" managed care was indeed extremely negative, good managed care could still be the solution. It might have been easy to create some consensus around what constituted good clinical care, yet evidence-based approaches, response times, access standards, and information systems were basically a loose connection of different data elements hidden within what amounted to a cottage industry. Very few standardized reports and quality metrics existed, and almost no clinical outcomes data in the realm of routine care (certainly not in an easily aggregatable and comparable format). Even as NCQA and HEDIS set off in the direction of creating definitions or benchmarks in quality that would allow for head-to-head comparisons, the focus was still at the beginning on processes rather than outcome data. For many, the course correction seemed too slow. The public and providers, having gained the attention of the media, took their case to the legislative process. These groups served as counters to "the clinical experts" in managed care who decided what should or should not be covered. Legislative bodies began not only to mandate benefits in terms of what should be covered, if there was any question, but also to mandate how. The rules of the game were changing, and many players tried to have a hand in writing the new policies. For example, in the realm of mental health, forces that had driven out excesses and abuses with regard to unnecessary hospitalization of many children and adolescents inherited the closing of multiple facilities and an increasing shortage of providers and treatment centers. Areas of development that had seemed attractive a decade before by promising easy access to money became subject to low-margin gains and increased bureaucracy. This new economic would have its own impact. As people began to look at outcomes, there emerged a greater awareness of cultural sensitivities. The recognition of differences in symptom expression and needed treatment among different ethnic groups and genders was becoming obvious. Although some of this began to be incorporated at the third stage, a wider understanding of the "sociology" of medicine would be clarified and integrated at a later time.

The Third Stage: Emphasis on Total Health Costs

As a result of the second-stage challenges, the system improved. There had again been real and measurable gains. There was a greater standardization around the metrics that should be evaluated as part of quality, and an improved consensus on data definition and gathering. This, in turn, allowed for greater understanding in comparability between plans. With the renewed emphasis on clinical outcomes and clinical quality, greater accountability in programs and utilization processes became a standard expectation. There was a chance to advocate that managed care done properly could not only provide answers to the economic crisis in health care but could also become a vehicle for improving health in general. The first HEDIS measure showed that within managed care there were improved vaccination rates and improved screenings for such conditions as breast cancer, changes that went beyond "business as usual." It was in part the aura of optimism created by these changes that made conditions ripe for "parity" to be floated before the legislators. In addition, "The Decade of the Brain" (the major research initiative of the National Institutes of Mental Health to provide greater credibility to treatment and outcomes research in mental health) began to show that treatments in many of the major mental health categories, such as depression, were more reliable and offered a better chance for remission of symptoms, cure, or management than many medical illnesses such as arthritis or diabetes. If managed care could now provide the oversight that would help ensure good clinical care to those who needed it, then concerns about the abuses of the previous period and the vulnerability to lack of scientific rigor could be set aside. If that were to be the case, the need for discriminatory benefits no longer existed, and parity could be returned. And so it was, although with stipulations that such legislation did not apply to all employers, only the larger ones. Also, in case the optimism was ill-founded, it was believed there should be a cap on the risk that employers would be taking. From our current position, it can be seen that the optimism was generally well founded, but the victory remained incomplete. Concerns about definitions or proof of success in substance abuse treatment brought reluctance to include chemical dependency within the umbrella of parity. The biases surrounding addiction, those who saw the issue as a problem of will, continued to impact the debate. Health researchers believed that even if there were gains in understanding of the neurochemistry of addiction, the ability to intervene with predictability remained elusive.

Clinically, the split between mind and body remained unaddressed. With the continuing focus on expense management, the definition of success continued to be aimed at managing the expenses within the "sickness" industry rather than on preventing illnesses in the first place.

On the economic front, the focus on quality metrics, standardization, and new data reporting would add a new layer of administrative expense. Managed care companies initially hoped this expense could be passed on to customers, and they sought to differentiate themselves by being better at or more focused on quality. They maintained such differentiation came at an additional expense, while employers attempted to point out that they thought they had been paying for a quality product all along and were not interested in paying more for what they should have been already getting. At the same time, a review of what employers were in fact getting was making some aware of problems with looking at the benefit world in silos. By focusing so heavily on "best in class" approaches, there was a tendency to see distinct areas as unrelated (with unique problems and unique solutions) rather than as an interdependent whole. This policy ignored all the research that demonstrated high comorbidity, when many physical and mental illnesses occur together in patterns. If the Pharmacy Benefit Manager (PBM) company was the focus, issues centered on rising costs and better expense management without any evaluation of the role played by medication in keeping people out of the hospital, helping them recover more quickly, or allowing them to get back to work sooner. Mental health and substance abuse expenses were thought to be solely in the carve-out, despite the facts that 70% of outpatient visits were occurring in primary care and that the psychopharmacy spend exceeded the total carve-out spend. Disability and workers' compensation were kept separate as well, and it was a rare company that could determine whether or not extending a hospital stay by half a day could result in a return to work two weeks earlier.

The relationship between benefits, health goals, and business goals came from the Washington Business Group on Health.

The Integrated Benefits Institute was the first agency to really articulate the values of looking at data in an integrated fashion, but companies were frequently set up with different departments managing different aspects of benefits. These departments were rewarded for managing their particular silo well and had little incentive to look at things in a new light, especially since the type of data needed to add an element of rationality to this endeavor was noticeably lacking. It was in this environment that the third stage began.

The new emphases spawned new technologies and new approaches, and in the era of the dot-com boom, a wealth of players tried to provide focused solutions in niche markets. On the medical side, there were the beginnings of a greater interest on prevention and broader services aimed at maintaining health. "Healthy Workforce 2010" (U.S. Department of Health and Human Services, 2001) came out with a series of positive stories of individual company successes; but despite these, continued skepticism meant the push toward prevention and early detection remained scattered. In mental health, however, there was progress with regard to employee assistance pro-

Health Plan Management	Total Health Management	Health and HR value
Managed care	Integrated benefits and programs	People value maximized
Discounted fees		Health aligned with business objectives
Utilization review	Management of direct and indirect costs	
Performance standards/TQM		Performance linked to key financial measures
	Value-based purchasing	
Reduced health care cost trend	*Total health-related cost management*	*People investments linked to company success*

FIGURE 13.2

Source: WBGH, Investing in People for Corporate Growth and Success, May 1998.

grams (EAP). Whereas traditional approaches had focused on early detection and treatment of substance abuse in the workplace, EAP was undergoing a major rebirth. Most families had two working adults, and as a result, there arose regular issues concerning child care and elder care. There were increasing numbers of bankruptcies, and thus the affordability of health care was a consideration, as well as redundancies, job losses abroad, and the impact of a falling stock market on pension and retirement security. The impact of stress on productivity, absenteeism, and "presenteeism" became clear. NIOSH (National Institute for Occupational Safety and Health, 1999) reported that 40% of workers rated their job as very or extremely stressful; 25% viewed their job as the number one stressor in their lives; 75% of employees believed workers have more on-the-job stress than a generation ago; 29% felt "quite a bit" or "extremely" stressed at work; 26% said they were "often" or "very often burned out or stressed" by their work; and in addition, job stress was more strongly associated with health complaints than financial or family problems. Likewise, a 2000 Integra (Integra Realty

The Third Stage

- Focus on prevention and broader services
- Impact of the Internet
- Concerns about escalating pharmacy costs
- Medical/behavioral integration
- Total health costs (including indirect, disability, etc.)
- Greater consumer empowerment/ knowledge

- Disease management
- Push for "real outcomes"
- Greater focus on children and adolescents
- Increased concerns about confidentiality
- Erosion of services (social HMO/child and adolescent)

Resources, 2000) study reported 65% of workers believing workplace stress had caused difficulties, and more than 10% describing these as having major effects; 10% said they worked in an atmosphere where physical violence had occurred because of job stress; 42% reported yelling and other verbal abuse was common; 29% had yelled at coworkers because of workplace stress; 14% said they worked where machinery or equipment had been damaged because of workplace rage; 2% admitted they had actually personally struck someone; 19% had quit a previous position because of job stress and nearly 25% had been driven to tears because of workplace stress; 62% routinely found they ended the day with work-related neck pain; 44% reported stressed-out eyes; 38% complained of hurting hands and 34% reported difficulty in sleeping because they were too stressed-out; 12% had called in sick because of job stress; over half said they often spent 12-hour days on work-related duties, and an equal number frequently skipped lunch because of the stress of job demands.

The impact of the World Trade Center attack on September 11, 2001, made "presenteeism" real in a way that employers could no longer ignore. For the first time, it was patently obvious what it meant for employees to come to work and be focused on anything but the duties of their employment. Whether it was watching the news on television or just talking with coworkers or e-mailing or calling friends and relatives, for a short period "present but distracted" was the norm and not the rarity.

Studies by Ron Goetzel and the Medstat group (Health Enhancement Research Organization, 2000) showed the single most significant health-related risk was stress, eclipsing obesity, smoking, and lack of exercise. It makes sense, since it is obvious that when stressed, people often do things that do not promote good health (drink too much, eat too much, smoke, don't exercise, get into fights, drive faster) and are much less likely to have the energy, focus, or desire to solve problems, take care of health, or have the patience to take care of others. Stress was responsible, according to the study, for 7.9% of total health spending.

What were some of the main stressors? The National Study of the Changing Workforce conducted by the Families and Work Institute (Bond, Galinsky, & Swanberg, 1998), a survey of 2,877 employees, showed the following statistics with regard to childcare:

- 46% of workers had children under 18;
- 29% of employed parents had at least 1 child care breakdown in the last 3 months;
- 19% of working parents were raising children alone; and
- 82% of employees were not aware of child care assistance services.

The study also showed the following in terms of elder care:

- 42% of the workforce anticipated elder care responsibilities in the next 5 years;
- 37% of those with elder care responsibilities had lost work time because of care-giving;
- These workers spent an average of 11 hours per week on elder care;
- 25% of workers had elder care responsibilities in the previous year; but only
- 25% of employees had or were aware of elder care assistance services.

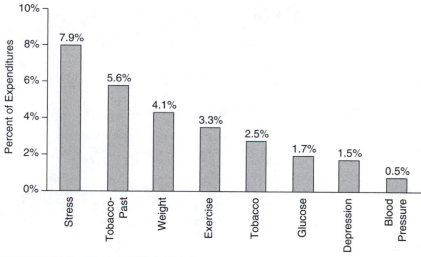

FIGURE 13.3 Types of High Risk Status

Impact of High-Risk Status on Organizational Health Care Costs

- High-risk status costs $465 per employee annually (1996 dollars)
- 27% of expenditures
- High-risk stress alone accounts for 7.9% of total health care costs

Ref: Anderson, D. R., Whitmer, R. W., Goetzel, R. Z., et al. *American Journal of Health Promotion, 15*:1, 45–52, September/October, 2000. Health care expenditures—1996 dollars. Independent effects after adjustment.

The top 10% of medical service utilizers account for the following:

- 29% of all PC visits;
- 52% of specialty visits;
- 40% of inpatient days;
- 26% of all prescriptions;
- 50% being psychologically distressed;
- Depressed 40.3%;
- Anxiety 21.8%;
- Somatization 20.2%;
- Panic 11.8%; and
- Alcohol 5%.
  (Katon, von Korffi & Lin, 1990)

Patients with adult onset diabetes have a 25% chance of being depressed. Approximately 70% of patients with diabetic complications are depressed. Conversely, depression doubles the risk for diabetes and is a significant risk factor for Type 2 diabetes.

The Depression Story

Depression and Cancer

25 percent of people with cancer have depression, but only 2 percent of cancer patients in one study were receiving antidepressant medication.

- People with cancer, as well as their doctors frequently misinterpret signs of depression, attributing them to the cancer itself.

Several factors increase the likelihood of depression co-occurring with cancer:
  advanced phases of the disease
  uncontrollable pain
  disability or disfigurement
  medications (chemotherapy agents)
  social isolation
  socioeconomic pressures

Cancer site/type	Prevalence
Pancreas	50%
Oropharynx	22–40%
Breast	10–26%
Colon	13–25%
Gynecologic	23%
Lymphoma	17%
Gastric	11%

Depression and Diabetes

- Approximately one in five (15–20%) patients with type 1 or 2 diabetes suffers from major depression.
- The odds of comorbid depression are significantly higher for women than men by the same ratio as in the general population.
- Lifetime prevalence is 3X higher than the general U.S. population. Depression is identified and treated in less than one third of the cases.
- The relapse rate of depression in patients with diabetes is 8X higher than for depressed patients who are physically healthy.
- Depression in patients with diabetes is associated with:
  Treatment noncompliance
  Missed appointments
  Poor glycemic control—the principle cause of diabetic complications.
- Depression doubles the risk of incident Type 2 diabetes independent of its association with other risk factors.

Depression and Heart Disease

- Depression is an independent risk factor for the development of heart disease, not just an emotional reaction to heart disease itself.
- Depression significantly increases the risk of developing CAD.
- The prevalence of depression in patients with coronary heart disease and an MI is estimated to be from 40%–65%.
- 18%–20% of patients with coronary heart disease without MI experience depression.
- Patients who are depressed following a myocardial infarction experience a 6-month and 18-month mortality rate 3.5 times and 5X higher than those who are not depressed, respectively.
- Patients with both coronary heart disease and depression have 2X the reduction in social functioning associated with either condition alone.

FIGURE 13.3A

Rini, Dunkel-Schetter, Wadhwa, and Pathik (1999) reported that women with better personal resources (mastery, self-esteem, optimism) had higher birth weight babies, whereas those with stress (state and pregnancy anxiety) had shorter durations of gestation. Further, socioeconomic resources did not buffer the effect of stress. In a study of the effect of job stress on pregnancy, Oths, Dunn, and Palmer (2001) reported that women with high (versus low) job strain had babies who were 190gm lower weight, a finding that remained even when covariates were adjusted. Examples of the detriment of splitting mind and body were not confined to the so-called medical area alone. Patients with eating disorders, developmental disorders, traumatic brain injury and Alzheimer's disease, as well as chemically dependent individuals, were likely to fall between the cracks. In some cases, such as with autism, advocacy groups were able to enlist legislators to help ensure adequate coverage, but in other areas, the lack of comprehensive coordination of benefits and care created and continues to create increased barriers to successful outcomes (once again demonstrating bad clinical effectiveness and bad economics). In the third stage, these issues became (and remain) front and central, and much of the new work was an attempt to better align clinical coordination and coordination of benefits.

Simply put, "Americans are demanding, and physicians are prescribing, a higher volume of medicines every year" (National Institute for Health Care Management, 2001). Between 1999 and 2000, there had been an 18.8% increase in pharmacy expenses (an increase that has not slowed). The drivers were a 42% increase in the number of prescriptions, a 36% shift to higher-cost drugs, and 22% price increases. Add to this the impact of direct-to-consumer advertising, the impending impact of pharmacogenetics with individually tailored drugs, improved processes in terms of the speed of bringing new drugs to market, and a rich pipeline and consolidation of pharmaceutical companies, the likelihood of continued double-digit inflationary trends seemed inevitable. Yet the more important question related to the value of such interventions and their impact on solving the health issues of employers, be they absenteeism, presenteeism, or disability.

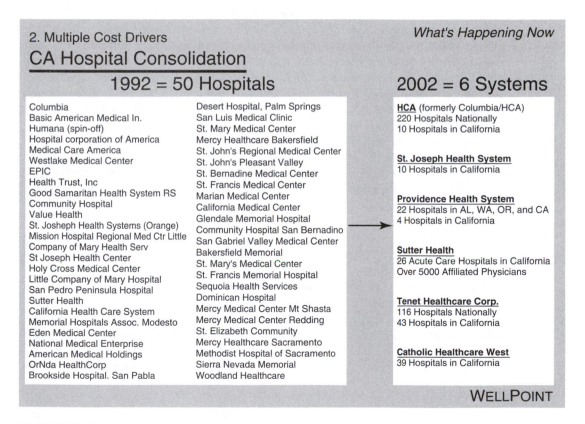

FIGURE 13.4

Consumers were fired by a combination of an increasing need to get involved, genuine interest in understanding their illnesses, and by looking for better health, to enjoy their leisure more actively. They responded to the availability of knowledge on the World Wide Web and the public debates and media interest in issues of access and privacy by becoming more insistent that their needs be met. Compared with the past, which saw insurance as an entitlement and "repair" coverage as an expectation, this new consumerism offered the possibility of creating more responsibility on the part of the consumers for decisions about medical treatment, as well as staying healthy in the first place. However, although this movement offered great promise, it has served most recently as a cover for solutions that aim to control employer expense by cost shifting to employees in the names of supporting empowerment and choice.

There was and continues to be an impact from an aging workforce and resultant chronic conditions. In 2010, 51% of the labor force will be over 40 (U.S Bureau of the Census, 2000). In 2003, Americans aged 55 and older made up approximately 12% of the workforce—the highest percentage ever recorded, according to the Bureau of Labor Statistics (2000). The aging labor force is expected to cause a 37% increase in the incidence of disability (Hewitt & Associates, 2001). Older workers are up to 5 times more likely to submit claims for short- or long-term disability, and are absent longer than the average employee (Hewitt & Associates, 2004). The 2003 Mercer/Marsh survey (Mercer Human Resources Consulting/Marsh & McLennan Companies, 2003) showed that approximately 125 million Americans currently suffer from at least one chronic condition, and the number is expected to climb to 157 million by 2020. The same study noted that in 2000, the U.S. spent $774 billion to treat chronic conditions—70% of the total spent on healthcare. Some 61% of adult Americans are overweight or obese (Johnson, 2003), and according to the Surgeon General's office (U.S. Department of Health and Human Services, 1999), the total cost of obesity in 2000 was estimated at $117 billion.

Analysis shows 12 of the most common mandates (minimum stay maternity, speech therapy, drug abuse treatment, mammography screening, well child care, podiatry, pap smears, vision exams, chiropractic, alcoholism, infertility, mental health care) combined could increase the cost of a family policy 15% to 30% (Milliman & Robertson, 1997).

Meanwhile, medical technology and pharmaceutical advances create the possibility of ever more sophisticated capabilities to eke out varying degrees of increased functioning, longevity, and repair. From stem cell research to the impact of the genome, the possibilities are vast, and their impact on an already overtaxed system is difficult to imagine. The writing was on the wall. Continuing to do more of the same, only louder, harder, and faster, was not going to work.

To add fuel to the fire, the other issue that had become obvious—quality within the health industry—was not being held to the same standard as other industries. The Institute of Medicine had come out with two landmark reports: "To Err Is Human: Building a Safer Health System," and "Crossing the Quality Chasm: A New Health System for the 21st Century."

An earlier report, "Ensuring Quality Cancer Care," concluded that "the burden of harm conveyed by the collective impact of all of our health care quality problems is staggering" (Hewitt & Simone, 1999). "To Err is Human" (Kohn, Corrigan, & Donaldson, 2000) put the spotlight on how tens of thousands of Americans die each year from medical errors and effectively put the issue of patient safety and quality on the radar screen of public and private policymakers.

The "Quality Chasm" report described broader quality issues: "The U.S. health-care system is in need of fundamental change . . . Healthcare today harms too frequently, and fails to deliver its potential benefits routinely" (Institute of Medicine, 2001, p. 1). "The performance of the healthcare system varies considerably. It may be exemplary, but often is not, and millions of Americans fail to receive effective care"; "A highly frag-mented delivery system that largely lacks even rudimentary clinical information capabil-ities results in poorly designed care processes characterized by unnecessary duplication of services and long waiting times and delays"(Institute of Medicine, 2001, p. 3).

The Institute of Medicine (2001, p. 61) also defined 6 aims—"care should be safe, effective, patient-centered, timely, efficient and equitable"—and 10 rules for care delivery redesign. These rules are as follows:

- Base care on continuous healing relationships.
- Customize care based on patient needs and values.
- The patient should be the source of control.
- Share knowledge and encourage the free flow of information.
- Utilize evidence-based decision making.
- Consider safety as a system priority.
- Emphasize the need for transparency.
- Anticipate needs.
- Strive for continuous decrease in waste.
- Enhance cooperation among clinicians.

Bruce Japsen, in a *Chicago Tribune* article on June 11, 2002, referred to these reports and their follow-up. He wrote the following:

Low quality health care in the U.S. is costing nearly $400 billion a year, or about 30 percent of the total $1.3 trillion spent annually on medical expenditures in the U.S.

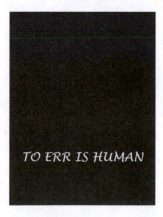

TO ERR IS HUMAN

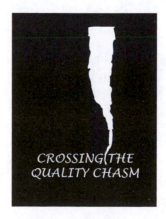

CROSSING THE QUALITY CHASM

From medical errors and unnecessary treatments to misused drugs and bureaucratic waste, new research suggests such problems compromise quality medical care and each year cost private employers between $1700 and $2000 per insured worker.

In looking at the world through a 6-sigma lens that defines the number of defects per million operations, 3 sigma allows 308,537 defects per million and 6 sigma 3.4. The benchmark industries strive to operate at a 6-sigma level. Placing health care under this light was revealing. Simply put, your luggage had a better chance of being handled well by the airlines than you yourself did of receiving the right medication as an in-patient in a U.S. hospital. Furthermore, as pointed out earlier, vocal provider and facility opposition to managed care had resulted in ill-conceived legislation such as the "any willing provider" law and a reimbursement methodology that reimbursed all procedures at the same rate regardless of the quality of the institution or the individual who performed them. In an article in *Medical Benefits* (Mulco, 2001), the 100 best-managed hospitals were compared with the average, and in these top hospitals mortality was 14% lower, complications 14% lower, average length of stay 7% lower, and costs 19% lower (Mulco, 2001). At the Washington Business Group Meeting, Bob Galvin (2003), the corporate medical director of General Electric, summed up the first issue well when he called the current health system the "most expensive repair and recovery health system in the world."

Although there had been talk of "health," the focus of managed care during its development had clearly been on the "sickness" industry. Utilization management, case management, and even disease management were all tools that played in the sickness area. To use a car analogy, it was as if there were an increasing concern about rising costs related to "burnt-out clutches." Demand for repairs had gone up, and some people were trying to get repairs earlier than needed or when not needed at all. At the same time, some unscrupulous repair shops were charging excessive amounts. Seemingly, there was a fix. In medical terms, it was "the medical necessity rule." Going back

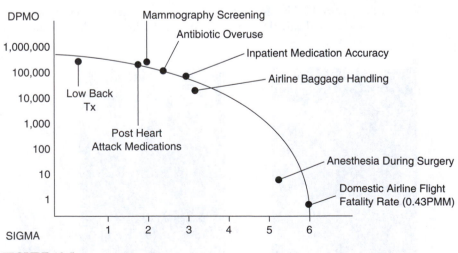

FIGURE 13.5

to the car analogy, it meant that no clutch would be repaired before its time—no semi-burnt-out clutches. Also, there would be no early maintenance—only bona fide disasters would be repaired. It was believed this method would save money. To stay with this analogy, discounts would be offered at garage chains across the country through aggressive contracting rates and by controlling access to the repair business. At the same time, the fact remained that regardless of whether the car would be repaired by a manufacturer's authorized dealer with 25 years of experience or done by a high-school student, the reimbursement would be the same.

The Fourth Stage: Keeping Healthy People Healthy

The beginning of the fourth stage was prompted by the general sentiment that business as usual was no longer possible. Returning to the car analogy, questions were starting to be raised as to why people weren't being taught how to drive in the first place to avoid repairs. Also, if repairs became needed, why not pay for performance and reward the better repair shops accordingly? In health terms, there was an increased emphasis on "keeping the healthy healthy" on one side and the "leap frog initiative" (which sought to create a "pay for performance" system for hospitals and providers) on the other.

Adults with multiple risk factors for disease (e.g., high blood pressure, smoking, and sedentary habits) are more likely to be high-cost employees in terms of health care use, absenteeism, disability, and overall productivity. Yet several of these important risk factors are controllable, often simply by modifying health habits. In other cases, the early detection of illness can simplify treatment and increase chances for a complete recovery.

Department of Health and Human Services (HHS) Secretary Tommy Thompson, on April 15, 2003, at the HHS' "Steps to a Healthier U.S.: Putting Prevention First" conference in Baltimore said the following:

> I am convinced that preventing disease by promoting better health is a smart policy choice for our future. Our current health care system is not structured to deal with the escalating costs of treating diseases that are largely preventable through changes in our lifestyle choices.

This approach lays the groundwork to see health as an investment in human capital and not just an expense or an entitlement. It seems that the key to financial success as a company is not just controlling the expense of benefits but also understanding that a healthy workforce may be the very key to competitive gains. Jim Loehr and Tony Schwartz (2001) in the *Harvard Business Review* wrote the following:

> In a corporate environment that is changing at warp speed, performing consistently at high levels is more difficult and more necessary than ever. High performance depends as much on how people renew and recover energy as on how they expend it, on how

they manage their lives as much as on how they manage their work. When people feel strong and resilient—physically mentally, emotionally, and spiritually—they perform better, with more passion for longer. They win, their families win, and corporations that employ them win." (Loehr & Schwartz, 2001, p. 128)

Emphasis on Health Psychology

A true focus on health delves into areas of human behavior with which many feel less comfortable. It is vital to become conversant in the paradigm of "health psychology" and to try to begin to understand the complicated psychological and sociological determinants of human behavior as they relate to health care purchasing and health care decisions, and in turn, to understand how to promote a new appreciation for health and prevention. In this arena, it may be that using approaches on a case-by-case basis can yield only piecemeal results and that real gains will come from shifts within communities. Early attempts at change, such as rewards for completing health risk assessments or engaging in health promotion programs, are baby steps within this arena; success may require a whole series of influences to change simultaneously.

Patients' Beliefs and Attitudes as Affecting Treatment Compliance

The literature on patient compliance is both compelling and alarming. Consider the following with regard to noncompliance with a short-term medication regimen:

- Patients do not fill their prescriptions 30% to 35% of the time.
- Patients stop taking medications after several days 25% of the time.
- Patients do not complete a 10-day course of treatment 75% to 80% of the time.

Consider the following with regard to noncompliance with a long-term medication regimen:

- Patients do not comply with long-term treatments 50% of the time.
- Compliance problems increase with the duration of an illness.
- Patients do not follow modest dietary recommendations 70% of the time.
- Patients do not stop using tobacco products 90% to 95% of the time after being advised to do so. (Stern, Fricchione, Cassem, Jellinek & Rosenbaum, 2004)

Practical barriers to compliance include ethnic/cultural barriers, patient disagreement with the diagnosis or treatment plan, patient's not understanding the treatment plan, patient's fear of getting dependent or getting better, side effects, patient runs out of pills or forget to take them, prohibitive cost, nonsupportive friends or family, patient's feeling that treatment is not working, patient hopelessness, or patient's simply wanting to discontinue.

Understanding patient beliefs is essential. Dissonance between a patient's model and a clinician's explanatory model of an illness can have a direct impact on compliance. Such dissonance must be recognized and discussed. Patients may voice concerns including the following:

- "I am not susceptible to illness and its consequences."
- "My illness is not serious."
- "My illness will resolve on its own."
- "The treatment prescribed for me is most likely ineffective."
- "The treatment recommended to me can be dangerous or cause problems."
- "I need less (or more) than the dose prescribed for me."
- "I am unable to follow the recommendations given to me."

PATH studies have consistently shown that 90% of the adults in the United States fall into one of these 9 PATH groups (Navarro & Wilkins, 2003):

- The Clinic Cynic (is generally distrustful of the medical profession);
- The Avoider (refrains from using health care services until very sick or injured);
- The Generic (tends to balance a concern for cost with a concern for quality);
- The Family-Centered (puts family health above all other matters);
- The Traditionalist (is willing to pay more for quality and tends to use the same providers);
- The Loyalist (is characterized by moderation in health care opinions and behaviors);
- The Ready User (actively seeks and uses health care services of all kinds);
- The Independently Healthy (is very actively involved in one's own health); and
- The Naturalist (has a propensity to use nontraditional or alternative health care methods).

Understanding which profile a person belongs to can better delineate whether he or she will act or be influenced from the outside and also can help determine the most likely method for success. Understanding "Protection Motivation Theory" (Prentice-Dunn & Rogers, 1986), the "Theory of Planned Behavior" (Ajzen, 1985), the "Health Belief Model" (Rosenstock, 1974), "Locus of Control" (Rotter, 1966), and "Readiness for Change" (Prochaska, DiClemente, & Norcross, 1992) are part of a new understanding that will be essential to success.

Future Directions in Managed Care

Systematic Stress Reduction.   Companies are realizing the need to reduce stress among workers as a means of lowering medical expenses and the broader costs of illness. While workshops targeting the staff are one option, another is to investigate the organizational climate. Managed care companies might begin to offer the services of industrial/organizational psychologists to review corporate structures, policies, procedures and communication patterns to reduce the stress caused by the manner in which business is conducted.

Incentives for Prevention.   As companies observe the cost effectiveness of prevention, human resources staff are collaborating with insurance providers to explore ways to reward managers for motivating their staff to participate in prevention activities. Cost effectiveness results only if workers attend these workshops.

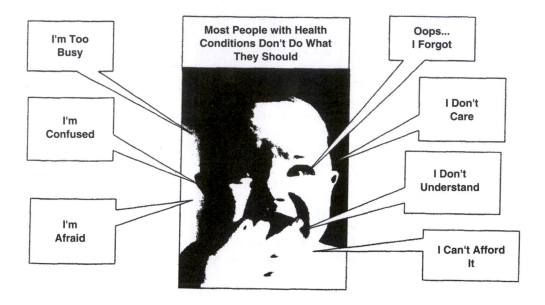

Universal Health Care Insurance.   The business community has changed its perspective on universal health care insurance over the past decade. With the cost of health care rising rapidly, providing worker benefits in this area is consuming larger chunks of corporate profits. Hiring American workers is becoming less cost effective and results in American made goods losing their competitive edge in the world market. Switching to a government single payer model for health care would reduce prices and develop a more favorable market for American products. In addition the nation would come closer to universal coverage for all residents and a guaranteed basic level of care. Research on genetic factors in illness could lead to matching workers to positions in which their health would not be in jeopardy.

Discrimination against workers due to likely illness would decrease as companies would no longer be responsible for the health care costs of their workers. As with any projection into the future, some of these themes might be incorporated into the nation's health care policy, and others might never be approved or implemented. Yet mental health professionals need to be aware of likely developments in order to participate more fully in planning the future of service delivery.

Conclusion

Current success in managing mental health and health in general is absolutely dependent upon advances in genetic medicine, basic science research, and improvements in defining evidence-based treatments that provide predictable outcomes. These are the basic tools of the trade and they grow in their scope and complexity as new fields and capabilities lead toward an increased understanding of the mechanisms behind normal and abnormal development. It is also important to understand how economics, financial rewards and incentives shift behavior, focus, leverage, and alliances. Essential, too, is the need to make sense of the conditions that operate in the environment, and also to be a player of impact in the real world. Likewise, it should be remembered that there exists a strong need to understand people. There are among individuals and groups a myriad of reasons for being. People hold dear a wide range of values and motivations, and a broad spectrum of interactions with the wider world. Ever-changing stressors like anthrax scares and terrorist attacks, job losses, homelessness, lack of insurance, divorce, violence, sexuality, or even hopes can lead mental health professionals to frustration.

As the country faces a health care system in crisis, it is important to acknowledge that the issues are unlikely to be changed solely through the application of biomedical techniques and interventions. The view of health, mental health, and health care must undergo a paradigm shift that acknowledges the role of behavioral, psychological, and social factors in health. This will be essential to guide continuing efforts to improve the health of the population.

Successful change and advances in mental health, both private and public, will come from collaborative work between many disciplines and perspectives. Hubris, at times, leads to overvaluation of some at the expense of others, as though a hierarchy will allow focus and quick solutions. In a way, this is part of the story in terms of managed care. As T. S. Eliot wrote in the *Four Quartets*, "The end of all our journeyings will be to return to the beginning and know the place for the first time." As mentioned at the outset, it is awareness that may better equip practitioners and consumers alike to cope with the frustrations of trying to operate successfully within the bounds of a complicated system. Awareness can also help people make the most of unique opportunities that the particular challenges of the time present.

DISCUSSION QUESTIONS

1. Why was psychiatry considered less "scientific" than the rest of medicine during health care policy shifts? How could this issue have been addressed? How is it currently addressed?

2. How did the initiation of a managed care system specifically affect those suffering from mental illness? What factors contributed to these changes, and do you think they were justified? If so, why? As a creative exercise, describe a fictional psychiatric patient and list 5 ways in which the beginning shift into managed care might have affected that patient in terms of his or her specific diagnosis.

3. Why was it so important to develop a basis for standardization of treatment guidelines? Do you think that this shift was primarily positive or negative? Why? How would this change have affected your fictional patient from the previous question?

4. Contrast a health care system focused on disease with a health system focused on health and prevention by listing positives and negative aspects for each. Which type of system do you think has the potential to be more cost-effective? Which has the potential to be more treatment-effective? Why?

5. How do patient beliefs and experiences affect treatment compliance, and how do these repercussions in turn affect the nature of the health care system? How can these issues be addressed? For example, would it be more effective to address poor medication compliance on a personal or societal level? In your opinion, whose responsibility is it to improve patient compliance rates? Why?

BIBLIOGRAPHY

Able-Boone, H., Goodwin, L. D., Sandall, S. R., Gordon, N., & Martin, D. G. (1992). Consumer based early intervention services. *Journal of Early Intervention, 16,* 201–209.

Adkins, G., Wong, M., Cunneff, T., Dagostino, M., Fowler, J., Green, M., Hazlett, C., Laudadio, M., Mandel, K., Mendel, S., Nussbaum, G., Perry, S., Roberts, R., Rodriguez, B., Rosza, L., Wihlborg, U., Wren, J. (November 22, 2004). Dr. Phil & Jay McGraw. *People,* 62 (21): 26.

Adler, N. J,. (1997). *International dimensions of organizational behavior,* 3rd ed. Cincinnati, OH; South-Western College Publishing.

Agazarian, Y., & Gantt, S. (2003). Phases of group development: Systems-centered hypotheses and their implications for research and practice. *Group Dynamics: Theory, Research & Practice, 7,* 238–252.

Albee, G. W. (1990). The futility of psychotherapy. *Journal of Mind and Behavior, 11,* (3–4), 369–384.

Albee, G. W. (1996). Revolutions and counterrevolutions in prevention. *American Psychologist, 51,* 1130–1133.

Albee, G. W. (1998). Fifty years of clinical psychology: Selling our souls to the devil. *Applied and Preventive Psychology, 7,* 189–194.

Albee, G. W. (2000). The Boulder model's fatal flaw. *American Psychologist, 55,* 247–248.

Albee, G. W., & Ryan-Finn, K. D. (1993). An overview of primary prevention. *Journal of Counseling and Development, 72,* 115–123.

Alcalde, J., & Walsh-Bowers, R. (1996). Community psychology values and the culture of graduate training: A self study. *American Journal of Community Psychology, 24*(3), 389–411.

Alinsky, S. D. (1972). *Rules for radicals.* New York: Vintage Books.

Allen, G., Chinsky, J., Larcen, S., Lockman, J., & Selinger, H. (1976). *Community psychology and the schools.* Hillsdale, NJ: Erlbaum.

Almanza, H., & Mosley, W. (1980). Curriculum adaptations and modifications for culturally diverse handicapped children. *Exceptional Children, 46,* 608–614.

Altman, I., & Rogoff, B. (1987). World views in psychology: Trait, organismic, and transactional perspectives. In D. Stokols & I. Altman (Eds.). *Handbook of environmental psychology* (pp. 7–40). New York: Wiley

American Psychiatric Association (1994*). Diagnostic and statistical manual for mental disorders* (4th ed.). Washington, D. C.: American Psychiatric Association Press.

American Psychological Association (2003). American Psychological Association applauds Senator Breaux for introducing the Positive Aging Act in the Senate: Press Release. Retrieved June 8, 2004, from (http://www.apa.org/releases/positiveaging.html.)

American Psychological Association (2004). Mental health care and older adults: Facts and policy recommendations. Retrieved May 25, 2004 from (http://www.apa.org/ppo/issues/oldermhfact03.html.)

Anderson, H., & Goolishian, H. A. (1992). The client is the expert: A not-knowing approach to therapy. In S. McNamee & K. J. Gergen (Eds.), *Therapy as social construction* (pp. 25–39). London: Sage & Publications.

Anderson, D., Whitmer R., Goetzel, R., Ozminkowski, R., Wasserman, and Serxner, S. (2000). The relationship between modifiable health risks and group-level health care expenditures. *American Journal of Health Promotion,* September/October, *15(1):*45–52. U.S. Government Printing Office.

Anderson, J. A., & Mohr, W. K. (2003). A developmental ecological perspective in systems of care for children with emotional disturbances and their families. *Education and Treatment of Children, 26,* 52–74.

Anderson, M. C. (1981). *Deinstitutionalized mentally retarded: A descriptive analysis of community residence settings for mentally retarded persons as it relates to the development of independent living skills.* Unpublished Ph.D. Dissertation, The Union Institute, Cleveland, Ohio.

Anthony, W.A. (1989). Psychiatric rehabilitation: achieving its promise. *Community Support Network News. 6* (10).

Anthony, W. A., Cohen, M. R., & Farkas, M. (1990). *Psychiatric Rehabilitation.* Boston: Center for Psychiatric Rehabilitation.

Anthony, W. A., Cohen, M. R., Farkas, M., & Gagne, C. V. (2002*). Psychiatric rehabilitation (second edition).* Boston, MA: Boston Univ. Center for Psychiatric Rehabilitation.

Antze, P. (1976). The role of ideologies in peer psychotherapy organizations: Some theoretical considerations and three case studies. *Journal of Applied Behavioral Science 12,* 323–346.

Appel, J. W. (1999, October). Fighting Fear. *American Heritage,* 22–30.

Aranda, M. P. (1990). Culture-friendly services for Latino elders. *Generations, 14*(1), 55–58.

Argyris, C. (1964). *Integrating the individual and the organization.* New York: Wiley.

Arias, E., and Smith, B. L. (2003). Deaths: Preliminary data for 2001. *National Vital Statistics Reports, 51(5).*

Arns, P. G., & Linney, J. A. (1993). Work, self, and life satisfaction for persons with severe and persistent mental disorders. *Psychosocial Rehabilitation Journal, 17,* 63–79.

Ajzen, I. (1985). From intentions to actions: A theory of planned behavior. In J. Kuhl & J. Beckmann (Eds.), *Action-control: From cognition to behavior* (pp. 11–39). Heidelberg: Springer.

Austen, K., & Butsford, A. (2000, March 18) *Assessing the needs and services of older people of Dutchess County: A study for the Dutchess County Office for the Aging.* Unpublished report. Poughkeepsie, NY: Marist College.

Avison, W. R., & Turner, R. J. (1992). Innovations in the measurement of life stress: Crisis Theory and the significance of event resolution. *Journal of Health and Social Behavior. 33 (1),* 36–50.

Babbie, E. (1990). *Survey research methods.* New York: Wadsworth.

Babinski, L. M., Rogers, D. L. (1998). Supporting new teachers through consultee-centered group consultation. *Journal of Eucational and Psychological Consultation (9),* 23–27.

Bahn, A. K., & Norman, V. B., (1957). Outpatient psychiatric clinics in the United States. *Public health Monograph* No. 49. Washington, D.C. 40.

Balk, D. E. (1996). Models for understanding adolescent coping with bereavement. *Death Studies, 20 (4),* 367–387.

Baltes, P. B., & Baltes, M. M. (1990). *Successful aging: Perspectives from the behavioral sciences.* New York: Cambridge University Press.

Barker, R. G. (1964). *Ecological psychology: Concepts and methods for studying the environment of human behavior.* Stanford, CA.: Stanford University Press.

Barker, R. G. (1968). *Ecological psychology.* Stanford, CA: Stanford University Press.

Barker, R. G., & Gump, P. V. (1964). *Big school, small school.* Stanford, CA.: Stanford University Press.

Baron, R. A. & Byrne, D. (1987). *Social psychology: Understanding human interaction.* (5th Ed.). Boston: Allyn and Bacon, Inc.

Beck, A. T., Rush, A. J., & Shaw, B. F. (1979). *Cognitive therapy of depression.* New York: Guilford.

Beers, C. W. (1960). *A mind that found itself.* Garden City, NY. Originally published in 1908.

Benes, K. M., Walsh, J. M., McMinn, M. R., Dominguez, A. W., & Aikins, D. C. (2000). Psychology and the church: An exemplar of psychologist—clergy collaboration. *Professional Psychology: Research and Practice, 31*, 515–520.

Bennett, C. (1989). Teaching students as they would be taught. In B. Shade (Ed.), *Culture, style, and the educative process* (pp. 71–86). Springfield, IL: Charles C. Thomas.

Bennis, W. G. (1966). *Changing organizations.* New York: McGraw Hill.

Berens, M. J. (1998) *Mentally ill vanish: A Windfall Appears. Chicago Tribune.* Sept. 28.

Ben-Zur, H., Duvdevany, I., Lury, L. (2005). Association of social support and hardiness with mental health aging among mothers of adult children with intellectual disability. *Journal of Intellectual Disability Research, 49 (1)*, 54–63.

Berman, A. L., & Jobes, D. A. (1995). Suicide prevention in adolescents. *Suicide and Life Threatening Behavior, 25*, 143–154.

Bernstein, B. L., Forrest, L., & Golston, S. S. (1994). Current practices of counseling psychology faculty in K-12 schools: A national survey. *Counseling Psychologist, 22*, 611–627.

Berreuta-Clement, J. R., Schweinhart, L. J., Barnett, M. W., Epstein, A. S., & Weikart, D. P. (1984). *Changed lives: The effects of the Perry preschool program on youth through age 19.* Ypsilanti, MI: High/Scope Educational Research Foundation.

Berscheid, E. (2003). Lessons in "greatness" from Kurt Lewin's life and works. In R. J. Sternberg (Ed.), *The anatomy of impact: What makes the great works of psychology great.* Washington, D.C.: American Psychological Association.

Bertalannffy, L. von (1968). *General systems theory.* (Rev. ed.). New York: George Braziller.

Beyene, Y. (1992) Medical disclosure and refugees: Telling bad news to Ethiopian patients. *Western Journal of Medicine, 157*(3), 328–332.

Bisconer, S. W., & Longo, D. A. (2003). Treatment of aggression of an adult diagnosed with schizophrenia at a public psychiatric hospital. *Professional Psychology: Research and Practice. 34* (2), 177–179.

Bitter, J. R., & Nicoll, W. G. (2000). Adlerian brief therapy with individuals: Process and practice. *Journal of Individual Psychology. 56* (1), 31–44.

Blair, C., Ramey, C. T., & Hardin, J. M. (1995). Early intervention for low birthweight, premature infants: Participation and intellectual development. *American Journal on Mental Retardation, 99*, 542–554.

Blatt, S. J., Pilkonis, P. A., Quinlan, D. M., & Zuroff, D. C. (1996). Interpersonal factors in brief treatment of depression: Further analyses of the National Institute of Mental Health Treatment of Depression Collaborative Research Program. *Journal of Consulting and Clinical Psychology. 64* (1), 162–171.

Blatter, C. W., & Jacobson, J. J. (1993). Older women coping with divorce: Peer support groups. *Women and Therapy, 14*, 145–155.

Bloom, B. L. (1984). *Community mental health: A general introduction* (2nd ed.). Monterey: Brooks/Cole.

Bonanno, G. A., Wortman, C. B., & Nesse, R. M. (2004). Prospective patterns of resilience and maladjustment during widowhood. *Psychology and Aging, 19:* 260–271.

Bonanno, G. A., Wortman, C. B., Lehman, D. R., Tweed, R. G., Haring, M., Sonnega, J., Carr, D., Nesse, R. M. (2002). Resilience to loss and chronic grief: A prospective study from preloss to 18-months postloss. *Journal of Personality and Social Psychology, 83* (5), 1150–1164.

Bond, Galinsky, & Swanberg (Families and Work Institute), 1998. The 1997 National Study of the Changing Workforce.

Bond, G. R., Drake, R. E., & Mueser, K. T. (1997). An update on supported employment for people with severe mental illness. *Psychiatric Services, 48:* 335–346.

Borduin, C. M., Mann, B. J., Cone, L. T., Henggeler, S. W., Fucci, B. R., Blaske, D. M., & Williams, R. A. (1995). Multisystemic treatment of serious juvenile offenders: Long-term prevention of criminality and violence. *Journal of Consulting and Clinical Psychology, 63*, 569–578.

Boss, R. W. (1983). Team building and the problem of regression: The Personal Management Interview as an intervention. *The Journal of Applied Behavioral Science, 19*, 67–83.

Bradley, R. H., Whiteside, L. Mundfrom, D. J., Casey, P. H., Caldwell, B. M., & Barrett, K. (1994). Impact of the Infant Health and Development Program (IHDP) on the home environments of infants born prematurely and with low birthweight. *Journal of Educational Psychology, 86*, 531–541.

Breckenridge, M. B. An exploration of the factors that influence leadership effectiveness in a corporate environment. *Dissertation Abstracts International Section A: Humanities & the Social Scences, 61 (5–A)*, 1720.

Breggin, P. R. (1991). *Toxic psychiatry*. New York: St. Martin Press.

Breslin, C., Sdao-Jarvie, K., Li, S., Tupker, E., & Ittig-Deland, V. (2002). Brief treatment for young substance abusers: A pilot study in an addiction treatment setting. *Psychology of Addictive Behaviors, 16* (1), 10–16.

Broadhead, R. S., Heckathorn, D. D., Grund, J. P. C., Stern, L. S., & Anthony, D. L. (1995). Drug users versus outreach workers in combating AIDS: Preliminary results of a peer-driven intervention. *The Journal of Drug Issue, 25*, 531–564.

Bronfenbrenner, U. (1979). *The ecology of human development: Experiments by nature and design*. Cambridge, MA: Harvard University Press.

Bronfenbrenner, U., & Ceci, S. J. (1994). Nature-nurture reconconceptualized in developmental perspective: A bioecological approach. *Psychological Review, 101*, 568–586.

Bronfenbrenner, U., & Evans, G. W. (2000). Developmental science in the 21st century: Emerging questions, theoretical models, research designs and empirical findings. *Social Development, 9*, 115–125.

Brooks, A. D. (1977) *Hospitalization of the Mentally Ill: The Legislative Role*. State Government 50. Boston, MA.

Burke, W. W. (2002). *Organization change; Theory and practice*. Thousand Oaks, CA: Sage.

Burke, W. W., & Litwin, G. H. (1992). A causal model of organizational performance and change. *Journal of Management, 18* (3), 532–545.

Butterfield, T. M., Ramseur, J. H. (2004). Research and case study findings in the area of workplace accommodations including provisions for assistive technology: A literature review. *Technology & Disability, 16*(4) 201–211.

Butzlaff, R. L. & Hooley, J. M. (1998). Expressed emotion and psychiatric relapse. *Archives of General Psychiatry 55*: 547–552.

Campbell, D. T., & Stanley, J. C. (1963). Experimental and quasi-experimental design for research on teaching. In N. L. Sage (Ed.), *Handbook of research on teaching*. Chicago: Rand Mc Nally.

Campinha-Bacote, J. (1994). Cultural competence in psychiatric mental health nursing: A conceptual model. *Nursing Clinics of North America, 29*(1), 1–8.

Caplan, G. (1964). *Principles of preventive psychiatry*. New York: Basic Books.

Caplan, G. (1970). *The theory and practice of mental health consultation*. New York: Basic Books.

Caplan, G. (1976). The family as a support system. In G. Caplan & M. Killea (Eds.), *Support systems and mutual help: Multidisciplinary explanations*. New York: Grune & Stratton.

Caplan, R. D., & Van Harrison, R. (1993). Person-environment fit theory: Some history, recent developments, and future directions. *Journal of Social Issues, 49*(4), 253–275.

Capuzzi, D., & Gross, D. R. (1995). *Counseling and psychotherapy: Theories and interventions.* Englewood Cliffs, NJ: Merrill.

Capuzzi, D., & Gross, D. R. (1996). *Youth at risk: A prevention resource for counselors, teachers, and Parents.* (2nd Ed.). Alexandria, VA: American Counseling Association.

Carlson, C. R., & Hoyle, R. H. (1993). Efficacy of abbreviated progressive muscle relaxation training: A quantitative review of behavioral medicine research. *Journal of Consulting and Clinical Psychology, 61*(6), 1059–1067.

Carlson, L., Sherwin, B., & Chertkow. (2000). Relationship between mood and estradiol (E2) levels in Alzheimer's disease (AD) patients. *The Journals of Gerontology: Psychological Sciences, 55B,* 47–53.

Carpinello, S., Knight, E., & Jatulis, L. (1992). A study of the meaning of self help, group processes, and outcomes. National Association of State Mental Health Program Directors, proceedings of the 3rd Annual National Conference of State Mental Health Agency.

Carpinello, S., Rosenberg, L., Stone, J., Schwager, M., & Felton, C. J., (2002). New York State's campaign to implement evidenced based practices for people with serious mental disorders. *Psychiatric Services, 53,* 153–155.

Carroll, W. (1993, June 18). The disabled succeed in local jobs. *Poughkeepsie Journal* (N. Y.), p. 12A.

Castenell, L., & Castenell, M. (1988). Norm-referenced testing and low-income blacks. *Journal of Counseling and Development, 67,* 205–206.

Castera, M. S., & Lund, D. A. (1996). Beyond bereavement support group meetings: Exploring outside social contacts among the members. *Death Studies, 20*(6), 537–556.

Catalano, R. F., Berglund, M. L., Ryan, J. A. M., Lóczak, H. S., & Hawkins, J. D. (2002). Positive youth development in the United States: Research findings on evaluations of positive youth development programs. *Prevention & Treatment, 5* (Article 15), 1–111.

Catalano, R. F., Haggerty, K. P., Oesterle, S., Fleming, C. B., Hawkins, J. D. (2004). The importance of bonding to school for healthy development: Findings from the Social Development Research Group. *Journal of School Health, 74*(7) 252–261.

Catalano, R. F., & Hawkins, J. D. (1992). *Communities that care.* San Francisco: Jossey-Bass.

Ceci, S. J., (2000). The contributions of Urie Bronfenbrenner. In A. Kazdin (Ed.), *Encyclopedia of psychology.* Washington, D.C.: APA Books.

Cepani, A., Riolli, L., & Savicki, V. (2002). Resilance in the face of catastrophe: Optimism, personality and coping in the Kosovo crisis. *Journal of Applied Social Psychology. 32* (8), 1604–1627.

Chadwick, P., Birchwood, M., & Trower, P. (1996). *Cognitive therapy for delusions, voices and paranoia.* West Sussex, England: Wiley & Sons.

Chamberlain, J., & Rogers, S. (1996). Self-Help Programs: A description of their characteristics and their numbers. *Psychiatric Rehabilitation Journal 19* (i) 3–33.

Chamberlain, J., Rogers, E. S., & Ellison, M. L. (1996). Self help programs: A description of their characteristics and their members. *Psychiatric Rehabilitation Journal, 19,* 33–42.

Chartrand, J. M. (1990). A causal analysis to predict the personal and academic adjustment of non-traditional students. *Journal of Counseling Psychology, 37,* 65–73.

Chavis, D. M. (2001). The Paradoxes and promises of Community Coalitions. *American Journal of Community Psychology, (29),* 135–143.

Checkland, P. (1997). Systems. In M. Warner (Ed.). *International encyclopedia of business and management,* 667–673. London: Thompson Business Press.

Cheng, A. (2001). Expressed emotion: A cross culturally valid concept? *British Journal of Psychiatry, 181:* 466–467.

Cherniss, C., Herzog, E. (1996). Impact of home-based family therapy on maternal and child outcomes in disadvantaged adolescent mothers. *Family Relations, 45* (1), 72–80.

Christensen, A., & Jacobson, N. (1994). Who or what can do psychotherapy: The status and challenge of nonprofessional therapies. *Psychological Science, 5*, 8–14.

Christensen, A. J., Raichle, K., Ehlers, S., L. & Bertolatus, J. A. (2002). Effect of family environment and donor source on patient quality of life following renal transplantation. *Health Psychology, 21*, 468–476.

Chu, F. & Trotter, S. (1974). *The madness experiment: Ralph Nadar's study group report on the Institute of Mental Health.* New York: Grossman Publishers.

Chung, T., Labouvie, E., Langenbucher, J., Moos, R. H., & Pandina, R. J. (2001). Changes in alcoholic patients coping responses predict 12-month treatment outcomes. *Journal of Consulting and Clinical Psychology, 69* (1), 92–100.

Cicirelli, V. G. (1969). *The impact of head start: An evaluation of the effects of head start on children's cognitive and affective development.* Washington, DC: National Bureau of Standard, Institute for Applied Technology.

Cnann, R. A., Blankertz, L., Messinger, K., & Gardner, J. R. (1989) Psychosocial rehabilitation: Towards a theoretical base. *Psychosocial Rehabilitation Journal, 1.3* (l0), 33–55.

Cohen, S., & Willis, T. A. (1985). Stress, social support and the buffering hypothesis. *Psychological Bulletin, 98*, 310–357.

Coleman, J. S., Campbell, E. Q., Hobson, C. J., Mc Partland, J., Mood, A. M., Weinfield, F. D., & York, R. L. (1966). *Equality of educational opportunity.* (U. S. Department of Health, Education and Welfare, Office of Education). Washington, DC: U. S. Government Printing Office.

Cook, D. D., McNally, K. T., Mulligan, M. J., Harrison, J. G., & Newman, S. P. (2001). Psychosocial interventions for caregivers of people with dementia: A systematic review. *Aging and Mental Health, 5* (2), 120–135.

Corcoran, J., Franklin, C., & Bennett, P. (2000). Ecological factors associated with adolescent pregnancy and parenting. *Social Work Research, 24*, 29–40.

Covey, S. R. (1989). *The seven habits of highly effective people: Restoring the character ethic.* New York: Simon and Schuster.

Covey, S. R. (1991). *Principle-centered leadership.* New York: Summit Books.

Cowen, E. L. (1977). Baby-steps toward primary prevention. *American Journal of Community Psychology, 5*, 1–22.

Cowen, E. L. (1980). The wooing of primary prevention. *American Journal of Community Psychology, 8*, 258–284.

Cowen, E. L. (1996). The ontogenesis of primary prevention: Lengthy strides and stubbed toes. *American Journal of Community Psychology, 24*, 235–249.

Cowen, E., Hightower, A., Pedro-Carroll, J., & Work, W. (1989). School based models for primary prevention programming with children. *Prevention in Human Services, 7*, 133–160.

Coyne, J. C. (1976) Depression and the response of others. *Journal of Abnormal Psychology, 85*, 186–193.

Craske, M. G., Gatz, M., & Wetherell, J. L. (2003). Treatment of generalized disorder in older adults. *Journal of Consulting and Clinical Psychology, 71* (1), 31–40.

Crispi, E. L., & Heitner, G. (2002). An activity-based intervention for family caregivers and residents with dementia in nursing homes. *Activities, Adaptation, and Aging, 26*(4), 61–72.

Crispi, E. L., & Rokeach, M. (2003). The buddy program: A mentoring team approach to improve quality of life of dementia residents in nursing homes. *Activities Directors' Quarterly for Alzheimer's & Other Dementia Patients, 4*(4), 27–36.

Crispi, E. L., Schiaffino, K., & Berman, W. H. (1997). The contribution of attachment to burden in adult children of institutionalized parents with dementia. *The Gerontologist, 37*, 52–60.

Crispi, E. L., Vangel, P., & Wetter, S. (2003, March). Community needs assessment for a college gerontology program. Poster presented at the conference "Teaching and Learning of Psychology: Ideas and Innovations," SUNY Farmingdale, Ellenville, NY.

Crockenberg, S. B. (1988). Stress and role satisfaction experienced by employed and nonemployed mothers with young children. *Lifestyles. Special issue: Socioeconomic stress in rural families, 9*(2), 97–110.

Crockenberg, S. C., Leerkes, E. M. (2004). Infant and maternal behaviors regulate infant reactivity to novelty at 6 months. *Developmental Psychology, 40* (6), 1123–1132.

Cruser, D. A. (Jan. 1995). Evaluating program design in the hospital setting. *Journal of Mental Health Administrations, 22,* 49–57.

Cuipers, P. (2002). Peer-led and adult-led school drug prevention: A meta-analytic comparison. *Journal of Drug Education, 32,* 107–119.

Cuipers, P. (2003). Examining the effects of prevention program on the incidence of new cases of mental disorders: The lack of statistical power. *American Journal of Psychiatry, 160,* 1385–1391.

Cumming, J., & Cumming, E. (1957). *Closed ranks.* Cambridge: Harvard University Press.

Cunningham, D. A. (2002). Application of Roy's adaptation model when caring for a group of women coping with menopause. *Journal of Community Health Nursing, 19*(1), 49–60.

Curwin, R. L. & Mendler, A. N. (2002). Preventing violence with values-based schools. *Journal of Emotional & Behavioral Problems, 9,* 41–44.

Cusack, S. A., Thompson, W. J. A., & Rogers, M. E. (2003). Mental fitness for life: Assessing the impact of an 8-week mental fitness program on healthy aging. *Educational Gerontology, 29,* 393–403.

Darlington, R. B., Royce, J. M., Snipper, A. S., Murray, H. W., & Lazar, I. (1980). Preschool programs and later school competence of children from low income families. *Science, 208,* 202–204.

Davidovitz, D., & Levenson, H. (2000). Brief therapy prevalence and training: A national Survey of psychologists. *Psychotherapy, 37* (4), 335–340.

Davidson, L., Shanhar, G., Stayner, D. A. (2004). Supported socialization for people with psychiatric disabilities: Lessons from a randomized controlled trial. *Journal of Community Psychology, 32* (4), 453–477.

Davis, M., Eshelman, E. R., & McKay, M. (1988). *The relaxation and stress reduction workbook* (3rd ed). Oakland, CA: New Harbinger Publications.

Davis, M., & Gidycz, C. A. (2000). Child sexual abuse programs: A meta-analysis. *Journal of Clinical Child Psychology, 29,* 257–265.

Deegan, P. (1992). The independent living movement and people with psychiatric disabilities: Taking back control of our lives. *Psychosocial Rehabilitation Journal, 15* (3), 3–19.

De La Sierra, M. D. (2001). Parent and child perceptions of the family-school relationship in a Hispanic population. *Dissertation Abstracts International: Section B: The Sciences and Engineering, 62* (5–B), 2533.

Deming, W. E. (1986). *Out of the crisis.* Cambridge: MIT Center for Advanced Engineering Study.

Denzin, N. K., & Lincoln, Y. S. (Eds.), (2000). *Handbook of qualitative research* (2nd ed.). Thousand Oaks, CA: Sage.

Deutsch, A. (1948). *The Shame of the states.* New York: Harcourt Brace.

Deutsch, A. (1949). *The mentally ill in America: A history of their care and treatment from colonial times.* New York: Columbia University Press.

Dittman, M. (2003). Geropsychologists are badly needed. *Monitor on Psychology, 34*(5)51.

Dohrenwend, B. S. (1978). Social stress and community psychology. *American Journal of Community Psychology, 6,* 1–14.

Dohrenwend, B. P., Neria, Y., Turner, J. B., Turse, N., Marshall, R., Lewis-Fernandez, R., Koene, K. C. (2004). Positive tertiary appraisals and post-traumatic stress disorder in U.S. male veterans of the war of Vietnam: The roles of positive affirmation positive reformulation and defensive denial. *Journal of Consulting and Clinical Psychology, 72* (3), 417–433.

Drake, R. E., Mercer-McFadden, & Mueser, K. T. (1998). Review of integrated mental health and substance abuse treatment for patients with dual disorders. *Schizophrenia Bulletin, 24:* 589–608.

Drewnowski, A., Monsen, E., Birkett, D., Gunther, S., Vendeland, S., Su, J., and Marshall, G. (2003). Health screening and health promotion programs for the elderly. *Dis Manage Health Outcomes 2003,* 11*(5),* 299–309.

Drisko, J. W. (1993). Special education teacher consultation: A student-focused, skill defining approach. *Social Work in Education, 15,* 19–28.

Durlak, J. A., & Wells, A. M. (1997). Primary prevention mental health programs for children and adolescents: A meta-analytic review. *American Journal of Community Psychology, 25*(2), 115–152.

Durlak, J. A., & Wells, A. M. (1997). Primary prevention mental health programs: The future is exciting. *American Journal of Community Psychology, 25*(2), 233–243.

Dyer, W. G. (1977). *Team building: Issues and alternatives.* Reading, MA: Arbor House.

Dyregrov, K. (2004). Micro-sociological analysis of social support following traumatic bereavement: Unhelpful and avoidant responses from the community. *Omega: Journal of Death and Dying, 48*(1) 23–45.

Eamon, M. K. (2001). The effects of poverty on children's socioeconomic development: An ecological systems analysis. *Social Work, 46,* 256–267.

Early, B. P. (1992). An ecological-exchange model of social work consultation within the work group of the school. *Social Work in Education, 14,* 207–214.

Eccles, J. S., Feldlaufer, H., MacIven, D., Midgley, C., Reuman, D., & Wigfield, A. (1993). Negative effects of traditional middle schools on students' motivation. *The Elementary School Journal, 93*(5), 553–571.

Eddy, J. M., Reid, J. B., & Fetrow, R. A. (2000). An elementary school-based prevention program targeting modifiable antecedents of youth delinquency and violence: Linking the interests of familes and teachers (LIFT). *Journal of Emotional & Behavioral Disorders, 8,* 165–177.

Elias, M., Gara, M., Schuyler, T., Branden-Muller, L., & Sayette, M. (1991). The promotion of social competence: Longitudinal study of a preventive school-based program. *American Journal of Orthopsychiatry, 61,* 409–417.

Ellis, A. (1969). *The essence of rational psychotherapy: A comprehensive approach to treatment.* New York: Institute for Rational Living.

Ellis, A (1975) *A new guide to rational living.* North Hollywood, CA: Wilshire Book Co.

Ellis, A. (1979). Rational-emotive therapy. In R. J. Corsini (Ed.), *Current psychotherapies* (pp. 197–237). Itasca, Ill.: Peacock.

Ellis, A. (1989). *Why some therapies don't work: The dangers of transpersonal psychology.* Amherst, NY: Prometheus.

Ellis, A. (1999). *How to make yourself happy and remarkably less disturbable.* North Fairfield, IA: Impact Publishers.

Ellis, A. (2003). Similarities and differences between rational emotive behavior therapy and cognitive therapy. *Journal of Cognitive Psychotherapy, 17*(3), 225–240.

Ennett, S. T., Ringwalt, C. L., Thorne, J., Rohrbach, L. A., Vincus, A., Simons-Rudolph, A., & Jones, S. (2003). A comparison of current practice in school-based substance use prevention programs with meta-analysis findings. *Prevention Science, 4,* 1–14.

Ennett, S. T., Tobler, N. S., Ringwalt, C. L, Flewelling, R. L. (1994). How effective is drug abuse resistance education? A meta-analysis of Project DARE outcome evaluations. *American Journal of Public Health, 84,* 1394–1401.

Erikson, E. H. (1950). *Childhood and society.* New York: Norton.

Erikson, E. H. (1980). *Identity and the life cycle.* New York: Norton.

Espiritu, Y. (1995). *Filipino American lives.* Philadelphia: Temple University Press.

Evanikoff, L. J. (1996). Russians. In Lipson, G. J., Dibble, S. L., Minarik, P.A. *Culture and nursing care: A pocket Guide.* San Francisco, CA: UCFS Nursing Press.

Fairweather, G. W. (Ed.) (1980). The Fairweather lodge society: A twenty-five year retrospective. *New directions for mental health service: A quarterly sourcebook.* San Francisco: Jossey-Bass.

Fairweather, G. W., & Davidson, W. S. (1986). *An introduction to community experimentation.* New York: McGraw Hill.

Fairweather, G. W., Sanders, D. H., Maynard, H., & Cressler, D. L. (1969). *Community life for the mentally ill.* Chicago: Aldine.

Federal Bureau of Investigation. (2000). *Crime in the United States.* Annual. Washington, D.C.: U.S. Department of Justice. (http://www.fbi.gov/ucr/ucr.htm.)

Federal Bureau of Investigation (2004) www.fbi.gov/ucr/cius-04

Fellin, P. A., & Powell, T. J. (1988). Mental health services and older adult minorities: An assessment. *Gerontologist, 28*(4), 442–447.

Fetterman, D. M., Kaftarian, S. J., & Wandersman, A. (Eds.). (1996). *Empowerment evaluation: Knowledge and tools for self assessment and accountability.* Thousand Oaks, CA: Sage Publications Inc.

Fetto, J. (2002) What seems to be the problem? Americans more accepting of psychotherapy after Sept. 11. *American Demographics,* April 1, 2002.

Fiedler, F. E. (1964). A contingency model of leadership effectiveness. In L. Berkowitz (Ed.). *Advances in experimental social psychology,* Vol. 1. NY: Academic Press.

Fiedler, F. E. (1967). *A theory of leadership effectiveness.* New York: McGraw Hill.

Fiedler, F. E. (1996). Research on leadership selection and training: One view of the future. *Administrative Science Quarterly, 41,* 241–250.

Fiedler, F. E. (2002). Proactive ways to improve leadership performance. In R. L. Lowman (Ed.), *Handbook of organizational consulting psychology: A comprehensive guide to theory, skills and technique.* San Francisco, CA: Jossey-Bass.

Fisher, D. B. (1994). Health care reform based on an empowerment model of recovery by people with psychiatric disabilities. *Hospital and Community Psychiatry, 45:*9, 913–915.

Fitz-Gibbon & Morris. (1987). How to design a program evaluation.

Flemming, A. S., Buchanan, J. G., Santos, J. F., & Rickards, L. D. (1984). Mental health services for the elderly: Report on a survey of community mental health centers. *Action committee to implement the mental health recommendations of the 1981 White House conference on aging. Vol. III.* Washington, DC: American Psychological Association.

Floyd, F. J., Haynes, S. N., Doll, E. R., Winemiller, D., Lemsky, C., Burgy, T. M., Werle, M., & Heilman, N. (1992). Assessing retirement satisfaction and perception of retirement experiences. *Psychology and Aging, 7*(4), 609–621.

Foa, E. B., & Emmelkamp, P. M. G. (1983). *Failures in behavior therapy.* New York: Wiley.

Foley, H. A. & Sharfstein, S. S. (1983). *Madness and the government.* Washington, DC: American Psychiatric Press.

Foos, P. W., & Clark, M. C. (2003). *Human aging.* Boston: Allyn & Bacon.

Fredrickson, B. L. (2001). The role of positive emotions in positive psychology: The broaden-and-build theory of positive emotions. *American Psychologist, 56:* 218–226.

Fredrickson, B. L., Larkin, G. R., Tugade, M. M., & Waugh, C. E. (2003).What good are positive emotions in crises? A prospective study of resilience and emotions following the terrorist attacks on the United States on September 11, 2001. *The Journal of Personality and Social Psychology, 84* (2), 365–376.

Freiman, M. P., Arons, B. S., Goldman, H. H., & Burns, B. J. (1990). Nursing home reform and the mentally ill. *Health Affairs, 9,* 47–60.

Freud, A. (1966). *The ego and the mechanisms of defense* (Rev. ed). New York: International Universities Press.

Freund, P. D. (1993). Professional roles in the empowerment process: "Working With" mental health consumers. *Psychosocial Rehabilitation Journal, 16*(3): 65–74.

Fuchs, D., Fuchs, L. S., Dulan, J., & Roberts, H. (1992). Where is the research on consultation effectiveness? *Journal of Educational and Psychological Consultation, 3,* 151–174.

Furlong, M., McCoy, M. L., Dincin, J., Clay, R., McClory, K., & Pavick, D. (2002). Jobs for people with the most severe psychiatric disorders: Thresholds Bridge North Pilot. *Psychiatric Rehabilitation Journal, 26,* 13–22.

Gatz, M. & Smyer, M. A. (1992). The mental health system and older: Adults in the 1990s. *American Psychologist, 47*(6), 741–751.

Gavin, D. (2003, March). *Business health agenda 2003: running out of time: What employers can do now to control costs and improve quality.* Business Health Agenda 2003, Washington, DC.

Geller, J. L. (2000). The last half century of psychiatric services as reflected in Psychiatric Services. *Psychiatric Services, 51*:41–67.

George, L. K. (1994). Caregiver burden and well-being: An elusive distinction. *The Gerontologist, 34,* 6–7.

George, L. K., & Gwyther, L. P. (1986). Caregiver well-being: A multidimensional examination of family caregivers of demented adults. *The Gerontologist, 26,* 253–259.

Gergin, K. J. (1973). Social psychology as history. *Journal of Personality and Social Psychology, 26,* 309–320.

Giarrusso, R., Silverstein, M., & Bengston, V. L. (1996). Family complexity and the grandparent role. *Generations, 20,* 17–23.

Gibbs, M. S., Lachenmeyer, J. R., & Sigal, J. (1992). *Community psychology and mental health.* New York: Gardner Press.

Gibson, B., & Werner, C. (1994). Airport waiting areas as behavioral settings: The role of legibility cues in communicating the setting program.. *Journal of Personality and Social Psychology, 66,* 1049–1060.

Gibson, G., & Chard, K. M. (1994). Quantifying the effects of community mental health consultation interventions. *Consulting Psychology Journal Practice and Research, 46,* 13–25.

Gifford, R., & Hine, D. W. (1997). I'm cooperative but you're greedy: Some cognitive tendencies in a commons dilemma. *Canadian Journal of Behavioral Science, 29,* 257–265.

Gillick, J. (1977). *Al-Anon: A self help group for co-alcoholics.* Unpublished doctoral dissertation, Department of Psychology, SUNY at Buffalo.

Gingerich, W. J., & Eisengart, S. (2000). Solution-focused brief therapy: A review of the outcome research. *Family Processes, 39* (4), 477–498.

Gladwell, M. (2000). *The tipping point: How little things can make a big difference.* Boston: Little Brown.

Glatzer, R. (1999). Longevity from America's healthiest state. *American Health,* 72–78.

Glittenberg, J. (1994). *To the mountain and back: The mysteries of Guatemalan highland family life.* Prospect Hights, IL: Waveland Press.

Golan, N. (1978). *Treatment in crisis situations.* New York: The Free Press.

Gold, S. (1992) Mental health and illness in Vietnamese refugees, *Western Journal of Medicine, 157,* 290–294.

Goldberg, D., & Huxley, P. (1980). *Mental illness in the community: The pathway to psychiatric care.* London: Tavistock.

Goodman, L. A., Johnson, M., Dutton, M. A., & Harris, M. (1997). Prevalence and impact of sexual and physical abuse. In M. Harris & C. L. Landis (Eds.), *Sexual abuse in the lives of women diagnosed with serious mental illness* (pp. 277–299). The Netherlands: Harwood Academic Publishers.

Goodwin, C. J. (1999). *A history of modern psychology.* New York: John Wiley & Sons, Inc.

Graham, T. L. (1993). Beyond direction: Education and the abused student. *Social Work in Education, 15,* 197–207.

Gray, A. J. (2001). Attitudes of the public to mental health: A church congregation. *Mental Health, Religion & Culture, 4,* 71–79.

Grob, G. N. (1994). *The Mad Among Us.* New York: Free Press.

Groth-Marnat, G., & Schumaker, J. (1995). Psychologists in disease prevention and health promotion. *Psychology, A Journal of Human Behavior, 32,* 1–10.

Group for the Advancement of Psychiatry. Circular newsletter No. 12 *Archives of psychiatry,* Nov. 20, 1946.

Grzywacz, J. G., & Marks, N. F. (2000). Reconceptualizing the work—family interface: An ecological perspective on the correlates of positive and negative spillover between work and family. *Journal of Occupational Health Psychology, 5,* 111–126.

Gullotta, T. P., & Bloom, M. (Eds.). (2003). *The encyclopedia of primary prevention and health promotion.* New York: Kluwer/Academic.

Gutkin, T. B. (1981). Relative frequency of consultee lack of knowledge, skills, confidence and objectivity in school settings. *Journal of School Psychology, 19,* 57–59.

Guydish, J., Bucardo, J., Clark, G., & Bernheim, S. (1998). Evaluating needle exchange: A description of client characteristics, health status, program utilization and HIV risk behavior. *Substance Use and Abuse, 33,* 1173–1196.

Haggard, E. A. (1954). Social status of intelligence. *Genetic Psychology Monographs, 49,* 141–186.

Hall, E. T. (1977). *Beyond culture.* Garden City: Ancho Press/Doubleday.

Hall, E. T. (1990). *Understanding cultural differences.* Yarmouth, ME: Intercultural Press.

Hamel, G., & Prahalad, C. K. (1994). *Competing for the future.* Boston: Harvard Business School Press.

Hankin, J. R. (2002). Fetal alcohol syndrome prevention research. *Alcohol Research and Health, 26,* 58–65.

Harman, J., & Reynolds, C. (2000). Removing the barriers to effective depression treatment in old age. *Journal of the American Geriatrics Society, 48:* 1012–1013.

Harrison, M., Loiselle, C. G., Duquette, A., Semenic, S. E. (2002). Hardiness, work support and psychological distress among nursing assistants and registered nurses in Quebec. *Journal of Advanced Nursing, 38* (6), 584–592.

Hatfield, A. B. (1999). Barriers to serving older adults with a psychiatric disability. *Psychiatric Rehabilitation Journal, 22,* 270–276.

Hawkins, J. D., Catalano, R. F., Kosterman, R., Abbott, R., & Hill, K. G. (1999). Preventing adolescent health risk behaviors by strengthening protection during childhood. *Archives of Pediatric Adolescent Medicine, 153,* 226–234.

Health Enhancement Research Organization. (2000). Study conducted by The Medstat Group. *American Journal of Health Promotion, 15:1,* 35–44.

Health Insurance Association of America (2001). Public opinion: Disability insurance. *Public Opinion Strategies, JHA Disability Fact Book,* 2001 Edition.

Hearn, G. (1969). *The general system approach: Contributions toward a holistic conception of social work.* New York: Council on Social Work Education.

Height, D. (1989). Family and community: Self-help, a black tradition. *The Nation, July 24,* 136–138.

Heiny, R. W., Stachowiak, R. J., & Shriner, S. C. (1975). *Resident-environment analysis by level scale: Experimental edition*. Nashville, TN: John F. Kennedy Center for Research and Development on Education and Human Development.

Heller, K. (1996). Coming of age of prevention science: Comments on the 1994 National Institute of Mental Health–Institute of Medicine Prevention reports. *American Psychologist, 51*, 1123–1127.

Heller, K, Jenkins, R. A., Steffen, A. M., & Swindle, R. W. (2000). Prospects for a viable community mental health system: Reconciling ideology, professional traditions, and political reality. In Rappaport, J., & Seidman, E. (Eds.), *Handbook of community psychology*. New York: Plenum.

Hellstrom, K., Lindwall, R., Ost, L-G., & Svensson, L. (2001). One-session treatment of specific phobias in youths: A randomized clinical trial. *Journal of Consulting and Clinical Psychology, 69* (5), 814–824.

Hendrick, J. B. (1990). *Early childhood*. In R. M. Thomas (Ed.), The encyclopedia of human development and education: Theory, research, and studies (p.p 181–184). Oxford: Pergamon Press.

Henggeler, S. W., Melton, G. B., & Smith, L. A. (1992). Family preservation using multisystemic therapy: An effective alternative to incarcerating serious juvenile offenders. *Journal of Consulting and Clinical Psychology, 60*, 953–961.

Henly, J. R., Danziger, S. K., Offer, S. (2005) The contribution of social support to the material well-being of low-income families. *Journal of marriage and the Family, 67* (1), 122–141.

Herman, J. L., & Yeh, J. P. (1980). *Some effects of parental involvement in schools*. Los Angeles: Center for the study of Evaluation. (ERIC Document Reproduction Service No. ED206–963).

Herrnstein, R. J., & Murray, C. (1994). *The bell curve*. New York: Free Press.

Hewitt, M., & Simone, J. V. (Eds.). (1999) *Ensuring quality cancer care*. Washington, DC: National Academy Press.

Hilliard, A. G. (1992). Behavioral Style, culture, and teaching and learning. *Journal of Negro Education, 61*, 370–377.

Hinrichsen, G. A. (1991). Adjustment of caregivers to depressed older adults. *Psychology and Aging, 6*(4), 631–639.

Hoff, L. E. (1984). *People in crisis: Understanding and helping* (2nd Ed.). California: Addison-Wesley Publishing Co.

Hofstede, G. (1984). Culture's consequences: International difference in work-related values. Beverly Hills California: Sage Publications.

Holahan, C. J. (2002). The contributions of Rudolf Moos. *American Journal of Community Psychology, 30*, 65–66.

Hollingshead, B. B., & Redlich, F. C. (1958). *Social class and mental illness: A community study*. New York: Wiley.

Holmes, T. H., & Rahe, R. H. (1967). The social readjustment rating scale. *Journal of Psychosomatic Research, 11*, 213–218.

Hooker, R. (1996). World civilizations. Retrieved from World Wide Web on April 24, 2004, at http://www.wsu.edu

Hooyman, N. R. and Kiyak, H. A. (1993). *Social gerontology: A multidisciplinary perspective*. Boston, MA: Allyn & Bacon.

Hornbrook, M. C., Stevens, V. J., Wingfield, D. J., Hollis, J. F., Greenlick, M. R., & Ory, M. G. (1994). Preventing falls among community dwelling older persons: Results from a randomized trial. *The Gerontologist, 34*, 16–23.

Horwath, E., Johnson, J., Klerman, G. L., & Weissman, M. M. (1992). Depressive symptoms as relative and attributable risk factors for first-onset major depression. *Archives of General Psychiatry, 49*(10), 817–823.

Horwath, E., Johnson, J., Klerman, G. L., & Weissman, M. M. (1994). What are the public health implications of subclinical depressive symptoms? *Psychiatric Quarterly, 65*, 323–337.

Hosmer, D. W., & Lemeshow, S. (1989). *Applied logical regression.* New York: Wiley.

Hosp, M. K. & Hosp, L. J. (2001). Behavior differences between African-American and Caucasian students: Issues for assessment and intervention. *Education & Treatment of Children, 24*, 336–350.

Hospital Closures (2003). The Olympian. Washington, Oct. 9.

Hostetler, M., & Fisher, K. (1997). Project C.A.R.E. substance abuse prevention program for high-risk youth: A longitudinal evaluation of program effectiveness. *Journal of Community Psychology, 25*(5), 397–419.

Howard, J. H. (1982). Adapting to retirement. *Journal of the American Geriatrics Society, 30*, 488–500.

Huey, S. J., & Henggeler, S. W. (2001). Effective community-based interventions for antisocial and delinquent adolescents. In Jan N. Hughes & A. M. La Greca (Eds.), *Handbook of psychological services for children and adolescents.* London: Oxford Univ. Press.

Huffstetler, B. (2001). Depression in older adults; Pervasive or preventable? *Adultspan, 3*(2), 61–70.

Hughes, J. N., & Hasbrouk, J. E. (1997). Television violence: Implications for violence prevention. *School Psychology Review, 25*(2), 134–151.

Humphreys, K., Finney, J. W., & Moos, R. H. (1994). Applying a stress and coping framework to research on mutual help organizations. *Journal of Community Psychology, 22*(4), 312–327.

Hunsley, J. (2002). *Cost-effectiveness of psychological interventions.* Ottawa, Ontario: Canadian Psychological Association.

Iivonen, M., Sonnenwald, D. H., & Parma, M. (1998). Analyzing and Understanding cultural differences: Experiences from education in library and information studies. Paper presented at the 64th IFLA General Conference August 16–August 21, 1998.

Institute of Medicine. (2001). *Crossing the quality chasm: A new health system for the 21st century.* Washington, DC: National Academy Press.

Institute of Science, Technology & Public Policy (2004). The congressional prevention coalition on stress prevention: Its impact on health and medical savings. Taken from www .istpp.org/stress prevention.html on February 3, 2004.

Integra Realty Resources, Inc. (2000, November). *Workplace stress study.* PR Newswire Association, Inc.

Ivens, J., & Thorne, H. (1999). Brief interventions with students with emotional and behavioral difficulties. *Educational Psychology in Practice. 15*(2), 122–125.

Jackson, D. D. (1960). *The Etiology of schizophrenia.* New York: Basic Books.

Jacobson, E. (1971). *Progressive relaxation.* Chicago: University of Chicago Press, 1929.

James, E. (2004). Financial hurdles confronting Baby Boomer women. *Harvard Generations Policy Journal, 1*, 45–52.

Janowiak, J. J., & Hackman, R. (1994). Meditation and college students' self-actualization and rated stress. *Psychological Reports, 75* (2), 1007–1010.

Japsen, B. (2002, June 11). Health-care woes cost billions; Study: Problems account for 30% of total U.S. tab. *Chicago Tribune.* p.1.

Jarrett, R. L., & Burton, L. M. (1999). Dynamic dimensions of family structure in low-income african american families: Emergent themes in qualitative research. *Journal of Comparative Family Studies (30)*, 177–181.

Jensen, A. R. (1969). How much can we boost IQ and scholastic achievement? *Harvard Educational Review, 39*, 1–123.

Jewler, A. J., & Gardner, J. N. (1987). *Step by step to college success.* Belmont, CA: Wadsworth.

Johnson, A. (2003, October 15). Why we can't wait to implement disease management. *Business and Health*, 21.

Johnson, A. B. (1990). *Out of bedlam*. Basic Books.

Johnson, C. L., & Catalano, D. J. (1983). A longitudinal study of family supports to impaired elderly. *The Gerontologist*, *26*(6), 612–618.

Johnson, D. W. (1970). *The social psychology of education*. New York: Holt, Rinehart and Winston.

Johnson, S. B., & Millstein, S. G. (2003). Prevention opportunities in health care settings. *American Psychologist*, *58*, 475–481.

Joint Commission on Mental Illness and Health (1961). *Action for mental health*. New York: Wiley.

Joniak, A. J., Puccio, G. J., & Talbot, R. J. (1993). Person-environment fit: Using commensurate scales to predict student stress. *British Journal of Educational Psychology*, *63*, 457–468.

Kamps, D., Kravitz, T., Rauch, J., Kamps, J. L., & Chung, N. (2000). A prevention program for students with or at risk for ED: Moderating effects of variation in treatment and classroom structure. *Journal of Emotional and Behavioral Disorders*, *8*, 141–156.

Kamps, D., Kravits, T., Stolze, J., & Swaggart, B. (1999). Prevention strategies for students at risk and identified as serious emotionally disturbed in urban, elementary settings. *Journal of Emotional and Behavioral Disorders*, *7*, (3) 178–188.

Kaslow, N. J. (2004). Competencies in professional psychology. *American Psychologist*, *59*, 774–781.

Kasschau, R. A. (1995). *Understanding psychology*. New York: McGraw Hill.

Katz, D., & Kahn, R. C. (1966). *The social psychology of organizations*. New York: Wiley.

Kelly, J. G. (1966). Ecological constraints on mental health services. *American Psychologist*, *21*, 535–539.

Kelly, J. G., Ryan, A. M., Altman, B. E., & Stelzman, S. P. (2000). Understanding and changing social systems. In Rappaport, J. & Seidman, E. (Eds.), *Handbook of community psychology*. New York: Plenum.

Kenardy, J., McCafferty, K., & Rosa, V. (2003). Internet delivered indicated prevention for anxiety disorders: A randomized controlled trial. *Behavioral & Cognitive Psychotherapy*, *31*, 279–289.

Kent, K. L. (1990). Elders & community mental-health centers. *Generations*, *14*(1), 19–21.

Kim, M. T. (1995). Cultural influences on depression in Korean Americans. *Journal of Psychosocial Nursing and Mental Health Services*, *33*(2), (13–18).

Kinzel, A., Nanson, J. (2000). Education and debriefing: Strategies for preventing crises in crisis-line volunteers. *Crisis*, *21* (3), 126–134.

Kluckhohn, F., & Strodtbeck, F. L. (1961). *Variations in Value-Orientations*. Connecticut: Greenwood Press.

Knight, B., Wollert, R. W., Levy, L. H., Frame, C. L., & Padgett, V. P. (1980). Self help groups: The members' perspectives. *American Journal of Community Psychology*, *8*, 53–56.

Ko, S. F., & Cosden, M. A. (2001). Do elementary school-based child abuse prevention programs work? A high school follow-up. *Psychology in the Schools*, *38*, 57–66.

Kobasa, S. C. (1993). 'Inquiries into Hardiness,' in Goldberger, L., and Breznitz, S. (Eds.), *Handbook of Stress: Theoretical and Clinical Aspects*. Free Press, New York.

Kobasa, S. (1979). Stressful life events, personality and health: An inquiry into hardiness. *Journal of Personality and Social Psychology*, *37*, 1–11.

Kobasa, S. C., & Maddi, S. R. (1985). Effectiveness of hardiness, exercise and social support as resources against illness. *Journal of Psychosomatic Research*, *29*(5), 525–533.

Koenig, H. G. (2000). Religion, well-being and health in the elderly: The scientific evidence for an association. In J. A. Thorson (Ed.), *Perspectives on spiritual well-being and aging*. Springfield, IL: Charles C. Thomas.

Kohn, L. T., Corrigan, J. M., & Donaldson, M. S. (Eds.). (2000). *To err is human: Building a safer health system*. Washington, DC: National Academy Press.

Kotter, K. P., & Cohen, D. S. (2002). *The heart of change; Real-life stories of how people change their organizations*. Boston, MA: Harvard Business School Press.

Kramer, B. J. (1996). American Indians. In Lipson, G. J., Dibble, S. L., Minarik, P. A. *Culture and Nursing Care: A pocket guide*. San Francisco, CA: UCFS Nursing Press.

Kramer, P. Anthony, W. A., Rogers, E. S., & Kennard, W. A. (2003). Another way of avoiding the "single model trap." *Psychiatric Rehabilitation Journal, 26*, 413.

Krause, N., and Shaw, B. A. (2002). Welfare participation and social support in late life. *Psychology and Aging, 17*(2): 260–270.

Kurdek, L. A. (2005). Gender and marital satisfaction early in marriage: A growth curve approach. *Journal of Marriage & the Family, 67*(1), 68–75.

Lachenmeyer, J. R. (1992). Consultation in M. S. Gibbs, J. R. Lachenmeyer, & J. Sigal (Eds.), *Community psychology and mental health*. New York: Gardner.

Laursen, B., & Williams, V. (2002). The role of ethnic identity in personality development. In L. Pulkkinen & A. Caspi (Eds.), *Paths to successful development: Personality in the life course*. New York: Cambridge University Press.

Lawrence, T., Aveyard, P., Cheng, K. K., Griffin, C., Croghan, E. (2005). Does stage-based smoking cessation advice in pregnancy result in long-term quitters? 18-month postpartum follow up of a randomized controlled trial. *Addiction, 100*(1), 107–117.

Lazarus, A. A. (1989). *The practice of multimodal therapy*. Baltimore, MD: Johns Hopkins University Press.

Lazarus, R. S. (1991). *Emotion and adaptation*. New York: Oxford University Press.

Lazarus, R. S. (1998). *Stress and emotion: A new synthesis*. London: Free Association Books.

Lee, E. (1999). A list of principles in cultural competency for health care clinicians: Found on the World Wide Web at http//:www.RAMS.org on March 13, 2004.

Lee, G. R., Dwyer, J. W., & Coward, R. T. (1993). Gender differences in parent care: Demographic factors and same-gender preferences. *Journal of Gerontology: Social Sciences, 48*, S9–S16.

Lehman, A. F., & Streinwachs, D. M. (1998). Translating research into practice: The Schizophrenia Patient Outcomes Research Team (PORT) treatment recommendations. *Schizophrenia Bulletin 24*, 1–10.

Lemme, B. H. (2002). *Development in Adulthood*. Boston, MA: Allyn and Bacon.

Lerner, R. M. (1995). *America's youth in crises: Challenges and options for programs and policies*. Thousand Islands, CA: Sage.

Lerner, R. M. (1998). Theories of human development: Contemporary perspectives. In R. M. Lerner (Ed.), *Theoretical models of human development. Handbook of Child Psychology* (5th ed.), Volume 1. New York: Wiley.

Lerner, R. M. (2002). *Concepts and theories of human development (third ed.)*. Mahwah, NJ: Lawrence Erlbaum Associates.

Lerner, R. M., Castellino, D. R., Terry, P. A., Villarruel, F. A., & McKinney, M. H. (1995). A developmental contextual perspective on parenting. In M. H. Bornstein (Ed.), *Handbook of Parenting: Biology and ecology of parenting* (Vol. 2, pp. 285–309). Hillsdale, NJ: Erlbaum.

Leung, J., Arthur, D. G. (2004). Clients and facilitators' experiences of participating in a Hong Kong self help group for people recovering from mental illness. *International Journal of Mental Health Nursing, 13*(4): 232–242.

Levenson, H., & Davidovitz, D. (2000). Brief therapy prevalence and training: A national survey of psychologists. *Psychotherapy, 37*, 335–340.

Levin, A. (2001). Conference Focuses on Mental Illness Stigma. *Psychiatric News 36 (9)*: 8–9.

Levine, M., & Perkins, D. V. (1987). *Principles of community psychology: Perspectives and Applications*. New York: Oxford University Press.

Levine, M., & Perkins, D. (1996). *Principles of community psychology: Perspectives and Applications*. New York: Oxford University Press.

Levo-Henriksson, R., (1994). Eyes upon wings—culture in Finish and U.S television news. Helsinki: Yleisradio.

Lewis, J. A., Lewis, M. D., Daniels, J. A., & D'Andrea, M. J. (1998). *Community counseling: Empowerment strategies for a diverse society*. (2nd Ed.). New York: Brooks/Cole.

Lewin, K. (1935). *Principles of topological psychology*. New York: McGraw Hill.

Lewin, K. (1951). *Field theory in social science*. New York: Harper.

Lewit, K. (1996). National Health Care Expenditures. *1995 Health Care Financing Review* 18 Fall.

Lichenstein, P., Gatz, M., Pedersen, N. L., Berg, S., & McClearn, G. E. (1996). A co-twin-control study of response to widowhood. *Journal of Gerontology: Psychological Sciences, 51*, 279–289.

Lieberman, M. A., & Snowden, L. R. (1993). Problems in assessing prevalence and membership characteristics of self-help group participants. *Journal of Applied Behavioral Science, 29*, 166–180.

Lieberman, R. P., DeRisi, W. J., & Mueser, K. T. (1989). *Social skills Training for psychiatric patients*. Needham Heights, MA: Allyn & Bacon.

Lincoln, Y. S., & Guba, E. G. (1985). *Naturalistic Inquiry*. Newbury Park, CA: Sage.

Lindemann, E. (1944). Symptomatology and management of acute grief. *American Journal of Psychiatry, 101*, 141–148.

Lipson, G. J., Dibble, S. L., Minarik, P. A (1996). *Culture and nursing care: A pocket guide*. San Francisco, CA: UCFS Nursing Press.

Litwin, G. H., Bray, J., & Brooke, K. L. (1996). *Mobilizing the organization: Bringing Strategy to Life*. London: Prentice-Hall.

Litwin, G., & Warner, B. W. (1992). A causal model of organizational performance and change. *Journal of Management, 18* (3): 523–545.

Litz, B. T., Bryant, R., Williams, L. Engel Jr., C. C., & Wang, J. (2004). A therapist assisted internet self-help program for traumatic stress. *Professional Psychology: Research and Practice, 35* (6): 628–635.

Locher, J. L., Ritchie, C. S., Roth, D. L., Baker, P. S., Bodner, E. V., & Allman, R. M. (2005). Social isolation, support and capital and nutritional risk in older sample: Ethnic and gender differences. *Social Science & Medicine, 60* (4): 747–763.

Loehr, J., Schwartz T. (2001) The making of a corporate athlete. *Harvard Business Review, 79*(1):120–128, 176.

Longo, D. A., & Bisconer, S. W. (2003). Treatment of aggression for an adult diagnosed with schizophrenia at a public psychiatric hospital. *Professional Psychology: Research and Practice, 34*(2), 177–179.

Lopez, M. A., & Silber, S. (1991). Stress management for the elderly: A preventive approach. *Clinical Gerontologist, 10*, 73–76.

Losel, F., & Beelmann, A. (2003). Effects of child skills training in preventing antisocial behavior: A systematic review of randomized evaluations. *Annals of the American Academy of Political & Social Science, 587*, 84–109.

Lounsbury, J. W., & DeNeui, D. (1996). Collegiate psychological sense of community in relation to size of college/university and extroversion. *Journal of Community Psychology, 24*(4), 381–394.

Love, J. M., Kisker, E. E., Ross, C. M., Schocket, P. Z., Brooks-Gunn, J., Paulsell, D. Boller, K., Cnstantine, J., Vogel, C., Fuligni, A. S., & Brady-Smith, C.. (2002). *Making a difference in the lives of infants and toddlers and their families: The impacts of Early Head Start.* Washington, DC: Department of Health and Human Services.

Lowey, N. (1996). The teenage pregnancy reduction act of 1996. [Online]. Available AOL: http://www.house.gov/lowey/pregact.htm

Luke, D., Roberts, L., & Rappaport, J. (1993). Individual, group context, and individual group fit predictors of self-help group attendance. *Journal of Applied Behavioral Science, 29,* 217–239.

Luria, A. (1976). *Cognitive development: Cultural and social foundations.* Cambridge, MA: Harvard University Press.

Lynch, E. W., & Hanson, M. J. (1992). Developing cross-cultural competence: A guide for working with young children and their families. Baltimore: Brookes.

Macpherson, C., & Macpherson, L. (1990) *Samoan medical belief and practice.* Auckland; Auckland University Press.

Maeroff, G. I. (1993). Building teams to rebuild schools. *Phi Delta Kappan 74,* 512–520.

Maira, A., & Scott-Morgan, S. P. (1996). *The accelerating organization.* New York: McGraw Hill.

Margolies, P. J. (1997). State Hospitals, the Future and Clinical Program Development. Paper presented at the 105th Annual American Psychological Association Convention, Chicago, Il.

Margolies, P. J. (1999). Identifying and teaching skills critical for success in the community. Paper presented at the 107th Annual American Psychological Association Convention, Boston, MA.

Margolies, P. J. (2000). Entry requirements of state-operated community residences: Staff and consumer perspectives. Paper presented at the NYS Office of Mental Health Research Conference, Albany, NY.

Margolies, P. J., & Columbia, N. S. (1997). Identifying Critical Skills for Success in Community Residential Settings. Paper presented at the tenth annual NYS Office of Mental Health Research Conference. Albany, NY.

Margolies, P. J., Glickman, H. S., & Devine, J. M. (1993). The Current Behavior Inventory: Clinical and programmatic applications of a psychiatric rehabilitation assessment instrument. Poster session at the 6th annual NYS Office of Mental Health Research Conference. Albany, NY.

Markman, H. J., Renick, M. J., Floyd, F. J., Stanley, S. M., & Clements, M. (1993). Preventing marital distress through communication and conflict management training: A 4-and 5-year follow-up. *Journal of Consulting and Clinical Psychology, 61,* 70–77.

Maslow, A. H. (1971). *The farther reaches of human nature.* New York: Viking.

Matano, R. A., Yalom, I. D., Schwartz, K. (1997). *Group Therapy for Medically ill patients.* New York: Guilford Press.

Maton, K. (1993). Moving beyond the individual level of analysis in mutual help group research: An ecological paradigm. *Journal of Applied Behavioral Science, 29,* 272–285.

Maton, K. I, Salem, D. A. (1995). Organizational characteristics of empowerment in community settings: A multiple case study approach. *American Journal of Community Psychology, 23,* 631–656.

May, P. A., & Gossage, J. P. (2001). Estimating the prevalence of fetal alcohol syndrome: A Summary. *Alcohol Research and Health, 25,* 159–167.

McArdle, P., Moseley, D., Quibell, T., Johnson, R., Allen, A., Hammal, D., & leCouteur, A. (2002). School-based indicated prevention: A randomized trial of group therapy. *Journal of Child Psychology & Psychiatry & Allied Disciplines, 43,* 705–712.

McConaughy, S. H., Kay, P. J., & Fitzgerald, M. (2000). How long is long enough? Outcomes for a school-based prevention program. *Exceptional Children, 67,* 21–34.

McFarlane, W. R., Lukens, E., & Link, B. (1995). Family Groups and psychoeducation in the treatment of schizophrenia. *Archives of General Psychiatry, 52:* 679–687.

McGarrity, M. (1993). *A guide to mental retardation.* New York: Crossroad.

McGrath, J. (2000). Universal interventions for the primary prevention of schizophrenia. *Australian & New Zealand Journal of Psychiatry, 34,* S58–S64.

McIntosh, D. N., Silver, R. C., & Wortman, C. B. (1993). Religions role in adjustment to a negative life event: Coping with the loss of a child. *Journal of Personality and Social Psychology, 65* (4), 812–821.

McKay, J. R., Alterman, A. I., & McLennan, A. T. (1994). Treatment goals, continuity of care, and outcome in a day hospital substance abuse rehabilitation program. *American Journal of Psychiatry, 151,* 254–259.

McMillan, D. W. (1996). Sense of community. *Journal of Community Psychology, 24*(4), 315–325.

McMillan, D. W., & Chavis, D. M. (1986). Sense of community: A definition and theory. *Journal of Community Psychology, 14,* 6–23.

McPhatter, A. R. (1997). Cultural competence in child welfare: What is it? How do we achieve it? What happens without it? *Child Welfare, 76* (1), 255–279.

Mechanic, D. (1995). Emerging trends in the application of the social sciences to health and medicine. *Social Science and Medicine, 40,* 1491–1496.

Mechanic, D. (1996). Emerging in international mental health services research. *Psychiatric Services, 47,* 371–375.

Mechanic, D. (2001). Removing barriers to care among persons with psychiatric symptoms. *Health Affairs, 21* (3): 137–147.

Mechanic, D., Schlesinger, M., & McAlpine, D. D. (1995). Management of mental health and substance abuse services: State of the art and early results. *Millbank Quarterly, 73,* 19–55.

Meckler, L. (1997, February 21). Aging nation grapples with soaring home care costs. *Poughkeepsie Journal,* p. 3a.

Medway, F., & Updyke, J. (1985). Meta-analysis of consultation outcome studies. *American Journal of Community Psychology, 13,* 489–506.

Meeks, S., Carstensen, L. L., & Stafford, P. B. (1990). Mental health needs of the chronically mentally ill elderly. *Psychology and Aging, 5*(2), 163–171.

Meeks, S., & Murrell, S. A. (1997). Mental Illness in late life: Socioeconomic conditions, psychiatric symptoms, and adjustments of long-term sufferers. *Psychology and Aging, 12*(2), 296–308.

Meissen, G., Warren, M. L., & Kendall, M. (1996). An assessment of college student willingness to use self-help groups. *Journal of College Student Development. 37*(4), 448–456.

Melan, E. H. (2004). Towards a contingency framework of intervention using systems-based methods. Unpublished doctoral dissertation, The management School at Lancaster University, England.

Meleis, A., Isenberg, M., Koerner, J., & Stern, P. (1995). *Diversity, marginalization, and cultural competent health care: Issues in knowledge development.* Washington, DC: American Academy of Nursing.

Melton, G. B. (2000). Community change, community stasis, and the law in *Handbook of Community Psychology,* Julian Rappaport, & Edward Seidman (Eds.). New York: Kluwer Academic/Plenum Publishers.

Mercer Human Resources Consulting/Marsh & McLennan Companies (2003, November). *Fourth Annual Survey of Employers Time-off and Disability Programs.*

Merrill, R. M., & Salazar, R. D. (2002). Relationship between church attendance and mental health among Mormons and non-Mormons in Utah. *Mental Health, Religion & Culture, 5,* 17–33.

Mervis, J. (2004). Efforts to boost diversity face persistent problems. *Science, 284*(5421), 1757–1759.

Meyer, N. G. (1976). Provisional patient movement and administrative data, State and County psychiatric inpatient services. *Mental Health statistical note no.132*. Rockville, MD.

Miles, M. B. (1964). Innovation in education: Some generalizations. In M. B. Miles (Ed.), *Innovation in Education*. New York: Teachers College Press, Columbia University, 631–663.

Milgram, S. (1967). A small world problem. *Psychology Today 1*, 60–67.

Miller, M. A., & Rahe, R. H. (1997). Life changes scaling for the 90's. *Journal of Psychosomatic Health*, 43: 279–292.

Milliman and Robertson (1997). *Increased health care cost.* (For the National Center for Policy Analysis).

Minkler, M. (1985). Building supportive ties and sense of community among the innercity elderly: The tenderloin senior outreach project. *Health Education Quarterly*, *12*(4), 303–314.

Miringoff, M. L. (1995). Toward a national standard of social health: The need for progress in social indicators. *American Journal of Orthopsychiatry*, *65*, 462–467.

Mitchell, R. E., & Trickett, E. J. (1980). Task force agent: Social networks as mediators of social support. *Community Mental Health Journal*, 16, 27–44.

Moos, R. H. (1972). Assessment of the psychosocial environments of community-oriented psychiatric treatment programs. *Journal of Abnormal Psychology*, 79, 9–18.

Moos, R. H. (1973). Conceptualization of human environments. *American Psychologist*, 28, 652–665.

Moos, R. H. (1976). *The human context: Environmental determinants of behavior.* New York: Wiley.

Moos, R. H. (1994). *The social climate scales: A user's guide* (2nd Edition). Palo Alto, CA: Consulting Psychologists Press.

Moos, R. H. (2002). The mystery of human context and coping: An unraveling of clues. *American Journal of Community Psychology*, *30*, 67–88.

Morgan, G. (1977). *Images of organizations.* Thousand Oaks, CA: Sage.

Morrissey, J. P, Tausig, M., & Lindsay, M. L. (1986) Interorganizational networks in mental health systems: Accessing community support programs for the chronically mentally ill. In W. R. Scott & B. L. Black (Eds.), *The organization of mental health services* (pp. 197–230). Beverly Hills, CA.

Moynahan, M. J. P. (1981). *Staff Development: The key to successful desegregation/integration implementation.* (ERIC Document Reproduction Service No. ED 207 156).

Moynihan, D. P. (1969). *Maximum feasible misunderstanding: Community action and the war on poverty.* New York: Free Press.

Mrazek, P. J., & Haggerty, R. J. (Eds.) (1994). *Reducing Risks for Mental Disorders: Frontiers for Preventive Intervention Research.* Washington, D.C.: National Academy Press.

Muclo, M. (Ed.). (2001). 100 best hospitals: Benchmarks for success. *Medical Benefits*, *18* (4). New York: Aspen Publishers, Inc.

Mueser, K. T., Bond, G. R., & Drake, R. E. (1998). Models of community care for severe mental illness: A review of research on case management. *Schizophrenia Bulletin*, 24:1998, 37–74.

Mueser, K.T., Bond, G. R., & Drake, R. E. (2001). Community based treatment of schizophrenia and other severerer mental disorders: Treatment outcomes. *Medscape General Medicine*, *3*(1).

Munoz, R. F., Mrazek, P. J., & Haggerty, R. J. (1996). Institute of Medicine report on prevention of mental disorders: Summary and commentary. *American Psychologist*, *51*, 1116–1122.

Murray, H. A. (1938). *Explorations in personality.* New York: Oxford University Press.

Murrell, S. A. (1973). *Community psychology and social systems.* New York: Behavioral Publications.

Mutchler, J. E., & Bullers, S. (1994). Gender differences in formal care use in later life. *Research on Aging*, *16*(3), 235–249.

Myers, I. (1962). *Manual: The Myers-BriggsType Indicator.* Palo Alto, CA: Consulting Psychologists Press.

Nabors, L. A., Reynolds, M. W., & Weist, M. D. (2000). Qualitative Evaluation of a high school mental health program. *Journal of Youth and Adolescence, (29)*1, 1–13.

Nash, J., Roynds, K., & Bowen, G. (1992). Level of parental involvement on early childhood intervention teams. *Families in Society: The Journal of Contemporary Human Services, 73*, 93–99.

Nash, K. B., & Kramer, K. D. (1993). Self-help for sickle cell disease in African American communities. Special Issue: Advances in understanding with self-help groups. *Journal of Applied Behavioral Science, 29*, 202–215.

Nation, M., Crusto, C., Wandersman, A., Kumpfer, K. L., Seybolt, D., Morrissey-Kane, E. & Davino, K. (2003). What works in prevention: Principles of effective prevention programs. *American Psychologist, 58*, 449–456.

National Center for Health Statistics. (1994*). Annual summary of births, deaths, marriages and divorces, 1994.* Washington, DC: U.S. Department of Health and Human Services.

National Center for Health Statistics, Centers for Disease Control (2002). Estimated life expectancy at birth years by race and sex. *National Vital Statistics Report 2002, 50*(6).

National Center for Health Statistics, Centers for Disease Control (2004). *Births, marriages, divorces and deaths: Provisional data for 2003.* Hyattsville, MD: National Center for Health Statistics (NCHS); National Vital Statistics Reports, *52* (22).

National Highway Traffic Safety Administration (1998). *Air bags & on-off switches: Information for an informed decision.* DOT HS 808 629. Washington, D.C.: U. S. Department of Transportation.

National Institute for Occupational Safety and Health (1999). *Stress . . . at work.* (DHHS(NIOSH) Publication No. 99-101) Cincinnati, OH.

National Institute for Health Care Management (2001). Prescription drug expenditures in 2001: The upward trend continues. *Health Care Focus, 1*, (2): 6.

National Institute of Mental Health Prevention Research Steering Committee (1994). *The Prevention of Mental Disorders: A national research agenda.* Washington DC: Author.

National Institute of Mental Health (2001). *The numbers count: Mental disorders in America: a summary of statistics describing the prevalence of mental disorders in America.* Washington DC: Author.

Navarro, F., & Wilkins, S. (2003*). Using PATH to increase the profitability of health plan member acquisition.* PATH Research Institute White Paper.

New York State Senate (1856). *Report and memorial of the County Superintendents of the Poor of this State on Lunacy and ITS Relation to Pauperism, and for the Relief of Insane Poor.* Albany, N.Y.: Jan. 23.

New York State Senate (1856). *Report of the Select Committee on Report and Memorial of County Superintendents of the poor, on Lunacy and its Relation to Pauperism.* Albany, N.Y.: March 5.

Nihira, K., Foster, R., Shellhaas, M., & Leland, H. (1974). *Adaptive behavior scale.* Washington, DC: American Association on Mental Deficiency.

Nissly, J. A., Barak, M. E. M., & Levin, A. (2005). Stress, social support and workers' intentions to leave their jobs in public child welfare. *Administration in Social Work, 29*(1):79–101.

Obsr, P., Smith, S. G., & Zinkiewicz, L. (2002). An exploration of sense of community. Part 3: Dimensions and predictors of psychological sense of community in geographical communities. *Journal of Community Psychology, 30* (1), 119–134.

O'Keefe, E. J., & Berger, D. S. (1993). *Self-management for college students: The ABC approach.* New York: Partridge Hill.

Olds, D. L., Eckenrode, J., Henderson, Jr., C. R., Kitzman, H., Powers, J., Cole, R., Sidora, K., Morris, P., Pettitt, L. M., & Luckey, D. (1997). Long-term effects of home visitation on maternal life course and child abuse and neglect: Fifteen year follow-up of a randomized trial. *Journal of the American Medical Association, 278*, 637–643.

Olds, D. L., Hill, P. L., Mihalic, S. F., & O'Brien, R. A. (1998). *Prenatal and home visitation by nurses*. Boulder, CO: Institute of Behavioral Science.

O'Leary, J., & Covell, K. (2002). The Tar Ponds kids: Toxic environments and adolescent well-being. *Canadian Journal of Behavioural Science, 34*, 34–43.

Omnibus Budget Reconciliation Act of 1987, PL 100–203.

Ordovensky, P. (1986, Feb. 16). Parents' involvement in education. *Poughkeepsie* (NY) *Journal*, 16A–17A.

Orford, J. (1987). Integration: A general account of families coping with disorder. In *Coping with disorder in the family*, J. Orford (Ed.). Croom Helm: Kent, pp. 266–293.

Orford, J. (1992). *Community psychology: Theory and practice*. Chichester, UK: Wiley.

Orme-Johnson, D. W. (1987). Medical care utilization and the transcendental medititation program. *Psychosomatic Medicine, 49*, 493–507.

Ornoy, A. (2002). The effects of alcohol and illicit drugs on the human embryo and fetus. *Israel Journal of Psychiatry & Related Sciences, 39*, 120–132.

Orstroff, C. (1993). Relationships between person-environment congruence and organizational effectiveness. *Group and Organizational Management, 18*, 103–122.

Ost, L. G., Svensson, L., Hellstrom, K., & Lindwall, R. (2001). One-session treatment of specific phobias in youths: A randomized clinical trial. *Journal of Consulting and Clinical Psychology, 69*(5):814–124.

Oths, K.S. Dunn, L. L., & Palmer, N. S. (2001). A prospective study of psychosocial job strain and birth outcomes. *Epidemiology, 12*(6):744.

Patil, R. (1999). *Life Positive Magazine*, March 1999, taken from http://www.lifepositive.com

Pelosi, N. (1996). Reducing risks of mental disorders. *American Psychologist, 51*, 1128–1129.

Perla, M. J. (1997). Public support for prevention. *American Psychologist, 52*, 1143.

Peterson, C., Maier, S. F., & Seligman, M. E. P. (1993). *Learned helplessnes: A theory for the age of personal control*. New York: Oxford University Press.

Peterson, M. D. (1984).*The writings of Thomas Jefferson*. New York: Literacy Classics of the U. S.

Peveler, R., Carson, A., & Rodin, G. (2002). Depression in medical inpatients. *Journal of Clinical Psychology, 41:* 337–344.

Plotnick, R. D. (1993). The effect of social policies on teenage pregnancy and childbearing. *Families in Society, 74*, 324–328.

Polich, J. M., Armor, D. J., & Braiker, H. B. (1981). *The course of alcoholism*. New York: Wiley.

Pope, K. S. (1990). Identifying and implementing ethical standards for primary prevention. *Prevention in Human Services, 8*, 43–64.

Posavac, E. J., & Carey, R. G. (2003). *Program evaluation: Methods and case studies*. Upper Saddle River, NJ: Prentice Hall.

Poughkeepsie Eagle (1905). *History of Poughkeepsie*. Platt and Platt.

Powell, T. J. (1993). Self help research and policy issues. *Journal of Applied Behavioral Science, 29*, 151–163.

Prentice-Dunn, S., & Rogers, R. W. (1986). Protection motivation theory and preventative health: Beyond the health belief model. *Health Education Research, Theory, and Practice, 1:* 153–161.

President's Commission on Mental Health. (1978). *Report to the President from the President's Commission on Mental Health* (Stock No. 040-000-003980-8, vol 1). Washington, DC: U.S. Government Printing Office.

Price, R. H., Cowen, E. L., Lorion, R. P., & Ramos-McKay, J. (Eds.) (1988). *14 ounces of prevention: A casebook for practitioners*. Washington, DC: American Psychological Association.

Prochaska, J. O., DiClemente, C. C., & Norcross, J. C. (1992). In search of how people change. *The American Psychologist, 47:*1102–1104.

Purcell, B. (2003). Elder abuse information: Senior depression may go undetected. Retrieved May 28, 2004, from http:/www.elder-abuse-information.com/news/news_091903_depression.htm

Quen, J. M. (1975). Learning from History. *Psychiatric Annuals 5:* 15–31.

Quinn, P. (2003, February/March). Race cleansing in America. *American Heritage*, 34–43.

Rahe, H., & Arthur, R J. (1968). Life change patterns surrounding illness experience. *Journal of Psychosomatic Research, 11*, 341–345.

Rahe, R. H., & Lind, E. (1971). Psychosocial factors and sudden cardiac death: A pilot study. *Journal of Psychomatic Research, 15*, 19–24.

Rajwani, R. (1996). South Asians. In Lipson, G. J., Dibble, S. L., Minarik, P. A. (1996). *Culture and Nursing Care: A pocket guide.* San Francisco, CA: UCFS Nursing Press.

Rappaport, J. (1977). *Community Psychology: Values, research, and action.* Chicago: Holt Rinehart and Winston.

Rappaport, J. (1984). Studies in empowerment: Introduction to the issue. *Prevention in Human Services 3*, 15–21.

Rappaport, J. (1993). Narrative studies, personal stories and identity transformation in the mutual help context. *Journal of Applied Behavioral Science, 29*(2), 239–256.

Reich, W. (1983, January 30). The world of soviet psychiatry. *The New York Times Magazine*, 20–26.

Repetti, R. L., Taylor, S. E., & Seaman, T. E. (2002). Risky families: Social environments and the mental and physical health of offspring. *Psychological Bulletin, 128*, 330–366.

Riegal, K. F. (1972). Influence of economic and political ideologies on the development of developmental psychology. *Psychological Bulletin, 78*, 129–141.

Rini, C. K., Dunkel-Schetter, C., Sandman, C. A., & Wadhwa, P. D. (1999). Psychological adaptation and birth outcomes: The role of personal resources, stress, and sociocultural context in pregnancy. *Health Psychology, 18*(4), 333–345.

Riolli, L. Savicki, V. & Cepani, A. (2002). Resilience in the face of catastrophe: Optimism, personality, and coping in the Kosovo crisis. *Journal of Applied Social Psychology, 32*, (8):1604–1627.

Ripple, C. H., & Zigler, E. (2003). Research, policy, and the federal role in prevention initiatives for children. *American Psychologist, 58*, 482–490.

Robb, C., Haley, W. E., Becker, M. A., Polivka, L. A., & Chwa, H.-J. (2003). Attitudes toward mental health care in younger and older adults: Similarities and differences. *Aging and Mental Health, 7*(2), 142–152.

Roberts, J., & Smith, J. (1994). From hospital community to the wider community: Developing a therapeutic environment on a rehabilitation ward. *Journal of Mental Health, 3*, 69–78.

Robertson, L. S. (1996). Reducing death on the road: The effects of minimum safety standards, publicized crash tests, seat belts, and alcohol. *American Journal of Public Health, 86*, 31–34.

Roesch, R. (1995). Creating change in the legal system: Contributions from community psychology. *Law and Human Behavior, 19*, 325–343.

Rogers, C. R. (1961). *On becoming a person.* Boston: Houghton Miffin Co.

Rosario, M., Salzinger, S., Feldman, R. S., Ng-Mak, D. S. (2003). Community violence exposure and delinquent behavior among youth: The moderating role of coping. Journal *of Community Psychology, 31*(5): 489–513.

Rosch, P. (1994) American Institute of Stress, Gannett News Service, December 29,1994.

Rosenbaum, Teitelbaum, J. (2002). *An analysis of the Medicaid IMD Exclusion.* Center for Health Services Research and Policy. George Washington University. Washington, D.C.

Rosenfield, S. (1991). Homelessness and re-hospitalization: The importance of housing for the chronically mentally ill. *Journal of Community Psychology, 19*, 60–69.

Rosenhan, D. (1973). On being sane in insane places. *Science, 179*, 250–258.

Rosenstock, I. M. (1974). *Historical* origins of the health belief model. *Health Education Monographs, 2*: 328–335.

Ross, L. (1977). The intuitive psychologist and his shortcomings: Distortions in the attribution process. In L. Berkowitz (Ed.), *Advances in experimental social psychology, vol. 10.* New York: Academic Press.

Ross, R. (1910). *The Prevention of Malaria.* N. Y.: Dutton.

Rossi, P. H., & Freeman, H. E. (1993). *Evaluation: A systematic approach.* Newbury Park, CA: Sage.

Rossi, P. H., Freeman, H. E., & Wright, S. R. (1978). *Evaluation: A systematic approach.* Beverly Hills, CA: Sage.

Rothman, D. J. (1971) *The discovery of the asylum: Social order and disorder in the New republic.* Boston: Little Brown.

Rotter, J. B. (1966). Generalized expectancies of internal versus external control of reinforcement. *Psychological Monographs, 80*:1–28.

Roy, C., & Andrews, H. A. (1999). *The Roy adaptation model* (2nd Ed.). Stamford, CN: Appleton & Lange.

Ryan, W. (1971). *Blaming the victim.* New York: Random House.

Sagarin, E. (1969). *Odd man in: Societies of deviants in America.* Chicago: Quadrangle Books.

Salyers, M. P., Bond, G. R., Teague, G. B., Cox, J. F., Smith, M. E., Hicks, M. L., & Koop, J. I. (2003). Is it ACT yet? Real-world examples of evaluating the degree of implementation for assertive community treatment. *The Journal of Behavioral Health Services & Research., 30*(3):304–320.

Salzinger, S. (1992). The role of social networks in adaptation throughout the life cycle. In M. S. Gibbs, J. R. Lachenmeyer, & J. Sigal (Eds.), *Community Psychology and Mental Health.* New York: Gardner Press.

Salzinger, S., Kaplan, S., & Artemyeff, C. (1983). Mothers' personal networks and child maltreatment. *Journal of Abnormal Psychology, 92,* 68–76.

Sarbin, T. R. (1970). A role theory perspective for community psychology: The structure of social identity. In D. Adelson & B. C. Kalis (Eds), *Community psychology and mental health: Perspectives and challenges.* Scranton, PA: Chandler.

Sarkadi, A., & Bremberg, S. (2005). Socially unbiased parenting support on the internet: A cross-sectional study of users of a large Swedish parenting website. *Care, Health, and Development, 31* (1): 43–53.

Sasa, I. K. (1999). Mechanism underlying the therapeutic effects of electroconvulsive therapy (ECT) on depression. *Journal of Pharmacology, 80* (3): 185–189.

Satcher, D. (2000). Mental health: A report of the Surgeon General: Executive summary. *Professional Psychology: Research and Practice, 31,* 5–13.

Sato, R. A., & Heiby, E. M. (1992). Correlates of depressive symptoms among battered women. *Journal of Family Violence, 7,* 229–245.

Sax, S. (1999). The Consultative Process. Found on the World Wide Web on February 23, 2004, at http://www.advancecounsulting.net

Schelkun, R. (2000). Community psychology in a community mental health setting. In Rappaport, J., & Seidman, E. (Eds.), *Handbook of community psychology.* New York: Plenum.

Schoenfeld, P., Halvey, J., Heemley-Van der Velden, E., & Ruhf, L. (1986). Long-term outcome of network therapy. *Hospital and Community Psychiatry, 37*(4), 373–376.

Schulz, R. (1996). A life span model of successful aging. *American Psychologist, 51*(7), 702–714.

Schwartz, K. D. (1997). FCC plan ensures dial tone for all. *InfoWorld, 19*(25), 75–76.

Schwartzberg, S. S. (1993). Struggling for meaning: How HIV-positive gay men make sense of AIDS. *Professional Psychology: Research and Practice, 24,* 483–490.

Schweinhart, L. J., Barnes, H. V., & Weikart, D. P. (1993*). Significant benefits: The High/Scope Perry Preschool study through age 27.* Ypsilanti, MI.: High Scope Press.

Schweinhart, L. J., & Weikart, D. P. (1989). The High/Scope Perry Preschool study: Implications for early childhood care and education. *Prevention in Human Services, 7*, 109–131.

Scileppi, J. A. (1976, April). *A systematic model for the promotion of community mental health and reservation development.* Paper presented at the annual meeting of the South Dakota Psychological Association. Rapid City, SD.

Scileppi, J. A. (1988). *A systems view of education: A model of change.* Lanham, MD: University Press of America.

Scileppi, J. A. (1998, April 20). Volunteers could bolster home health care. *Poughkeepsie (NY) Journal,* 4a.

Scileppi, J. A. (1999). *A proposal for a national self-insurance plan to provide volunteer caregivers for the homebound elderly.* A poster presentation for the Society for Community Research and Action (APA Division 27) Biennial Conference, Yake University, New Haven, CT.

Scileppi, J. A., & Montalto, L. A. (1986, October). *Primary prevention in the workplace: Offering problem-solving skills workshops to employee groups.* Paper presented at the Third Annual Northeast Regional Community Psychology Conference, Lowell, MA.

Seeman, T. E., Dubin, L. F., & Seeman, M. (2003). Religiosity/spirituality and health: A critical review of the evidence for biological pathways. *American Psychologist, 58* (1), 53–63.

Seidman, E., & French, S. E. (1998). Community mental health. In H. S. Friedman (Ed.), *Encyclopedia of Mental Health,* Vol. 1. New York: Academic Press.

Selye, H. (1956). *The stress of life.* New York: McGraw-Hill.

Selye, H. (1974). *Stress without distress.* Philadelphia: J. B. Lippincott Company.

Selye, H. (1976). *The stress of life, revised edition.* New York: McGraw Hill.

Senge, P. (1994). *The fifth discipline: The act and practice of the learning organization.* New York: Doubleday.

Sharfstein, S. S.(2000). Whatever happened to community mental health? *Psychiatric Services 51,* 616–620.

Sherman, M. D. (2003). *Support and family education (SAFE) program: Mental health facts for families.* Oklahoma City VA Medical Center. (2nd ed.).

Silver, E., Mulvey, E. P., & Swanson, J. W. (2002). Neighborhood structural characteristics and mental disorder: Faris and Dunham revisited. *Social Science & Medicine, 55,* 1457–1470.

Simons, L. S. (1989). Privatization and the mental health system. *American Psychologist, 44,* 1138–1141.

Smith, D. (2002). APA advocates for new funding for graduate training. *Monitor on Psychology, 33*(4). Retrieved May 25, 2004, from http://www.apa.org/monitor/apr02/advocates.html

Sohn, A. (November 22, 2004). The enablers. *New York, 37* (41), 66–68.

Sommer, R., & Ross, H. (1958). Social interaction on a geriatric ward. *International Journal of Social Psychiatry, 4,* 128–133.

Speaker, K. M. & Peterson, G. J. (2000). School violence and adolescent suicide: Strategies for effective intervention. *Educational Review, 52,* 65–73.

Sperry, L., Brill, P., Howard, K., and Grissom, G. (1996). *Treatment outcomes in psychotherapy and psychiatric interventions.* New York: Brunner/Mazel.

Sperry, L., & Carlson, J. (1996). *Psychopathology and psychotherapy: From diagnosis to treatment of DSM-IV disorders. (Sec. ed.).* Philadelphia: Taylor & Francis/Accelerated Development.

State of New York (1868). *First Annual Report of the Managers of the Hudson River State Hospital for the Insane.* Van benthuysen and sons. Feb. 6.

Stein, L. I., & Test, M. A. (1980). Alternative to mental hospital treatment. *Archives of General Psychiatry, 37*, 392–397.

Stein, L. I., Test, M. A., & Marx, A. J. (1975). Alternative to the hospital: A controlled study. *American Journal of Psychiatry, 132*, 419–422.

Stephens, R. S., Roffman, R. A., & Curtin, L. (2000). Comparison of extended versus brief treatments for marijuana use. *Journal of Consulting and Clinical Psychology, 68* (5), 898–908.

Stern, T. A., Fricchione, G. L., Cassem, N. H., Jellinek, M., & Rosenbaum, J. F. (Eds.). *Massachusetts General Hospital handbook of general hospital psychiatry, (5th ed).* Mosby: St. Louis, MO.

Stewart, K. E., Cianfrini, L. R., & Walker, J. F. (2005). Stress, social support and housing are related to health status among HIV-positive persons in the deep south of the United States. *AIDS Care, 17* (3), 350–9.

Stiffman, A. R., & Hadley-Ives, E. (1999). Impact of environment on adolescent mental health and behavior: Structural equation modeling. *American Journal of Orthopsychiatry, 68*, 468–478.

Sutherland, A. (1992). Gypsies and health care. *Western Journal of Medicine, 157*(3), 276–280.

Swazy, J. P. (1974). *Chlorpromazine in Psychiatry: A study in therapeutic intervention.* Cambridge, MA: MIT Press.

Swift, C. (1987). Prevention planning in community mental health centers. In H. Jared & J. A. Morell (Eds.), *Prevention planning in mental health.* Newbury Park, CA: Sage.

Swisher, S. L. (2001). Your faith has made you whole: The correlation between faith and wellness. *Dissertation Abstracts International Section A: Humanities & Social Sciences, 62*, 1091.

Szasz, T. S. (1970*). The manufacture of madness: A comparative study of the inquisition and the health movement.* New York: Harper & Row.

Szcipocznik, J., & Kurtines, W. (1993). Family psychology and cultural diversity. *American Psychologist, 48*, 400–407.

Talbott, J. A. (1975). Current clichés and platitudes in vogue in psychiatric vocabularies. *Hospital and Community Psychiatry, 26*, 530.

Talbott, J. A. (1978). *Death of the Asylum.* Grune & Stratton.

Talbott, J. A. (1984). The chronic mental patient: A national perspective. In Mirabi, M. (Ed). *The chronically mentally Ill: Research and services.* New York: Spectrum Publications.

Tannenbaum, C. B., Nasmith, L., & Mayo, N. (2003). Understanding older women's health care concerns: A qualitative study. *Journal of Women and Aging, 15*(1), 3.

Tate, D. C., Reppucci, N. D., & Mulvey, E. P. (1995). Violent juvenile delinquents. *American Psychologist, 50*, 777–781.

Teed, E. L. (1996). Report to Dutchess County, NY HIV Health Services Planning Council.

Tervalon, M., & Murray-Garcia, J. (1998). Cultural humility versus cultural competence: A critical distinction in defining physician training outcomes in multicultural education. *Journal of Health Care Poor Underserved, 9*(2), 117–125.

Thompson, T. (2003, April). Public Health Action Plan for Prevention and Treatment of Heart Disease and Stroke. *Steps to a healthier US: Putting prevention first conference.* U.S. Department of Health and Human Services (HHS), Press Release, April 15, 2003. Baltimore, MD.

Thorne, H., & Ivens, J. (1999). Brief interventions with students with emotional and behavioural difficulties. *Educational Psychology in Practice, 15* (2).

Thurston, W. E., Graham, J., Hatfield, J. (2003). Evaluability assessment: A catalyst for program change and improvement. *Evaluation & the Health Professions, 26* (2), 206–216.

Tobler, N. S. (2000). Lessons learned. *Journal of Primary Prevention, 20*, 261–274.

Tobler, N. S., Lessard, T., Marshall, D., Ochshorn, P., & Roona, M. (1999). Effectiveness of school-based drug prevention programs for marijuana use. *School Psychology International, 20*, 105–137.

Tobler, N. S., Roona, M. R., Ochshorn, P., Marshall, D. G., Streke, A. V. & Stackpole, K. M. (2000). School-based adolescent drug prevention programs: 1998 meta-analysis. *Journal of Primary Prevention, 20,* 275–336.

Tobler, N. S., & Stratton, H. H. (1997). Effectiveness of school-based drug prevention programs: Ameta-analysis of the research. *Journal of Primary Prevention, 18,* 71–128.

Toward, J. I., & Ostwald, S. K. (2002). Exploring mental health service needs for the elderly: Results of a modified Delphi study. *Community Mental Health Journal, 38*(2), 141–149.

Trickett, E. J., & Buchanan, R. M. (2001). The role of personal relationships in transitions: Contributions of an ecological perspective. In B. R. Sarason & S. Duck (Eds.), *Personal relationships: Implications for clinical and community psychology.* New York: Wiley.

Trickett, E. J., & Mitchell, R. E. (1992). An ecological metaphor for research and intervention. In Gibbs, M. S., Lachenmeyer, J. R., & Sigal, J. (Eds.), *Community psychology and mental health.* New York: Gardner Press.

Trompenaars, F. (1993). *Riding the waves of culture.* London: The Economist Books.

Tseng, V., Chesire-Teran, D., Becker-Klein, R., Chan, M. L., Duran, Roberts, A., & Bardoliwalla, N. (2002). Promotion of social change: A conceptual framework. *American Journal of Community Psychology, 30.*

Tudge, J. R. H., Odero, D. A., Hogan, D. M., & Etz, K. E. (2003). Relations between the everyday activities of preschoolers and their teachers' perceptions of their competence in the first years of school. *Early Childhood Research Quarterly, 18,* 42–64.

Tugade, M. M., & Fredrickson, B. L. (2004). Resilient individuals use positive emotions to bounce back from negative emotional experiences. *Journal of Personality and Social Psychology, 86,* 320–333.

Turner, J. C., Midgley, C., Meyer, D. K. Gheen, M., Anderman, E. M. Kang, Y. & Patrick, H. (2000). The classroom environment and students' report of avoidance strategies in mathematics: A multimethod study. *Journal of Educational Psychology, 94,* 88–106.

Turner, R. J., & Avison, W. R. (1992). Innovations in the measurement of life stress: Crisis theory and the significance of event resolution. *Journal of Health and Social Behavior, 33*(1), 36–50.

United Nations International Labor Organization (1993). Stress at work. *World Labor Report, 6,* Geneva, Switzerland: United Nations International Labor Office, 1993.

U.S. Bureau of the Census. (1995). Population profile of the United States: 1995. *Current Population Reports, Series P-23-189.* Washington, DC: U.S.Government Printing Office.

U.S. Bureau of the Census (2000). *Projections of the total resident population by 5-year age groups, race, and Hispanic origin, with special age categories: Middle series, 1999–2100.* Washington, DC: U.S. Government Printing Office.

U.S. Department of the Interior (1989). National Registry of Historical Places. Bearss, E. C., Washington, D.C. Feb.21.

U.S. Department of Health and Human Services (1999). Mental health: A report of the Surgeon General. Rockville, MD: U.S. Department of Health and Human Services, National Institute of Mental Health.

U.S. Department of Health and Human Services (2000). *Healthy people 2010.* (2nd Ed.). Washington, DC: U.S. Government Printing Office.

U.S. Department of Health and Human Services. (2001). *Healthy workforce 2010: Essential health promotion sourcebook for employers, large and small.* Washington, DC: U.S. Government Printing Office.

U.S. Department of Labor (2003) www.dol.gov

U.S. Department of Labor, Bureau of Labor Statistics (2000). *State and regional unemployment, 1999 Averages.* Released February 2000. http://www.bls.gov/bls/newsrels.htm.

U.S. Department of Labor and Statistics (1996). *Occupational outlook handbook 1996–97 edition.* Lanham Maryland: Bernan Press.

U.S. General Accounting Office (1977). *Returning the mentally disabled to the community: Government needs to do more.* U.S. Government Printing Office, 10–11.

U.S. General Accounting Office (1997*). Head Start: Research provides little information on impact of current program* (GAO No. GAO/HEHS-97-59). Washington, DC: Author.

Vailiant, G. E. (1977). *Adaptation to life: How the best and the brightest came of age.* Boston, MA: Little Brown.

Vailiant, G. E. (1983). *The natural history of alcoholism.* Cambridge: Harvard University Press.

Van Ornum, W. (1997). *A Thousand frightening fantasies: Understanding and healing scrupulosity and obsessive compulsive disorder.* New York: Crossroad.

Vaupel, J. W. (1998). Demographic analysis of aging and longevity. *American Economic Review, 88,* 242–247.

Walsh, F. (1996). The concept of family resilience: Crisis and challenge. *Family Process, 35* (3), 261–281.

Wandersman, A., & Florian, P. (2003). Community interventions and effective prevention. *American Psychologist, 58,* 441–449.

Ward, M. J. (1947) *The Snake Pit.* London: Cassell & Company.

Warren, D. I. (1983). Using helping networks: A key social bond of urbanites. In D. E. Biegel & A. J. Naparsteck (Eds.), *Community support systems and mental health.* New York: Springer.

Watson, J. (1924). *Behaviorism.* Chicago: University of Chicago Press.

Watzlawick, P., Weakland, J. H., & Fisch, R. (1974). *Change: Principles of problem formation and problem resolution.* New York: Norton.

Webster-Stratton, C., Reid, M. J., & Hammond, M. (2001). Preventing conduct problems, promoting social competence: A parent and teacher training partnership in Head Start. *Journal of Clinical Child Psychology, 30,* 283–302.

Weiner-Davis, M., deShazer, S., & Gingerich, W. (1987). Building on pre treatment change to construct the therapeutic solution: An exploratory study. *Journal of Marital and Family Therapy, 13*(4): 359–363.

Weiss, C. (1998). *Evaluation* (2nd Ed.). NJ: Prentice Hall.

Weissberg, R. P., Gullotta, T. P., Adams, G. R., Hampton, R. L., & Ryan, B. A. (Eds.) (1997a). *Healthy children 2010: Enhancing Children's Wellness.* Thousand Oaks, CA: Sage.

Weissberg, R. P., Gullotta, T. P., Adams, G. R., Hampton, R. L., & Ryan, B. A. (Eds.) (1997b). *Healthy children 2010: Establishing preventive services.* Thousand Oaks, CA: Sage.

Weissberg, R. P., Kumpfer, K. L., & Seligman, M. E. P. (2003). Prevention that works for children and youth. *American Psychologist, 58,* 425–432.

Wetherell, J. L., Gatz, M., & Craske, M. G. (2003). Treatment of generalized anxiety disorder in older adults. *Journal of Consulting and Clinical Psychology, 71*(1):31–40.

Whitbourne, S. K. (2005). *Adult development and aging: Biopsychosocial perspectives.* New York: Wiley.

Wilcox, B. C. (1981). Social support in adjusting to marital disruption: A network analysis. In B. H. Gottlieb (Ed.), *Social networks and social support.* Beverly Hills, CA: Sage.

Willer, B., & Intagliata, J. (1984*). Promises and realities for mentally retarded citizens: Life in the community.* Baltimore: University Park Press.

Williams, W. M., & Ceci, S. J. (1997). A person-process-context-time approach to understanding intellectual development. *Review of General Psychology, 1,* 288–310.

Wilson, D. B., Gottfredson, D. C., & Najaka, S. S. (2001). School-based prevention of problem behaviors: A meta-analysis. *Journal of Quantitative Criminality, 17,* 247–272.

Wilson, S. J., Lipsey, M. W. & Derzon, J. H. (2003). The effects of school-based intervention programs on aggressive behavior: A meta-analysis. *Journal of Consulting and Clinical Psychology*, *71* (1), 136–149.

Winkel, F. W., & Vrij, A. (1993). Facilitating problem and emotion-focused coping in victims of burglary: Evaluating a police crisis intervention program. *Journal of Community Psychology*, *21*, 97–112.

Wojtaszek, M. M. (2005) *A community psychology oriented agency profile of Time & Space Limited, Hudson, NY.* Unpublished manuscript, Marist College, Poughkeepsie, NY.

Wolkenstein, B. H., & Sterman, L. (1998). Unmet needs of older women in a clinic population: The discovery of possible long-term sequelae of domestic violence. *Professional Psychology: Research and Practice*, *29*(4), 341–348.

Wrosch, C., Heckhausen, J., & Lachman, M. E. (2000). Primary and secondary control strategies for managing health and financial stress across adulthood. *Psychology and Aging*, *15*(3), 387–399.

Wykle, M. L., & Musil, C. M. (1993). Mental health of older persons: Social and cultural factors. In M. A. Smyer (Ed.), *Mental health and aging: Progress and prospects* (pp. 3–17). New York: Springer Publishing Company.

Zarit, S. H., & Leitsch, A. (2001). Developing and evaluating community-based intervention programs for Alzheimer's patients and their caregivers. *Aging and Mental Health*, *5*, S84–S98.

Zarit, S. H., & Teri, L. (1991). Interventions and services for family caregivers. *Annual Review of Gerontology and Geriatrics*, *11*, 287–310.

Zeidner, M., & Hammer, A. L. (1992). Coping with missile attack: Resources, strategies and outcomes. *Journal of Personality*, *60*, 709–746.

Zigler, E., Taussig, C., & Black, K. (1992). Early childhood intervention: A promising preventative for juvenile delinquency. *American Psychologist*, *47*, 997–1006.

Zigler, E., & Valentine, J. (Eds.) (1979). *Project Head Start: A legacy on the wave of poverty.* New York: Free Press.

Zimmerman, M. A. (2000). Empowerment Theory, *Handbook of Community Psychology.* New York: Plenum Publishers.

INDEX

A

Abbreviated progressive muscle relaxation training (APRT), 139

Acceptance, of change, 258–61
    decree from high authority, 258
    demonstration projects, 260–61
    information, presentation of, 258–59
    personnel, replacement of, 258
    sensitivity group training, 259–60
    skill training, 259
    survey feedback method, 260
    team building, 259–60

Accidental falls, in elderly, 117

Action plans, 264

Activities for daily living (ADL), 16, 72, 76, 107

Adaptation, 71
    for children, 85
    in crisis intervention, 133–35

Adler, Alfred, 149

Adlerian Brief Therapy, 149–50

Adolescents
    crisis intervention in, 125
    health care providers and, 118
    networks for, 163
    pregnancy in, 82, 160

Adults
    marijuana use in, 151
    networks for, 163–64
    prevention programs for, 116–18

African American
    Behavioral Style (AABS), 183
    beliefs about illness, 187

Agency policy, 198

Aging
    future trends, 289–90
    model of successful, 290
    social networks and, 164

AIDS prevention, 94
    program, 70

Alcoholics Anonymous (AA), 60, 166, 168, 172, 193

Alzheimer's Association, work agreement for, 216

Alzheimer's disease, 196
    bilingual support group for, 280
    community-based interventions for, 274–75

American Association of Retired Persons (AARP), 285, 286

American Civil Liberties Union (ACLU), 13

American Counseling Association, 195

American Institute of Stress, 142

American Managed Behavioral Association (AMBHA), 298

American Medical Association (AMA), 43

American Psychiatric Association, 9, 43, 44

American Psychological Association, 19, 101, 142, 195, 272, 274

Americans with Disabilities Act of 1991 (ADA), 12, 52, 72, 250

Antibiotic medication, 35

Ascribed role status, *versus* Sarbins' achieved, 74–75

Assertive community treatment (ACT), 40, 50, 67, 108, 193, 194

Association for Retarded Children (ARC), 14

Asylums, 30, 31, 34, 41

Attributable risk, 96